ntroduction

he only factor in choosing a new car.
riced autos aren't the best values in the
y aren't as durable or reliable as more
either is price the best way to choose a
ys to shop around, talk to friends and
anizations such as the Better Business
utations of car dealers in your area. If a
ge a little more than others, but has a
ustomer service, maybe that dealer de-

nore that, for most buyers, price is the
oosing a new car. Thus, the price lists
f the most valuable services we provide
r readers to compare the costs of differ-
s at home, away from the pressures of
m.

latest available at publication time.
has not yet announced 1989 prices, we
the case of a new car not yet on sale at
n, there's no price to list. Where dealer
are unavailable, we print only retail

ICATIONS

e or sedan with a separate trunk.
or sedan with a rear liftgate. Wheel-
veen the front and rear wheels. Curb
base models, not including optional
s: **ohv** = overhead valve; **ohc** = over-
uble overhead cam; **I** = inline engine;
onfiguration; **flat** = horizontally op-
. = barrel (carburetor); **TBI** = throt-
t) fuel injection; **PFI** = port (multi-
rpm = revolutions per minute; **S** =
nal; **OD** = overdrive transmission;

CONSUMER GUIDE®

CONSUMER GUIDE®

1989 CARS

Contents

Price shouldn't be
Some of the lowest
long run because t
costly competitors.
new-car dealer. It
relatives, and ask o
Bureau about the re
dealer seems to cha
reputation for good
serves a higher pric

None of this is to
governing factor in
in this issue are one
because they allow o
ent models and optic
the new-car showro

Our prices are th
Where an automake
list '88 prices. And i
the time of publicati
invoice and low pric
prices.

KEY TO SPECIF

Notchback = cou
Hatchback = coupe
base = distance bet
weight = weight o
equipment. **Engine**
head cam; **dohc** = d
V = cylinders in V o
posed cylinders; **bb**
tle-body (single-poin
point) fuel injection
standard; O = optic
NA = not available.

Invoice prices are those the dealer pays to buy the car from the factory. On most domestic cars, the manufacturer includes in the invoice price the cost of preparing the car for delivery, advertising fees and other expenses. Most import makers do not include such costs in their invoice price.

Our Low Price is an estimate based on national market conditions. Supply, demand and competition rule the market, and market conditions vary greatly for different cars in different parts of the country. Our Low Price is only a guide. You'll have to determine the best price in your area by shopping for the same car at three or more dealers.

Note that car companies are free to change prices at any time, and frequently do. Market conditions and the fluctuating value of the U.S. dollar against foreign currencies are often the cause.

If a dealer claims our prices are incorrect, contact us and we'll do our best to help you out. We have everything to gain by giving you the right information; a dealer might gain by doing otherwise. Still, dealers are free to sell their cars for whatever the market will bear, even if it's higher than suggested retail price.

Federal law requires that all cars sold in the U.S. have a manufacturer's price sticker posted in a window. It must show the suggested retail price for the vehicle and for all factory-installed options, plus the destination charge for shipping the vehicle to the dealer and the EPA fuel economy estimates. This law does not apply to light trucks. Some passenger vans and most 4-wheel-drive vehicles are classified as trucks.

Most dealers add a second window sticker showing accessories they have installed (pinstripes, rustproofing, "protection packages," burglar alarms, etc.), plus a variety of other charges. Question these charges! Many are illegitimate. For example, some dealers add a "prep charge" for preparing domestic cars for delivery, even when the manufacturer's price sticker clearly states that those charges are included in the suggested retail price. Others levy an "advertising fee," ostensibly to cover the dealer's share of the manufacturer's national or regional ad campaign. Balk at paying this charge. You don't know if the dealer is indeed participating in the manufacturer's ad program. Anyway, advertising is part of the dealer's cost of doing business, not yours, so don't pay it.

Other examples: A $900 "import tariff" on a Honda; no such tariff exists, so this is merely added dealer profit. A charge of $319 for "ocean freight" and $225 for "inland destination" (on top of the $255 for destination listed on the manufacturer's price sticker), on a Hyundai Excel.

Charging for rustproofing, "paint shields" and "protection packages" are dealer ploys that can add hundreds to the price of a car. If you're buying a car that's backed by a 6-year/100,000-mile factory corrosion warranty, you don't need extra-cost rustproofing. Refuse to pay for it. Many manufacturers flatly state in new-car ownership papers that post-factory anti-corrosion measures are unnecessary and may even void your new-car warranty.

Stick with the manufacturer's price sticker and bargain from that, not the inflated price posted by the dealer.

Most of the information in the individual model reports comes from the manufacturers and, like prices, is subject to change. The specifications for the cars are also provided by the manufacturers (except for EPA fuel economy estimates).

Before you start shopping, get a quote on a car loan from your bank, credit union, insurance company or other lending institution. You'll thus have something to compare against a new-car dealer's offer to finance your purchase.

Trading in your old car is both a convenient way to dispose of it and a way to finance your new-car downpayment. But a host of pitfalls lurk here. Dealers can make it appear they are paying you well for your used car, while in reality jacking up the cost of the new-car purchase. The worst thing to do is trade in your old car before it's paid for. The dealer will gladly pay off your old loan, use any value left from your trade-in as a down payment, and write you another loan for the new car. And, he'll make money on each part of the deal. If possible, try and sell your used car outright to a private buyer. And in any case, negotiate a price for your new car before telling the dealer you have a possible trade in.

The editors invite your questions and comments. Address them to:

CONSUMER GUIDE®
7373 N. Cicero Ave.
Lincolnwood, IL 60646

Acura Integra

Acura Integra LS 3-door

American Honda's upscale division will bring out an all-new Integra in spring 1989 as an early 1990 model, so last year's versions are unchanged for 1989. Integra debuted in spring 1986 as the sporty, small Acura, using a front-drive platform derived from the Honda Civic. It comes in 3- and 5-door hatchback body styles and two trim levels, RS or LS. All versions have a dual-overhead cam, 16-valve 1.6-liter 4-cylinder engine. Transmission choices are a 5-speed manual or a 4-speed overdrive automatic. The 1990 Integra reportedly will have a 1.8-liter engine for more power and be positioned slightly upmarket from today's car. Integra is quick, agile, well built and stylish, with the right sound and feel to enthrall enthusiasts. Its silky engine begs for rushes to the redline, though you'll have to rev it above 3500 rpm or so to draw out its real punch, which means sports-minded drivers ought to avoid the automatic transmission. Cornering benefits from responsive power-assisted steering, minimal body roll and good tire grip. The brakes feel strong. The taut suspension can be jarring over rougher pavement. Road, engine and wind noise can be intrusive if you're not in a sporting mood, and the air conditioner can't seem to cool the glassy interior sufficiently on hot days. Still, the cabin is a paragon of driver-oriented efficiency, and there's reasonable room in the rear seat considering the sporty-coupe design. The 5-door's longer wheelbase gives it slightly more rear-seat room than the 3-door's. In finesse and price, Integra fits neatly between the quick but raw-edged 2-seat Honda CRX Si and the more refined and expensive Prelude Si sports coupe. That's not a bad place to be.

Specifications

	3-door hatchback	5-door hatchback
Wheelbase, in.	96.5	99.2
Overall length, in.	168.5	171.3
Overall width, in.	65.6	65.6
Overall height, in.	53.0	53.0
Turn diameter, ft.	31.5	32.1
Curb weight, lbs.	2326	2390
Cargo vol., cu. ft.	16.0	16.0
Fuel capacity, gal.	13.2	13.2
Seating capacity	5	5
Front headroom, in.	37.5	37.5
Front shoulder room, in.	NA	NA
Front legroom, max., in.	40.7	40.7
Rear headroom, in.	35.8	36.3
Rear shoulder room, in.	NA	NA
Rear legroom, min., in.	33.3	33.9

Engines

	dohc I-4
Size, liters/cu. in.	1.6/97
Fuel delivery	PFI
Horsepower @ rpm	118 @ 6250
Torque (lbs./ft.) @ rpm	99 @ 5500
Availability	S

EPA city/highway mpg

5-speed OD manual	26/30
4-speed OD automatic	25/30

Prices

Acura Integra	Retail Price	Dealer Invoice	Low Price
RS 3-door hatchback, 5-speed	$11260	$9458	$10960
RS 3-door hatchback, automatic	11870	9970	11570
RS 5-door hatchback, 5-speed	12060	10130	11760
RS 5-door hatchback, automatic	12670	10642	12370
LS 3-door hatchback, 5-speed	13070	10978	12770
LS 3-door hatchback, automatic	13680	11491	13380

Prices are accurate at time of printing; subject to manufacturer's change.

CONSUMER GUIDE®

	Retail Price	Dealer Invoice	Low Price
LS 5-door hatchback, 5-speed	13900	11676	13600
LS 5-door hatchback, automatic	14510	12188	14210
Destination charge	295	295	295

Standard Equipment:

RS: 1.6-liter PFI 16-valve 4-cylinder engine, 5-speed manual or 4-speed automatic transmission, power steering, power 4-wheel disc brakes, cloth reclining front bucket seats, split folding rear seat, tilt steering column, digital clock, tachometer, coolant temperature gauge, intermittent wipers, bodyside molding, remote mirrors, tinted glass, rear defogger and wiper/washer, remote hatch and fuel door releases, center console, front door pockets, right visor mirror, cargo area light, cargo tiedown straps, cargo area cover, Yokohama 195/60R14 tires. **LS 3-door** adds: power sunroof, cassette storage in console, cruise control, AM/FM ST ET cassette, Michelin MXV tires on alloy wheels. **LS 5-door** deletes sunroof and adds power windows and locks.

OPTIONS are available as dealer-installed accessories.

Acura Legend

Acura Legend LS 4-door

Few visible changes have been made to these Honda-made imports, but the Legend Sedan gets the Coupe's double-wishbone rear suspension and all Legends now have a driver-side air bag as standard. The Sedan's new rear sus-

Prices are accurate at time of printing; subject to manufacturer's change.

pension is intended to improve ride and handling. The air bag—a passive safety device designed to inflate in a frontal collision—was previously standard only on the top-rung LS versions of the Sedan and Coupe. Both the 4-door sedan and 2-door coupe body styles are powered by a 2.7-liter V-6 engine. All are front-drive and have 4-wheel disc brakes as standard; L and LS models add anti-lock systems. A 5-speed manual transmission is standard; a 4-speed overdrive automatic is available at extra cost. The Coupe's wheelbase is two inches shorter and its rear track is wider than the Sedan's, plus its suspension is tuned for a firmer ride. Acura reportedly is planning to introduce a larger sedan with a V-8 engine as a flagship companion to the Legend, but the company says it won't be sold during the '89 model year. The present Sedan debuted for 1986 and the Coupe followed a

Specifications	2-door notchback	4-door notchback
Wheelbase, in.	106.5	108.6
Overall length, in.	188.0	189.4
Overall width, in.	68.7	68.3
Overall height, in.	53.9	54.7
Turn diameter, ft.	36.5	36.1
Curb weight, lbs.	3089	3077
Cargo vol., cu. ft.	14.7	16.6
Fuel capacity, gal.	18.0	18.0
Seating capacity	5	5
Front headroom, in.	37.2	37.2
Front shoulder room, in.	55.4	55.8
Front legroom, max., in.	42.9	42.3
Rear headroom, in.	36.3	36.1
Rear shoulder room, in.	54.3	55.4
Rear legroom, min., in.	30.3	34.2

Engines	ohc V-6
Size, liters/cu. in.	2.7/163
Fuel delivery	PFI
Horsepower @ rpm	161 @ 5900
Torque (lbs./ft.) @ rpm	162 @ 4500
Availability	S

EPA city/highway mpg

5-speed OD manual	19/23
4-speed OD automatic	18/22

year later. To get the Legend's wonderfully smooth and powerful engine, thoughtful interior design, solid construction, sport-sedan road manners and commendable quality in a European car, you'd have to pay lots more. Plus, independent surveys show Acura has an impressive record of owner satisfaction. Flaws include an automatic transmission that shifts abruptly and harshly at times. Torque peaks at a high 4500 rpm and bursts of speed require quicker downshifts than the automatic transmission provides. The mid-level L series, with its standard anti-lock brakes, is probably the best value in a car line packed with it.

Prices

Acura Legend	Retail Price	Dealer Invoice	Low Price
Sedan			
4-door notchback, 5-speed	$22600	$18532	$22400
4-door notchback, automatic	23400	19188	23200
4-door notchback w/sunroof, 5-speed . . .	23485	19257	23285
4-door notchback w/sunroof, automatic . .	24285	19913	24085
L 4-door notchback, 5-speed	25900	21238	25700
L 4-door notchback, automatic	26700	21894	26500
L w/leather trim, 5-speed	26850	22017	26650
L w/leather trim, automatic	27560	22673	27450
LS 4-door notchback, 5-speed	29160	23911	28960
LS 4-door notchback, automatic	29960	24567	29760
Coupe			
2-door notchback, 5-speed	24760	20303	24560
2-door notchback, automatic	25560	20959	25360
L 2-door notchback, 5-speed	27325	22406	27125
L 2-door notchback, automatic	28125	23062	27925
L w/leather trim, 5-speed	28275	23185	28075
L w/leather trim, automatic	29075	23841	28875
LS 2-door notchback, 5-speed	30040	24632	29840
LS 2-door notchback, automatic	30840	25288	30640
Destination charge	295	295	295

Standard Equipment:

4-door: 2.7-liter SOHC 24-valve PFI V-6, 5-speed manual or 4-speed automatic transmission, power steering, power 4-wheel disc brakes, driver's side airbag, air conditioning, cruise control, power windows and locks, tilt steering column, remote fuel door and trunk releases, door pockets, lighted visor mirrors, rear defogger, map lights, illuminated entry system, reclining front

Prices are accurate at time of printing; subject to manufacturer's change.

bucket seats, moquette upholstery, driver's seat lumbar and thigh support adjustments, rear armrest, AM/FM ST ET cassette with EQ and power diversity antenna, maintenance interval reminder, tachometer, coolant temperature gauge, trip odometer, intermittent wipers, Michelin MXV 205/60HR14 tires on alloy wheels; 2-door has power sunroof, V-rated tires. **L 4-door** has: anti-lock braking system, memory power driver's seat, security system; 2-door adds power driver's seat, heated mirrors, driver's seatbelt presenter, driver's information center. **LS** has: automatic climate control, power passenger seat, Bose sound system, driver's information center.

OPTIONS are available as dealer-installed accessories.

Audi 80/90

Audi 80 Quattro

Audi's smallest sedans are unchanged for 1989 after dumping their 4000-series designation in 1988 and picking up new sheetmetal in the style of the larger Audi 100/200 line. Two developments are expected later in the '89 model year, however: a 20-valve, 160-horsepower version of the 5-cylinder engine is scheduled to debut in the 4-wheel-drive 90 Quattro, and a coupe version of the 80/90 may be introduced. Until then, the 80 and 90 continue to share the same notchback body. The more-expensive 90 is distinguished by a higher level of standard equipment, including a leather-and wood-trimmed interior and power sunroof. Audi 90s equipped with a 5-speed manual transmission get a 2.3-liter 5-cylinder engine; those with a 3-speed automatic get the 2.0-liter four that's standard on the 80. Both models are available as Quattros, Audi's term for its permanent 4-wheel drive system. All Quattros have the 5-cylinder and 5-speed. Four-wheel disc brakes are standard; an anti-lock system is standard on 90 models, optional on the 80 Quattro. Audi has positioned the 80/90 to take on such tough rivals as the Acura Legend and the BMW 3-Series. Among its ammunition is a refined, sport-sedan manner, distinct styling, an ergonomically sound interior, fine build quality, a wide array of standard equipment and 4WD availability. Steep prices make perceived value a problem, however. The 80 models have lackluster performance with automatic transmission. And all 80s and 90s are hampered by very small

---

Specifications

	4-door notchback
Wheelbase, in.	100.2
Overall length, in.	176.3
Overall width, in.	66.7
Overall height, in.	55.0
Turn diameter, ft.	33.8
Curb weight, lbs.	2568[1]
Cargo vol., cu. ft.	10.2
Fuel capacity, gal.	17.9[2]
Seating capacity	5
Front headroom, in.	NA
Front shoulder room, in.	NA
Front legroom, max., in.	NA
Rear headroom, in.	NA
Rear shoulder room, in.	NA
Rear legroom, min., in.	NA

1. 2904 lbs, Quattro   2. 18.5 gals, Quattro

Engines

	ohc I-4	ohc I-5
Displacement, l/cu. in.	2.0/121	2.3/141
Fuel delivery	PFI	PFI
Horsepower @ rpm	108 @ 5300	130 @ 5700
Torque (lbs./ft.) @ rpm	121 @ 3200	140 @ 4500
Availability	S	S

EPA city/highway mpg

5-speed OD manual	22/30	20/26
3-speed automatic	23/27	

trunks, which limits their appeal as all-around family cars. Fallout from unintended-acceleration allegations leveled at Audi 5000s have hurt sales of all Audis. Audi responds this year with the "Audi Advantage," a comprehensive new warranty and service program that also guarantees the resale value of '89 Audis traded for future Audi models.

Prices

Audi 80/90 (1988 prices)	Retail Price	Dealer Invoice	Low Price
80 4-door notchback, 5-speed	$19160	—	—
80 4-door notchback, automatic	19685	—	—
80 Quattro 4-door notchback	23380	—	—
90 4-door notchback, 5-speed	25060	—	—
90 4-door notchback, automatic	25060	—	—
90 Quattro 4-door notchback, 5-speed	28550	—	—
Destination charge	NA	NA	NA

Dealer invoice and low price not available at time of publication.

Standard Equipment:

80: 2.0-liter PFI 4-cylinder engine, 5-speed manual or 3-speed automatic transmission, power steering, power 4-wheel disc brakes, air conditioning, tinted glass, rear defogger, cruise control, power windows and locks, AM/FM ST ET with diversity antenna, power mirrors, velour reclining front bucket seats with height adjusters, rear head restraints and lap/shoulder belts, automatic front seatbelt tensioners, tachometer, coolant temperature gauge, trip odometer, digital clock, intermittent wipers, lighted right visor mirror,

Audi 90

Prices are accurate at time of printing; subject to manufacturer's change.

lockable fuel cap, 175/70SR14 SBR tires. **80 Quattro** adds: 2.3-liter PFI 4-cylinder engine, close-ratio 5-speed, permanent 4-wheel drive, rear spoiler, 195/60VR14 tires on alloy wheels. **90** has: 2.3-liter 5-cylinder engine with 5-speed or 2.0-liter 4-cylinder with 3-speed automatic, anti-lock braking system, fog lights, clearcoat metallic paint, leather interior, wood dashboard trim, power sunroof, individual passenger reading lamps, Auto Check, cassette stereo, 195/60VR14 tires (H-rated on 4-cylinder).

Optional Equipment:	Retail Price	Dealer Invoice	Low Price
Anti-lock brakes, 80 Quattro	1150	1035	1093
Leather interior, 80	1090	NA	NA
Clearcoat or pearlescent paint	375	300	338
California equipment	90	90	90
Sport seats, exc. 90 Quattro	295	236	266
Power sunroof, 80/80 Quattro	795	668	732
Auto Check System, 80/80 Quattro	100	80	90
Trip computer	245	196	221
Heated front seats	225	180	203
Heated front & rear seats	375	300	338
Cassette stereo, 80/80 Quattro	495	396	446
Ski sack	120	96	108

Audi 100/200

Audi's biggest car drops its 5000-series designation and gains an updated interior. Models with the naturally aspirated 2.3-liter 5-cylinder engine are now called the 100; those with the turbocharged and intercooled 2.2-liter five are 200s. The name change standardizes the German automaker's worldwide badging. Meanwhile, Audi announced that the 200 will form the basis for the Audi V-8, a 240-horsepower, $50,000 flagship sedan coming to the U.S. in mid-1989. The V-8 will come standard with Audi's permanently engaged Quattro 4-wheel drive system. Only exterior details—flush door handles, new wheels—distinguish the 100/200 from the 5000-series. The interior, however, is much more luxurious, with a new dashboard and tasteful wood inlays. Automatic-transmission shift levers now move through a gated pattern; Audi's Automatic Shift Lock continues to require the driver to depress the brake pedal before shifting out of park. Like the 5000 series, 100s and 200s come as 4-door-notchback sedans and 5-door wagons in either front-drive or

Prices are accurate at time of printing; subject to manufacturer's change.

Audi 100 4-door

Specifications

	4-door notchback	5-door wagon
Wheelbase, in.	105.8	105.8
Overall length, in.	192.7	192.7
Overall width, in.	71.4	71.4
Overall height, in.	54.7	55.7
Turn diameter, ft.	34.2	34.2
Curb weight, lbs.	2932[1]	3042[1]
Cargo vol., cu. ft.	16.8	38.5
Fuel capacity, gal.	21.1	21.1
Seating capacity	5	5
Front headroom, in.	37.5	37.5
Front shoulder room, in.	NA	NA
Front legroom, max., in.	NA	NA
Rear headroom, in.	36.5	36.5
Rear shoulder room, in.	NA	NA
Rear legroom, min., in.	NA	NA

1. 3306 lbs, Quattro   2. 3439 lbs, Quattro

Engines

	ohc I-5	Turbo ohc I-5
Size, liters/cu. in.	2.3/141	2.2/136
Fuel delivery	PFI	PFI
Horsepower @ rpm	130 @ 5600	158 @ 5500
Torque (lbs./ft.) @ rpm	140 @ 4000	166 @ 3000
Availability	S	S

EPA city/highway mpg

5-speed OD manual	18/25	18/26
3-speed automatic	19/22	18/22

Quattro variants. An entry-level 100E Automatic model is new. The 100 and 200 models add anti-lock brakes and plusher interiors. A driver-side air bag is now standard on 200s, optional on 100s. Under any name, these Audis are exemplary sport sedans, with a distinctive and functional design, lots of standard equipment, a fine ride, composed road manners and quality workmanship. The naturally aspirated 2.3 has sub-par muscle for this class, however, while the turbo 2.2 gives outstanding performance. Allegations of unintended acceleration in automatic-transmission Audi 5000s crippled Audi's U.S. sales. The company hopes to reverse the trend with help from its "Audi Advantage," a comprehensive new warranty and service plan.

Prices

Audi 100/200	Retail Price	Dealer Invoice	Low Price
100E 4-door notchback, automatic	$24980	—	—
100 4-door notchback, 5-speed	27480	—	—
100 4-door notchback, automatic	28030	—	—
100 5-door wagon, 5-speed	28960	—	—
100 5-door wagon, automatic	29510	—	—
100 Quattro 4-door notchback, 5-speed . .	30805	—	—
200 Turbo 4-door notchback, 5-speed . . .	33405	—	—
200 Turbo 4-door notchback, automatic . .	33955	—	—
200 Quattro 4-door notchback, 5-speed . .	37305	—	—
200 Quattro 5-door wagon, 5-speed	38805	—	—
Destination charge	NA	NA	NA

Dealer invoice and low price not available at time of publication.

Audi 100 wagon

Prices are accurate at time of printing; subject to manufacturer's change.

Standard Equipment:

100E: 2.3-liter PFI 5-cylinder engine, 3-speed automatic transmission, power steering, power 4-wheel disc brakes, air conditioning, power windows and locks, heated power mirrors, velour reclining bucket seats with driver's side height adjustment, folding rear armrest, outboard rear lap/shoulder belts, reading lamps, lighted visor mirrors, anti-theft alarm, tinted glass, rear defogger, cruise control, intermittent wipers, AM/FM ST ET cassette with diversity antenna, manual sunroof, 185/70HR14 SBR tires. **100** adds: 5-speed manual or 3-speed automatic transmission, anti-lock braking system, automatic climate control, Zebrano wood inlays, rear head restraints, 10-function check system, front seatback pockets, leather-wrapped steering wheel, shift knob and boot, power sunroof, 205/60VR15 SBR tires on alloy wheels. **Wagon** deletes rear head restraints, rear armrest and diversity antenna and adds: heavy-duty suspension, asymmetrically split rear seatback, rear wiper/washer. **100 Quattro** has permanent 4-wheel drive. **200** adds to 100: 2.2-liter turbocharged PFI 5-cylinder engine, trip computer, chenille velour upholstery, ski sack, driver's side air bag (delayed introduction), Audi/Bose music system (delayed introduction). **200 Quattro** has permanent 4-wheel drive, leather upholstery.

Optional Equipment:	Retail Price	Dealer Invoice	Low Price
Anti-lock braking system, 100E	1215	—	—
Driver's side airbag, 100 exc.E	950	—	—
Airbag pkg., 100E	1600	—	—
Driver's side airbag, automatic climate control, wood interior trim, leather-wrapped steering wheel, 10-function check system.			
California compliance equipment	95	—	—
Partial leather upholstery, 200 Turbo	900	—	—
Leather upholstery (NA 100E)	1250	—	—
Clearcoat paint, 100s	450	—	—
Pearlescent paint, 200s	450	—	—
Sport seats, 100, 200 Turbo	350	—	—
Cold weather pkg., 100s	350	—	—
200s	500	—	—
Heated front seats, windshield washer nozzles and door lock cylinders.			
Power front seats, 100	825	—	—
Roof rails, wagons	225	—	—
Ski sack, 100s exc. wagon	125	—	—
Trip computer, 100	260	—	—

BMW 3-Series

All 3-Series BMWs save the 325i Convertible get new body-color bumpers that trim overall length 5.4 inches, and all but the super-performance M3 now employ a 168-horsepower

Prices are accurate at time of printing; subject to manufacturer's change.

BMW 325i 2-door

2.5-liter six. The 2.5 ousts the economy-oriented 127-horse-power "eta" engine from the base 325 2- and 4-door, which become 325i models for 1989. They're priced slightly above last year's 325 and well below the 325is. The sporty 325is 2-door adds front air dam, rear spoiler, wider wheels, firmer suspension, limited-slip differential (optional elsewhere), and sport seats. The 325i Convertible's only change is a slimmer center rear brake lamp. Introduced last year as a 2-door with manual-shift only, the all-wheel-drive 325iX is now offered with four doors, optional automatic transmission and, as a price-capper, fewer standard features. Except for losing its roof antenna for one in the windshield, the M3 is a carryover. Powered by a 2.3-liter dual-overhead-cam-shaft, 16-valve four rated at 192 horsepower, it's now the only 3-Series BMW limited to a 5-speed manual transmission. Sales of the 3-Series are down following several price increases the past two years. For '89, BMW has repositioned its entry-level models with stronger engines and more features. Price increases on the 325is ($550) and Convertible ($1350) rate as modest. These are model sports sedans in any guise, though passenger and cargo space are limited, cabins are a bit austere for the price and fuel economy is mediocre. Still, the powerful engine is a smooth delight. Handling and control are outstanding and the is ride firm but comfortable. Standard anti-lock braking is a plus. The potent but high-strung M3 is for wealthy would-be racers, and the 4WD 325iX feels glued to the pavement.

Specifications

	2-door notchback	4-door notchback	2-door conv.
Wheelbase, in.	101.2	101.2	101.2
Overall length, in.	170.2	170.2	175.2
Overall width, in.	64.8	64.8	64.8
Overall height, in.	54.3	54.3	53.9
Turn diameter, ft.	34.4	34.4	34.4
Curb weight, lbs.	2811[1]	2855	3055
Cargo vol., cu. ft.	14.3	14.3	11.0
Fuel capacity, gal.	16.4	16.4	16.4
Seating capacity	5	5	4
Front headroom, in.	37.7	37.7	NA
Front shoulder room, in.	52.0	52.0	NA
Front legroom, max., in.	NA	NA	NA
Rear headroom, in.	36.4	36.4	NA
Rear shoulder room, in.	52.4	52.4	NA
Rear legroom, min., in.	NA	NA	NA

1. 2865 lbs., M3; 3010 lbs., 325iX

Engines

	ohc I-6	dohc I-4
Size, liters/cu. in.	2.5/152	2.3/140
Fuel delivery	PFI	PFI
Horsepower @ rpm	168 @ 5800	192 @ 6750
Torque (lbs./ft.) @ rpm	164 @ 4300	170 @ 4750
Availability	S	S[1]

EPA city/highway mpg

5-speed OD manual	18/23	17/29
4-speed OD automatic	18/22	

1. M3

Prices

BMW 3-Series	Retail Price	Dealer Invoice	Low Price
325i 2-door notchback	$24650	—	—
325i 4-door notchback	25450	—	—
325is 2-door notchback	28950	—	—
325i 2-door convertible	33850	—	—
325iX 2-door notchback	29950	—	—
325iX 4-door notchback	30750	—	—
M3 2-door notchback	34950	—	—
Destination charge	325	325	325

Dealer invoice and low price not available at time of publication.

Prices are accurate at time of printing; subject to manufacturer's change.

Standard Equipment:

325i: 2.5-liter PFI 6-cylinder engine, 5-speed manual transmission, power steering, power 4-wheel disc brakes, anti-lock braking system, air conditioning, cloth or leatherette reclining bucket seats with height/tilt adjustments, outboard rear lap/shoulder belts, power windows and locks, cruise control, power mirrors, AM/FM ST ET cassette, power antenna, tinted glass, Service Interval Indicator, Active Check Control, digital clock, manual sunroof, toolkit, 195/65VR14 tires on alloy wheels. **Convertible** adds: leather sport seats with adjustable thigh support, map lights, trip computer, premium sound system. **325is** adds: limited-slip differential, front and rear spoilers, power sunroof. **325iX** has: permanent 4-wheel drive, sill extensions, leatherette upholstery, manual sunroof, folding rear armrest with ski sack, 205/55VR15 tires. **M3** has 325is equipment plus 2.3-liter DOHC PFI 4-cylinder engine, sport suspension, 205/55VR15 tires.

Optional Equipment:	Retail Price	Dealer Invoice	Low Price
4-speed automatic transmission (NA M3) .	645	—	—
Metallic paint	375	—	—
Limited-slip differential (std. 325is, M3) . .	370	—	—
Heated front seats, 325iX & conv.	200	—	—
Hardtop, convertible	3500	—	—

BMW 5-Series

BMW 535i

BMW's redesigned midrange 5-Series sedan replaces a model that came to the U.S. in 1975. The rear-drive 4-door borrows the general look and many features from the revamped 7-Series that bowed here in '87. The new 5-Series has a 5.4-inch longer wheelbase than its predecessor. Its

Prices are accurate at time of printing; subject to manufacturer's change.

body is wider by two inches, but shorter by 3.2 and fractionally lower. It's also 260-300 pounds heavier. Two models are offered. The 525i, powered by the 2.5-liter straight six introduced in last year's 3-Series, takes over for the economy-oriented 528e. A new 535i replaces the previous 535i and 535is. It has the 3.4-liter six used in the 735i/735iL sedans and 635CSi coupe. Both are available with 5-speed manual or extra-cost 4-speed automatic transmission. A high-performance M5 model with a sport suspension and BMW Motorsport's 3.5-liter 24-valve six should appear for 1990. Initial driving impressions suggest the added weight has taken the edge off the 535i's standing-start acceleration and midrange passing ability, especially with automatic transmission. We

Specifications

	4-door notchback
Wheelbase, in.	108.7
Overall length, in.	185.8
Overall width, in.	68.9
Overall height, in.	55.6
Turn diameter, ft.	37.7
Curb weight, lbs.	3395[1]
Cargo vol., cu. ft.	16.2
Fuel capacity, gal.	21.1
Seating capacity	5
Front headroom, in.	NA
Front shoulder room, in.	NA
Front legroom, max., in.	NA
Rear headroom, in.	NA
Rear shoulder room, in.	NA
Rear legroom, min., in.	NA

1. 525i; 3530 lbs., 535i

Engines

	ohc I-6	ohc I-6
Size, liters/cu. in.	2.5/152	3.4/209
Fuel delivery	PFI	PFI
Horsepower @ rpm	168 @ 5800	208 @ 5700
Torque (lbs./ft.) @ rpm	164 @ 4300	225 @ 4000
Availability	S[1]	S[2]

EPA city/highway mpg

5-speed OD manual	18/24	15/23
4-speed OD automatic	18/23	15/19

1. 525i   2. 535i

Prices are accurate at time of printing; subject to manufacturer's change.

haven't driven a 525i yet, but it weighs only about 100 pounds less and lacks strong low-end torque, so it's likely to be even more strained. Handling is fluid and responsive, grip ample, body roll well checked, the ride taut but comfortable, and noise levels quite low.

Prices

BMW 5-Series	Retail Price	Dealer Invoice	Low Price
525i 4-door notchback	$37000	—	—
535i 4-door notchback	43600	—	—
Destination charge	325	325	325
Gas Guzzler Tax, 535i 5-speed	650	650	650
535i automatic	850	850	850

Dealer invoice and low price not available at time of publication.

Standard Equipment:

525i: 2.5-liter PFI 6-cylinder engine, 5-speed manual or 4-speed automatic transmission, power steering, power 4-wheel disc brakes, anti-lock braking system, air conditioning with individual temperature controls, leather power front bucket seats, folding center armrests, rear armrest with storage, outboard rear lap/shoulder belts, power windows and locks, heated power mirrors, fog lights, adjustable steering wheel, tinted glass, tachometer and coolant temperature gauge, rear defogger, seatback pockets, front and rear reading lights, dual LCD trip odometers, Service Interval Indicator, fuel economy indicator, trip computer, power sunroof, toolkit, 205/65VR15 tires on alloy wheels. **535i** adds: 3.5-liter engine, leather-wrapped steering wheel, driver's side airbag, automatic climate control, 225/60VR15 tires.

Optional Equipment:

Limited-slip differential	390	—	—
CD changer	775	—	—
Heated front seats	200	—	—

BMW 7-Series

BMW debuted its redesigned 7-Series in the spring of '87 by introducing the 6-cylinder 735i as an early 1988 model. Last winter brought the 750iL, a stretched-wheelbase version powered by a 5.0-liter V-12. Arriving last summer was the

BMW 735i

Specifications

	735i 4-door notchback	735iL/750iL 4-door notchback
Wheelbase, in.	111.5	116.0
Overall length, in.	193.3	197.8
Overall width, in.	72.6	72.6
Overall height, in.	55.6	55.1
Turn diameter, ft.	38.1	39.4
Curb weight, lbs.	3835	4015[1]
Cargo vol., cu. ft.	17.6	17.6
Fuel capacity, gal.	21.5	24.0
Seating capacity	5	5
Front headroom, in.	NA	NA
Front shoulder room, in.	NA	NA
Front legroom, max., in.	NA	NA
Rear headroom, in.	NA	NA
Rear shoulder room, in.	NA	NA
Rear legroom, min., in.	NA	NA

1. 4235 lbs., 750iL

Engines	ohc I-6	ohc V-12
Size, liters/cu. in.	3.4/209	5.0/304
Fuel delivery	PFI	PFI
Horsepower @ rpm	208 @ 5700	300 @ 5200
Torque (lbs./ft.) @ rpm	225 @ 4000	332 @ 4100
Availability	S	S[1]

EPA city/highway mpg

5-speed OD manual	15/23	
4-speed OD automatic	14/19	12/17

1. 750iL

735iL, basically the 735's 6-cylinder in the long 750 body. For 1989, all three rear-drive 4-door sedan models get infrared remote control for their standard central locking/anti-theft system, plus power-steering assist that now varies with vehicle speed, not engine speed. Automatic-transmission 6-cylinder models get a revised final drive ratio for better acceleration. As before, only the 735i offers a 5-speed manual transmission as a no-charge option. Otherwise, you get a 4-speed automatic with "Sport," "Economy" and "Manual" shift modes. A trunk-mounted compact-disc player/changer is now standard on the 750iL and a dealer-installed option for the 735iL. The latest 7-Series is tremendously impressive—a good thing for BMW, because it's the blueprint design for the all-new 5-Series, the coming 8-Series coupe and, ultimately, the next 3-Series. All are big, heavy, quiet and smooth-riding cars with ample room, especially the limousine-like long-wheelbase models. Alas, they're also gas guzzlers. More worrisome is their complexity. There's a lot to go wrong with so many electric and electronic gizmos. But whether you're behind the mighty V-12 or the smooth six, any 7-Series will eat highway miles in a hurry and with great comfort. They're surprisingly capable on tight, twisty roads, too, with a nimbleness that belies their bulk. Overall, we prefer the 7-Series to the aging Mercedes-Benz S-Class sedans.

Prices

BMW 7-Series	Retail Price	Dealer Invoice	Low Price
735i 4-door notchback	$54000	—	—
735iL 4-door notchback	58000	—	—
750iL 4-door notchback	70000	—	—
Destination charge	325	325	325
Gas Guzzler Tax, 735i 5-speed	650	650	650
735i automatic	850	850	850
735iL	850	850	850
750iL	1850	1850	1850

Dealer invoice and low price not available at time of publication.

Standard Equipment:

3.4-liter PFI 6-cylinder engine, 5-speed manual or 4-speed automatic transmission, power steering, power 4-wheel disc brakes, anti-lock braking system, driver's side airbag, automatic climate control system with separate left and right controls, outboard rear lap/shoulder belts, cruise control, fog lamps, speed-sensitive intermittent wipers, heated wiper parking area, heated windshield washer jets, heated power mirrors, heated driver's door lock, central locking including trunk, power windows, leather-wrapped steering wheel, 8-way power front seats with 3-position driver's side memory (including outside mirrors), driver's side airbag, rear head restraints, leather seating, front center armrests, rear armrest with storage compartment, Bubinga wood trim, time-delay courtesy light, map lights, rear reading lights, tinted glass, tachometer and coolant temperature gauge, LCD main and trip odometers, Service Interval Indicator, fuel economy indicator, Active Check Control, trip computer, rear defogger, cruise control, roll-up rear sunshade, power two-way sunroof, AM/FM ST ET cassette, power antenna, lockable glovebox, toolkit, 225/60VR15 tires on cast alloy wheels. **735iL** adds: power rear seat, self-leveling rear suspension. **750iL** adds: 5.0-liter PFI V-12, anti-theft warning device, additional leather trim, Elmwood trim, cellular telephone, forged alloy wheels.

Optional Equipment:	Retail Price	Dealer Invoice	Low Price
Limited-slip differential	390	—	—
Heated front seats (std. 750iL)	200	—	—
CD changer	775	—	—

Buick Century/
Oldsmobile Cutlass Ciera

Fresh exterior styling and a new V-6 grace the Century and Cutlass Ciera, front-drive intermediates built from GM's A-body design. Both the Buick and the Olds get new grilles and flush composite headlamps. Their rear windows are more convex and less steeply sloped and, combined with new roof pillars, trunk lid and taillamps, give the cars a rounded, more aero-look at the rear. Century also gains Buick's new Dynaride suspension, which uses deflected-disc shock absorber valving that Buick says improves its ride. The new V-6 is GM's 3.3-liter "3300" rated at 160 horsepower and 185 pound/feet torque. It replaces a 3.8-liter V-6 (150 horsepower, 200 pound/feet torque) as the models' top available engine. An optional 125-horsepower 2.8-liter V-6 returns unchanged for the Cutlass Ciera, but is no longer offered on the Century. Both cars retain the base 2.5-liter

Buick Century Custom 2-door

Specifications

	2-door notchback	4-door notchback	5-door wagon
Wheelbase, in.	104.9	104.9	104.9
Overall length, in.	190.3	190.3	194.4
Overall width, in.	69.5	69.5	69.5
Overall height, in.	54.1	54.1	54.5
Turn diameter, ft.	38.1	38.1	38.1
Curb weight, lbs.	2736	2764	2913
Cargo vol., cu. ft.	15.8	15.8	74.4
Fuel capacity, gal.	15.7	15.7	15.7
Seating capacity	6	6	8
Front headroom, in.	38.6	38.6	38.6
Front shoulder room, in.	55.9	55.9	56.2
Front legroom, max., in.	42.1	42.1	42.1
Rear headroom, in.	37.6	38.0	38.9
Rear shoulder room, in.	56.9	55.9	56.2
Rear legroom, min., in.	35.8	35.8	NA

Engines

	ohv I-4	ohv V-6	ohv V-6
Size, liters/cu. in.	2.5/151	2.8/173	3.3/204
Fuel delivery	TBI	PFI	PFI
Horsepower @ rpm	110 @ 5200	125 @ 4500	160 @ 5200
Torque (lbs./ft.) @ rpm	135 @ 3200	160 @ 3600	185 3200
Availability	S	O[1]	O[2]

EPA city/highway mpg

3-speed automatic	23/30		
4-speed OD automatic		20/29	20/29

1. Cutlass Ciera   2. Standard on Cutlass Ciera I-Series

4-cylinder, which makes 110 horsepower this year, a gain of 12 after alterations to the cylinder head and fuel-injection system. As with all 1989 GM cars, rear shoulder belts are standard. A power sunroof is a new Cutlass Ciera option and wheel locks now come with the optional aluminum wheels. Both cars continue in three body styles: 2-door coupe, 4-door sedan and 5-door wagon. They share their basic design with the less-expensive Chevrolet Celebrity and Pontiac 6000, neither of which offers the 2-door body style or the new 3.3-liter V-6. The 3.3 should be more fuel efficient than the previous 3.8 without much noticeable loss of performance. And it's certainly smoother than the 2.8 or the standard 4-cylinder. These conservative GM intermediates don't have the modern look or over-the-road feel of the newer Ford Taurus/Mercury Sable, but they're roomy and competent nonetheless. The International Series version of the Olds adds a touch of sportiness with a suspension and tire package designed to upgrade handling.

Prices

Buick Century	Retail Price	Dealer Invoice	Low Price
Custom 4-door notchback	$12429	$10726	$11578
Custom 2-door notchback	12199	10528	11364
Custom 5-door wagon	13156	11354	12255
Limited 4-door notchback	13356	11526	12441
Estate 5-door wagon	13956	12044	13000
Destination charge	450	450	450

Standard Equipment:

Custom: 2.5-liter TBI 4-cylinder engine, 3-speed automatic transmission, power steering, power brakes, dual outside mirrors, bumper guards and rub strips, tinted glass, map lights, instrument panel courtesy lights, engine compartment and trunk lights, cloth notchback bench seats, AM/FM ST ET, headlamps-on chime, deluxe wheel covers, P185/75R14 all-season SBR tires. **Wagon** adds: split folding rear seatback, two-way tailgate. **Limited and Estate** add: moldings (windsplit, wide rocker panel), 55/45 notchback cloth seat, armrest with storage, trunk trim (4-door).

Optional Equipment:

3.3-liter PFI V-6	710	604	653
4-speed automatic transmission (V-6 req.) .	175	149	161

Prices are accurate at time of printing; subject to manufacturer's change.

	Retail Price	Dealer Invoice	Low Price
HD engine & transmission cooling, w/A/C .	40	34	37
w/o A/C	70	60	64
Rear defogger	145	123	133
California emissions pkg.	100	85	92
Decklid luggage rack, exc. wagons	115	98	106
AM/FM ST ET cassette	122	104	112
Power antenna	70	60	64
Bodyside stripes	45	38	41
HD suspension, wagon	27	23	25
195/75R14 WSW tires, 2- & 4-doors	61	52	56
Wagons	34	29	31
Cloth 55/45 seat w/storage armrest, Custom	183	156	168
Locking wire wheel covers	199	169	183
Styled steel wheels	99	84	91
Alloy wheels	199	169	183
Rear wiper/washer, wagons	125	106	115
Woodgrain applique, wagons	350	298	322
Gran Touring Pkg. (NA wagons)	500	425	460

Gran Touring Suspension, leather-wrapped steering wheel, 215/60R14 Goodyear Eagle GT tires.

Popular Pkg. SB, Custom 2- & 4-door . . .	700	595	644

Air conditioning, rear defogger, tilt steering column, intermittent wipers.

Premium Pkg. SC, Custom 2-door	1125	956	1035
Custom 4-door	1185	1007	1090

Pkg. SB plus cruise control, 55/45 seat, AM/FM ST ET cassette, carpet savers, seatback recliners, power door locks, door edge guards.

Luxury Pkg. SD, Custom 2-door	1492	1268	1373
Custom 4-door	1627	1383	1497

Pkg. SC plus wire wheel covers, lighted right visor mirror, power windows.

Prestige Pkg. SE, Custom 2-door	1780	1513	1638
Custom 4-door	1915	1628	1762

Pkg. SD plus power mirrors, power driver's seat, power antenna, power trunk release.

Special Pkg. SJ, Custom 2-door	925	786	851
Custom 4-door	1010	859	929

Air conditioning, rear defogger, tilt steering column, intermittent wipers, door edge guards, power windows.

Special Pkg. SK, Custom 2-door	1065	905	980
Custom 4-door	1115	948	1026

Deletes power windows and door edge guards from Pkg. SJ and adds carpet savers, power door locks, cruise control.

Premium Pkg. SC, Limited	965	820	888

Air conditioning, rear defogger, tilt steering column, carpet savers, cruise control, intermittent wipers, power door locks.

Luxury Pkg. SD, Limited	1336	1136	1229

Pkg. SC plus AM/FM ST ET cassette, seatback recliners, wire wheel covers, door edge guards, power windows.

Prices are accurate at time of printing; subject to manufacturer's change.

	Retail Price	Dealer Invoice	Low Price
Prestige Pkg. SE, Limited	1826	1552	1680

Pkg. SD plus power mirrors, lighted right visor mirror, power drivers' seat, power antenna, power trunk release, front reading lights, premium rear speakers.

Popular Pkg. 1SB, Custom wagon	815	693	750

Air conditioner, rear defogger, roof rack, intermittent wipers, tilt steering column.

Premium Pkg. SC, Custom wagon	1602	1362	1474

Pkg. SB plus carpet savers, power door locks, power tailgate release, cruise control, AM/FM ST ET cassette, third seat, swing-out rear quarter windows, front seatback recliners, 55/45 front seat, rear window air deflector, door edge guards.

Luxury Pkg. SD, Custom wagon	2044	1737	1880

Pkg. SC plus wire wheel covers, power windows, lighted right visor mirror.

Prestige Pkg. SE, Custom wagon	2282	1940	2099

Pkg. SD plus power mirrors, power driver's seat, power antenna.

Premium Pkg. SC, Estate	1220	1037	1122

Air conditioning, rear defogger, roof rack, intermittent wipers, tilt steering column, carpet savers, power door locks, power tailgate release, cruise control, front seatback recliners.

Luxury Pkg. SD, Estate	1881	1599	1731

Pkg. SC plus AM/FM ST ET cassette, third seat, swing-out rear quarter windows, rear window air deflector, door edge guards, wire wheel covers, power windows, power antenna, lighted right visor mirror.

Prestige Pkg. SE, Estate	2158	1834	1985

Pkg. SD plus power driver's seat, power mirrors, front reading lights, premium rear speakers.

Oldsmobile Cutlass Ciera

	Retail	Dealer	Low
2-door notchback	$11695	$10327	$11011
4-door notchback	12195	10524	11360
SL 2-door notchback	12695	11210	11953
SL 4-door notchback	13495	11646	12571
I Series 2-door notchback	15995	14124	15060
I Series 4-door notchback	16795	14494	15645
Cruiser 5-door wagon	12995	11215	12105
Cruiser SL 5-door wagon	13995	12078	13037
Destination charge	450	450	450

Standard Equipment:

2.5-liter TBI 4-cylinder engine, 3-speed automatic transmission, power steering and brakes, front bench seat with armrest, left remote and right manual mirrors, outboard rear lap/shoulder belts, AM/FM ST ET, tinted glass, 185/75R14 all-season SBR tires. **SL** adds: 55/45 front seat, Convenience Group

Prices are accurate at time of printing; subject to manufacturer's change

(reading lamps, lighted right visor mirror, chime tones, misc. lights), AM/FM ST ET cassette, rear parcel shelf storage bin, power decklid release. **International Series** adds: 3.3-liter PFI V-6, 4-speed automatic transmission, FE3 suspension, front air dam with fog lights, center console with floorshift, Driver Information System (trip computer, service reminder), rallye instruments (tachometer, coolant temperature, oil pressure, voltmeter, trip odometer), tilt steering column, leather-wrapped steering wheel, intermittent wipers, 215/60R14 tires on alloy wheels.

Optional Equipment:

	Retail Price	Dealer Invoice	Low Price
2.8-liter V-6, exc. I Series	610	519	561
3.3-liter V-6, exc. I Series	710	604	653
4-speed auto trans, exc. I Series	175	149	161
Option Pkg. 1SB, base	631	536	581
Air conditioning, tilt steering column, intermittent wipers, Convenience Group.			
Option Pkg. 1SC, base 2-door	891	757	820
Base 4-door	1026	872	944
Pkg. 1SB plus power windows and locks, floormats, door edge guards, power antenna.			
Option Pkg. 1SD, base 2-door	1252	1064	1152
Base 4-door	1387	1179	1276
Pkg. 1SC plus Molding Pkg., seatback recliners, remote mirrors, power driver's seat.			
Option Pkg. 1SB, SL 2-door	885	752	814
SL 4-door	895	761	823
Air conditioning, tilt steering column, intermittent wipers, floormats, door edge guards, cruise control, power antenna.			
Option Pkg. 1SC, SL 2-door	1250	1063	1150
SL 4-door	1385	1177	1274
Pkg. 1SB plus power windows and locks, seatback recliners, remote mirrors, power driver's seat.			
Option Pkg. 1SB, I Series 2-door	870	740	800
I Series 4-door	995	846	915
Power windows and locks, cruise control, power driver's seat, power antenna.			
Option Pkg. 1SB, base wagon	1163	989	1070
Air conditioning, cruise control, tilt steering column, intermittent wipers, door edge guards, luggage rack, divided bench seat with storage armrest, floormats.			
Option Pkg. 1SC, base wagon	1841	1565	1694
Pkg. 1SB plus power windows and locks, Convenience Group, rear-facing third seat, power antenna.			
Option Pkg. 1SD, base wagon	2202	1872	2026
Pkg. 1SC plus Molding Pkg., seatback recliners, remote mirrors, power driver's seat.			

Prices are accurate at time of printing; subject to manufacturer's change

	Retail Price	Dealer Invoice	Low Price
Option Pkg. 1SB, SL wagon	1590	1352	1463

Air conditioning, tilt steering column, intermittent wipers, cruise control, luggage rack, floormats, door edge guards, power windows and locks, power antenna, power driver's seat, remote mirrors, seatback recliners.

	Retail Price	Dealer Invoice	Low Price
Divided bench seat, base	183	156	168
Reclining bucket seats, base	347	295	319
45/45 front seat, SL	275	234	253
Seatback recliners (each), base & SL . . .	45	38	41
Power locks, 2-doors	145	123	133
4-doors	195	166	179
Wagons	245	208	225
Power windows, 2-doors	210	179	193
4-doors & wagons	285	242	262
Rear defogger	145	123	133
Power sunroof, SL & I Series	775	659	713
Accent stripe, exc. I Series	45	38	41
FE2 suspension pkg., base & SL	30	26	28
FE3 suspension pkg., base & SL	455	387	419
Engine block heater	18	15	17
Cruise control, base	175	149	161
Wire wheel covers, SL	267	227	246
Super Stock wheels, base	99	84	91
Alloy wheels, base & SL	283	241	260
185/75R14 WSW tires, base & SL	68	58	63
Rallye instruments, base & SL	142	121	131
AM/FM ST ET cassette, base	147	125	135
w/EQ, SL & I Series	150	128	138
HD cooling, w/A/C	70	60	64
w/o A/C	70	60	64
Decklid luggage rack, base & SL	115	98	106
California emissions pkg.	100	85	92
Vinyl woodgrain paneling, wagons	290	247	267
w/Option Pkg	260	221	239

Buick Electra/
Oldsmobile Ninety-Eight

Both these front-drive, full-size luxury 4-doors have a host of equipment changes for '89, while Buick will use the Electra as the basis for a new flagship sedan, the Park Avenue Ultra, to be introduced at mid-year. Among Ultra's features is a

Prices are accurate at time of printing; subject to manufacturer's change

Buick Electra T Type

leather interior with 20-way power adjustments for the front seats. It will join the Electra Limited, plusher Park Avenue and sporty Electra T Type. Among options new to all these models is remote keyless entry system that uses radio waves. It doesn't require that the signal be aimed at a receiver inside the car and can lock or unlock doors or trunk from as far away as 30 feet. On the Olds side, steering-wheel controls for most climate and stereo system functions are a new option on Ninety-Eight and standard on the top-line Touring Sedan, Olds' European-style luxury effort. A driver's-side air bag is a new option for Ninety-Eight (the steering-wheel controls render it unavailable on the Touring Sedan). Both Olds and Buick models have standard automatic front seat belts and 3-point rear shoulder belts. Buick makes anti-lock brakes standard on the T Type and Ultra, optional on the others; Olds puts them on the Touring Sedan and makes them optional on Ninety-Eights. The only available powertrain is a 3.8-liter V-6 and a 4-speed automatic transmission. The engine provides brisk acceleration, though it isn't the smoothest V-6, plus it uses too much gas (expect 15-18 mpg around town). Both Buick and Olds editions are roomy and posh executive cars. The T Type and Touring Sedan sacrifice some comfort for a firmer ride and better handling, though without the all-around competence of European rivals. This basic design is used for the Buick LeSabre, Oldsmobile 88 Royale, Pontiac Bonneville and Cadillac De Ville/Fleetwood. We suspect many Buick and

Olds buyers would be as well served by the mechanically similar but less-expensive LeSabre and 88, especially since both can be had with optional anti-lock brakes.

Specifications

	4-door notchback
Wheelbase, in.	110.8
Overall length, in.	196.9
Overall width, in.	72.4
Overall height, in.	54.3
Turn diameter, ft.	39.4
Curb weight, lbs.	3289
Cargo vol., cu. ft.	16.4
Fuel capacity, gal.	18.0
Seating capacity	6
Front headroom, in.	39.3
Front shoulder room, in.	58.9
Front legroom, max., in.	42.4
Rear headroom, in.	38.1
Rear shoulder room, in.	58.8
Rear legroom, min., in.	41.5

Engines

	ohv V-6
Size, liters/cu. in.	3.8/231
Fuel delivery	PFI
Horsepower @ rpm	165 @ 4800
Torque (lbs./ft.) @ rpm	210 @ 2000
Availability	S

EPA city/highway mpg

4-speed OD automatic	19/28

Prices

Buick Electra	Retail Price	Dealer Invoice	Low Price
Limited 4-door notchback	$18525	$15987	$17256
T Type 4-door notchback	21325	18403	19864
Park Avenue 4-door notchback	20460	17657	19059
Ultra 4-door notchback	NA	NA	NA
Destination charge	550	550	550

Standard Equipment:

Limited: 3.8-liter PFI V-6 engine, 4-speed automatic transmission, power steering and brakes, air conditioning, 55/45 cloth front seat with storage

Prices are accurate at time of printing; subject to manufacturer's change

armrest, power driver's seat, tilt steering column, power windows, left remote and right manual mirrors, headlamps-on tone, trip odometer, remote fuel door release, tinted glass, front reading and courtesy lights, engine compartment and trunk lights, bodyside moldings, AM/FM ST ET, automatic front seat belts, outboard rear lap/shoulder belts, automatic level control, 205/75R14 all-season SBR tires. **T Type** adds: anti-lock braking system, Gran Touring Suspension, sport steering wheel, carpet savers, overhead console, quartz analog gauge cluster (includes tachometer, voltmeter, coolant temperature and oil pressure, low-fuel warning), rear headrests, lighted visor mirrors, power mirrors, 45/45 front seat with console and armrest, leather-wrapped steering wheel, 215/65R15 Goodyear Eagle GT + 4 tires on alloy wheels. **Park Avenue** adds to base: cruise control, power door locks, power mirrors, intermittent wipers, coach lamps, rear reading and courtesy lights, lighted right visor mirror, added sound insulation, carpet savers, upgraded carpet, WSW tires. **Ultra** adds: anti-lock braking system, 55/45 leather front seat with 20-way power adjustments, two-tone paint, rear armrest, 205/70R15 tires on alloy wheels.

Optional Equipment:

	Retail Price	Dealer Invoice	Low Price
Anti-lock braking system, Ltd & Park Ave	925	786	851
HD engine & transmission cooling (std. T Type)	40	34	37
California emissions pkg.	100	85	92
Rear defogger (SA Pkg. req.)	145	123	133
Quartz analog gauges, Ltd & Park Ave	126	107	116
Electronic instrumentation, Park Ave & Ultra	299	254	275
Decklid luggage rack	115	98	106
Firemist paint (exc. T Type)	210	179	193
AM/FM ST ET cassette	132	112	121
AM/FM ST ET cassette w/EQ	352	299	324
Delco/Bose music system	905	769	833
Power antenna, Park Ave & Ultra	70	60	64
Astroroof	1230	1046	1132
Bodyside stripes	45	38	41
Theft deterrent system	159	135	146
Heavily padded vinyl top, Ltd & Park Ave	260	221	239
Leather/vinyl 55/45 seat, Park Ave	425	361	391
T Type	325	276	299
Alloy wheels, Ltd	255	217	235
Park Ave	220	187	202
Gran Touring Pkg., Ltd	548	466	504
Park Ave	447	380	411

Gran Touring Suspension, 215/65R15 Goodyear Eagle GT tires on alloy wheels, 2.97 axle ratio, HD cooling, leather-wrapped steering wheel.

Popular Pkg. SB, Ltd	877	745	807

Rear defogger, 205/75R14 WSW tires, intermittent wipers, cruise control, power door locks, AM/FM ST ET cassette, wire wheel covers.

Prices are accurate at time of printing; subject to manufacturer's change

	Retail Price	Dealer Invoice	Low Price
Premium Pkg. SC, Ltd	1170	995	1076

Pkg. SB plus carpet savers, lighted right visor mirror, power antenna, power trunk release, door edge guards, passenger seatback recliner.

	Retail Price	Dealer Invoice	Low Price
Luxury Pkg. SD, Ltd	1562	1328	1437

Pkg. SC plus power passenger seat, automatic climate control, HD battery, power mirrors, door courtesy and warning lights.

Prestige Pkg. SE, Ltd	2652	2254	2440

Pkg. SD plus AM/FM ST ET cassette w/EQ, cornering lights, lamp monitors, Twilight Sentinel, illuminated entry, automatic power door locks, automatic day/night mirror, lighted left visor mirror, power driver's seatback recliner, self-sealing tires, remote keyless entry system.

Popular Pkg. SB, Park Ave	341	290	314

AM/FM ST ET cassette, rear defogger, wire wheel covers.

Premium Pkg. SC, Park Ave	1042	886	959

Pkg. SB plus power antenna, door edge guards, HD battery, power passenger's seatback recliner, power passenger seat, automatic climate control, Concert Sound speakers, Twilight Sentinel.

Luxury Pkg. SD, Park Ave	1517	1289	1396

Pkg. SC plus illuminated driver's door lock and interior light control, four-note horn, low fuel and washer fluid indicators, cornering lights, light monitors, low fuel indicator, power decklid pulldown, remote keyless entry system, lighted left visor mirror, automatic power door locks.

Prestige Pkg. SE, Park Ave	2223	1890	2045

Pkg. SD plus AM/FM ST ET cassette w/EQ, automatic day/night mirror, power mirrors with heated left, power driver's seatback recliner, memory power driver's seat, self-sealing tires, deluxe trunk trim with mat.

Popular Pkg. SB, T Type	722	614	664

Intermittent wipers, cruise control, rear defogger, power door locks, AM/FM ST ET cassette, power antenna, power trunk release.

Premium Pkg. SC, T Type	1293	1099	1190

Pkg. SB plus door edge guards, power passenger seatback recliner, power passenger seat, automatic climate control, HD battery, Concert Sound speakers.

Prestige Pkg. SE, T Type	2482	2110	2283

Pkg. SD plus automatic power door locks, AM/FM ST ET cassette w/EQ, automatic day/night mirror, power mirrors with heated left, power driver's seatback recliner, memory power driver's seat, deluxe trunk trim with mat.

Oldsmobile Ninety-Eight

4-door notchback	$19295	$16652	$17974
Brougham 4-door notchback	20495	17687	19091
Touring Sedan 4-door notchback	25995	22434	24215
Destination charge	550	550	550

Prices are accurate at time of printing; subject to manufacturer's change

Standard Equipment:

3.8-liter PFI V-6, 4-speed automatic transmission, power steering and brakes, air conditioning, tinted glass, power windows and locks, 55/45 seat with power driver's side and storage armrest, automatic front seatbelts, outboard rear lap/shoulder belts, remote mirrors, opera lamps, front and rear armrests, right visor mirrors, trip odometer, reading lamp, AM/FM ST ET cassette, automatic load leveling, 205/75R14 all-season SBR tires, wire wheel covers. **Brougham** adds: automatic climate control, cruise control, tilt steering column, cornering lamps, sail panel reading lamps, intermittent wipers, opera lamp, alloy wheels. **Touring Sedan** adds: anti-lock braking system, FE3 suspension, 215/65R15 Goodyear Eagle GT + 4 tires on alloy wheels, front console with storage, Driver Information System (trip computer, service reminder), gauge cluster including tachometer, fog lamps, illumination package, power mirrors with heated left, AM/FM ST ET cassette w/EQ, Twilight Sentinel, steering wheel touch controls, power decklid and fuel door releases.

Optional Equipment:

	Retail Price	Dealer Invoice	Low Price
Anti-lock brakes, base & Brougham	925	786	851
Inflatable restraint (airbag), base & Brougham	850	723	782
Option Pkg. 1SB, base	629	535	579
Floormats, intermittent wipers, cruise control, tilt steering column, power decklid release, power antenna, lighted visor mirrors.			
Option Pkg. 1SC, base	1721	1463	1583
Pkg. 1SB plus seatback recliners, automatic climate control, power passenger seat, cornering lamps, Driver Information System, Convenience Value Group.			
Option Pkg. 1SB, Brougham	684	581	629
Power decklid release and pulldown, floormats, lighted visor mirrors, power antenna, power passenger seat, seatback recliners.			
Option Pkg. 1SC, Brougham	1490	1267	1371
Pkg. 1SB plus Driver Information System, Convenience Value Group, steering wheel touch controls, leather-wrapped steering wheel, automatic power locks.			
Seatback recliners (each), base & Brougham	45	38	41
Padded vinyl roof, base & Brougham . . .	260	221	239
Power sunroof, Brougham & Touring . . .	1230	1046	1132
Rear defogger, base & Brougham	145	123	133
Accent stripe, base	45	38	41
FE3 suspension pkg., base	289	246	266
Brougham	246	209	226
Engine block heater	18	15	17
Wire wheel covers, Brougham (credit) . . .	(33)	(28)	(28)
Alloy wheels, base	53	45	49
Steering wheel touch controls, base	179	152	165
AM/FM ST ET cassette w/EQ, base & Brougham	235	200	216

Prices are accurate at time of printing; subject to manufacturer's change

	Retail Price	Dealer Invoice	Low Price
AM/FM ST ET w/CD player, base & Brougham	359	305	330
Delco/Bose music system, Touring	523	445	481
Instrument panel cluster, base & Brougham .	66	56	61
Electronic instruments, Brougham	245	208	225
HD cooling, base & Brougham	66	56	61
Glamour metallic paint, base & Brougham .	210	179	193
Custom leather trim, base & Brougham . .	433	368	398
California emissions pkg.	100	85	92

Buick Estate/
Oldsmobile Custom Cruiser/
Pontiac Safari

Buick Le Sabre Estate

These full-size, rear-drive stations wagons share with the Chevrolet Caprice wagon a design that dates from 1977. Changes for '89 are minimal. A new 5000-pound trailer-towing package is optional for both Buick versions, the LeSabre Estate and plusher Electra wagons. Leather seats are a new option for the Electra model. The new towing package includes heavy-duty engine and transmission cooling, automatic level control, limited slip differential, and a 3.23 final drive ratio. The Custom Cruiser and Safari already had that towing option, and this year join the Buick with standard 3-point shoulder belts for outboard rear seating positions.

Prices are accurate at time of printing; subject to manufacturer's change

All use a carbureted 5.0-liter V-8 engine and 4-speed overdrive automatic transmission. With a standard rear-facing
fold-down rear seat that gives them 8-passenger capacity,
and with nearly 90 cubic feet of cargo space, these big
wagons exceed the capabilities of mid-size, front-drive
rivals, and nearly match the minivans. They may in fact
come out a little cheaper than a fully equipped minivan.
GM's full-size wagons have impressive reputations for occu-
pant protection. But at well over 4000 pounds, they're too
heavy for their 140-horsepower engine, so gas mileage and
acceleration both are poor. They also suffer clumsy, boat-
like handling and a mushy, poorly controlled ride, though
the trailering package cures some of that. While these aren't
our favorites, they serve a market niche that calls for a
luxurious beast of burden in a traditional station-wagon
format.

Specifications

	5-door wagon
Wheelbase, in.	115.9
Overall length, in.	220.5
Overall width, in.	79.3
Overall height, in.	59.3
Turn diameter, ft.	41.4
Curb weight, lbs.	4209
Cargo vol., cu. ft.	87.9
Fuel capacity, gal.	22.0
Seating capacity	8
Front headroom, in.	39.6
Front shoulder room, in.	60.9
Front legroom, max., in.	42.2
Rear headroom, in.	39.3
Rear shoulder room, in.	61.0
Rear legroom, min., in.	37.2

Engines

	ohv V-8
Size, liters/cu. in.	5.0/307
Fuel delivery	4 bbl.
Horsepower @ rpm	140 @ 3200
Torque (lbs./ft.) @ rpm	255 @ 2000
Availability	S

EPA city/highway mpg

4-speed OD automatic	17/24

Prices

Buick Le Sabre/ Electra Estate

	Retail Price	Dealer Invoice	Low Price
LeSabre Estate 5-door wagon	$16770	$14473	$15622
Electra Estate 5-door wagon	19860	17139	18500
Destination charge	550	550	550

Standard Equipment:

LeSabre: 5.0-liter 4bbl. V-8, 4-speed automatic transmission, power steering and brakes, air conditioning, 55/45 cloth front seat with armrest, reclining passenger-side backrest, headlamps-on tone, trip odometer, tinted glass, outboard rear lap/shoulder belts, low fuel and washer fluid indicators, AM/FM ST ET, 225/75R15 all-season SBR tires. **Electra** adds: power windows and locks, roof rack, power driver's seat, woodgrain vinyl applique.

Optional Equipment:

Rear defogger	145	123	133
California emissions pkg	100	85	92
AM/FM ST ET cassette, LeSabre	132	112	121
AM/FM ST ET cassette w/EQ, Electra	282	240	259
Power passenger seat, Electra	240	204	221
Trailer Towing Pkg.	315	268	290
3.23 axle ratio, HD engine and transmission cooling, automatic level control, limited-slip differential.			
Leather/vinyl 55/45 front seat, LeSabre ..	525	446	483
Electra	425	361	391
Locking wire wheel covers	199	169	183
Vinyl woodgrain applique, LeSabre	345	293	317
Popular Pkg. SB, LeSabre	870	740	800
Power door locks, remote tailgate release, tilt steering column, roof rack, cruise control, intermittent wipers, rear defogger.			
Premium Pkg. SC, LeSabre	1747	1485	1607
Pkg. SB plus power windows, door edge guards, AM/FM ST ET cassette, air deflector, carpet savers, Molding Pkg., power driver's seat.			
Luxury Pkg. SD, LeSabre	2030	1726	1868
Pkg. SC plus power antenna, lighted right visor mirror, halogen headlamps, bodyside moldings, power seatback recliner.			
Popular Pkg. SB, Electra	790	672	727
Cruise control, AM/FM ST ET cassette, air deflector, carpet savers, power antenna, lighted right visor mirror, rear defogger, moldings (rocker panel, lower fender, bodyside).			
Premium Pkg. SC, Electra	1233	1048	1134
Pkg. SB plus halogen headlamps, power seatback recliner, automatic climate control, door courtesy and warning lights, front light monitors, power mirrors.			

Prices are accurate at time of printing; subject to manufacturer's change

	Retail Price	Dealer Invoice	Low Price
Luxury Pkg. SD, Electra	1578	1341	1452

Pkg. SC plus cornering lights, Twilight Sentinel, illuminated driver's door lock and interior light control, AM/FM ST ET cassette w/EQ.

Oldsmobile Custom Cruiser

5-door wagon	$16795	$14494	$15645
Destination charge	505	505	505

Standard Equipment:

5.0-liter 4bbl. V-8, 4-speed automatic transmission, power steering and brakes, power tailgate window, air conditioning, tinted glass, left remote mirror, trip odometer, AM/FM ST ET, right visor mirror, chime tones, rear storage compartment lock, 55/45 bench seat, outboard rear lap/shoulder belts, rear-facing third seat, P225/75R15 tires.

Optional Equipment:

Option Pkg. 1SB	1072	911	986

Intermittent wipers, cruise control, tilt steering column, wire wheel covers, door edge guards, floormats, power mirrors, passenger recliner, power antenna, Reminder Pkg., rear defogger, accent stripe.

Option Pkg. 1SC	2493	2119	2294

Pkg. 1SB plus power windows and locks, luggage rack, bodyside moldings, lighted visor mirrors, power driver's seat, AM/FM ST ET cassette, side paneling.

Option Pkg. 1SD	3095	2631	2847

Pkg. 1SC plus automatic climate control, dome/reading lamps, Illumination Pkg., cornering lamps, exterior lamp monitor, automatic day/ night mirror, power passenger seat.

Passenger recliner	45	38	41
Power locks	245	208	225
Power windows	285	242	262
Automatic leveling	175	149	161
Limited-slip differential	100	85	92
Engine block heater	18	15	17
Instrument panel cluster	66	56	61
Trailering Pkg.	96	82	88
California emissions pkg.	100	85	92

Pontiac Safari

5-door wagon	$15659	$13514	$14587
Destination charge	505	505	505

Prices are accurate at time of printing; subject to manufacturer's change

Standard Equipment:

5.0-liter 4bbl. V-8 engine, 4-speed automatic transmission, power steering and brakes, air conditioning, tinted glass, courtesy lights, left remote and right manual mirrors, bodyside moldings, AM/FM ST ET, cloth split bench seat with center armrest, rear-facing third seat, outboard rear lap/shoulder belts, custom wheel covers, 225/75R15 tires.

Optional Equipment:	Retail Price	Dealer Invoice	Low Price
Option Pkg. 1SA	402	342	370
Tilt steering column, Lamp Group, cruise control, intermittent wipers.			
Option Pkg. 1SB	1434	1219	1319
Pkg. 1SA plus power windows and locks, power driver's seat, sidewall and tailgate carpet, cornering lamps, remote mirrors, bumper guards, lighted right visor mirror, halogen headlamps.			
HD cooling	40	34	37
Rear defogger	145	123	133
California emissions pkg.	100	85	92
Instrument cluster gauges	71	60	65
Roof luggage rack	155	132	143
Power locks	245	208	225
Power windows	285	242	262
AM/FM ST ET cassette	122	104	112
w/EQ	272	231	250
Power antenna	70	60	64
55/45 seat	133	113	122
Right seatback recliner	45	38	41
Requires 55/45 seat.			
Super-lift shock absorbers	64	54	59
7-lead trailer wiring harness	30	26	28
Wire wheel covers	214	182	197
Simulated woodgrain siding	345	293	317

Buick LeSabre/ Oldsmobile 88 Royale/ Pontiac Bonneville

For the first time, anti-lock brakes are available for all versions of these full-size front-drive family cars built off GM's H-body platform. The LeSabre line, Buick's most popular, includes 2- and 4-door body styles in a choice of trim levels. A sporty T Type package is again available for the base coupe,

Buick Le Sabre Custom 2-door

while a Gran Touring suspension package can be ordered with any model. A tilt steering column and trip odometer are now standard on all LeSabres, new speedometer graphics have readings up to 100 mph instead of 85, and Custom and Limited models get more fake wood interior trim. The "Delta" name, used since 1965 on Oldsmobile 88 models, has disappeared, so the moniker is now "88 Royale." As before, base and Brougham trim levels are available on either the 2-door coupe or 4-door sedan. The 4-door is one of the least expensive cars available in the U.S. with both a driver's-side air bag and anti-lock brakes. Bonneville is available as a 4-door only. Base LE and mid-level SE editions gain optional anti-lock brakes this year. The flagship SSE retains them as standard, but gets some new interior appointments, including a center console that houses relocated power controls for the reshaped front bucket seats and two auxiliary jacks that can be used for operating radar detectors, portable computers and other electrically powered appliances. Steering-wheel controls for the stereo system, standard on the SSE and now optional on both SE and LE, are simplified and now also cover most climate-system functions. All three of these H-bodies are roomy cars adept at family transport. T Type LeSabres and SSE Bonnevilles have European luxury-performance cues without the imports' sky-high price tags. One thing all three share is a mandatory powertrain: 3.8-liter V-6 and 4-speed automatic transmission. They also are lower-priced versions of the same design used for the Oldsmobile Ninety-Eight and Buick Electra, which are costlier and posher, but no more efficient or capable.

Specifications

	2-door notchback	4-door notchback
Wheelbase, in.	110.8	110.8
Overall length, in.	196.5	196.5
Overall width, in.	72.4	72.4
Overall height, in.	54.7	55.4
Turn diameter, ft.	40.0	40.0
Curb weight, lbs.	3227	3267
Cargo vol., cu. ft.	15.7	16.4
Fuel capacity, gal.	18.0	18.0
Seating capacity	6	6
Front headroom, in.	38.1	38.9
Front shoulder room, in.	59.0	59.5
Front legroom, max., in.	42.4	42.4
Rear headroom, in.	37.6	38.3
Rear shoulder room, in.	57.8	59.5
Rear legroom, min., in.	37.0	38.7

Engines

	ohv V-6
Size, liters/cu. in.	3.8/231
Fuel delivery	PFI
Horsepower @ rpm	165 @ 4800
Torque (lbs./ft.) @ rpm	210 @ 2000
Availability	S

EPA city/highway mpg

4-speed OD automatic	19/28

Prices

Buick Le Sabre	Retail Price	Dealer Invoice	Low Price
2-door notchback	$15425	$13312	$14369
Custom 4-door notchback	15330	13230	14280
Limited 4-door notchback	16730	14438	15584
Limited 2-door notchback	16630	14352	15491
Destination charge	505	505	505

Standard Equipment:

Base and Custom: 3.8-liter PFI V-6, 4-speed automatic transmission, power steering and brakes, air conditioning, tilt steering column, cloth split bench seat with armrest, trip odometer, tinted glass, AM/FM ST ET, automatic front seatbelts, outboard rear lap/shoulder belts, 205/75R14 all-season SBR tires. **Limited** adds: 55/45 front seat with storage armrest, reclining seatbacks, wide lower bodyside moldings.

Prices are accurate at time of printing; subject to manufacturer's change.

Optional Equipment:

	Retail Price	Dealer Invoice	Low Price
Anti-lock braking system	925	786	851
HD engine & transmission cooling	40	34	37
Rear defogger	145	123	133
California emissions pkg.	100	85	92
Gauges & tachometer	110	94	101
Decklid luggage rack	115	98	106
AM/FM ST ET cassette	132	112	121
AM/FM ST ET cassette w/EQ	367	312	338
Power antenna	70	60	64
Bodyside stripes	45	38	41
Automatic level control	175	149	161
Full vinyl top, 4-doors	200	170	184
55/45 seat, base & Custom	183	156	168
Leather/vinyl 55/45 seat, Ltd	425	361	391
Leather/vinyl 45/45 seat, base & T Type ..	325	276	299
Alloy wheels, 14"	255	217	235
Styled steel wheels	99	84	91
Locking wire wheel covers, exc. T Type ..	199	169	183
Gran Touring Pkg.	548	466	504

Gran Touring Suspension, 215/65R15 tires on alloy wheels, 2.97 axle ratio, HD cooling, leather-wrapped steering wheel.

T Type Pkg., base	1902	1617	1750

Gran Touring Pkg., cruise control, intermittent wipers, gauges, 45/45 seat, operating console, AM/FM ST ET cassette with Concert Sound speakers.

T Type Popular Pkg. SF	2422	2059	2228

T Type Pkg., rear defogger, rear carpet savers, power windows and locks, front seatback recliners.

T Type Premium Pkg. SG	2623	2230	2413

Pkg. SF plus power driver's seat, power antenna, power mirrors.

T Type Luxury Pkg. SH	2771	2355	2549

Pkg. SG plus lighted right visor mirror, power passenger seat.

Popular Pkg. SB, base & Custom	618	525	569

Rear defogger, intermittent wipers, cruise control, 205/75R14 WSW tires, bodyside molding, rear bumper guards, 55/45 front seat with storage armrest.

Premium Pkg. SC, base 2-door	989	841	910
Custom 4-door	1039	883	956

Pkg. SB plus carpet savers, power door locks, AM/FM ST ET cassette, wire wheel covers.

Luxury Pkg. SD, base 2-door	1454	1236	1338
Custom 4-door	1589	1351	1462

Pkg. SC plus power windows, door edge guards, power driver's seat, front seatback recliners.

Prestige Pkg. SE, base 2-door	1708	1452	1571
Custom 4-door	1843	1567	1696

Pkg. SD plus power trunk release, lighted visor mirror, power antenna, power mirrors, Concert Sound speakers.

Prices are accurate at time of printing; subject to manufacturer's change

	Retail Price	Dealer Invoice	Low Price
Special Pkg. SJ, base 2-door	823	700	757
Custom 4-door	948	806	872

Rear defogger, intermittent wipers, cruise control, 205/75R14 WSW tires, bodyside molding, rear bumper guards, 55/45 front seat with storage armrest, power windows and locks.

Special Pkg. SK, base 2-door	955	812	879
Custom 4-door	1080	918	994

Pkg. SJ plus AM/FM ST ET cassette.

Popular Pkg. SB, Ltd 2-door	1073	912	987
Ltd 4-door	1198	1018	1102

Rear defogger, intermittent wipers, cruise control, 205/75R14 WSW tires, carpet savers, power door locks, AM/FM ST ET cassette, power windows, power driver's seat.

Premium Pkg. SC, Ltd 2-door	1265	1075	1164
Ltd 4-door	1400	1190	1288

Pkg. SB plus wire wheel covers, door edge guards, power trunk release, lighted right visor mirror, power antenna.

Luxury Pkg. SD, Ltd 2-door	1592	1353	1465
Ltd 4-door	1797	1527	1653

Pkg. SC plus power mirrors, power passenger seatback recliner, deluxe trunk trim, automatic climate control, front and rear reading and courtesy lights, door courtesy and warning lights.

Prestige Pkg. SD, Ltd 2-door	1967	1672	1810
Ltd 4-door	2102	1787	1934

Pkg. SD plus power passenger seat, AM/FM ST ET cassette w/EQ.

Oldsmobile 88 Royale

	Retail Price	Dealer Invoice	Low Price
2-door notchback	$15195	$13113	$14154
4-door notchback	15295	13200	14248
Brougham 2-door notchback	16295	14063	15179
Brougham 4-door notchback	16395	14149	15272
Destination charge	505	505	505

Standard Equipment:

Royale: 3.8-liter PFI V-6 engine, 4-speed automatic transmission, power steering and brakes, air conditioning, tinted glass, headlamps-on warning, left remote mirror, AM/FM ST ET, bench seat with center armrests, automatic front lap/shoulder belts, rear lap/shoulder belts, 205/75R14 all- season tires. **Brougham** adds: Convenience Group (lamps, right visor mirror, chime tones), 55/45 front seat with storage armrest, power decklid release.

Optional Equipment:

Inflatable Restraint System, 4-doors	850	723	782
Anti-lock brakes	925	786	851

Prices are accurate at time of printing; subject to manufacturer's change.

	Retail Price	Dealer Invoice	Low Price
Option Pkg. 1SB, base	559	475	514

Split bench seat, intermittent wipers, cruise control, tilt steering column, Convenience Group.

	Retail Price	Dealer Invoice	Low Price
Option Pkg. 1SC, base 2-door	1374	1168	1264
Base 4-door	1509	1283	1388

Pkg. 1SB plus power windows and locks, floormats, door edge guards, power antenna, seatback recliners, power driver's seat.

	Retail Price	Dealer Invoice	Low Price
Option Pkg. 1SD, base 2-door	1823	1550	1677
Base 4-door	1958	1664	1801

Pkg. 1SC plus power decklid release, Reminder Pkg., Convenience Value Group.

	Retail Price	Dealer Invoice	Low Price
Option Pkg. 1SB, Brougham 2-door	1162	988	1069
Brougham 4-door	1297	1102	1193

Power windows and locks, intermittent wipers, cruise control, tilt steering column, floormats, door edge guards, power antenna, Reminder Pkg., power driver's seat.

	Retail Price	Dealer Invoice	Low Price
Option Pkg. 1SC, Brougham 2-door	1806	1535	1662
Brougham 4-door	1941	1650	1786

Pkg. 1SB plus seatback recliners, automatic climate control, opera lamps, Convenience Value Group.

	Retail Price	Dealer Invoice	Low Price
Power passenger seat, Brougham	240	204	221
Seatback recliners (each)	45	38	41
Power locks, 2-doors	145	123	133
4-doors	195	166	179
Power windows, 2-doors	210	179	193
4-doors	285	242	262
Rear defogger	145	123	133
Vinyl roof, Brougham 4-door	200	170	184
Accent stripe	45	38	41
FE2 suspension pkg.	271	230	249
FE3 suspension pkg.	729	620	671
Engine block heater	18	15	17
15" alloy wheels	318	270	293
WSW tires	76	65	70
AM/FM ST ET cassette	122	104	112
w/EQ, Brougham	357	303	328
AM/FM ST ET w/CD player, Brougham . . .	481	409	443
Instrument panel cluster	66	56	61
High-capacity cooling	66	56	61
Custom leather trim, Brougham	433	368	398

Pontiac Bonneville

	Retail Price	Dealer Invoice	Low Price
LE 4-door notchback	$14829	$12797	$13813
SE 4-door notchback	17199	14842	16012
SSE 4-door notchback	22899	19762	21331
Destination charge	505	505	505

Prices are accurate at time of printing; subject to manufacturer's change

Standard Equipment:

LE: 3.8-liter PFI V-6, 4-speed automatic transmission, power steering and brakes, air conditioning, tinted glass, cloth bench seat, outboard rear lap/shoulder belts, left remote and right manual mirrors, wide bodyside moldings, AM/FM ST ET, coolant temperature gauge, 205/75R14 tires. **SE adds:** 2.97 axle ratio, 45/55 seat with recliners and storage armrest, cargo security net, intermittent wipers, cruise control, tilt steering column, tachometer and trip odometer, power windows, AM/FM ST ET cassette, Rally Tuned Suspension, 215/65R15 Eagle GT+4 tires on alloy wheels. **SSE adds:** 3.33 axle ratio, anti-lock braking system, Electronic Ride Control, automatic air conditioning with steering wheel controls, electronic compass, Driver Information System, heated power mirrors, headlamp sentinel, headlamp washers, power seat adjustments (including lumbar support, recliners and head restraints), automatic seatbelts, fog lamps, aero bodyside extensions, AM & FM ST ET cassette with EQ and Touch Control, power antenna, rear armrest with storage, rear defogger, lighted visor mirrors, leather steering wheel trim, illuminated entry, remote decklid release, power door locks, first aid and accessory kits, uprated suspension, 215/60R16 Eagle GT+4 tires.

Optional Equipment:

	Retail Price	Dealer Invoice	Low Price
Anti-lock brakes, LE & SE	925	505	505
Option Pkg. 1SA, LE	259	220	238
Tilt steering column, intermittent wipers, Lamp Group.			
Option Pkg. 1SB, LE	434	369	399
Pkg. 1SA plus cruise control.			
Option Pkg. 1SC, LE	1325	1126	1219
Pkg. 1SB plus power windows and locks, power driver's seat, power decklid release, lighted right visor mirror.			
Option Pkg. 1SD, LE	1793	1524	1650
Pkg. 1SC plus leather-wrapped steering wheel, illuminated entry, remote fuel door release, power mirrors, power passenger seat.			
Option Pkg. 1SA, SE	274	233	252
Lamp Group, power locks.			
Option Pkg. 1SB, SE	675	574	621
Pkg. 1SA plus power driver's seat, power decklid release, lighted right visor mirror, fog lamps.			
Option Pkg. 1SC, SE	1153	980	1061
Pkg. 1SB plus illuminated entry, remote fuel door release, power mirrors, power passenger seat, Twilight Sentinel.			
Value Option Pkg., LE	424	360	390
205/70R15 tires on alloy wheels, 45/55 seat, AM/FM ST ET cassette.			
Value Option Pkg., SE	327	278	301
45/45 seat, AM/FM ST ET cassette, power antenna.			
Rear defogger, SE & LE	145	123	133
Rally gauge cluster, LE	100	85	92
Tachometer and trip odometer.			
Power locks, LE & SE	195	166	179

Prices are accurate at time of printing; subject to manufacturer's change.

	Retail Price	Dealer Invoice	Low Price
Power windows, LE	355	302	327
AM/FM ST ET cassette, LE & SE	122	104	112
AM/FM ST ET cassette w/EQ, LE w/o VOP .	722	614	664
LE w/VOP	600	510	552
LE w/Pkg. 1SD, w/o VOP	672	571	618
LE w/Pkg. 1SD & VOP	550	468	506
SE w/o VOP	672	571	618
SE w/VOP	480	408	442
AM/FM ST ET w/CD & EQ, LE w/o VOP ..	926	787	852
LE w/VOP	804	683	740
LE w/Pkg. 1SD, w/o VOP	876	745	806
LE w/Pkg. 1SD & VOP	754	641	694
SE w/o VOP	876	745	806
SE w/VOP	684	581	629
SSE	204	173	188
Stereos w/EQ include power antenna.			
Performance Sound System, SE & LE ...	100	85	92
Requires power windows.			
Seatback recliners, LE w/o Custom Trim ..	90	77	83
45/55 seat, LE w/o Custom Trim or VOP .	133	113	122
45/45 seat w/console, SE	235	200	216
Leather 45/45 seat, SSE	379	322	349
Custom Interior Trim, LE w/o VOP	608	517	559
LE w/VOP	475	404	437
LE w/Pkg. 1SC or 1SD, w/o VOP	253	215	233
LE w/Pkg. 1SC or 1SD & VOP	120	102	110
45/45 seat with recliners, power windows, trunk security net.			
Power glass sunroof, LE & SE	1284	1091	1181
LE & SE w/Option Pkg. (exc. VOP) ...	1230	1046	1132
205/75R14 WSW tires, LE	76	65	70
205/70R15 tires, LE	48	41	44
205/70R15 WSW tires, LE w/o VOP	114	97	105
LE w/VOP	66	56	61
215/65R15 tires & Y99 suspension,			
LE w/o VOP	164	139	151
LE w/VOP	116	99	107
All 15-inch tires require alloy wheels on LE.			

Buick Reatta

Buick introduced its 2-seater in January 1988 with a $25,000 base price and by July, dealers had snapped up the entire 3000-unit 1988 production run. The base price is up by $1,700 for '89, but not much else has changed. A new stan-

Prices are accurate at time of printing; subject to manufacturer's change.

Buick Reatta

dard keyless entry system uses a hand-held radio transmitter to lock or unlock the doors and trunk from up to 30 feet away. The electrically operated glove box door is supplanted by a manual one and cloth upholstery is no longer available as an alternative to leather. Reatta is built on a shortened Riviera front-drive platform and uses the same drivetrain: a 3.8-liter V-6 and 4-speed overdrive automatic transmission. It shares the Riv's instrument panel, including the Electronic Control Center, which uses a touch-sensitive video display screen instead of conventional controls for the climate system, stereo and other functions. The only two extra-cost options are an electric sunroof and 16-way power driver's seat. A convertible version is planned, but probably won't arrive until the 1990 model year. Reatta is a distinctively styled luxury coupe that can sprint to 60 mph in about 10 seconds. Its short chassis carries two-thirds of its weight at the front, but thanks to a taut suspension and high-performance tires, road manners are far more athletic than you'd expect from a Buick. Its ride can be choppy, however, and while the cabin is comfortable for two, it isn't well insulated against tire and exhaust noise. Standard anti-lock disc brakes stop it short and true. Our only real complaints are that the controls for lights and wiper/washer are unnecessarily complex; the automatic climate system is inflexible, and the video screen is an ill-advised and distracting substitute for traditional buttons and switches.

Specifications

	2-door notchback
Wheelbase, in.	98.5
Overall length, in.	183.5
Overall width, in.	73.0
Overall height, in.	51.2
Turn diameter, ft.	38.0
Curb weight, lbs.	3394
Cargo vol., cu. ft.	10.3
Fuel capacity, gal.	18.2
Seating capacity	2
Front headroom, in.	36.9
Front shoulder room, in.	57.0
Front legroom, max., in.	43.1
Rear headroom, in.	—
Rear shoulder room, in.	—
Rear legroom, min., in.	—

Engines

	ohv V-6
Size, liters/cu. in.	3.8/231
Fuel delivery	PFI
Horsepower @ rpm	165 @ 4800
Torque (lbs./ft.) @ rpm	210 @ 2000
Availability	S

EPA city/highway mpg

4-speed OD automatic	19/28

Prices

Buick Reatta	Retail Price	Dealer Invoice	Low Price
2-door notchback	$26700	$23042	$26000
Destination charge	550	550	550

Standard Equipment:

3.8-liter PFI V-6 engine, 4-speed automatic transmission, power steering, power 4-wheel disc brakes, anti-lock braking system, automatic climate control air conditioning, power windows and locks, power front bucket seats with recliners, leather upholstery, remote keyless entry, touch-sensitive Electronic Control Center, trip odometer, tinted glass, intermittent wipers, AM/FM ST ET cassette with EQ and power antenna, full-length console, lighted visor mirrors, intermittent wipers, tilt steering column, leather-wrapped steering wheel, rear defogger, digital clock, cruise control, head-lamps-on and turn-signal reminder tones, remote fuel door and trunk re-

Prices are accurate at time of printing; subject to manufacturer's change.

leases, cornering lamps, fog lamps, theft deterrent system, map lights, illuminated driver's door lock and interior light control, 215/65R15 Goodyear Eagle GT + 4 tires on alloy wheels.

Optional Equipment:

	Retail Price	Dealer Invoice	Low Price
California emissions pkg.	100	85	92
Power sunroof	895	761	823
16-way power driver's seat	680	578	626

Buick Regal

Buick Regal Custom

Anti-lock braking is a new option for the mid-size Regal, which is due for a new engine at mid-year. A 3.1-liter V-6 is to replace the standard 2.8-liter V-6. The 3.1 produces 140 horsepower (10 more than the 2.8) and 190 pound/feet of torque (20 more than the 2.8). Like the 2.8, it will come only with a 4-speed overdrive automatic and should address one of Regal's prime shortfalls: too little power for 3000 pounds of curb weight. Regal is in its second year as an aero-styled front-drive coupe. It's built under the GM W-body program that also produced the similar '88 Oldsmobile Cutlass Supreme and Pontiac Grand Prix. Regal base prices are up nearly $2000 since last fall, mostly for new standard features, including air conditioning, rear shoulder belts, AM/FM stereo radio and tilt steering column. Joining the $925 anti-lock brakes as '89 options are a compact disc player, a power sunroof and auxiliary radio controls mounted in

Prices are accurate at time of printing; subject to manufacturer's change.

the steering wheel. Also available at extra cost is a new remote keyless entry system that uses radio signals to lock or unlock the doors and trunk from up to 30 feet away. Regal also gains Buick's Dynaride suspension, which is designed to soften the ride without hurting handling. The optional Gran Touring suspension included in the Gran Touring Package and Regal Gran Sport package also has been tuned for a softer ride, while the tires that come with those packages are a size larger. Nothing has been done to improve the poorly designed instrument cluster, however, and optional digital gauges at $299 are no better. Regal and the similar GM coupes are competent if underpowered cruisers. A 4-door version of the Regal is planned for 1990 or 1991, but the 4-door Chevrolet Lumina due next spring will be built from this design.

Specifications

	2-door notchback
Wheelbase, in.	107.5
Overall length, in.	192.2
Overall width, in.	72.5
Overall height, in.	53.0
Turn diameter, ft.	39.0
Curb weight, lbs.	3144
Cargo vol., cu. ft.	15.5
Fuel capacity, gal.	16.5
Seating capacity	6
Front headroom, in.	37.8
Front shoulder room, in.	57.6
Front legroom, max., in.	42.3
Rear headroom, in.	37.1
Rear shoulder room, in.	56.8
Rear legroom, min., in.	34.8

Engines

	ohv V-6	ohv V-6
Size, liters/cu. in.	2.8/173	3.1/190
Fuel delivery	PFI	PFI
Horsepower @ rpm	130 @ 4500	140 @ 4500
Torque (lbs./ft.) @ rpm	170 @ 3600	190 @ 3600
Availability	S	S

EPA city/highway mpg

4-speed OD automatic	20/29	NA

Prices

Buick Regal

	Retail Price	Dealer Invoice	Low Price
Custom 2-door notchback	$14214	$12267	$13241
Limited 2-door notchback	14739	12720	13730
Destination charge	455	455	455

Standard Equipment:

2.8-liter PFI V-6, 4-speed automatic transmission, power steering and brakes, cloth split bench seat with armrest and recliners, headlamps-on tone, tilt steering column, tinted glass, digital speedometer, optical horn, left remote and right manual mirrors, black lower bodyside moldings, AM/FM ST ET, automatic front seatbelts, outboard rear lap/shoulder belts, 205/70R14 all-season SBR WSW tires. **Limited** adds: upgraded carpet, bright wide bodyside moldings, 55/45 seat with storage armrest.

Optional Equipment:

Anti-lock braking system	925	786	851
Rear defogger	145	123	133
Electronic digital/graphic instruments	299	254	275
Remote keyless entry, Gran Sport	125	106	115
Decklid luggage rack, Custom	115	98	106
Lower accent paint	205	174	189
AM/FM ST ET cassette w/EQ	272	231	250
CD player	396	337	364
Power glass sunroof	650	553	598
Steering-wheel-mounted radio controls			
w/o Four Seater, Gran Touring,			
or Gran Sport	125	106	115
w/Four Seater, Gran Touring or Gran Sport	29	25	27
Cloth 55/45 seat w/storage armrest, Custom	183	156	168
Cloth reclining buckets w/console, Custom	105	89	97
Leather/vinyl 55/45 seat w/recliners, Ltd	395	336	363
Locking wire wheel covers	199	169	183
Styled aluminum wheels	199	169	183
Styled steel wheels	99	84	91
Gran Touring Pkg., w/o Four Seater	600	510	552
w/Four Seater	504	428	464
Gran Touring Suspension, 215/60R16 tires on alloy wheels, leather-wrapped steering wheel.			
Four Seater Pkg., Custom	700	595	644
Limited	600	510	552
Gran Sport	409	348	376
Front and rear bucket seats, rear armrest with storage, console with cassette storage, leather-wrapped steering wheel, rear headrests.			

Prices are accurate at time of printing; subject to manufacturer's change.

	Retail Price	Dealer Invoice	Low Price
Gran Sport Pkg., Custom	1205	1024	1109

Gran Touring Pkg., bucket seats with console, blackout exterior, fog lamps, aero rocker panels, wide bodyside moldings, front spoiler.

Popular Pkg. SB, Custom	171	145	157

Rear defogger, white stripe tires.

Premium Pkg. SC, Custom	761	647	700

Pkg. SB plus AM/FM ST ET cassette w/EQ, intermittent wipers, cruise control, carpet savers, door edge guards, 55/45 front seat with storage armrest, power antenna, power door locks.

Luxury Pkg. SD, Custom	908	772	835

Pkg. SC plus power windows, wire wheel covers, lighted right visor mirror.

Prestige Pkg. SE, Custom	1499	1274	1379

Pkg. SD plus power driver's seat, power mirrors, power trunk release, Concert Sound speakers, steering-wheel-mounted redundant accessory controls.

Special Pkg. SJ, Custom	486	413	447

Rear defogger, white stripe tires, intermittent wipers, cruise control, door edge guards, power windows.

Premium Pkg. SC, Ltd	373	317	343

Rear defogger, white stripe tires, AM/FM ST ET cassette, intermittent wipers, cruise control.

Luxury Pkg. SD, Ltd	1165	990	1072

Pkg. SC plus carpet savers, door edge guards, power antenna, power windows and locks, wire wheel covers, lighted right visor mirror, power driver's seat.

Prestige Pkg. SE, Ltd	1441	1225	1326

Pkg. SD plus power mirrors, power trunk release, Concert Sound speakers, steering-wheel-mounted redundant accessory controls, remote keyless entry.

Special Pkg. SM, Gran Sport	1547	1315	1423

Rear defogger, AM/FM ST ET cassette, intermittent wipers, cruise control, carpet savers.

Popular Pkg. SF, Gran Sport	2405	2044	2213

Pkg. SM plus electronic digital/graphic instruments, power antenna, power windows and locks, lighted right visor mirror, power driver's seat, power mirrors, power trunk release, Concert Sound speakers.

Buick Riviera

Buick has grafted 11 inches to the Riviera's body, a measure it hopes will rekindle sales by recapturing the spirit of previous models. Wheelbase remains 108 inches, but with an overall length of 198.3 inches, Riviera now has Buick's long-

Buick Riviera

est front-drive body, stretching 1.4 inches beyond Electra's. Most of the added length is at the rear, where a sloping posterior replaces the 1986-88 models' chopped rump. Rear roof pillars are wider and the rear window has more rake. There's a new grille and more chrome trim everywhere. Whitewall tires and wire wheel covers replace blackwalls and aluminum wheels as standard. Buick's new Dynaride suspension is standard in an effort to give the Riv a softer, more isolated ride. The T Type option package with its taut suspension is dropped, though a firmed-up suspension is available as part of the $49 Gran Touring Package. Inside, imitation wood replaces much of the vinyl dashboard and console trim. The touch-screen Electronic Control Center continues to supplant a host of traditional gauges and switches, though the electrically released glove box door has given way to a manual one. A remote keyless entry system is a new option and anti-lock brakes are a carried-over option. Little has changed under the hood, though heavy duty engine and transmission cooling are now standard. A 3.8-liter V-6 and 4-speed overdrive automatic transmission is the only available drivetrain. Riviera shares its basic design with the Cadillac Eldorado and Oldsmobile Toronado. Styling aside, there's little unique about Riviera, but it does offer plenty of luxury and convenience features and adequate space for four people and their luggage. Acceleration is brisk, while ride control and handling are at least competent.

Specifications

	2-door notchback
Wheelbase, in.	108.0
Overall length, in.	198.3
Overall width, in.	71.7
Overall height, in.	53.6
Turn diameter, ft.	37.5
Curb weight, lbs.	3436
Cargo vol., cu. ft.	13.9
Fuel capacity, gal.	18.2
Seating capacity	5
Front headroom, in.	37.8
Front shoulder room, in.	57.9
Front legroom, max., in.	42.7
Rear headroom, in.	37.8
Rear shoulder room, in.	57.4
Rear legroom, min., in.	35.6

Engines

	ohv V-6
Size, liters/cu. in.	3.8/231
Fuel delivery	PFI
Horsepower @ rpm	165 @ 4800
Torque (lbs./ft.) @ rpm	210 @ 2000
Availability	S

EPA city/highway mpg

4-speed OD automatic	19/28

Prices

Buick Riviera	Retail Price	Dealer Invoice	Low Price
2-door notchback	$22540	$19452	$20996
Destination charge	550	550	550

Standard Equipment:

3.8-liter PFI V-6, 4-speed automatic transmission, power steering, power 4-wheel disc brakes, power windows and locks, automatic level control, cloth reclining bucket seats, power driver's seat, AM/FM ST ET cassette, power antenna, outboard rear lap/shoulder belts, carpet savers, full-length console, cruise control, rear defogger, intermittent wipers, door edge guards, touch-sensitive Electronic Control Center, remote fuel door and trunk releases, tinted glass, tilt steering column, leather-wrapped steering wheel, illuminated driver's door lock and interior light control, digital instru-

Prices are accurate at time of printing; subject to manufacturer's change.

ments, trip odometer, low fuel indicator, cornering lamps, coach lamps, door courtesy and warning lights, power mirrors, lighted visor mirrors, 205/70R15 all-season SBR tires, locking wire wheel covers.

Optional Equipment:

	Retail Price	Dealer Invoice	Low Price
Anti-lock braking system	925	786	851
Lower accent paint	190	162	175
Delco/Bose music system	703	598	647
Astroroof	1230	1046	1132
Cellular telephone	1975	1679	1817
Heavily padded vinyl roof	695	591	639
Leather & suede trim	487	414	448
16-way leather & suede driver's seat	1167	992	1074
Styled alloy wheels	NC	NC	NC
Gran Touring Pkg.	49	42	45

Gran Touring Suspension, 2.97 axle ratio, 215/65R15 Goodyear Eagle GT + 4 tires on alloy wheels, leather-wrapped sport steering wheel and shift handle, fast-ratio power steering.

Appearance Pkg.	150	128	138

Platinum beige Firemist lower accent paint, bodyside stripe, painted aluminum wheels.

Popular Pkg. SB, w/o 16-way seat	435	370	400
w/16-way seat	360	306	331

AM/FM ST ET cassette w/EQ, power passenger seat.

Premium Pkg. SC, w/o 16-way seat	840	714	773
w/16-way seat	765	650	704

Pkg. SB plus power decklid pulldown, remote keyless entry and automatic power door locks, Twilight Sentinel.

Luxury Pkg. SD, w/o 16-way seat	1189	1011	1094
w/16-way seat	1114	947	1025

Pkg. SC plus theft deterrent system, power mirrors with heated left, automatic rear-view mirror, electronic compass.

Buick Skyhawk

Rear shoulder belts, additional sound insulation and Buick's new Dynaride suspension are standard for 1989 on this front-drive subcompact. Buick says Dynaride adjusts shock absorbers to soften a car's rough-road ride without compromising handling. Skyhawk is again available as a 2-door coupe, 4-door sedan and 5-door wagon. Buick has dropped the 96-horsepower overhead cam 4-cylinder engine previously used in Skyhawk and all models now have the 90-horsepower 2.0-liter overhead valve 4-cylinder from the similar

Prices are accurate at time of printing; subject to manufacturer's change.

Buick Skyhawk 4-door

Specifications

	2-door notchback	4-door notchback	5-door wagon
Wheelbase, in.	101.2	101.2	101.2
Overall length, in.	179.3	181.7	181.7
Overall width, in.	65.0	65.0	65.0
Overall height, in.	54.0	54.0	54.4
Turn diameter, ft.	34.3	34.3	34.3
Curb weight, lbs.	2420	2469	2551
Cargo vol., cu. ft.	12.6	13.5	64.4
Fuel capacity, gal.	13.6	13.6	13.6
Seating capacity	5	5	5
Front headroom, in.	37.4	38.2	38.3
Front shoulder room, in.	53.7	53.7	53.7
Front legroom, max., in.	42.1	42.2	42.2
Rear headroom, in.	36.3	37.6	38.8
Rear shoulder room, in.	52.6	53.8	53.8
Rear legroom, min., in.	31.8	34.3	33.7

Engines

	ohv I-4
Size, liters/cu. in.	2.0/121
Fuel delivery	TBI
Horsepower @ rpm	90 @ 5600
Torque (lbs./ft.) @ rpm	108 @ 3200
Availability	S

EPA city/highway mpg

5-speed OD manual	26/36
3-speed automatic	25/32

Chevrolet Cavalier. A 5-speed manual transmission is standard and a 3-speed automatic optional. Optional on 2-door Skyhawks is an S/E package that includes hidden headlamps, sport trim, gauge cluster, Gran Touring suspension, and high-performance tires on 14-inch alloy wheels. Skyhawk is part of the J-car family GM introduced for 1982. The Cadillac Cimarron and Oldsmobile Firenza have been dropped, but the Cavalier and the Pontiac Sunbird survive while Skyhawk stays around as an entry-level model to draw young buyers to the Buick fold. Cavalier and Sunbird are similar cars at lower prices, and you're likely to find a bigger selection at Chevy and Pontiac dealers. Buick buyers will find Skyhawk to be economical, but lacking in performance, smoothness, and the packaging efficiency of more modern and sophisticated Japanese competitors. Most Skyhawks are sold with automatic transmission, which dulls the already marginal acceleration.

Prices

Buick Skyhawk	Retail Price	Dealer Invoice	Low Price
4-door notchback	$9285	$8570	$8928
2-door notchback	9285	8570	8928
5-door wagon	10230	9442	9836
Destination charge	425	425	425

Standard Equipment:

2.0-liter TBI 4-cylinder engine, 5-speed manual transmission, power steering and brakes, reclining cloth front bucket seats, left remote and right manual mirrors, tinted glass, full-length console, coin holder, headlamps-on tone, AM/FM ST ET, outboard rear lap/shoulder belts, 185/80R13 all-season SBR WSW tires. **Wagon** has: air deflector, luggage rack, split folding rear seatback.

Optional Equipment:

3-speed automatic transmission	415	353	382
Air conditioning	675	574	621
Rear defogger	145	123	133
California emissions pkg.	100	85	92
S/E Pkg., 2-door	1095	931	1007

Gran Touring Suspension, 215/60R14 Goodyear Eagle GT + 4 tires on alloy wheels, leather-wrapped steering wheel, carpet savers, gauges and tachometer, blackout exterior moldings, concealed headlamps, fog lamps.

Prices are accurate at time of printing; subject to manufacturer's change.

	Retail Price	Dealer Invoice	Low Price
Popular Pkg. SB	617	524	568

3-speed automatic transmission, tilt steering column, intermittent wipers, cruise control, AM/FM ST ET cassette, 4-way manual driver's seat, console armrest, rear defogger.

Premium Pkg. SC, 2-door	617	524	568
4-door	667	567	614
Wagon	717	609	660

Deletes rear defogger from Pkg. SB and adds power door locks.

Luxury Pkg. SD, 2-door	662	563	609
4-door	712	605	655
Wagon	762	648	701

Pkg. SC plus rear defogger.

S/E Popular Pkg. SF, 2-door	1412	1200	1299

S/E Pkg., 3-speed automatic transmission, tilt steering column, intermittent wipers, cruise control, AM/FM ST ET cassette, 4-way manual driver's seat, console armrest, rear defogger.

S/E Premium Pkg. SG, 2-door	1412	1200	1299

Deletes rear defogger from Pkg. SF and adds power door locks.

S/E Luxury Pkg. SH, 2-door	1457	1238	1340

Pkg. SG plus rear defogger.

Buick Skylark/ Oldsmobile Cutlass Calais

Buick Skylark Limited 4-door

A larger V-6 engine is now optional for these corporate cousins, and the Cutlass Calais gets a facelift as well. Built as 2-door coupes and 4-door sedans, these GM N-body front-drive compacts are similar to the Pontiac Grand Am. Their new V-6, called "3300" by GM, has 160 horsepower and 185 pound/feet of torque. Dropped is last year's 3.0-liter V-6, which had 125 horsepower and 150 pound/feet of torque. A 2.5-liter 4-cylinder remains standard, but horsepower is up to 110, from 98. The 150-horsepower Quad 4 double-overhead cam 2.3-liter 4-cylinder is optional in either model and will become standard in the sporty Cutlass Calais International Series model set for introduction later in the model year. Optional in the I Series will be a new 185-horsepower High Output version of the Quad 4. Buick offers only a 3-speed automatic transmission, while Olds offers a 5-speed manual with either 4-cylinder. Skylark sedans now have the coupe's flush composite headlamps and a split front bench seat is standard on all models in place of the now-optional buckets. As with all '89 GM cars, rear shoulder belts are

Specifications

	2-door notchback	4-door notchback
Wheelbase, in.	103.4	103.4
Overall length, in.	180.0	180.0
Overall width, in.	66.6	66.6
Overall height, in.	52.1	52.1
Turn diameter, ft.	37.8	37.8
Curb weight, lbs.	2583	2640
Cargo vol., cu. ft.	13.4	13.4
Fuel capacity, gal.	13.6	13.6
Seating capacity	6	6
Front headroom, in.	37.7	37.7
Front shoulder room, in.	54.6	54.3
Front legroom, max., in.	42.9	42.9
Rear headroom, in.	37.1	37.1
Rear shoulder room, in.	55.2	54.1
Rear legroom, min., in.	34.3	34.3

Engines

	ohv I-4	dohc I-4	ohv V-6
Size, liters/cu. in.	2.5/151	2.3/138	3.3/204
Fuel delivery	TBI	PFI	PFI
Horsepower @ rpm	110 @ 5200	150 @ 5200	160 @ 5200
Torque (lbs./ft.) @ rpm	135 @ 3200	160 @ 4000	185 @ 2000
Availability	S	O	O

EPA city/highway mpg

3-speed automatic	23/30	23/32	20/27

standard. The base suspension this year is Buick's new Dynaride system, which Buick says gives a soft ride with no sacrifice in handling ability. Olds has dropped the Firenza subcompact, so Calais is the smallest, least expensive model in its '89 lineup. A new entry-level Value Leader (VL) Calais comes only with the 2.5-liter four and limited options. All Calais models have new grilles, front and rear fascias, exterior trim and taillamps. The International Series will add aero body trim, monochromatic paint and fog lamps. A power sunroof is a new option. Skylark and Cutlass Calais are conservative cars and, compared to such Japanese rivals as the Honda Accord and Toyota Camry, not particularly refined or roomy.

Prices

Buick Skylark	Retail Price	Dealer Invoice	Low Price
Custom 4-door notchback	$11115	$9926	$10521
Custom 2-door notchback	11115	9926	10521
Limited 4-door notchback	12345	11024	11685
Limited 2-door notchback	12345	11024	11685
Destination charge	425	361	391

Standard Equipment:

Custom: 2.5-liter TBI 4-cylinder engine, 3-speed automatic transmission, power steering and brakes, reclining cloth split bench seat, headlamps-on tone, remote fuel door release, tinted glass, trip odometer, AM/FM ST ET, automatic front seatbelts, outboard rear lap/shoulder belts, right visor mirror, 185/80R13 all-season SBR tires. **Limited** adds: front and rear center armrests, front and rear courtesy lights, narrow rocker panel moldings, wheel opening moldings.

Optional Equipment:

2.3-liter Quad 4 4-cylinder engine	660	561	607
3.3-liter PFI V-6	710	604	653
Rear defogger	145	123	133
California emissions pkg.	100	85	92
Engine block heater	18	15	17
Decklid luggage rack	115	98	106
Lower accent paint	195	166	179
Bodyside stripes	45	38	41
205/70R13 blackwall tires	124	105	114
205/70R13 WSW tires	190	162	175

Prices are accurate at time of printing; subject to manufacturer's change.

	Retail Price	Dealer Invoice	Low Price
Cloth bucket seats & console	180	153	166
13″ styled alloy wheels	229	195	211
Locking wire wheel covers	199	169	183
Gran Touring Pkg.	592	503	545

215/60R14 Goodyear Eagle GT + 4 tires on alloy wheels, Gran Touring Suspension, leather-wrapped steering wheel.

	Retail Price	Dealer Invoice	Low Price
Exterior Sport Pkg., Custom 2-door	374	318	344
Ltd 2-door	318	270	293

Blackout moldings, front air dam, aero rocker moldings, wide bodyside moldings, Touring Suspension, leather-wrapped steering wheel.

	Retail Price	Dealer Invoice	Low Price
S/E Pkg., Custom	1123	955	1033

Bucket seats and console, left remote and right manual mirrors, bodyside and wheel opening moldings, AM/FM ST ET cassette, leather-wrapped steering wheel, 215/60R14 Goodyear Eagle GT + 4 tires on alloy wheels, Gran Touring Suspension.

	Retail Price	Dealer Invoice	Low Price
Popular Pkg. SB, Custom	576	490	530

Air conditioning, tilt steering column, 185/80R13 WSW tires, left remote and right manual mirrors, rear defogger, wide bodyside moldings, wheel opening moldings.

	Retail Price	Dealer Invoice	Low Price
Premium Pkg. SC, Custom	1025	871	943

Pkg. SB plus cruise control, intermittent wipers, carpet savers, AM/FM ST ET cassette, wire wheel covers, 4-way manual driver's seat.

	Retail Price	Dealer Invoice	Low Price
Luxury Pkg. SD, Custom 2-door	1180	1003	1086
Custom 4-door	1305	1109	1201

Pkg. SC plus power windows and locks.

	Retail Price	Dealer Invoice	Low Price
Prestige Pkg. SE, Custom 2-door	1357	1153	1248
Custom 4-door	1482	1260	1363

Pkg. SD plus power driver's seat, power antenna, lighted right visor mirror, power trunk release, front and rear courtesy lights.

	Retail Price	Dealer Invoice	Low Price
Special Pkg. SJ, Custom	639	543	588

Air conditioning, tilt steering column, 185/80R13 WSW tires, left remote and right manual mirrors, rear defogger, wide bodyside moldings, wheel opening moldings, cruise control, intermittent wipers, carpet savers.

	Retail Price	Dealer Invoice	Low Price
Premium Pkg. SC, Ltd	606	515	558

Air conditioning, tilt steering column, 185/80R13 WSW tires, variable intermittent wipers, carpet savers, cruise control, wide bodyside moldings, rear defogger.

	Retail Price	Dealer Invoice	Low Price
Luxury Pkg. SD, Ltd 2-door	1197	1017	1101
Ltd 4-door	1322	1124	1216

AM/FM ST ET cassette, wire wheel covers, power windows and locks, 4-way manual driver's seat.

	Retail Price	Dealer Invoice	Low Price
Prestige Pkg. SE, Ltd 2-door	1310	1114	1205
Ltd 4-door	1435	1220	1320

Pkg. SD plus power driver's seat, power antenna, lighted right visor mirror, power trunk release, wide rocker panel moldings.

	Retail Price	Dealer Invoice	Low Price
S/E Popular Pkg. SF	1568	1333	1443

S/E Pkg., air conditioning, tilt steering column, rear defogger.

Prices are accurate at time of printing; subject to manufacturer's change.

CONSUMER GUIDE®

	Retail Price	Dealer Invoice	Low Price
S/E Premium Pkg. SG	1766	1501	1625

Pkg. SF plus cruise control, intermittent wipers, carpet savers, 4-way manual driver's seat.

	Retail Price	Dealer Invoice	Low Price
S/E Luxury Pkg. SH, 2-door	2091	1777	1924
4-door	2216	1884	2039

Pkg. SG plus power windows and locks, power antenna.

Oldsmobile Cutlass Calais

	Retail Price	Dealer Invoice	Low Price
2-door notchback	$9995	$9225	$9610
4-door notchback	9995	9225	9610
S 2-door notchback	10895	9729	10312
S 4-door notchback	10995	9819	10407
SL 2-door notchback	11895	10622	11259
SL 4-door notchback	11995	10712	11354
I Series 2-door notchback	14395	12855	13625
I Series 4-door notchback	14495	12944	13720
Destination charge	425	425	425

Standard Equipment:

2.5-liter TBI 4-cylinder engine, 5-speed manual transmission, power steering and brakes, cloth front bucket seats (reclining on 2-door), AM/FM ST ET, trip odometer, dual outside mirrors, tinted glass, automatic front seatbelts, outboard rear lap/shoulder belts, 185/80R13 all-season SBR tires. **S** adds: full-length console with armrest and storage bin, left remote mirror, reclining front seatbacks. **SL** adds: Convenience Group (reading lights, lighted right visor mirror, misc. lights), 4-way driver's seat, split folding rear seat, upgraded steering wheel, two-tone paint. **International Series** adds: 2.3-liter DOHC PFI Quad 4 engine, FE3 suspension, air conditioning, door pockets, floormats, fog lamps, rocker panel extensions and wheel flares, Driver Information System (trip computer, service reminder), rallye instruments (tachometer, coolant temperature, oil pressure, voltmeter), AM/FM ST ET cassette, tilt steering column, leather-wrapped steering wheel and shift handle, power decklid release, intermittent wipers, 205/55R16 tires on alloy wheels.

Optional Equipment:

	Retail	Dealer	Low
2.3-liter Quad 4, S & SL	660	561	607
3.3-liter V-6, S & SL	710	604	653
3-speed automatic transmission, base . . .	380	323	350
Others	490	417	451
Column shift, SL 4-door (credit)	(110)	(94)	(94)
Option Pkg. 1SB, base 2-door	338	287	311
Base 4-door	388	330	357

Tilt steering column, floormats, 4-way driver's seat, power locks.

Prices are accurate at time of printing; subject to manufacturer's change

	Retail Price	Dealer Invoice	Low Price
Option Pkg. 1SC, base 2-door	513	436	472
Base 4-door	563	479	518
Pkg. 1 plus air conditioning.			
Option Pkg. 1SB, S	484	411	445
Tilt steering column, floormats, intermittent wipers, Convenience Group, air conditioning.			
Option Pkg. 1SC, S 2-door	809	688	744
S 4-door	934	794	859
Pkg. 1SB plus power windows and locks, power antenna, 4-way driver's seat, remote mirrors, power decklid release.			
Option Pkg. 1SB, SL	633	538	582
Tilt steering column, floormats, intermittent wipers, cruise control, air conditioner, power antenna.			
Option Pkg. 1SC, SL 2-door	1208	1027	1111
SL 4-door	1333	1133	1226
Pkg. 1SB plus power decklid release, power windows and locks, remote mirrors, power driver's seat, Driver Information System.			
Option Pkg. 1SB, I Series 2-door	845	718	777
I-Series 4-door	970	825	892
Power windows and locks, power driver's seat, remote mirrors, cruise control, power antenna.			
Power locks, 2-doors	145	123	133
4-doors	195	166	179
Rear defogger	145	123	133
Touring Car Ride & Handling Pkg., S . . .	491	417	452
SL	397	337	365
Removable sunroof (NA base)	350	298	322
Power windows (NA base), 2-doors	220	187	202
4-doors	295	251	271
Cruise control (NA base)	175	149	161
Rallye instruments, S & SL	126	107	116
AM/FM ST ET cassette, S & SL	147	125	135
w/EQ, SL	297	252	273
w/EQ, I Series	150	128	138
Decklid luggage rack (NA base)	115	98	106
Quad 4 Appearance Pkg., S & SL	1130	961	1040

Cadillac Allante

Cadillac has made a host of changes in its ultra-luxury 2-seater in an effort to stimulate sales that have lagged since its 1987 introduction. It began by replacing the previous 4.1-liter V-8 with a performance-tuned 4.5-liter V-8. Horse-

Prices are accurate at time of printing; subject to manufacturer's change.

Cadillac Allante

Specifications

	2-door conv.
Wheelbase, in.	99.4
Overall length, in.	178.6
Overall width, in.	73.5
Overall height, in.	52.2
Turn diameter, ft.	36.1
Curb weight, lbs.	3492
Cargo vol., cu. ft.	16.2
Fuel capacity, gal.	22.0
Seating capacity	2
Front headroom, in.	37.3
Front shoulder room, in.	57.6
Front legroom, max., in.	43.1
Rear headroom, in.	—
Rear shoulder room, in.	—
Rear legroom, min., in.	—

Engines

	ohv V-8
Size, liters/cu. in.	4.5/273
Fuel delivery	PFI
Horsepower @ rpm	200 @ 4300
Torque (lbs./ft.) @ rpm	270 @ 3200
Availability	S

EPA city/highway mpg

4-speed OD automatic	15/23

power increases from 170 to 200, torque from 230 pounds/feet to 265. Cadillac says 0-60 mph now takes 8.3 seconds, 1.5 seconds less than before. On the downside, Allante's 22.5 mpg combined city/highway average makes it the first GM car subject to a federal gas guzzler tax. The levy is $650 on top of the $56,533 base price, which is unchanged from last year. Chassis revisions include electronics that automatically alter shock-absorber damping to "compliant," "normal" or "firm" depending on vehicle speed and accelerative and braking forces. Wheel diameter goes from 15 inches to 16, suspension components are revised for less impact harshness and the power steering is now variable assist, depending on speed. A redesigned standard manual folding soft top can now be raised or lowered by one person in about 20 seconds. The Recaro leather seats are reshaped and softer, and charcoal has been added to tan and maroon as an interior color. A theft-deterrent system that can disable the starter and electric fuel pump is now standard. The changes dramatically improve Allante's performance and feel. Its engine is more substantial and more responsive, and we doubt Allante buyers will balk at the guzzler tax. Both high-speed stability and low-speed ride comfort are improved, the steering is sharper, the body feels more rigid.

Prices

Cadillac Allante	Retail Price	Dealer Invoice	Low Price
2-door convertible	$57183	$48873	$51700
Destination charge	550	550	550

Price includes $650 Gas Guzzler Tax.

Standard Equipment:

4.5-liter PFI V-8 engine, 4-speed automatic transmission, power steering, power 4-wheel disc brakes, anti-lock braking system, removable hardtop, folding convertible top, ten-way power Recaro seats with leather upholstery and driver's side position memory, Delco-GM/Bose Symphony music system, tilt/telescopic steering column, dual power mirrors, intermittent wipers, automatic day/night mirror, power decklid pulldown, theft deterrent system, 225/55VR16 Goodyear Eagle VL tires on alloy wheels.

Optional Equipment:

California emissions pkg.	99	84	91
Analog instrument cluster	NC	NC	NC

Prices are accurate at time of printing; subject to manufacturer's change

	Retail Price	Dealer Invoice	Low Price
Mobile cellular telephone	NA	NA	NA
Provisions for above	NA	NA	NA
California emissions pkg.	100	84	92
Cellular mobile telephone	1975	1659	1807
Provision for above	395	332	361
Analog instrument cluster	NC	NC	NC

Cadillac Brougham

Cadillac Brougham

The biggest Cadillac—and the only one with rear-wheel drive—gets a restyled grille and a few new standard features, but otherwise is a carryover for '89. Cruise control, intermittent wipers and a power trunk lid become standard as Cadillac continues to trim its optional-equipment lists. Brougham, offered only as a 4-door sedan, was last redesigned for the 1977 model year in GM's first round of downsizing. With an overall length of 221 inches, it's the longest production car made in America, edging the arch-rival Lincoln Town Car by nearly two inches. Cadillac says its front-drive De Ville/Fleetwood can hit 60 mph in less than 10 seconds. Brougham, with its carbureted 5.0-liter V-8, requires 14.3 seconds. That's slower than many economy cars and Brougham struggles to merge safely into expressway traffic. This Cadillac appeals to traditional American luxury-car buyers because it's big, posh, and can carry six people and their golf clubs. The tepid performance, dismal fuel economy and clumsy road manners leave us cold, however.

Prices are accurate at time of printing; subject to manufacturer's change

This year's larger De Ville/Fleetwood sedans are closer in exterior and interior dimensions to the Brougham, and far superior in acceleration, ride and handling.

Specifications

	4-door notchback
Wheelbase, in.	121.5
Overall length, in.	221.0
Overall width, in.	76.5
Overall height, in.	56.7
Turn diameter, ft.	40.5
Curb weight, lbs.	4190
Cargo vol., cu. ft.	19.5
Fuel capacity, gal.	25.0
Seating capacity	6
Front headroom, in.	39.0
Front shoulder room, in.	59.4
Front legroom, max., in.	42.0
Rear headroom, in.	38.1
Rear shoulder room, in.	59.4
Rear legroom, min., in.	41.2

Engines

	ohv V-8
Size, liters/cu. in.	5.0/307
Fuel delivery	4 bbl.
Horsepower @ rpm	140 @ 3200
Torque (lbs./ft.) @ rpm	255 @ 2000
Availability	S

EPA city/highway mpg

4-speed OD automatic	17/24

Prices

Cadillac Brougham	Retail Price	Dealer Invoice	Low Price
4-door notchback	$25699	$21921	$23510
Destination charge	550	550	550

Standard Equipment:

5.0-liter 4bbl. V-8 engine, 4-speed automatic transmission, power steering and brakes, Dual Comfort 55/45 front seats, illuminated entry system, front

Prices are accurate at time of printing; subject to manufacturer's change

and rear center armrests, headlights-on warning, power windows and locks, automatic climate control, outboard rear lap/shoulder belts, front and rear lamp monitors, cornering lights, sunshade support and door courtesy lights, power decklid release, cruise control, carpeted litter receptacle, low fuel and washer fluid indicators, dual remote mirrors, front seatback pockets, power driver's seat, tinted glass, trip odometer, padded sunvisors, AM/FM ST ET with power antenna, tilt/telescopic steering column, full padded vinyl roof, front bumper guards, door sill plates, full carpeting, opera lamps, automatic parking brake release, P225/75R15 Uniroyal Royal Seal all-season SBR tires.

Optional Equipment:

	Retail Price	Dealer Invoice	Low Price
Astroroof	1255	1054	1148
Rear defogger	170	143	156
D'Elegance Pkg., w/cloth upholstery	2146	1803	1964
w/leather	2706	2273	2476
50/50 dual comfort front seats, power passenger seat, lighted visor mirrors, illuminated entry, rear reading lamps.			
Automatic power door locks	185	155	169
HD Ride Pkg.	120	101	110
Leather seating area	560	470	512
Automatic day/night mirror	80	67	73
AM/FM ST ET cassette	309	260	283
Power passenger seatback recliner	160	134	146
w/d'Elegance	95	80	87
Premier Formal Vinyl Roof	1095	920	1002
Leather-trimmed steering wheel	115	97	105
Theft deterrent system	200	168	183
Trailer Towing Pkg.	299	251	274
HD springs and shock absorbers, upgraded transmission cooling, 3.23 axle ratio, trailer wiring harness.			
Locking wire wheel discs	400	336	366
Wire wheels	940	790	860
Option Pkg. B	385	323	352
Door edge guards, floormats, power passenger seat, trunk mat.			
Option Pkg. C	743	624	680
Pkg. B plus lighted visor mirrors, rear reading lamps, power decklid pulldown, Twilight Sentinel.			

Cadillac De Ville/Fleetwood

Cadillac has lengthened its most popular cars in an effort to appease traditional buyers who equate size and weight with value. In the lineup are the Coupe and Sedan De Ville; the plusher Fleetwood Sedan and, after a 2-year absence, the

Prices are accurate at time of printing; subject to manufacturer's change

Cadillac Coupe de Ville

Fleetwood Coupe. The limited-production 4-door Fleetwood Sixty Special also returns. The coupes retain their 110.8-inch wheelbase, but their bodies are lengthened by 5.8 inches, to 202.2. Sedan wheelbases grow three inches, to 113.8, and their bodies stretch 8.8 inches, to 205.2. The added wheelbase increases rear leg room by two inches. The Sixty Special actually loses two inches from its wheelbase (formerly 115.8 inches) to share the one used for the De Ville and Fleetwood sedans, but overall length is increased 3.7 inches to match that of its siblings. Trunk capacity is up from 16.1 cubic feet to 18.1 on the coupe and to 18.4 on the sedan, and base curb weights are up by about 100 pounds. Standard rear fender skirts on the Fleetwood and Sixty Special sedans help emphasize their new length. Front fenders are now a rust-proof nylon composite alloy that weighs less than steel. All models have standard rear shoulder belts, while the sedans also get integral rear headrests. The Sixty Special gains redesigned heated leather seats. Anti-lock brakes, previously standard only on the Sixty Special, are now standard on the Fleetwood Coupe and Sedan. They remain optional on De Ville. All models are powered by a 4.5-liter V-8. A driver's-side air bag, heated windshield and a revised theft-deterrent system are new options for all models. This year's size increases are a reaction to the 1985 downsizing and conversion to front-wheel drive that alienated some long-time Cadillac fans. We expect the '89 restyle, plus Cadillac's improved assembly quality (as indicated by independent industry polls), to help bring buyers back. These boulevard cruisers have their place in the market and we're happy to see better quality, anti-lock brakes and air bags among their attributes.

Specifications

	2-door notchback	4-door notchback
Wheelbase, in.	110.8	113.8
Overall length, in.	202.3	205.3
Overall width, in.	72.5	72.5
Overall height, in.	55.0	55.0
Turn diameter, ft.	40.0	42.6
Curb weight, lbs.	3397	3470
Cargo vol., cu. ft.	18.1	18.4
Fuel capacity, gal.	18.0	18.0
Seating capacity	6	6
Front headroom, in.	39.3	39.3
Front shoulder room, in.	59.0	59.0
Front legroom, max., in.	42.4	42.4
Rear headroom, in.	38.0	38.1
Rear shoulder room, in.	57.6	59.3
Rear legroom, min., in.	40.3	43.3

Engines

	ohv V-8
Size, liters/cu. in.	4.5/273
Fuel delivery	TBI
Horsepower @ rpm	155 @ 4000
Torque (lbs./ft.) @ rpm	240 @ 2800
Availability	S

EPA city/highway mpg

4-speed OD automatic	17/25

Prices

Cadillac De Ville/Fleetwood	Retail Price	Dealer Invoice	Low Price
Coupe De Ville 2-door notchback	$24960	$21291	$22626
Sedan de Ville 4-door notchback	25435	21696	23066
Fleetwood 2-door notchback	29825	25441	27133
Fleetwood 4-door notchback	30300	25846	27573
Fleetwood Sixty Special 4-door notchback	34230	29198	31214
Destination charge	550	550	550

Standard Equipment:

4.5-liter TBI V-8 engine, 4-speed automatic transmission, power steering and brakes, automatic level control, air adjustable rear struts, power driver's

Prices are accurate at time of printing; subject to manufacturer's change

seat, manual recliners, power windows and locks, tilt/telescopic steering column, cruise control, Dual Comfort seat with power driver's side, intermittent wipers, power trunk release, automatic climate control, AM/FM ST ET, power mirrors, sail panel courtesy/reading lights, rear head restraints, Michelin 205/70R15 all-season SBR tires. **Fleetwood** adds: anti-lock braking system, padded vinyl roof (2-door), formal cabriolet roof (4-door), power seats, storage armrest, power decklid release, power decklid pulldown, illuminated entry, Twilight Sentinel, lighted visor mirrors, trunk mat, power mirrors, rear reading lamps, overhead assist handles, AM/FM ST ET cassette w/EQ, digital instrument cluster, locking wire wheel discs. **Sixty Special** adds: leather interior, heated front seats with power lumbar, thigh and lateral supports, automatic day/night mirror, rear passenger footrests, rear overhead console, vinyl top.

Optional Equipment:	Retail Price	Dealer Invoice	Low Price
Anti-lock braking system, De Ville	925	777	846
Supplemental Inflatable Restraint	NA	NA	NA
Front storage armrest, De Ville	70	59	64
Astroroof (NA Sixty Special)	1255	1054	1148
Rear defogger	170	143	156
Heated windshield	250	210	229
Automatic power door locks	185	155	169
Digital instruments, De Ville	238	200	218
Leather seating area (std. Sixty Special) . .	525	441	480
Memory power driver's seat (NA De Ville) .	235	197	215
Automatic day/night mirror	80	67	73
Firemist paint	240	202	220
Delco-Bose sound system w/cassette	576	484	527
w/CD player	872	732	798
Power recliners, Fleetwood (each)	95	80	87
Formal cabriolet roof, De Ville 2-door	713	599	652
Padded vinyl roof, De Ville 4-door	713	599	652
Full cabriolet roof, De Ville 2-door	995	836	910
Leather-trimmed steering wheel, De Ville .	115	97	105
Theft deterrent system	200	168	183
Trunk mat, De Ville	36	30	33
Wire wheel discs, De Ville	320	269	293
Alloy wheels, De Ville	435	365	398
Fleetwood	115	97	105
Accent striping, De Ville	65	55	59
De Ville Option Pkg. B	324	272	296
Door edge guards, floormats, power passenger seat.			
De Ville Option Pkg. C	739	621	676
Pkg. B plus illuminated entry, lighted visor mirrors, power decklid pulldown, Twilight Sentinel.			
De Ville Option Pkg. D	894	751	818
Pkg. C plus remote fuel door release, manual driver's seatback recliner, trumpet horn.			

Prices are accurate at time of printing; subject to manufacturer's change.

Cadillac Eldorado/Seville

Cadillac Eldorado

Cadillac's front-drive 2-door Eldorado and its Seville 4-door cousin get trim and equipment alterations for '89. This follows last year's exterior remake that added three inches to their overall length and reversed falling sales. The sporty Seville Touring Sedan (STS), introduced for a limited run of 1500 in late '88, becomes a regular option for '89 with a production of 3000 planned. STS has a monochrome exterior, shorter final-drive ratio for quicker acceleration, Touring Suspension, high-performance tires, alloy wheels, leather seats, burl elm interior trim and 4-passenger seating. New standard equipment on the base Seville includes 6-way power front seats, maple interior trim, stereo cassette player, graphic equalizer and a revised theft-deterrent system that can prevent unauthorized starts. For '89, Eldo gets the same new standard features as Seville, though maple trim is standard only with the extra-cost Biarritz package and optional on the base model. Eldorado and Seville use Cadillac's 4.5-liter V-8, introduced last year and shared with the De Ville/Fleetwood line. The engine gave the cars a needed 25 additional horsepower. The improvement was pronounced, and now these luxury cars have the smooth power delivery and driveability demanded of the class. They remain slightly cramped inside, with an especially crowded rear seat and only marginal luggage space. The optional

Touring Suspension and its stickier tires make them the best-handling Cadillacs ever and worthy road cars, but at a serious loss of ride comfort. Anti-lock brakes are a boon, but fuel economy is poor and prices are creeping up. Still, these cars deserve a look from anyone shopping in the $30,000 range, even committed import buyers.

Specifications	2-door notchback	4-door notchback
Wheelbase, in.	108.0	108.0
Overall length, in.	190.8	191.4
Overall width, in.	70.9	71.7
Overall height, in.	53.7	53.7
Turn diameter, ft.	40.3	40.3
Curb weight, lbs.	3422	3422
Cargo vol., cu. ft.	14.1	14.1
Fuel capacity, gal.	18.8	18.8
Seating capacity	5	5
Front headroom, in.	37.8	37.8
Front shoulder room, in.	57.2	57.6
Front legroom, max., in.	42.5	42.5
Rear headroom, in.	37.9	37.8
Rear shoulder room, in.	57.2	57.5
Rear legroom, min., in.	36.1	36.1

Engines	ohv V-8
Size, liters/cu. in.	4.5/273
Fuel delivery	TBI
Horsepower @ rpm	155 @ 4000
Torque (lbs./ft.) @ rpm	240 @ 2800
Availability	S

EPA city/highway mpg

4-speed OD automatic	17/25

Cadillac Eldorado/Seville	Retail Price	Dealer Invoice	Low Price
Eldorado 2-door notchback	$26738	$22808	$24473
Seville 4-door notchback	29750	25377	27264
Destination charge	550	550	550

Standard Equipment:

Eldorado: 4.5-liter TBI V-8 engine, power steering, power 4-wheel disc brakes, automatic climate control, power windows and locks, retained acces-

Prices are accurate at time of printing; subject to manufacturer's change.

sory power system, cruise control, Twilight Sentinel, Pass Key theft deterrent system, power mirrors, reclining cloth and leather bucket seats w/power adjustments, outboard rear lap/shoulder belts, digital instrument cluster including tachometer, coolant temperature gauge and voltmeter, low fuel warning light, trip computer, outside thermometer, fold-down center armrest with storage bins, rotating cup holder and coin retainer, leather-wrapped steering wheel with tilt and telescope feature, lamp monitors, AM/FM ST ET cassette w/EQ, dual spot/map lights with retainer for garage door opener, reversible floormats, 215/65R15 Goodyear Eagle GT + 4 tires on alloy wheels. **Seville** adds: Birdseye maple trim, two-tone paint.

Optional Equipment:

	Retail Price	Dealer Invoice	Low Price
Anti-lock braking system	925	777	846
Birdseye maple appliques, Eldorado	245	206	224
Astroroof	1255	1054	1148
Biarritz Pkg. w/leather upholstery, Eldorado .	3180	2671	2910
w/cloth	2770	2327	2535

Power front recliners and lumbar support adjusters, power passenger seat, seatback pockets, walnut on instrument panel, console and door panels, cabriolet roof with opera lamps, two-tone paint, closed-in backlight treatment, wire wheel discs, accent molding, reversible floormats.

	Retail Price	Dealer Invoice	Low Price
STS Pkg., Seville	5754	4833	5265

Anti-lock braking system, 3.31 axle ratio, leather interior with elm burl accents, rear console, automatic power locks, illuminated entry, lighted visor mirrors, theft deterrent system, 215/65R15 Goodyear Eagle GT + 4 tires.

	Retail Price	Dealer Invoice	Low Price
Cellular mobile telephone	1975	1659	1807
Provision for cellular phone	395	332	361
Rear defogger	170	143	156
Automatic power door locks	185	155	169
Engine block heater	45	38	41
Leather seating area	410	344	375
Automatic day/night mirror	80	67	73
Firemist paint	240	202	220
Firemist paint, primary	190	160	174
Secondary	50	42	46
White diamond paint	240	202	220
Two-tone paint, Seville	225	189	206
Delco-Bose music system w/cassette	576	484	527
w/CD player	872	732	798
Power passenger seatback recliner, Eldorado	95	80	87
Padded vinyl roof, Eldorado	995	836	910
Full cabriolet roof, Eldorado	995	836	910
Phaeton roof, Eldorado	1095	920	1002
Theft deterrent system	200	168	183
215/65R15 tires	76	64	70
Touring Suspension	155	130	142
Locking wire wheel discs	190	160	174

Prices are accurate at time of printing; subject to manufacturer's change.

Chevrolet Astro/GMC Safari

Chevrolet Astro

Anti-lock rear brakes are now standard on all passenger versions of Astro and Safari, GM's compact rear-drive vans. The anti-lock system modulates braking pressure to the rear wheels to keep them from locking in panic stops. Astro, sold by Chevrolet dealers, and Safari, sold by GM dealers with GMC truck franchises, are identical except for names and series designations. Power steering, a front stabilizer bar and 27-gallon fuel tank, all optional last year, are standard this year on passenger models. So are shoulder belts for all outboard seating positions except the one next to the sliding side door. And standard instrumentation now includes more gauges. Five-passenger seating is standard; the optional 4-seat package has been dropped for '89, leaving 7-and 8-passenger arrangements available. A sport suspension package that was promised last year but not delivered is promised again for mid-1989; it includes gas-pressurized shock absorbers, rear stabilizer bar and 245/60HR15 tires. All passenger Astros and Safaris are powered by a 150-horsepower 4.3-liter V-6, with a choice of 5-speed manual or extra-cost 4-speed automatic transmissions. Base payload is 1000 pounds and the Astro/Safari can be equipped to tow up to 6000 pounds. These minivans are similar to the Ford Aerostar in design and concept. They're smaller interpretations of the traditional truck-based van, whereas the front-drive Dodge Caravan and Plymouth Voyager are more like enlarged station-wagon cars. With their extra brawn, Astro and Safari are good choices for hauling and towing, but the Caravan and Voyager remain better passenger vehicles. GM plans to introduce a front-drive minivan for the 1990 model year and will tailor it for passenger use.

Specifications

	5-door van
Wheelbase, in.	111.0
Overall length, in.	176.8
Overall width, in.	77.0
Overall height, in.	71.7
Turn diameter, ft.	40.2
Curb weight, lbs.	3084
Cargo vol., cu. ft.	151.8
Fuel capacity, gal.	27.0
Seating capacity	8
Front headroom, in.	NA
Front shoulder room, in.	NA
Front legroom, max., in.	NA
Rear headroom, in.	NA
Rear shoulder room, in.	NA
Rear legroom, min., in.	NA

Engines

	ohv V-6
Size, liters/cu. in.	4.3/262
Fuel delivery	TBI
Horsepower @ rpm	155 @ 4000
Torque (lbs./ft.) @ rpm	230 @ 2400
Availability	S

EPA city/highway mpg

5-speed OD manual	17/24
4-speed OD automatic	17/22

Prices

Chevrolet Astro Passenger Van	Retail Price	Dealer Invoice	Low Price
CS 4-door van	$11900	$10627	$11263
CL 4-door van	12633	11281	11957
LT 4-door van	14144	12631	13388
Destination charge	465	465	465

Prices are accurate at time of printing; subject to manufacturer's change.

Standard Equipment:

CS: 4.3-liter TBI V-6 engine, 5-speed manual transmission, anti- lock rear brakes, full instrumentation (coolant temperature and oil pressure gauges, voltmeter, trip odometer), swing-out side windows, high-back bucket seats, 5-passenger seating, rubber floor covering, inside fuel door release, lighted visor mirrors, under-floor spare tire carrier, 195/75R15 tires. **CL** adds: trip odometer, voltmeter, oil pressure and coolant temperature gauges, custom steering wheel, wheel trim rings, auxiliary lighting, carpet. **LT** adds: air dam with fog lamps, luxury velour seat and door panel trim, upgraded front bucket seats with recliners, integrated armrests and adjustable headrests, split-back center bench seat with integrated armrests, headrests, recliners and fold-down center console with convenience tray and cup pockets; right-hand seat folds forward for access to rear.

Optional Equipment:	Retail Price	Dealer Invoice	Low Price
4-speed automatic transmission	610	519	561
Air conditioning, front	736	626	677
Front & rear	1320	1122	1214
Optional axle ratio	38	32	35
Locking differential	252	214	232
Operating Convenience Pkg	.411	349	378
Power windows and locks.			
Power door locks	211	179	194
7-passenger seating, CS	1069	909	983
CL	981	834	903
LT	878	746	808
8-passenger seating, CS	344	292	316
CL	396	337	364
LT	878	746	808
Custom vinyl bucket seats, w/8-pass	.158	134	145
w/5-pass	.106	90	98
Custom cloth bucket seats, w/8-pass	.158	134	145
w/5-pass	.106	90	98
Special two-tone paint, CS & CL	251	213	231
LT	172	146	158
Sport two-tone paint, CS & CL	172	146	158
California emissions pkg	.100	85	92
Air dam with fog lamps, CS & CL	115	98	106
Deluxe chromed bumpers, CS	128	109	118
CL, LT	76	65	70
Color-keyed bumpers, CS	52	44	48
Luggage carrier	126	107	116
Engine oil cooler	126	107	116
HD radiator	56	48	52
HD radiator & trans oil cooler, w/o A/C . .	118	100	109
w/A/C	63	54	58
Cold Climate Pkg	.46	39	42

Prices are accurate at time of printing; subject to manufacturer's change.

	Retail Price	Dealer Invoice	Low Price
Roof console	83	71	76
Convenience Group	326	277	300
Cruise control, tilt steering column.			
Complete body glass	128	109	118
Tinted glass, w/o complete body glass . . .	75	64	69
w/complete body glass	104	88	96
Tinted windshield	40	34	37
Deep tinted glass, w/o complete body glass .	236	201	217
w/complete body glass	365	310	336
w/light tinted rear window, w/o body glass	185	157	170
w/body glass	308	262	283
Swing-out rear door glass, CS & CL	59	50	54
Rear heater	267	227	246
Electronic instruments	88	75	81
Auxiliary lighting	128	109	118
Dual outside mirrors	52	44	48
Power mirrors	150	128	138
Lighted right visor mirror	43	37	40
Black bodyside moldings, CS	59	50	54
AM radio	122	104	112
AM/FM ST ET	293	249	270
w/seek/scan & clock	347	295	319
AM/FM ST ET cassette	474	403	436
w/EQ	624	530	574
Front recliners & armrests	241	205	222
Power driver's seat	240	204	221
HD shock absorbers	36	31	33
Cruise control	205	174	189
Custom steering wheel, CS	28	24	26
Sport steering wheel, CS	35	30	32
CL	7	6	6
Sport suspension, CS	509	433	468
CL	467	397	430
LT	417	354	384
Puncture sealant tires	184	156	169
HD Trailering Special Equipment, w/o A/C .	555	472	511
w/A/C	498	423	458
LD Trailering Special Equipment	109	93	100
Bright wheel covers, CS	42	36	39
Rally wheels, CS	92	78	85
CL	50	43	46
Aluminum wheels, CS or w/o sport			
suspension	316	269	291
CL	274	233	252
CS w/sport suspension or LT	224	190	206
Intermittent wipers	59	50	54

Prices are accurate at time of printing; subject to manufacturer's change.

Chevrolet Camaro/ Pontiac Firebird

Chevrolet Camaro IROC-Z

The hottest news about these similar rear-drive pony cars is the 20th Anniversary Trans Am. Using the turbocharged 3.8-liter V-6 from Buick's defunct Regal Grand National, Pontiac says the 250-horsepower anniversary edition does 0-60 mph in 5.4 seconds or less, and the quarter mile in under 13 seconds. Only about 1500 will be built and all will have a white exterior and tan interior. Other Trans Am changes include 4-wheel disc brakes as standard for all models. Air conditioning becomes standard for Formula and Trans Am versions, and the GTA gets "Z" speed rated tires (over 149 mph) instead of a "V" rating (over 130 mph). GTA is available as a 3-door hatchback or 2-door notchback; the others come as a hatchback only. On the Camaro side, a new RS model replaces the Sport Coupe as a lower-cost running mate to the high-performance IROC-Z. Both the RS and IROC-Z are available as a 3-door hatchback or 2-door convertible. The RS imitates the IROC's exterior styling, but has a standard 135-horsepower 2.8-liter V-6, a measure intended

82   CONSUMER GUIDE®

to lower insurance premiums for young drivers compared to the IROC. The V-6 also is in the base Firebird, and both lines offer 5.0- and 5.7-liter V-8s of between 170 and 230 horsepower, depending on model and transmission choice. Later in the model year, an extra-cost exhaust system with reduced back pressure will be available with IROC's two optional V-8s to boost horsepower to as much as 240. Camaros and Firebirds are among America's most frequently stolen cars and this year all models gain a standard anti-theft system similar to that which has helped reduce Corvette thefts since 1985. The car won't start if a resistor pellet in the ignition key doesn't match ignition-lock coding. These cars

Specifications	2-door notchback	3-door hatchback	2-door conv.
Wheelbase, in.	101.1	101.1	101.1
Overall length, in.	190.3	190.3	192.0
Overall width, in.	72.4	72.4	72.8
Overall height, in.	49.8	49.8	50.3
Turn diameter, ft.	36.9	36.9	36.9
Curb weight, lbs.	3458	3083	3116
Cargo vol., cu. ft.	12.3	34.8	5.2
Fuel capacity, gal.	15.5	15.5	15.5
Seating capacity	4	4	4
Front headroom, in.	37.0	37.0	37.1
Front shoulder room, in.	57.7	57.7	58.6
Front legroom, max., in.	43.0	43.0	42.9
Rear headroom, in.	35.6	35.6	36.1
Rear shoulder room, in.	56.3	56.3	48.1
Rear legroom, min., in.	28.6	29.8	28.3

Engines	ohv V-6	ohv V-8	ohv V-8	ohv V-8
Size, liters/cu. in.	2.8/173	5.0/305	5.0/305	5.7/350
Fuel delivery	PFI	TBI	PFI	PFI
Horsepower @ rpm	135 @ 4900	170 @ 4000	220 @ 4400	230 @ 4400
Torque (lbs./ft.) @ rpm	160 @ 3900	255 @ 2400	290 @ 3200	330 @ 3200
Availability	S[1]	S[2]	O[3]	O[3]
EPA city/highway mpg				
5-speed OD manual	18/27	17/25	17/26	
4-speed OD automatic	19/27	17/26	16/25	17/25

1. Camaro RS coupe and base Firebird   2. Camaro RS conv. & IROC-Z, Firebird Formula & Trans Am; optional on Camaro RS coupe   3. Camaro IROC-Z, Firebird Formula, Trans AM & GTA   4. Firebird GTA; optional on Camaro IROC-Z

can be exciting to drive, but their insurance rates are sky-rocketing, so check with your agent before buying either. Choosing between them is a matter of taste (and whether you want a convertible). Both trade extroverted styling for poor interior room, good handling for a terrible ride, and substantial rear-drive power for lousy wet-road traction.

Prices

Chevrolet Camaro	Retail Price	Dealer Invoice	Low Price
RS 3-door hatchback	$11495	$10265	$10780
RS 2-door convertible	16995	15177	15986
IROC-Z 3-door hatchback	14145	12631	13288
IROC-Z 2-door convertible	18945	16918	17832
Destination charge	439	439	439

Standard Equipment:

RS: 2.8-liter PFI V-6 engine (hatchback; convertible has 5.0-liter TBI V-8), 5-speed manual transmission, power steering and brakes, AM/FM ST ET, left remote and right manual mirrors, reclining front bucket seats, cloth upholstery, outboard rear lap/shoulder belts, headlamps-on tone, folding rear seat, automatic hatch pulldown, tachometer, coolant temperature and oil pressure gauges, voltmeter, 215/65R15 all-season SBR tires on alloy wheels. **IROC-Z** adds: 5.0-liter TPI V-8 engine, right visor mirror, fog lamps, performance tires.

Optional Equipment:

5.0-liter PFI (TPI) V-8	745	633	685
5.0-liter TBI V-8, RS 3-door	400	340	368
5.7-liter PFI V-8	1045	888	961
4-speed automatic transmission	490	417	451
Custom cloth bucket seats	277	235	255
Custom leather bucket seats	750	638	690
Air conditioning	775	659	713
Limited-slip differential	100	85	92
4-wheel disc brakes	179	152	165
Locking rear storage cover	80	68	74
Rear defogger	145	123	133
Power door locks	145	123	133
California emissions pkg	100	85	92
Power hatch release	50	43	46
Engine block heater	20	17	18
Rear window louvers	210	179	193

Prices are accurate at time of printing; subject to manufacturer's change.

	Retail Price	Dealer Invoice	Low Price
Deluxe luggage compartment trim, RS 3-door	164	139	151
IROC-Z 3-door	84	71	77
Power mirrors	91	77	84
Door edge guards	15	13	14
Removable glass roof panels	866	736	797
Split folding rear seatbacks	50	43	46
245/50VR16 tires on alloy wheels	468	398	431
AM/FM ST ET cassette, RS 3-door	122	104	112
w/EQ	272	231	250
w/Delco/Bose	885	752	814

Sound system prices are for base models; prices vary with option package content.

RS Coupe Preferred Equipment Group 1 . .	255	217	235

HD battery, tinted glass, auxiliary lighting, bodyside moldings.

RS Coupe Preferred Equipment Group 2 . .	1687	1434	1552

Group 1 plus air conditioning, power door locks, floormats, AM/FM ST ET cassette, cruise control, tilt steering column, intermittent wipers.

RS Coupe Preferred Equipment Group 3 . .	2014	1712	1853

Group 2 plus cargo cover, halogen headlamps, reading lamps, power windows.

IROC-Z Preferred Equipment Group 1, w/o 5.7	255	217	235
w/5.7	229	195	211

Tinted glass, auxiliary lighting, bodyside moldings.

IROC-Z Preferred Equipment Group 2, w/o 5.7	1737	1476	1598
w/5.7	1711	1454	1574

Group 1 plus air conditioning, power door locks, floormats, power hatch release, AM/FM ST ET cassette, cruise control, tilt steering column, intermittent wipers.

IROC-Z Preferred Equipment Group 3, w/o 5.7	2545	2163	2341
w/5.7	2519	2141	2317

Group 2 plus cargo cover, halogen headlamps, reading lamps, power mirrors, power driver's seat, power windows.

RS Conv. Preferred Equipment Group 1 . .	206	175	190

HD battery, tinted glass, bodyside moldings.

RS Conv. Preferred Equipment Group 2 . .	1638	1392	1507

Group 1 plus air conditioning, power door locks, floormats, AM/FM ST ET cassette, cruise control, tilt steering column, intermittent wipers.

RS Conv. Preferred Equipment Group 3 . .	1873	1592	1723

Group 2 plus power windows, halogen headlamps.

IROC-Z Conv. Preferred Equipment Group 1 .	206	175	190

HD battery, tinted glass, bodyside moldings.

IROC-Z Conv. Preferred Equipment Group 2 .	1638	1392	1507

Group 1 plus air conditioning, power door locks, floormats, AM/FM ST ET cassette, cruise control, tilt steering column, intermittent wipers.

IROC-Z Conv. Preferred Equipment Group 3 .	2354	2001	2166

Halogen headlamps, power mirrors, AM/FM ST ET cassette w/EQ, power driver's seat, power windows.

Prices are accurate at time of printing; subject to manufacturer's change.

Pontiac Firebird

	Retail Price	Dealer Invoice	Low Price
3-door hatchback	$11999	$10715	$11357
Formula 3-door hatchback	13949	12457	13203
Trans Am 3-door hatchback	15999	14287	15143
Trans Am GTA 3-door hatchback	20339	18163	19251
Destination charge	439	439	439

Standard Equipment:

2.8-liter PFI V-6, 5-speed manual transmisson, power steering and brakes, cloth reclining front bucket seats, outboard rear lap/shoulder belts, power hatch pulldown, AM/FM ST ET, gauge cluster including tachometer, Pass Key theft-deterrent system, 215/65R15 tires on alloy wheels. **Trans Am** adds: 5.0-liter TBI V-8, F41 suspension. **Formula** adds: dual exhaust, air conditioning, WS6 performance suspension, 245/50ZR16 tires on alloy wheels. **GTA** adds: 5.7-liter PFI V-8, 4-speed automatic transmission, 4-wheel disc brakes, limited-slip differential, rear defogger, power windows and locks, tinted glass, cruise control, tilt steering column, articulated bucket seats with inflatable lumbar support and thigh bolsters, floormats, upgraded upholstery, cargo cover, AM/FM ST ET cassette with EQ and Touch Control.

Optional Equipment:

Notchback roof, GTA	700	595	644
5.0-liter TBI V-8, base	400	340	368
5.0-liter PFI (TPI) V-8, Formula & T/A ...	745	633	685
GTA (credit)	(300)	(255)	(255)
Requires limited-slip differential.			
5.7-liter PFI V-8, Formula & T/A	1045	888	961
Requires automatic transmission, engine oil cooler, 4-wheel disc brakes, limited-slip differential and 245/50ZR16 tires.			
5-speed manual transmission, GTA (credit) .	(490)	(417)	(417)
4-speed auto trans, base, Formula & T/A .	490	417	451
Air conditioning, base	775	659	713
Limited-slip differential, Formula & T/A ..	100	85	92
Dual exhaust	155	132	143
Engine oil cooler, Formula & T/A	110	94	101
4-wheel disc brakes, Formula	179	152	165
Option Pkg. 1SA, base (credit)	(331)	(281)	(281)
Air conditioning, bodyside moldings, Lamp Group.			
Option Pkg. 1SB, base	137	116	126
Pkg. 1SA plus power windows and locks, 4-way driver's seat, door pockets, cruise control, power decklid release, reading lamps.			
Option Pkg. 1SA, Formula & T/A (credit)	(721)	(613)	(613)
Bodyside moldings, Lamp Group, power windows and locks, door pockets.			

Prices are accurate at time of printing; subject to manufacturer's change.

	Retail Price	Dealer Invoice	Low Price
Option Pkg. 1SB, Formula & T/A (credit) .	(547)	(465)	(465)
Pkg. 1SA plus 4-way driver's seat, cruise control, power liftgate release, reading lamps, power mirrors.			
Value Option Pkg., base & Formula	802	682	738
T-top roof, AM/FM ST ET cassette.			
Value Option Pkg., T/A	1089	926	1002
T-top roof, Custom Interior Trim, AM/FM ST ET cassette, cargo screen.			
Value Option Pkg., GTA	945	803	869
T-top roof, leather interior.			
Rear defogger, exc. GTA	145	123	133
California emissions pkg.	100	85	92
T-top roof	920	782	846
Two-tone paint, base	150	128	138
Power locks, exc. GTA	145	123	133
Power windows, exc. GTA	240	204	221
AM/FM ST ET cassette, exc. GTA	122	104	112
AM/FM ST ET cassette w/EQ, exc. GTA . .	282	240	259
w/VOP	150	128	138
w/Touch Control, base w/o VOP	447	380	411
Base w/VOP	315	268	290
AM/FM ST ET w/CD & EQ, exc. GTA	447	380	411
w/VOP	394	335	362
GTA	79	67	73
Power antenna, exc. GTA	70	60	64
Cargo security screen, exc. GTA	69	59	63
Luxury Interior Trim, T/A	293	249	270
Luxury seats and door panels, split folding rear seat.			
Leather articulated seats, GTA	375	319	345
245/50ZR16 tires & WS6 suspension, T/A .	385	327	354

Chevrolet Caprice

All Caprices come with air conditioning and a V-8 engine for '89, perhaps the last year for this venerable design that dates to 1977. Chevy has prepared an aerodynamically styled, all-new, but still rear-wheel-drive replacement, possibly as a 1990 model. For '89, the 140-horsepower V-6 that had been standard in the Caprice sedan is dropped in favor of a fuel-injected 170-horsepower 5.0-liter (305-cubic-inch) eight. The station wagon retains its carbureted 140-horsepower 307-cubic-inch V-8. Air conditioning was optional on 4-doors last year, and making it standard accounts for part

Prices are accurate at time of printing; subject to manufacturer's change.

Chevrolet Caprice Classic 4-door

Specifications

	4-door notchback	5-door wagon
Wheelbase, in.	116.0	116.0
Overall length, in.	212.2	215.7
Overall width, in.	75.4	79.3
Overall height, in.	56.4	58.2
Turn diameter, ft.	38.7	39.7
Curb weight, lbs.	3693	3770
Cargo vol., cu. ft.	20.9	87.9
Fuel capacity, gal.	24.5	22.0
Seating capacity	6	8
Front headroom, in.	39.5	39.6
Front shoulder room, in.	60.5	60.5
Front legroom, max., in.	42.2	42.2
Rear headroom, in.	38.2	39.3
Rear shoulder room, in.	60.9	60.9
Rear legroom, min., in.	39.1	37.2

Engines

	ohv V-8	ohv V-8
Size, liters/cu. in.	5.0/305	5.0/307
Fuel delivery	TBI	4 bbl.
Horsepower @ rpm	170 @ 4000	140 @ 3200
Torque (lbs./ft.) @ rpm	255 @ 2400	255 @ 2000
Availability	S[1]	S[2]

EPA city/highway mpg

4-speed OD automatic	17/24	17/24

1. Sedans   2. Wagon

of the nearly $2000 increase in 1989 base prices. Three-point rear shoulder belts are now standard also, and an elasticized cargo restraint net is a new sedan option. The 4-door comes in base, Classic, Brougham or LS trim, while the 3-seat/8-passenger wagon comes only in Classic trim. Buick, Oldsmobile and Pontiac offer similar wagons, but Caprice is the only rear-drive family sedan in the GM stable. As such, it serves buyers who want a big car with V-8 power at reasonable cost. The only direct rivals are the Ford LTD Crown Victoria and nearly identical Mercury Grand Marquis, which we find a little more pleasant to drive, thanks to a slightly more refined V-8 engine. A well-equipped Caprice can be had for $15,500 to $17,000—probably less with a dealer discount. That's cheaper than many mid-size cars and even some Japanese compacts. Fuel economy is poor and the car isn't a nimble handler, but this is a full-size package that insurance statistics rate high for occupant protection.

Prices

Chevrolet Caprice	Retail Price	Dealer Invoice	Low Price
4-door notchback	$13865	$11966	$12916
Classic 4-door notchback	14445	12466	13456
Classic Brougham 4-door notchback	15615	13476	14546
Classic Brougham LS 4-door notchback	16835	14529	15682
Classic 5-door wagon	15025	12967	13996
Destination charge	505	505	505

Standard Equipment:

5.0-liter (305-cid) TBI V-8 engine (4-doors; 307-cid 4bbl. on wagon), 4-speed automatic transmission, power steering and brakes, air conditioning, left remote and right manual mirrors, tinted glass, outboard rear lap/shoulder belts, AM/FM ST ET, knit cloth bench seat, 205/75R15 all-season SBR tires (4-doors; wagon has 225/75R15). **Classic** adds: wheel opening moldings, Quiet Sound Group, vinyl door pull straps, bright wide lower bodyside moldings, headlamps-on tone, hood ornament, carpeted lower door panels. **Brougham** adds: upgraded carpet, front door courtesy lights, vinyl roof, 55/45 cloth front seat with center armrest. **LS** adds: Landau-style vinyl roof, sport mirrors, tinted glass.

Optional Equipment:

Limited-slip differential	100	85	92
Performance axle ratio	21	18	19

Prices are accurate at time of printing; subject to manufacturer's change.

	Retail Price	Dealer Invoice	Low Price
Vinyl bench seat, base	28	24	26
Wagon (credit)	(172)	(146)	(146)
50/50 vinyl seat, base	305	259	281
Wagon	103	88	95
50/50 cloth seat	275	234	253
45/55 leather seat	550	468	506
Custom two-tone paint	141	120	130
Vinyl roof	200	170	184
Air deflector, wagon	65	55	60
Trunk cargo net	30	26	28
HD cooling	40	34	37
Rear defogger	145	123	133
Power door locks, 4-doors	195	166	179
Wagon	255	217	235
California emissions pkg	100	85	92
Estate equipment	307	261	282
Engine block heater	20	17	18
Pinstriping	61	52	56
HD suspension, F40 (std. wagon)	26	22	24
Sport suspension, F41	49	42	45
Inflatable rear shock absorbers	64	54	59
WSW tires	76	65	70
225/70R15 WSW tires	188	160	173
Custom wheel covers, base	65	55	60
Locking wire wheel covers, Brougham	134	114	123
Others	199	169	183
AM/FM ST ET cassette	122	104	112
w/EQ	232	197	213

Sound system prices are for base model; prices vary with option package content.

Preferred Group 1, base	196	167	180

HD battery, floormats, bodyside and wheel opening moldings, extended-range speakers.

Preferred Group 2, base	796	677	732

Group 1 plus power door locks, auxiliary lighting, cruise control, tilt steering column, intermittent wipers.

Classic Sedan Preferred Group 1	709	603	652

HD battery, floormats, auxiliary lighting, remote mirrors, bodyside moldings, extended-range speakers, cruise control, tilt steering column, WSW tires, power decklid release, intermittent wipers.

Classic Sedan Preferred Group 2,

w/50/50 seat	1970	1675	1812
w/bench seat	1490	1267	1371

Group 1 plus power door locks, deluxe luggage compartment trim, lighted right visor mirror, AM/FM ST ET cassette, power windows, power seats (w/50/50 seat).

Prices are accurate at time of printing; subject to manufacturer's change.

	Retail Price	Dealer Invoice	Low Price
Wagon Preferred Group 1	237	201	218

HD battery, load floor carpet, auxiliary lighting, remote mirrors, bodyside moldings.

Wagon Preferred Group 2	1484	1261	1365

Group 1 plus roof carrier, floormats, AM/FM ST ET cassette, cruise control, tilt steering column, power windows, intermittent wipers.

Wagon Preferred Group 3, w/50/50 seat . .	2343	1992	2156
w/bench seat	1863	1584	1714

Group 2 plus gauge package with trip odometer, Twilight Sentinel, cornering lamps, lighted right visor mirror, deluxe rear compartment decor.

Brougham Preferred Group 1	496	422	456

HD battery, floormats, gauge package with trip odometer, Twilight Sentinel, lighted right visor mirror, remote mirrors, bodyside moldings, extended-range speakers, WSW tires, power decklid release.

Brougham Preferred Group 2	2251	1913	2071

Group 1 plus power door locks, cornering lamps, deluxe luggage compartment trim, AM/FM ST ET cassette, power seats, cruise control, tilt steering column, wire wheel covers, power windows, intermittent wipers.

LS Preferred Group 1	2137	1816	1966

HD battery, power door locks, floormats, gauge package with trip odometer, Twilight Sentinel, lighted right visor mirror, remote mirrors, bodyside moldings, AM/FM ST ET cassette, power seats, cruise control, tilt steering column, WSW tires, power decklid release, wire wheel covers, power windows, intermittent wipers.

LS Preferred Group 2	2361	2007	2172

Group 1 plus cornering lamps, deluxe luggage compartment trim.

Chevrolet Cavalier

A steering wheel designed to reduce crash injuries debuts as standard equipment in Cavalier, Chevrolet's version of the J-car front-drive subcompact. An energy-absorbing hub with six deformable metal legs brings the wheel parallel to the driver's chest in a collision, spreading the force of the impact. Volvo has used similar technology for several years. This year's other changes are modest compared to the restyle Cavalier got for '88. The RS 2-door coupe and 4-door sedan are dropped and RS option packages are instead offered on base versions of the coupe, sedan and 5-door wagon. RS packages include sport suspension, 14-inch tires on rally

Chevrolet Cavalier Z24

Specifications	2-door notchback	4-door notchback	5-door wagon	2-door conv.
Wheelbase, in.	101.2	101.2	101.2	101.2
Overall length, in.	178.4	178.4	174.5	178.7
Overall width, in.	66.0	66.3	66.3	66.0
Overall height, in.	52.0	52.1	52.8	52.7
Turn diameter, ft.	34.7	34.7	34.7	34.7
Curb weight, lbs.	2418	2423	2478	2729
Cargo vol., cu. ft.	13.2	13.7	64.4	10.4
Fuel capacity, gal.	13.6	13.6	13.6	13.6
Seating capacity	5	5	5	4
Front headroom, in.	37.9	39.7	38.3	39.1
Front shoulder room, in..	53.7	53.7	53.7	53.7
Front legroom, max., in..	42.9	42.2	42.2	42.9
Rear headroom, in.	36.1	37.9	38.8	37.4
Rear shoulder room, in. .	52.0	53.7	53.7	38.0
Rear legroom, min., in. .	30.5	34.3	33.7	31.1

Engines	ohv I-4	ohv V-6
Size, liters/cu. in.	2.0/121	2.8/173
Fuel delivery	TBI	PFI
Horsepower @ rpm	90 @ 5600	130 @ 4500
Torque (lbs./ft.) @ rpm	108 @ 3200	160 @ 3600
Availability	S	S[1]

EPA city/highway mpg

5-speed OD manual	26/36	18/29
3-speed automatic	25/32	20/27

1. *Z24; optional, wagon*

wheels, power steering and a gauge package with tachometer. Other models are a VL ("value leader") coupe and a high-performance Z24 coupe and convertible. A 2.0-liter 4-cylinder is standard on all models except the Z24, which comes with a 2.8-liter V-6. The V-6 is a station wagon option. Rear shoulder belts are standard on all models for '89. Z24s gain gas-pressurized shock absorbers and, on the coupe, a split folding rear seatback. All GM divisions introduced J-cars for 1982. Cadillac and Oldsmobile dropped theirs for '89, but the Buick Skyhawk and Pontiac Sunbird survive. Cavalier isn't as roomy or technically sophisticated as newer Japanese subcompacts, yet it offers good value for the money. The 4-cylinder is economical but lethargic, especially with automatic transmission. The V-6 is essential to adequate hauling capability in the wagon and, along with the sport suspension and wider tires, helps turn the Z24 into a mini-muscle car. Note that some rivals have a 4-speed overdrive automatic, which makes for quieter, more economical cruising than Cavalier's 3-speed.

Prices

Chevrolet Cavalier	Retail Price	Dealer Invoice	Low Price
VL 2-door notchback	$7375	$6955	$7165
Base 2-door notchback	8395	7749	8072
Base 4-door notchback	8595	7933	8264
Base 5-door wagon	8975	8284	8630
Z24 2-door notchback	11325	10113	10719
Z24 2-door convertible	16615	14837	15726
Destination charge	425	425	425

Standard Equipment:

VL: 2.0-liter TBI 4-cylinder engine, 5-speed manual transmission, power brakes, vinyl reclining front bucket seats, outboard rear lap/shoulder belts, 185/80R13 all-season SBR tires on styled steel wheels. **Base** adds: easy-entry passenger seat (2-door), ashtray and glovebox lights, headlights-on tone, AM/FM ST ET. **Z24** adds: 2.8-liter PFI V-6 engine, custom cloth interior with contoured front seats, split folding rear seatback (3-door), center console, FE3 sport suspension, 215/60R14 Goodyear Eagle GT + 4 tires on aluminum wheels.

Optional Equipment:

2.8-liter PFI V-6, wagon	660	561	607
3-speed automatic transmission	415	353	382

Prices are accurate at time of printing; subject to manufacturer's change.

	Retail Price	Dealer Invoice	Low Price
Air conditioning	675	574	621
Cloth bucket seats	28	24	26
Sport cloth bucket seats, 2-door	459	390	422
4-door	483	411	444
Wagon	383	326	352
Roof luggage carrier, wagon	115	98	106
Decklid luggage carrier, 4-door	115	98	106
Rear defogger	145	123	133
Power door locks, 2-door	145	123	133
4-door	195	166	179
California emissions pkg	100	85	92
Floormats	33	28	30
Tinted glass	105	89	97
Engine block heater	20	17	18
Electronic instrument cluster	156	133	144
Bodyside moldings	50	43	46
Removable sunroof	350	298	322
FE2 sport suspension	27	23	25
WSW tires	68	58	63
195/70R14 tires	129	110	119
215/60R14 OWL tires, Z24	102	87	94
Power decklid release	50	43	46
Wheel trim rings	39	33	36
Alloy wheels	212	180	195
Power windows (std. conv.)	285	242	262
AM/FM ST ET	332	282	305
AM/FM ST ET cassette	454	386	418

Sound system prices are for VL; prices vary with model and option package content.

	Retail Price	Dealer Invoice	Low Price
VL Preferred Group 1, w/5-speed	303	258	279
w/automatic	277	235	255

Auxiliary lighting, power steering.

	Retail Price	Dealer Invoice	Low Price
VL Preferred Group 2, w/5-speed	544	462	500
w/automatic	518	440	477

Group 1 plus floormats, tinted glass, left remote and right manual mirrors, bodyside moldings.

	Retail Price	Dealer Invoice	Low Price
VL Preferred Group 3, w/5-speed	1574	1338	1448
w/automatic	1548	1316	1424

Group 2 plus air conditioning, cruise control, tilt steering column, intermittent wipers.

	Retail Price	Dealer Invoice	Low Price
Base Preferred Group 1, 2- & 4-door			
w/5-speed	303	258	279
Wagon w/2.8	309	263	284
2- & 4-door w/automatic	277	235	255
Wagon w/2.0 & automatic	283	241	260

Auxiliary lighting, power steering.

	Retail Price	Dealer Invoice	Low Price
Base Preferred Group 2, 2- & 4-door			
w/5-speed	544	462	500
Wagon w/2.8	550	468	506
2- & 4-door w/automatic	518	440	477
Wagon w/2.0 & automatic	524	445	482

Group 1 plus floormats, tinted glass, left remote and right manual mirrors, bodyside moldings.

	Retail Price	Dealer Invoice	Low Price
Base Preferred Group 3, 2- & 4-door			
w/5-speed	1574	1338	1448
Wagon w/2.8	1695	1441	1559
2- & 4-door w/automatic	1548	1316	1424
Wagon w/2.0 & automatic	1669	1419	1535

Group 2 plus air conditioning, cruise control, tilt steering column, intermittent wipers, roof rack (wagon).

	Retail Price	Dealer Invoice	Low Price
Base Preferred Group 4, 2-door w/5-speed .	2051	1743	1887
4-door w/5-speed	2176	1850	2002
2-door w/automatic	2025	1721	1863
4-door w/automatic	2150	1828	1978

Group 3 plus power windows and locks, AM/FM ST ET cassette.

	Retail Price	Dealer Invoice	Low Price
RS Pkg., 2-door	695	591	639
4-door	705	599	649

Black exterior accents, dual mirrors, FE2 sport suspension, power steering, gauges including tachometer and trip odometer, 195/70R14 SBR tires on rally wheels.

	Retail Price	Dealer Invoice	Low Price
RS Preferred Group 1, 2-door w/5-speed .	911	774	838
4-door w/5-speed	921	783	847
Wagon w/5-speed or 2.8	927	788	853
2-door w/automatic	885	752	814
4-door w/automatic	895	761	823
Wagon w/2.0 & automatic	901	766	829

RS Pkg. plus floormats, tinted glass, auxiliary lighting.

	Retail Price	Dealer Invoice	Low Price
RS Preferred Group 2, 2-door w/5-speed .	1941	1650	1786
4-door w/5-speed	1951	1658	1795
Wagon w/5-speed or 2.8	1957	1663	1800
2-door w/automatic	1915	1628	1762
4-door w/automatic	1925	1636	1771
Wagon w/2.0 & automatic	1931	1641	1777

Group 1 plus air conditioning, cruise control, tilt steering column, intermittent wipers.

	Retail Price	Dealer Invoice	Low Price
RS Preferred Group 3, 2-door w/5-speed .	2583	2196	2376
4-door w/5-speed	2603	2213	2395
Wagon w/5-speed or 2.8	2674	2273	2460
2-door w/automatic	2557	2173	2352
4-door w/automatic	2577	2190	2371
Wagon w/2.0 & automatic	2648	2251	2436

Group 2 plus decklid luggage carrier (2-door), roof luggage carrier (wagon), power windows and locks, AM/FM ST ET cassette, power decklid release.

Prices are accurate at time of printing; subject to manufacturer's change.

		Retail Price	Dealer Invoice	Low Price
Z24 Coupe Preferred Group 1		850	723	782
Air conditioning, HD battery, tinted glass, auxiliary lighting.				
Z24 Coupe Preferred Group 2		1360	1156	1251
Group 1 plus AM/FM ST ET cassette, cruise control, tilt steering column, intermittent wipers.				
Z24 Coupe Preferred Group 3		1915	1628	1762
Group 2 plus power windows and locks, power decklid release, AM/FM ST ET cassette w/EQ.				
Z24 Convertible Preferred Group 1		838	712	771
Air conditioning, HD battery, auxiliary lighting, AM/FM ST ET cassette.				
Z24 Convertible Preferred Group 2		1426	1212	1312
Group 1 plus AM/FM ST ET cassette w/EQ, power decklid release, cruise control, tilt steering column, intermittent wipers.				

Chevrolet Celebrity/
Pontiac 6000

Chevrolet Celebrity Eurosport 4-door

Celebrity loses its slow-selling 2-door coupe and 6000 gets a
rear-end restyle as these front-drive intermediate twins
head into their eighth season. Both lines now consist of 4-
door sedans and 5-door wagons, though the Celebrity sedan
is to be replaced after the '89 model year by the new 1990
Lumina 4-door. The Celebrity wagon is expected to remain
in production. As for the 6000, all sedans get a rounded rear

window, and a new roof, trunklid and taillamps. It's a restyle similar that given the corporate-companion Buick Century and Oldsmobile Cutlass Ciera. LE and S/E 6000 sedans and 5-door wagons also gain the 6-lamp treatment (quad headlamps plus integrated fog lamps) used on the top-line STE. A body-color grille and moldings further the resemblance. The front-drive version of the STE has disappeared, leaving only the All-Wheel Drive model that arrived last year. STE comes only as a 4-door with a 3.1-liter V-6 and anti-lock brakes, both of which are unavailable on other 6000s or Celebritys. Changes common to both lines include the addition of rear-seat shoulder belts. The base 2.5-liter 4-cylinder engine is due for mid-year internal revisions that will boost horsepower from 98 to 110. And a 5-speed manual transmission that had been offered with the available 2.8-liter V-6 dies of

Specifications

	4-door notchback	5-door wagon
Wheelbase, in.	104.9	104.9
Overall length, in.	188.3	190.8
Overall width, in.	69.3	69.3
Overall height, in.	54.1	54.3
Turn diameter, ft.	38.7	38.7
Curb weight, lbs.	2751	2888
Cargo vol., cu. ft.	16.2	75.1
Fuel capacity, gal.	15.7	15.7
Seating capacity	6	8
Front headroom, in.	38.6	38.6
Front shoulder room, in.	56.2	56.2
Front legroom, max., in.	42.1	42.1
Rear headroom, in.	38.0	38.9
Rear shoulder room, in.	56.2	56.2
Rear legroom, min., in.	36.4	35.6

Engines

	ohv I-4	ohv V-6
Size, liters/cu. in.	2.5/151	2.8/173
Fuel delivery	TBI	PFI
Horsepower @ rpm	98 @ 4800	125 @ 4500
Torque (lbs./ft.) @ rpm	135 @ 3200	160 @ 3600
Availability	S	O

EPA city/highway mpg

3-speed automatic	23/30	20/27
4-speed OD automatic		20/29

poor sales, leaving only 3- and 4-speed automatics. We still recommend these cars as good mid-size values. Passenger and cargo room are comparable to the more modern Ford Taurus and Mercury Sable, the V-6s furnish sufficient power and the upgraded suspension on Celebrity Eurosport and 6000 S/E models gives capable handling. The 4WD STE is a budget Audi Quattro, and dealer and factory incentives mean both the Pontiac and Chevy are often priced attractively.

Prices

Chevrolet Celebrity	Retail Price	Dealer Invoice	Low Price
4-door notchback	$11495	$9920	$10708
5-door 2-seat wagon	11925	10291	11108
5-door 3-seat wagon	12175	10507	11341
Destination charge	450	450	450

Standard Equipment:

2.5-liter TBI 4-cylinder engine, 3-speed automatic transmission, power steering and brakes, front bench seat with center armrest, cloth upholstery, outboard rear lap/shoulder belts, AM/FM ST ET, bodyside moldings, day/night mirror, left remote and right manual mirrors, headlamps-on tone, 185/75R14 all-season SBR tires.

Optional Equipment:

2.8-liter PFI V-6	610	519	561
4-speed automatic transmission (2.8 req.) .	175	149	161
Air conditioning	775	659	713
Cloth bucket seats w/console	257	218	236
Cloth 55/45 seat	133	113	122
Custom cloth 55/45 seat, 4-door	385	327	354
w/split folding middle seat, wagon	435	370	400
Custom cloth 45/45 seat w/console, 4-door .	335	285	308
w/split folding middle seat, wagon	385	327	354
Custom two-tone paint, w/option pkg . . .	93	79	86
w/o option pkg	148	126	136
Air deflector, wagon	40	34	37
HD cooling, w/o A/C	70	60	64
w/A/C	40	34	37
Rear defogger	145	123	133
Power door locks	195	166	179
California emissions pkg	100	85	92

Prices are accurate at time of printing; subject to manufacturer's change.

	Retail Price	Dealer Invoice	Low Price
Front floormats	17	14	16
Rear floormats	12	10	11
Gauge Pkg	64	54	59
Coolant temperature gauge, voltmeter, trip odometer.			
Exterior Molding Pkg	55	47	51
Deluxe rear compartment decor	40	34	37
Power driver's seat	240	204	221
Reclining front seatbacks	90	77	83
Cargo Area Security Pkg	44	37	40
Inflatable rear shock absorbers	64	54	59
HD suspension, F40	26	22	24
WSW tires	68	58	63
195/70R14 tires	90	77	83
Sport wheel covers	65	55	60
Locking wire wheel covers	199	169	183
Alloy wheels	143	122	132
Rally wheels	56	48	52
Intermittent wipers	125	106	115
AM/FM ST ET cassette	122	104	112
Preferred Group 1, 4-door w/2.5	911	774	838
4-door w/2.8	937	796	862
Wagon w/2.5	903	768	831
Wagon w/2.8	929	790	855
Air conditioning, floormats, auxiliary lighting, Exterior Molding Pkg.			
Preferred Group 2, 4-door w/2.5	1525	1296	1403
4-door w/2.8	1551	1318	1427
Wagon w/2.5	1682	1430	1547
Wagon w/2.8	1708	1452	1571
4-door: Group 1 plus power door locks, Gauge Pkg., cruise control, tilt steering column, intermittent wipers. Wagon adds luggage rack, power liftage release.			
Preferred Group 3, 4-door w/2.5	2012	1710	1851
4-door w/2.8	2038	1732	1875
Wagon w/2.5	2203	1873	2027
Wagon w/2.8	2229	1895	2051
4-door: Group 2 plus remote mirrors, AM/FM ST ET cassette, power decklid release, power windows. Wagon adds deluxe rear compartment decor, Cargo Area Security Pkg.			
Eurosport Equipment Group	230	196	212
Sport suspension, quick-ratio steering, blackout exterior trim, padded sport steering wheel, 195/75R14 all-season SBR tires on rally wheels.			
Eurosport Preferred Group 1, 4-door w/2.5 .	1141	970	1050
4-door w/2.8	1167	992	1074
Wagon w/2.5	1133	963	1042
Wagon w/2.8	1159	985	1066
Eurosport Equipment plus air conditioning, floormats, auxiliary lighting, Exterior Molding Pkg.			

Prices are accurate at time of printing; subject to manufacturer's change.

	Retail Price	Dealer Invoice	Low Price
Eurosport Preferred Group 2, 4-door w/2.5 .	1755	1492	1615
4-door w/2.8	1781	1514	1639
Wagon w/2.5	1912	1625	1759
Wagon w/2.8	1938	1647	1783

4-door: Group 1 plus power door locks, Gauge Pkg., cruise control, tilt steering column, intermittent wipers. Wagon adds luggage rack, power liftgate release.

	Retail Price	Dealer Invoice	Low Price
Eurosport Preferred Group 3, 4-door w/2.5 .	2242	1906	2063
4-door w/2.8	2268	1928	2087
Wagon w/2.5	2433	2068	2238
Wagon w/2.8	2459	2090	2262

4-door: Group 2 plus remote mirrors, AM/FM ST ET cassette, power decklid release, power windows. Wagon adds deluxe rear compartment decor, Cargo Area Security Pkg.

Pontiac 6000

	Retail Price	Dealer Invoice	Low Price
LE 4-door notchback	$11969	$10329	$11149
LE 5-door wagon	13769	11883	12826
S/E 4-door notchback	15399	13289	14344
S/E 5-door wagon	16999	14411	15705
STE All Wheel Drive 4-door notchback . . .	22599	19503	21051
Destination charge	450	450	450

Standard Equipment:

LE: 2.5-liter TBI 4-cylinder engine, 3-speed automatic transmission (4-door); wagon has 2.8-liter PFI V-6 and 4-speed automatic transmission), power steering and brakes, AM/FM ST ET, tinted glass, cloth front seat with armrest, split folding second seat (wagon), rear defogger (wagon), outboard rear lap/shoulder belts, 185/75R14 SBR tires. **S/E adds:** 2.8-liter PFI V-6, 4-speed automatic transmission, tachometer, trip odometer, voltmeter, coolant temperature and oil pressure gauges, intermittent wipers, power windows and locks, AM/FM ST ET cassette, rear defogger, luggage rack (wagon), cloth reclining bucket seats, leather-wrapped steering wheel, sport suspension, Electronic Ride Control (wagon), 195/70R14 Goodyear Eagle GT + 4 tires on aluminum wheels. **STE All Wheel Drive** adds: 3.1-liter V-6, 3-speed automatic transmission, permanent, full-time 4-wheel drive, 4-wheel disc brakes, anti-lock braking system, accessory kit (flares, first aid kit, raincoat, gloves, spotlight), air conditioning, cruise control, power windows and locks, Driver Information Center, tire inflator, Lamp Group, intermittent wipers, Electronic Ride Control, AM/FM ET cassette with EQ and Touch Control, power antenna, power trunk release, rear defogger, electronic instruments, front reading lamps, lighted right visor mirror, fog lamps, 195/70R15 Goodyear Eagle GT + 4 tires on alloy wheels.

Prices are accurate at time of printing; subject to manufacturer's change.

Optional Equipment:

	Retail Price	Dealer Invoice	Low Price
2.8-liter PFI V-6, LE 4-door	610	519	561
4-speed automatic transmission, LE 4-door .	175	149	161
Requires 2.8-liter V-6.			
Air conditioning	775	659	713
Option Pkg. 1SA, LE	605	514	557
Air conditioning, tilt steering column, intermittent wipers.			
Option Pkg. 1SB, LE 4-door	730	621	672
LE wagon	865	735	796
Pkg. 1SA plus cruise control.			
Option Pkg. 1SC, LE 4-door	1141	970	1050
LE wagon	1131	961	1041
Pkg. 1SB plus power windows and locks, Lamp Group, remote decklid release, power driver's seat, lighted right visor mirror, reading lamps.			
Option Pkg. 1SA, S/E 4-door	238	202	219
S/E wagon	188	160	173
Air conditioning, remote decklid release, power driver's seat, reading lamps.			
Value Option Pkg., LE 4-door	345	293	317
45/55 seat, AM/FM ST ET cassette, alloy wheels.			
Rear defogger, LE 4-door	145	123	133
Two-tone paint	115	98	106
Power locks, LE 4-door	195	166	179
Power windows, LE 4-door	300	255	276
AM/FM ST ET cassette, LE	122	104	112
AM/FM ST ET cassette w/EQ, S/E 4-door . .	350	298	322
S/E wagon	315	268	290
AM/FM ST ET w/CD & EQ, S/E 4-door . . .	554	471	510
S/E wagon	519	441	477
STE	204	173	188
45/55 seat, LE	133	113	122
Custom Interior Trim, LE	493	419	454
LE w/VOP	360	306	331
45/55 seat with recliners, gauges.			
WSW tires, LE	68	58	63
Alloy wheels, LE	215	183	198
Simulated woodgrain siding, LE wagon . .	295	251	271

Chevrolet Corsica/Beretta

A new 5-door hatchback and a new top-line LTZ 4-door join the Corsica ranks, while the base Beretta has upgraded trim. Corsica and the Beretta 2-door coupe share the same platform, but differ in exterior styling, interior furnishings

Prices are accurate at time of printing; subject to manufacturer's change.

Chevrolet Beretta GT

and chassis components. Chevy counts them as a single model, a practice that has the front-drive compacts No. 1 in U.S. sales. For '89, base Berettas sport last year's GT exterior trim and the GT becomes a regular model instead of an option package. It also gets new 15×7-inch alloy wheels. The Corsica hatchback gets a rear seatback that folds to create 39 cubic feet of cargo area. A new 60/40 split rear seatback is standard on the LTZ 4-door and is scheduled to become optional on the hatchback and base 4-door. Corsica's new LTZ includes the basic ingredients of the Beretta GT: 130-horsepower V-6 engine, sport suspension, high-performance tires, 15-inch alloy wheels and a trunk-lid luggage rack. New 195/70R14 all-season tires are standard on the base Beretta, while the GT gets new cloth interior trim and a 60/40 split folding rear seatback with an armrest. All Corsicas and Berettas come with 3-point rear shoulder belts. Neither car has any outstanding features, but both are generally competent and, properly outfitted, earn our recommendation. Forget the base 90-horsepower 2.0-liter 4-cylinder engine. Its performance is leaden. Go with the optional V-6 and 3-speed automatic transmission; the standard 5-speed manual lacks precision and driveability. We also prefer the sport suspension and 195/70R14 tires for a balance of handling and ride. A Corsica with the V-6, automatic and top LT option package is $14,000; a base Beretta with the same powertrain and option group 3 is about $13,400. That's good value.

Specifications

	2-door notchback	4-door notchback	5-door hatchback
Wheelbase, in.	103.4	103.4	103.4
Overall length, in.	187.2	183.4	183.4
Overall width, in.	68.2	68.2	68.2
Overall height, in.	55.3	56.2	56.2
Turn diameter, ft.	34.8	34.8	34.8
Curb weight, lbs.	2631	2595	2648
Cargo vol., cu. ft.	13.5	13.5	39.1
Fuel capacity, gal.	13.6	13.6	13.6
Seating capacity	5	5	5
Front headroom, in.	38.0	38.1	38.1
Front shoulder room, in.	55.3	55.4	55.4
Front legroom, max., in.	43.4	43.4	43.4
Rear headroom, in.	36.6	37.4	37.4
Rear shoulder room, in.	55.1	55.6	55.6
Rear legroom, min., in.	34.6	35.0	35.0

Engines

	ohv I-4	ohv V-6
Size, liters/cu. in.	2.0/121	2.8/173
Fuel delivery	TBI	PFI
Horsepower @ rpm	90 @ 5600	130 @ 4700
Torque (lbs./ft.) @ rpm	108 @ 3200	160 @ 3600
Availability	S	O[1]

EPA city/highway mpg

5-speed OD manual	24/34	18/29
3-speed automatic	24/31	20/27

1 - Standard Corsica LTZ and Beretta GT

Prices

Chevrolet Corsica	Retail Price	Dealer Invoice	Low Price
4-door notchback	$9985	$8917	$9601
5-door hatchback	10375	9265	9970
LTZ 4-door notchback	12825	11453	12289
Destination charge	425	425	425

Standard Equipment:

2.0-liter TBI 4-cylinder engine, 5-speed manual transmission, power steering, power brakes, cloth reclining front bucket seats, door pockets, automatic front seatbelts, outboard rear lap/shoulder belts, headlamps-on warning, AM/FM ST ET, P185/75R14 all-season SBR tires on steel wheels; hatchback has sliding package tray, cargo cover. **LTZ** adds: 2.8-liter PFI V-6, FE3 sport

Prices are accurate at time of printing; subject to manufacturer's change.

suspension, luggage rack, 205/60R15 Goodyear Eagle GT tires, on alloy wheels, sport steering wheel, custom cloth interior with center console, 60/40 split rear seatback with center armrest, gauge package with tachometer, overhead console.

Optional Equipment:

	Retail Price	Dealer Invoice	Low Price
2.8-liter PFI V-6, base & LT	660	561	607
3-speed automatic transmission	490	417	451
Air conditioning, base & LT	750	638	690
Custom cloth CL bucket seats, 4-door . . .	425	361	391
5-door	275	234	253
Custom two-tone paint	123	105	113
HD battery	26	22	24
Decklid luggage carrier	115	98	106
Floor console	60	51	55
Rear defogger	145	123	133
Power door locks	195	166	179
California emissions pkg	100	85	92
Gauge Pkg. (std. LTZ)	139	118	128
Tachometer, voltmeter, coolant temperature and oil pressure gauges, trip odometer.			
Auxiliary lighting, 4-door	64	54	59
5-door	56	48	52
Bodyside striping	57	48	52
F41 sport suspension, base	49	42	45
195/70R14 tires, base	93	79	86
WSW tires, base	68	58	63
Styled wheels, base	56	48	52
Alloy wheels, base	215	183	198
LT	159	135	146
Intermittent wipers	55	47	51
AM/FM ST ET cassette	122	104	112
AM/FM ST ET cassette w/EQ	272	231	250
Sound system prices vary with option package content.			
Preferred Group 1, base 4-door	243	207	224
Base 5-door	235	200	216
HD battery, floormats, tinted glass, auxiliary lighting.			
Preferred Group 2, base 4-door	1348	1146	1240
Base hatchback	1340	1139	1233
Group 1 plus air conditioning, cruise control, tilt steering column, intermittent wipers.			
Preferred Group 3, base 4-door	2000	1700	1840
Base 5-door	1992	1693	1833
Group 2 plus power windows and locks, AM/FM ST ET cassette, power decklid release.			
LT Equipment Group, base	244	207	224
F41 sport suspension, 195/70R14 Goodyear Eagle GA tires, blackout exterior trim, sport steering wheel.			

Prices are accurate at time of printing; subject to manufacturer's change.

	Retail Price	Dealer Invoice	Low Price
LT Preferred Group 1, 4-door	487	414	448
5-door	479	407	441

LT Group plus HD battery, floormats, tinted glass, auxiliary lighting.

LT Preferred Group 2, 4-door	1731	1471	1593
5-door	1723	1465	1585

Group 1 plus air conditioning, Gauge Pkg., cruise control, tilt steering column, intermittent wipers.

LT Preferred Group 3, 4-door	2383	2026	2192
5-door	2375	2019	2185

Group 2 plus power windows and locks, AM/FM ST ET cassette, power decklid release.

Preferred Group 1, LTZ	534	454	491

HD battery, floormats, tinted glass, cruise control, tilt steering column, intermittent wipers.

Preferred Group 2, LTZ	1186	1008	1091

Group 1 plus power windows and locks, AM/FM ST ET cassette, power decklid release.

Chevrolet Beretta

	Retail Price	Dealer Invoice	Low Price
2-door notchback	$10575	$9443	$10159
GT 2-door notchback	12685	11328	12157
Destination charge	425	425	425

Standard Equipment:

2.0-liter TBI 4-cylinder engine, 5-speed manual transmission, power steering and brakes, cloth reclining front bucket seats, automatic front seatbelts, console with storage armrest, outboard rear lap/shoulder belts, tachometer, coolant temperature and oil pressure gauges, voltmeter, trip odometer, headlamps-on warning, left remote and right manual mirrors, AM/FM ST ET, console, tinted glass, F41 sport suspension, P195/70R14 Goodyear GA all-season SBR tires on steel wheels. **GT** adds: 2.8-liter PFI V-6, FE3 sport suspension, sport steering wheel, 60/40 split folding rear seatback, custom cloth trim, overhead consolette, power decklid release, 205/60R15 Goodyear Eagle GT tires on styled steel wheels.

Optional Equipment:

2.8-liter PFI V-6, base	660	561	607
3-speed automatic transmission	490	417	451
Air conditioning, base	750	638	690
Custom two-tone paint	123	105	113
HD battery	26	22	24
Decklid luggage carrier	115	98	106
Rear defogger	145	123	133
Power door locks	145	123	133

Prices are accurate at time of printing; subject to manufacturer's change.

	Retail Price	Dealer Invoice	Low Price
California emissions pkg	100	85	92
Engine block heater	20	17	18
Electronic instrumentation	156	133	144
Auxiliary lighting	32	27	29
Removable sunroof	350	298	322
Alloy wheels	159	135	146
Intermittent wipers	55	47	51
AM/FM ST ET cassette	122	104	112
AM/FM ST ET cassette w/EQ	272	231	250

Sound system prices vary with option package content.

Preferred Group 1, base	91	77	84

HD battery, floormats, auxiliary lighting.

Preferred Group 2, base	1196	1017	1100

Group 1 plus air conditioning, cruise control, tilt steering column, intermittent wipers.

Preferred Group 3, base	1723	1465	1585

Group 2 plus power windows and locks, AM/FM ST ET cassette, power decklid release.

Preferred Group 1, GT	446	379	410

HD battery, floormats, auxiliary lighting, cruise control, tilt steering column, intermittent wipers.

Preferred Group 2, GT	973	827	895

Group 1 plus AM/FM ST ET cassette, power windows and locks, power decklid release.

Chevrolet Corvette

A new ZR1 package puts Corvette among the world's fastest production cars, while a new 6-speed manual transmission becomes available on all 1989 'Vettes. ZR1 is a limited-production option built around the new LT5 engine, a double-overhead cam, 32-valve 5.7-liter aluminum V-8 jointly developed by Chevrolet and Group Lotus, the British car company now owned by GM. Chevy wasn't saying, but LT5 horsepower is estimated at around 385, some 140 more than the standard Corvette V-8. Top speed is an estimated 185 mph, with 0-60 mph times around 4.2 seconds. A special "valet" key limits the power output, for times ZR1 owners lend their car to others. Unofficially dubbed the "King of the Hill," only 2000 to 3000 ZR1s will be built annually, all of them coupes. A price hadn't been announced at press time,

Chevrolet Corvette

Specifications	3-door hatchback	2-door conv.
Wheelbase, in.	96.2	96.2
Overall length, in.	176.5	176.5
Overall width, in.	71.0	71.0
Overall height, in.	46.7	46.4
Turn diameter, ft.	40.4	40.4
Curb weight, lbs.	3229	3269
Cargo vol., cu. ft.	17.9	6.6
Fuel capacity, gal.	20.0	20.0
Seating capacity	2	2
Front headroom, in.	36.4	36.5
Front shoulder room, in.	54.1	54.1
Front legroom, max., in.	42.6	42.6
Rear headroom, in.	—	—
Rear shoulder room, in.	—	—
Rear legroom, min., in.	—	—

Engines

	ohv V-8
Size, liters/cu. in.	5.7/350
Fuel delivery	PFI
Horsepower @ rpm	245 @ 4300
Torque (lbs./ft.) @ rpm	340 @ 3200
Availability	S

EPA city/highway mpg

6-speed OD manual	16/25
4-speed OD automatic	17/25

but a ZR1 will likely cost around $50,000. They're set apart visually from other 'Vettes by their convex tail panels, rectangular taillamps and by bulging rear fenders needed to accommodate steamroller 315/35ZR17 tires, which are 1.5 inches wider than standard Corvette tires. ZR1 meets the government's combined city/highway standard of 22.5 mpg and thus avoids a gas guzzler tax. Chevy credits the new ZF 6-speed manual, which is madatory on ZR1s and a no-cost option in place of the 4-speed automatic on other Corvettes. To preserve fuel, a pin in the ZF's linkage forces the shift lever to bypass second and third gears and to go directly from first to fourth. This occurs only in certain light throttle applications; most of the time it operates like a traditional manual transmission. Standard on ZR1 will be the Z51 Performance Handling Package and the new FX3 Delco-Bilstein Selective Ride Control system, which can alter shock-absorber damping. The Z51 package is optional on all 'Vettes, and 6-speed models so equipped are eligible for the FX3 option. Elsewhere in the Corvette lineup, a fiberglass removable hardtop with heated glass rear window will become available for convertibles later in the model year. Corvettes are expensive, rough riding, impractical and, in the wrong hands, dangerously fast. Driven sensibly, they're high-excitment image machines that rival the performance of imported exotics costing much more.

Prices

Chevrolet Corvette	Retail Price	Dealer Invoice	Low Price
3-door hatchback	$31545	$26592	$29069
2-door convertible	36785	31010	33898
Destination charge	500	500	500

Standard Equipment:

5.7-liter PFI V-8 engine, 6-speed manual or 4-speed automatic transmission, power steering, power 4-wheel disc brakes, anti-lock braking system, Pass Key theft deterrent system, air conditioning, AM/FM ST ET cassette, power antenna, tinted glass, power mirrors, tilt/telescopic steering column, power windows, intermittent wipers, 275/40ZR17 Goodyear Eagle GT tires on cast alloy wheels.

Prices are accurate at time of printing; subject to manufacturer's change.

Optional Equipment:

	Retail Price	Dealer Invoice	Low Price
Z51 Performance Handling Pkg	.NA	NA	NA
FX3 Selective Ride Control System	NA	NA	NA
Leather seats	400	332	368
Electronic control air conditioning	150	125	138
Performance axle ratio	22	18	20
Engine oil cooler	110	91	101
California emissions pkg	100	83	92
Radiator cooling boost fan	75	62	69
Engine block heater	20	17	18
Low tire pressure warning indicator	325	270	299
Lighted right visor mirror	58	48	53
HD radiator	40	33	37
Removable roof panel	615	510	566
Dual removable roof panels	915	759	842
Power seats (each)	240	199	221
Delco/Bose music system	773	642	711
Preferred Group 1	1163	965	1070

Electronic air conditioning, Delco/Bose music system, power driver' seat.

Chevrolet Lumina

1990 Chevrolet Lumina

Lumina is a new front-drive intermediate scheduled to arrive in the late spring of 1989 as the first 4-door sedan from the GM10, or W-body, design that produced the 1988 Buick Regal, Oldsmobile Cutlass Supreme and Pontiac Grand Prix 2-door coupes. Lumina, to be introduced as an early 1990 model, will ride the same 107.5-inch wheelbase as the W-

Prices are accurate at time of printing; subject to manufacturer's change.

body coupes and come with the 140-horsepower 3.1-liter V-6 and 4-speed overdrive automatic transmission also used in those cars. Lumina's wheelbase is three inches longer than Celebrity's, Chevy's front-drive, mid-size offering since 1982. The Celebrity 4-door will be dropped after '89 to make room for Lumina. The Celebrity station wagon is expected to continue. By 1990, Chevy will get a 2-door version of the W-body to replace the rear-drive Monte Carlo, which was discontinued after 1988. The other three divisions will get 4-door sedan W-bodies, though styling is supposed to be different on all models. Chevrolet hasn't released additional information and we have not driven a Lumina.

Specifications and prices not available at time of publication.

Chrysler Conquest TSi/ Mitsubishi Starion

Chrysler Conquest TSi

These twin rear-drive sports coupes, built by Chrysler-partner Mitsubishi, are carried over virtually unaltered in preparation for an all-new version due for 1990. Changes common to both include an automatic-down feature for the driver's power window, shoulder belts for rear passengers, new standard-seat trim and a higher capacity rear defroster. In addition, the optional 4-speed automatic transmission is now available only on the Conquest; all Starions have the 5-speed manual. These cars use a turbocharged and intercooled 2.6-liter 4-cylinder engine. Standard equipment includes 4-wheel disc brakes with anti-lock rear brakes, cruise control, power windows and door locks and a cassette stereo with graphic equalizer. Motorized automatic front shoulder belts with manual lap belts also are standard. The suspension is all independent and carries tires wider at the rear than at the front. An optional handling package adds adjustable shock absorbers and a mix of even wider front and rear tires. A broad-shouldered stance, low seating, taut ride and throaty exhaust lend these 3-door hatchbacks a masculine air. Acceleration is satisfying and turbocharger lag is minimal. Control is good, but the ride is extremely firm and

Specifications

	3-door hatchback
Wheelbase, in.	95.9
Overall length, in.	173.2
Overall width, in.	66.3
Overall height, in.	51.8
Turn diameter, ft.	31.5
Curb weight, lbs.	2822
Cargo vol., cu. ft.	NA
Fuel capacity, gal.	19.8
Seating capacity	4
Front headroom, in.	36.6
Front shoulder room, in.	52.4
Front legroom, max., in.	40.7
Rear headroom, in.	35.4
Rear shoulder room, in.	51.2
Rear legroom, min., in.	29.1

Engines

	Turbo ohc I-4
Size, liters/cu. in.	2.6/156
Fuel delivery	TBI
Horsepower @ rpm	188 @ 5000
Torque (lbs./ft.) @ rpm	223 @ 2500
Availability	S

EPA city/highway mpg

5-speed OD manual	18/22
4-speed OD automatic	18/24

we'd like anti-lock brakes all around, not just at the rear. The supportive front bucket seats have adjustable side bolsters and the driver's positioning before the pedals and tilt steering wheel is businesslike. The rear seat is suitable only for children and cargo room is subpar, despite the hatchback design. Starion is an aging but quick 2+2.

Prices

Chrysler Conquest TSi	Retail Price	Dealer Invoice	Low Price
3-door hatchback	$18974	$15938	$17456
Destination charge	255	255	255

Standard Equipment:

2.6-liter turbocharged, intercooled TBI 4-cylinder engine, 5-speed manual transmission, power steering, power brakes, anti-lock rear braking system, limited-slip differential, power windows and locks, cruise control, tilt steering column, digital clock, tachometer, trip odometer, coolant temperature gauge and oil pressure gauges, voltmeter, cloth reclining front bucket seats with adjustable side bolsters, split folding rear seatback, cargo area security panel, rear defogger, anti-theft system, AM/FM ST ET cassette w/EQ and power antenna, fog lamps, remote fuel filler and hatch releases, bronze tinted glass, optical horn, automatic headlamp shutoff, warning lights (low fuel and washer fluid, door or liftgate ajar), lighted visor mirrors, heated power mirrors, variable intermittent wipers, 205/55VR16 front and 225/50VR16 rear tires on aluminum wheels.

Optional Equipment:

4-speed automatic transmission	718	596	657
Automatic air conditioning	955	793	874
Leather seats	372	309	341
Sunroof	292	242	267
Performance Handling Pkg.	205	170	188
225/50VR16 front and 245/45VR16 rear tires on alloy wheels, adjustable shock absorbers.			
Carpet protectors	28	23	26

Mitsubishi Starion

ESI-R 3-door hatchback	$19859	—	—
Destination charge	265	265	265

Dealer invoice and low price not available at time of publication.

Prices are accurate at time of printing; subject to manufacturer's change

Standard Equipment:

2.6-liter TBI turbocharged, intercooled 4-cylinder engine, 5-speed manual transmission, power steering, power 4-wheel disc brakes, anti-lock rear brakes, limited-slip differential, automatic climate control, power windows and locks, heated power mirrors, cruise control, automatic-off headlamps, velour reclining front bucket seats, motorized front shoulder belts with manual lap belts, outboard rear lap/shoulder belts, split folding rear seat, door pockets, tilt steering column, bronze-tinted glass, rear defogger and wiper/washer, leather-wrapped steering wheel, removable cargo cover, remote fuel door and liftgate releases, speed-sensitive intermittent wipers, right visor mirror, console with armrest and storage, tachometer, coolant temperature and oil pressure gauges, voltmeter, boost gauge, trip odometer, digital clock, AM/FM ST ET cassette w/EQ, power antenna, audio controls in steering wheel hub, theft protection device, 205/55VR16 front and 225/50VR16 rear tires on alloy wheels.

Optional Equipment:	Retail Price	Dealer Invoice	Low Price
Leather seats	626	—	—
Sunroof	303	—	—
Sports Handling Pkg.	386	—	—

225/50VR16 front and 245/45VR16 rear tires on wider alloy wheels, adjustable shock absorbers.

Chrysler Fifth Avenue/ Dodge Diplomat/ Plymouth Gran Fury

A standard driver's-side air bag was added in mid-1988 and continues this fall as Chrysler's only rear-drive sedans head into their swan-song season. Chrysler plans a front-drive replacement for the Fifth Avenue as a 1990 model. It will be based on the New Yorker and will use that car's Mitsubishi-made V-6 engine. Its body will be about six inches longer than the current Fifth Avenue's and its sister ship will be a new Imperial model. No replacement is planned for the Diplomat or Gran Fury. The current trio's air bag supplements a conventional lap/shoulder belt and is contained in the steering wheel hub. The Chrysler and Dodge versions are among the few cars with both tilt steering columns and air bags.

Prices are accurate at time of printing; subject to manufacturer's change

Chrysler Fifth Avenue

Specifications

	4-door notchback
Wheelbase, in.	112.6
Overall length, in.	206.7
Overall width, in.	72.4
Overall height, in.	55.0
Turn diameter, ft.	40.7
Curb weight, lbs.	3556
Cargo vol., cu. ft.	15.6
Fuel capacity, gal.	18.0
Seating capacity	6
Front headroom, in.	39.3
Front shoulder room, in.	56.0
Front legroom, max., in.	42.5
Rear headroom, in.	37.7
Rear shoulder room, in.	55.5
Rear legroom, min., in.	37.0

Engines

	ohv V-8
Size, liters/cu. in.	5.2/318
Fuel delivery	2 bbl.
Horsepower @ rpm	140 @ 3600
Torque (lbs./ft.) @ rpm	265 @ 2000
Availability	S

EPA city/highway mpg

3-speed automatic	16/22

Among the few changes for '89, Fifth Avenue and Diplomat get a new leather-wrapped steering wheel as part of their optional Luxury Equipment packages. Only one powertrain is available with these cars, a carbureted 5.2-liter V-8 and 3-speed automatic transmission. All are 6-passenger, 4-door sedans that can tow up to 2000 pounds. Some might mourn this trio's passing, but not us. The Fifth Avenue in particular heaps on the comfort and convenience features, but that doesn't atone for an ancient rear-drive chassis that dates to the 1976 Plymouth Volare/Dodge Aspen. These cars bounce and buck over bumps and have slow, uncertain responses to the steering wheel. They lean heavily in turns and nosedive in normal braking. Interior room is adequate for five, but there's not much luggage space. The proven drivetrain is among the few redeeming features. The V-8 isn't especially powerful and is not fuel efficient, but it usually runs smoothly.

Prices

Chrysler Fifth Avenue	Retail Price	Dealer Invoice	Low Price
4-door notchback	$18345	$15793	$17069
Destination charge	505	505	505

Standard Equipment:

5.2-liter 2bbl. V-8 engine, 3-speed automatic transmission, power steering and brakes, driver's side air bag, automatic air conditioning, power windows, AM & FM ST ET, rear defogger, tinted glass, 60/40 bench seat with folding armrest and driver's seatback recliner, tilt steering column, power mirrors, cloth upholstery, coolant temperature gauge, ammeter, trip odometer, headlamps-on tone, intermittent wipers, padded landau roof, P205/75R15 SBR WSW tires.

Optional Equipment:

Power Convenience Pkg	680	578	626
Cruise control, power decklid release, power locks, power driver's seat.			
Luxury Equipment Discount Pkg.	1921	1633	1767
Power Convenience Pkg. plus vinyl bodyside molding, floormats, illuminated entry, leather/vinyl seats, leather-wrapped steering wheel, overhead console with compass and outside temperature readouts, power antenna, lighted visor mirrors, wire wheel covers.			
Pearl coat paint	41	35	38
California emissions pkg.	100	85	92

Prices are accurate at time of printing; subject to manufacturer's change

	Retail Price	Dealer Invoice	Low Price
Power passenger seat . . . . *Requires Luxury Pkg.*	262	223	241
AM & FM ST ET cassette	262	223	241
Conventional spare tire	96	82	88
Power sunroof . . . . *Requires Luxury Pkg.; deletes overhead console.*	928	789	854
HD suspension	27	23	25
Undercoating	44	37	40
Wire wheel covers	212	180	195

Dodge Diplomat

	Retail Price	Dealer Invoice	Low Price
Salon 4-door notchback	$11995	$10706	$11351
SE 4-door notchback	14795	12726	13761
Destination charge	505	505	505

Standard Equipment:

Salon: 5.2-liter 2bbl. V-8 engine, 3-speed automatic transmission, power steering, power brakes, driver's-side air bag, tinted glass, AM/FM ST ET, tilt steering column, bench seat with center armrest, cloth and vinyl upholstery, ammeter, coolant temperature gauge, headlamps-on tone, intermittent wipers, P205/75R15 tires. **SE** adds: automatic air conditioning, vinyl roof, 60/40 front seat with driver's seatback recliner, cloth upholstery, rear center armrest, rear defogger, cruise control, remote mirrors, lighted right visor mirror, trunk dress-up, upgraded sound insulation.

Optional Equipment:

Automatic air conditioning, Salon	855	727	787
Popular Equipment Discount Pkg., Salon .	1147	975	1055
Automatic air conditioning, rear defogger, power mirrors, cruise control, premium wheel covers.			
Protection Pkg., Salon	185	157	170
Bodyside moldings, rear bumper guards, floormats, undercoating.			
Light Pkg., Salon	133	113	122
SE	122	104	112
Luxury Equipment Discount Pkg., SE . . .	1202	1022	1106
Light group, power decklid release, power windows and locks, power driver's seat, leather-wrapped steering wheel, lighted visor mirrors, wire wheel covers.			
Pearl/clear coat paint	41	35	38
Rear defogger, Salon	149	127	137
California emissions pkg	100	85	92
Illuminated entry, SE . . . . *Requires Luxury Pkg.*	78	66	72
Power mirrors, Salon	164	139	151
Power door locks . . . . *Requires power mirrors or Popular Pkg.*	201	171	185

Prices are accurate at time of printing; subject to manufacturer's change

	Retail Price	Dealer Invoice	Low Price
Power windows	294	250	270
Requires power locks; Salon requires power mirrors or Popular Pkg.			
AM & FM ST ET cassette	262	223	241
Power antenna, SE	72	61	66
Requires Luxury Pkg.			
HD suspension	27	23	25
Power sunroof, SE	1108	942	1019
Trunk dress-up, Salon	58	49	53
Requires Popular Pkg.			
Conventional spare tire	96	82	88
Vinyl roof	206	175	190
Salon requires Popular Pkg.			
Wire wheel covers, SE	231	196	213

Plymouth Gran Fury

	Retail Price	Dealer Invoice	Low Price
Salon 4-door notchback	$11995	$10706	$11351
Destination charge	505	505	505

Standard Equipment:

5.2-liter 2bbl. V-8 engine, 3-speed automatic transmission, power steering and brakes, driver's side air bag, tinted glass, AM ET, cloth and vinyl bench seat with center armrest, ammeter, coolant temperature gauge, headlamps-on tone, 205/75R15 tires.

Optional Equipment:

	Retail Price	Dealer Invoice	Low Price
Automatic climate control	855	727	787
Popular Equipment Pkg	1147	975	1055
Automatic climate control, rear defogger, power mirrors, cruise control, premium wheel covers.			
Luxury Equipment Pkg.	2835	2410	2608
Popular Pkg. plus Light Group, upper door frame molding, power decklid release, power windows and locks, 60/40 cloth seat with recliners, leather-wrapped steering wheel, trunk dress-up, lighted visor mirrors, vinyl roof, wire wheel covers.			
Protection Pkg.	185	157	170
Light Pkg.	133	113	122
Requires Popular Pkg.			
60/40 cloth seat w/recliners	353	300	325
Requires Popular Pkg.			
Rear defogger	149	127	137
California emissions pkg.	100	85	92
Power mirrors	164	139	151
Power locks	201	171	185
Requires power mirrors.			

Prices are accurate at time of printing; subject to manufacturer's change

	Retail Price	Dealer Invoice	Low Price
Power windows	294	250	270
Requires power mirrors and locks.			
AM/FM ST ET cassette	262	223	241
HD suspension	27	23	25
Trunk dress-up	58	49	53
Requires Popular Pkg.			
Conventional spare tire	96	82	88
Vinyl roof	206	175	190
Requires Popular Pkg.			

Chrysler LeBaron

Chrysler LeBaron GTC Coupe

The 4-door notchback sedan and the station wagon have been dropped for '89 and production will cease on the 5-door hatchback as Chrysler pares its LeBaron line to the carried-over coupe and convertible. Chrysler will stop building the slow-selling hatchback and its corporate twin Dodge Lancer in March, though inventories of unsold cars mean dealers are likely to have them available though most of the '89 model year. All 1989 LeBarons get a new 2.5-liter turbocharged engine and the coupe and convertible also get standard 4-wheel disc brakes and a driver's-side air bag. Performance versions are identified this year by a GTC suffix for the coupe and convertible and a GTS suffix for the hatchback. They come with special exterior graphics, low-profile tires on alloy wheels and a handling suspension. The standard GTC/GTS engine is a turbocharged and intercooled 2.2-liter 4-cylinder rated at 174-horsepower, a 28-horsepower increase over last year's non-intercooled 2.2 turbo. Chrysler designates this the Turbo II engine and makes it available only with a 5-speed manual transmission. A credit option on GTC/GTS cars is the Turbo I, a 150-horsepower 2.5 mated to a 3-speed automatic. This engine also is optional on other LeBarons. All other models except the base sedan come standard with a naturally aspirated 2.5 rated at 100 horsepower, up four from last year. The base sedan has a naturally aspirated 2.2, with the 2.5 optional. The road manners, quality of assembly and interior materials of these front-drive cars don't measure up to their attractive looks, a discrepancy that's true especially for the convertible and coupe. The hatchback is unrefined, though its design is prac-

Specifications	2-door notchback	2-door conv.	5-door hatchback
Wheelbase, in.	100.3	100.3	103.1
Overall length, in.	184.9	184.9	180.4
Overall width, in.	68.4	68.4	68.3
Overall height, in.	50.9	52.2	53.0
Turn diameter, ft.	38.1	38.1	36.2
Curb weight, lbs.	2769	2860	2659
Cargo vol., cu. ft.	33.4	14.0	42.6
Fuel capacity, gal.	14.0	14.0	14.0
Seating capacity	5	4	5
Front headroom, in.	37.6	38.3	38.3
Front shoulder room, in.	55.9	55.9	55.8
Front legroom, max., in.	43.1	43.1	41.1
Rear headroom, in.	36.3	37.0	37.9
Rear shoulder room, in.	56.3	45.7	55.9
Rear legroom, min., in.	33.0	33.0	36.5

Engines	ohc I-4	ohc I-4	Turbo ohc I-4	Turbo ohc I-4
Size, liters/cu. in.	2.2/135	2.5/153	2.5/153	2.2/135
Fuel delivery	TBI	TBI	PFI	PFI
Horsepower @ rpm	93 @ 4800	100 @ 4800	150 @ 4800	174 @ 5200
Torque (lbs./ft.) @ rpm	122 @ 3200	135 @ 2800	180 @ 2000	200 @ 2400
Availability	S	S	O	S[1]

EPA city/highway mpg				
5-speed OD manual	24/34	24/34	20/25	20/28
3-speed automatic	24/28	23/29	18/23	

1. LeBaron GTC/GTS with 5-speed manual trans.

tical and its price reasonable. The naturally aspirated 2.5 is easier to live with than the raucous but quick turbo engines. GTC/GTS models improve handling, but their stiff suspensions offer little comfort or bad-pavement control.

Prices

Chrysler LeBaron	Retail Price	Dealer Invoice	Low Price
5-door hatchback	$11495	$10266	$10731
Premium 5-door hatchback	13495	12026	12611
GTS 5-door hatchback	17095	15194	15995
Destination charge	450	450	450

Standard Equipment:

2.2-liter TBI 4-cylinder engine, 5-speed manual transmission, power steering and brakes, cloth reclining bucket seats, tachometer, coolant temperature and oil pressure gauges, voltmeter, trip odometer, front console with storage, tinted glass, variable intermittent wipers, rear defogger, message center, remote mirrors, visor mirrors, remote fuel door and liftgate releases, wide bodyside moldings, AM & FM ST ET, removable shelf panel, 195/70R14 all-season SBR touring tires. **Premium** adds: 2.5-liter engine, air conditioning, power locks, power mirrors, lighted visor mirrors, floormats, Light Group. **GTS** adds: 2.2-liter intercooled Turbo II engine, power windows, illuminated entry, overhead console with compass and outside temperature readout, AM & FM ST ET cassette, cruise control, rear spoiler, tilt steering column, leather-wrapped steering wheel, sport suspension, 205/60R15 performance tires on alloy wheels.

Optional Equipment:

2.5-liter engine, base	279	237	257
2.5-liter turbo engine, base	536	456	493
Premium	678	576	624
GTS w/automatic	NC	NC	NC
Base requires Popular or Luxury Pkg.			
3-speed automatic transmission, base & Premium	536	456	493
GTS (credit w/2.5 Turbo I)	(175)	(149)	(149)
Air conditioning, base	775	659	713
Basic Equipment Pkg., base	873	742	803
Air conditioning, console extension with armrest, Light Group.			
Popular Equipment Pkg., base w/5-speed	1443	1227	1328
Base incl. automatic or turbo	1879	1597	1729
Base incl. automatic & turbo	2315	1968	2130
Basic Pkg. plus 2.5-liter engine, cruise control, floormats, illuminated entry, AM & FM ST ET cassette, tilt steering column, undercoating.			

Prices are accurate at time of printing; subject to manufacturer's change

	Retail Price	Dealer Invoice	Low Price
Luxury Equipment Pkg., base	2064	1754	1899
Premium	1371	1165	1261
Premium incl. 2.5 turbo	1924	1635	1770

Base: Popular Pkg. plus power windows and locks, heated power mirrors, leather-wrapped steering wheel, lighted visor mirrors. Premium adds: overhead console with compass and outside temperature readout, AM & FM ST ET cassette with Infinity speakers, power driver's seat.

	Retail Price	Dealer Invoice	Low Price
Power Convenience Pkg., base	514	437	473

Power windows and locks, heated power mirrors.

Deluxe Convenience Pkg., base & Premium .	300	255	276

Cruise control, tilt steering column; base requires Basic Pkg.

Sport Handling Pkg., base	153	130	141
Base w/Luxury Pkg., Premium	94	80	86

Sport suspension, leather-wrapped steering wheel, all-season performance tires; base requires Popular or Premium Pkg.

Power locks, base	195	166	179

Requires Basic, Luxury or Sport Handling Pkg.

Electronic instruments, Premium	299	254	275

Requires Electronic Navigator.

California emissions pkg.	100	85	92
Electronic Navigator, Premium & GTS . . .	272	231	250

Premium requires Luxury Pkg.

Power driver's seat	240	204	221

Base requires Basic, Popular or Luxury Pkg.

Power windows, Premium	285	242	262
AM & FM ST ET cassette, base	152	129	140

Requires Basic, Popular or Luxury Pkg.

AM & FM ST ET cassette, Premium	458	389	421
Premium w/Popular or Luxury Pkg . . .	306	260	282
Cassette stereo w/EQ, Premium & GTS . .	210	179	193

Premium requires Luxury Pkg.

Power sunroof, base w/Luxury Pkg.,			
Premium	776	660	714
Premium w/Luxury Pkg., GTS	601	511	553
205/60R15 tires on alloy wheels, Premium .	584	496	537
Premium w/Sport Handling Pkg	516	439	475

Requires Luxury Pkg.

14" alloy wheels, base & Premium	322	274	296

Base requires Popular or Luxury Pkg.

Liftgate wiper/washer	122	104	112

Chrysler LeBaron
Coupe & Convertible

Highline 2-door notchback	$11695	$10325	$11110
Highline 2-door convertible	14195	12500	13448
Premium 2-door notchback	14695	12935	13915

Prices are accurate at time of printing; subject to manufacturer's change

	Retail Price	Dealer Invoice	Low Price
Premium 2-door convertible	18195	15980	17188
GTC 2-door notchback	17519	15392	16556
GTC 2-door convertible	19680	17272	18576
Destination charge	440	440	440

Standard Equipment:

Highline: 2.5-liter TBI 4-cylinder engine, 5-speed manual transmission, power steering, power 4-wheel disc brakes, cloth reclining front bucket seats, tachometer, coolant temperature and oil pressure gauges, voltmeter, trip odometer, trip computer, center console, remote fuel door and decklid releases, tinted glass, variable intermittent wipers, message center, remote mirrors, visor mirrors, wide bodyside moldings, AM & FM ST ET, 195/70R14 SBR tires. **Convertible** adds: power top, power windows. **Premium** adds to Highline coupe: 3-speed automatic transmission, automatic air conditioning, overhead console with compass and outside temperature readouts, power locks, electronic instrument cluster, floormats, cornering lights, heated power mirrors, leather-wrapped steering wheel, two-tone paint. **Premium convertible** deletes overhead console and adds: illuminated entry, trunk dress-up, lighted visor mirrors, AM & FM ST ET cassette with Infinity speakers and power antenna, power driver's seat, cruise control, tilt steering column, undercoating. **GTC** deletes electronic instruments and cornering lights and adds: 2.2-liter intercooled Turbo II 4-cylinder engine and heavy-duty 5-speed manual transmission (2.5-liter Turbo I and automatic may be substituted at no charge), performance suspension, quick-ratio power steering, decklid luggage rack, 205/55R16 unidirectional SBR tires on alloy wheels.

Optional Equipment:

2.5-liter turbo engine, Highline & Premium .	698	593	642
3-speed automatic transmission, Highline .	552	469	508
Manual air conditioning, Highline	798	678	734
Deluxe Convenience Pkg	309	263	284
Cruise control, tilt steering column; standard on Premium convertible and GTC.			
Light Pkg., Highline, Premium coupe . . .	203	173	187
Power Convenience Pkg. I, Highline	243	207	224
Power locks, heated power mirrors; requires Popular Pkg.			
Power Convenience Pkg. II, Highline	459	390	422
Pkg. I plus power windows.			
Popular Equipment Pkg., Highline coupe .	1028	874	946
Highline conv.	1368	1163	1259
Coupe: Manual air conditioning, floormats, cruise control, tilt steering column, undercoating. Convertible adds: headlights with time delay, illuminated entry, lighted visor mirrors, power locks, heated power mirrors.			

Prices are accurate at time of printing; subject to manufacturer's change

	Retail Price	Dealer Invoice	Low Price
Luxury Equipment Pkg., Highline coupe ..	1898	1613	1746
Premium coupe	697	592	641
Manual air conditioning, floormats, headlights with time delay, illuminated entry, lighted visor mirrors, power windows and locks, heated power mirrors, power driver's seat, cruise control, tilt steering column, undercoating, leather-wrapped steering wheel.			
Electronic Discount Pkg., Premium	494	420	454
Electronic Monitor, Electronic Navigator; coupe requires Luxury Pkg.			
Pearl coat paint, Highline	41	35	38
Two-tone paint, Highline	233	198	214
Leather seats, Premium coupe	646	549	594
Requires Luxury Pkg.			
Premium leather seats w/power left,			
Premium conv	1112	945	1023
Enthusiast leather power seats, GTC cpe .	646	549	594
California emissions pkg.	102	87	94
Electronic Navigator, GTC	280	238	258
Power driver's seat, Highline,			
Premium coupe	247	210	227
Power windows, Premium coupe	216	184	199
AM/FM ST ET cassette, Highline	157	133	144
w/seek/scan, Premium coupe	569	484	523
CD player, Premium & GTC coupes	412	350	379
AM/FM ST ET cassette w/EQ, Highline . . .	754	641	694
w/seek/scan & EQ, Premium coupe . . .	785	667	722
Premium conv., GTC	216	184	199
Removable glass sunroof, Highline coupe .	409	348	376
w/o overhead console, Premium coupe .	229	195	211
Overhead console, Premium coupe	268	228	247
195/75R14 WSW touring tires, Highline &			
Premium	74	63	68
14" alloy wheels, Highline & Premium . . .	322	274	296
Sport suspension, Highline, Premium conv.	59	50	54
w/premium wheel covers, Highline	329	280	303
w/alloy wheels, Premium	651	553	599

Chrysler New Yorker

Chrysler's flagship is refined for '89 with more power, a new 4-speed overdrive automatic transmission and some new convenience options. New Yorker was reintroduced as an all-new, front-drive 6-passenger sedan for 1988. It continues in a single 4-door notchback body style in base and Landau

Prices are accurate at time of printing; subject to manufacturer's change

Chrysler New Yorker

trim. A redesigned intake manifold and exhaust-flow improvements help boost the horsepower of its Mitsubishi-made 3.0-liter V-6 from 136 to 141 this year. Replacing a 3-speed automatic as the only available transmission is a new 4-speed automatic. Four-wheel disc brakes with an anti-lock feature continue as an option in place of the standard front disc/rear drum setup. Among new options are an 8-way power driver's seat, a new anti-theft system and an electronic information center that warns if a turn signal is left on inadvertently. The Landau has a vinyl landau roof, automatic power door locks that activate when the car reaches about 15 mph, 6-way power driver's seat, cruise control and a leather-wrapped steering wheel with a tilt column. A conservative sedan that evokes Chrysler's big-car luxury heritage, the New Yorker is smooth, quiet and unexciting. The V-6 has adequate power, but not much more. Around-town handling is good, but the car succumbs to tire-squealing body lean at the first hint of spirited cornering. The chassis filters out most bumps, yet the New Yorker doesn't float excessively at speed. The available anti-lock brakes are a big plus. The interior will seat five adults in true comfort, though three in front is a bit of a squeeze. Dashboard controls are generally easy to reach and well labeled. Trunk space is good. Overall, Chrysler took aim at the middle of the road, and hit it.

Specifications

	4-door notchback
Wheelbase, in.	104.3
Overall length, in.	193.6
Overall width, in.	68.5
Overall height, in.	53.5
Turn diameter, ft.	40.5
Curb weight, lbs.	3214
Cargo vol., cu. ft.	16.5
Fuel capacity, gal.	16.0
Seating capacity	6
Front headroom, in.	38.3
Front shoulder room, in.	56.4
Front legroom, max., in.	41.9
Rear headroom, in.	37.8
Rear shoulder room, in.	55.9
Rear legroom, min., in.	38.7

Engines

	ohc V-6
Size, liters/cu. in.	3.0/181
Fuel delivery	PFI
Horsepower @ rpm	141 @ 5000
Torque (lbs./ft.) @ rpm	171 @ 2800
Availability	S

EPA city/highway mpg

4-speed OD automatic	18/26

Prices

Chrysler New Yorker	Retail Price	Dealer Invoice	Low Price
4-door notchback	$17416	$15004	$16310
Landau 4-door notchback	19509	16783	18246
Destination charge	495	495	495

Standard Equipment:

3.0-liter PFI V-6 engine, 4-speed automatic transmission, power steering and brakes, automatic air conditioning, 50/50 cloth bench seat with armrest, front seatback storage pockets, power windows, tinted glass, heated power mirrors, intermittent wipers, optical horn, coolant temperature and oil pressure gauges, voltmeter, low-fuel light, message center, visor mirrors, AM & FM ST ET, cornering lights, 195/75R14 SBR WSW tires. **Landau** adds: landau vinyl roof, automatic rear load leveling, power driver's seat, speed-ac-

Prices are accurate at time of printing; subject to manufacturer's change

tivated power door locks, cruise control, tilt steering column, leather-wrapped steering wheel, electronic instruments, trip computer, upgraded wheel covers.

Optional Equipment:

	Retail Price	Dealer Invoice	Low Price
Anti-lock 4-wheel disc brakes	954	811	878
Base requires Luxury Pkg.			
Luxury Equipment Pkg., base	1557	1323	1432
Landau	1962	1668	1805
Base: automatic power locks, bodyside molding, electronic instruments, cruise control, floormats, illuminated entry, lighted visor mirrors, leather-wrapped steering wheel, automatic rear load leveling, tilt steering column, trip computer, undercoating, wire wheel covers. Landau adds: overhead console with electronic information center, power antenna, memory power seats.			
Mark Cross Edition, base	2140	1819	1969
Landau	2545	2163	2341
Luxury Pkg. plus leather/vinyl 50/50 power front seats, upgraded door panels.			
Interior Illumination Pkg.	197	167	181
Illuminated entry, lighted visor mirrors.			
Deluxe Convenience Pkg., base	309	263	284
Cruise control, tilt steering column.			
Overhead console w/electronic info center, base	690	587	635
Requires Luxury Pkg.			
Automatic power locks, base	294	250	270
California emissions pkg	102	87	94
AM/FM ST ET cassette	262	223	241
AM/FM Cassette Pkg., Landau w/Luxury Pkg.	497	422	457
Base or Landau w/o Luxury Pkg.	569	484	523
Includes 6 Infinity speakers and power antenna.			
AM/FM Cassette w/EQ Pkg., Landau	713	606	656
Base	785	667	722
Requires Luxury or Mark Cross Pkg.			
Security alarm	150	128	138
Requires power locks.			
Power driver's seat, base	247	210	227
Memory power seats, base	351	298	323
Requires Luxury Pkg.			
Power sunroof	799	679	735
Base requires Luxury Pkg.			
Automatic rear load leveling, base	185	157	170
Conventional spare tire	85	72	78
Wire wheel covers, Landau	231	196	213
Alloy wheels, base w/Luxury or Mark Cross Pkg.	42	36	39
Landau	273	232	251

Prices are accurate at time of printing; subject to manufacturer's change.

Daihatsu Charade

1988 Daihatsu Charade CSX

Daihatsu had a limited presence in 1988, its first year in the U.S., when imports were limited to 11,500 Charade minicompacts available in Hawaii and 10 continental states in the south and west. For 1989, Daihatsu's allotment under Japan's voluntary quota system grows to 17,000 cars, and the company plans to expand into several southeastern states. A 90-horsepower 1.3-liter 4-cylinder and a 3-speed automatic transmission are scheduled to arrive in January for the front-drive Charade. Until then, all Charades will come only with a 53-horsepower 1.0-liter 3-cylinder engine and a 5-speed manual. In January, the lineup changes as follows: A base CES model will use the 3-cylinder and the 5-speed. A mid-level CLS will be available with either the 3-cylinder or the new 4-cylinder. A top-line CLX will come only with the 4-cylinder. The new automatic transmission will be optional with the 4-cylinder engine on the CLS and CLX. Daihatsu has positioned Charade as an upscale small car, not an entry-level, low-budget model. But for the price of even a top-line CSX, you could buy a Honda Civic hatchback with a smoother and livelier 4-cylinder engine, sportier road manners and equal or better economy. Charade's 3-cylinder engine is willing, but too underpowered to be acceptable all-around transportation. Charade hops and skates through bumpy bends and rides rough on all but smooth roads. It's very cramped inside and though well equipped, it's just overpriced for an urban commuter car. In the summer of '89, Daihatsu plans to introduce a 4-door sedan that's larger than Charade, followed by a new 4-wheel-drive sport utility vehicle called Rocky II. Eventually, Daihatsu plans to offer a full line of vehicles in the U.S.

1988 Specifications

	3-door hatchback
Wheelbase, in.	92.1
Overall length, in.	144.9
Overall width, in.	63.6
Overall height, in.	54.5
Turn diameter, ft.	31.5
Curb weight, lbs.	1775
Cargo vol., cu. ft.	33.0
Fuel capacity, gal.	10.6
Seating capacity	4
Front headroom, in.	37.5
Front shoulder room, in.	51.1
Front legroom, max., in.	41.1
Rear headroom, in.	35.7
Rear shoulder room, in.	51.9
Rear legroom, min., in.	31.8

Engines

	ohc I-3
Size, liters/cu. in.	1.0/61
Fuel delivery	PFI
Horsepower @ rpm	53 @ 5200
Torque (lbs./ft.) @ rpm	58 @ 3600
Availability	S

EPA city/highway mpg

5-speed OD manual	38/42

Prices

Daihatsu Charade (1988 prices)	Retail Price	Dealer Invoice	Low Price
CLS 3-door hatchback	$6397	$5822	$6110
CLX 3-door hatchback	7650	6733	7192
w/Automatic Restraint System	7725	6798	7262
CSX 3-door hatchback	9232	8124	8678
Destination charge	257	257	257

Prices are accurate at time of printing; subject to manufacturer's change.

Standard Equipment:

1.0-liter PFI 3-cylinder engine, 5-speed manual transmission, power brakes, cloth reclining front bucket seats, folding rear seat, tinted windshield, remote fuel door and liftgate releases, visor mirrors, rear defogger, intermittent wipers, trip odometer, 145/80R13 tires. **CLX** adds: digital clock, door pockets, power mirrors, bodyside moldings, front mud guards, sport front seats, tachometer, rear wiper/washer, 155/80R13 tires, wheel covers. **CSX** adds: air conditioning, AM/FM ST ET cassette, 165/70R13 tires on alloy wheels.

Optional Equipment:	Retail Price	Dealer Invoice	Low Price
Power Option Pkg.	305	253	279
Power windows and locks.			
Air conditioning, CLS & CLX	695	591	643
Air conditioning delete (credit), CSX	(695)	(591)	(591)
AM/FM ST ET cassette, CLS, CLX	295	245	270
Premium AM/FM cassette, CLS, CLX	395	328	362

Dodge Aries America/ Plymouth Reliant America

Dodge Aries 4-door

Dodge drops the station wagon and makes only minor changes in its K-car sedans for '89. The Aries and Reliant are identical cars sold with the same equipment at the same prices. The front-drive 2- and 4-door notchbacks now wear the "America" label, denoting Chrysler's program to reduce manufacturing and retail costs by offering a single trim

Prices are accurate at time of printing; subject to manufacturer's change.

level with most options grouped into packages. The base engine remains a 2.2-liter 4-cylinder. A 5-speed manual transmission is standard; a 3-speed automatic is optional. Available at extra cost is a 2.5-liter four, which goes from 96 to 100 horsepower this year. It's available only with the automatic transmission. Both engines get slight internal modifications that Chrysler says makes them run quieter. The K-cars also have new front-suspension components intended to reduce ride harshness. Among the few new features for '89 are identifying paint markings for underhood service points such as the dipstick. There's also a new 4-speaker stereo system. Chrysler is known to be planning a K-car successor, so this could be the last year for the Aries/Reliant. K-cars offer few frills and few thrills, providing

Specifications

	2-door notchback	4-door notchback
Wheelbase, in.	100.3	100.3
Overall length, in.	178.9	178.9
Overall width, in.	67.9	67.9
Overall height, in.	52.5	52.5
Turn diameter, ft.	34.8	34.8
Curb weight, lbs.	2317	2323
Cargo vol., cu. ft.	15.0	15.0
Fuel capacity, gal.	14.0	14.0
Seating capacity	6	6
Front headroom, in.	38.2	38.6
Front shoulder room, in.	55.0	55.4
Front legroom, max., in.	42.4	42.2
Rear headroom, in.	37.0	37.8
Rear shoulder room, in.	58.8	55.9
Rear legroom, min., in.	35.1	35.4

Engines

	ohc I-4	ohc I-4
Size liters/cu. in.	2.2/135	2.5/153
Fuel delivery	TBI	TBI
Horsepower @ rpm	93 @ 4800	100 @ 4800
Torque (lbs./ft.) @ rpm	122 @ 3200	135 @ 2800
Availability	S	O

EPA city/highway mpg

5-speed OD manual	25/34	
3-speed automatic	24/30	23/28

Prices are accurate at time of printing; subject to manufacturer's change.

instead functional transportation at a reasonable price. The optional 2.5-liter engine is smoother, quieter and provides stronger acceleration without using much more gas than the standard 2.2. The automatic is likewise preferable to the poor-shifting 5-speed manual. K-cars have modest handling ability and are best driven gently. Rough pavement reveals an undisciplined ride. The front bench seat (a no-cost option) ups passenger capacity to six, but has a fixed seatback that's so reclined it forces an uncomfortable driving position.

Prices

Dodge Aries/Plymouth Reliant	Retail Price	Dealer Invoice	Low Price
2-door notchback	$7595	$6935	$7365
4-door notchback	7595	6935	7365
Destination charge	454	454	454

Standard Equipment:

2.2-liter TBI 4-cylinder engine, 5-speed manual transmission, power brakes, reclining front bucket seats (bench seat may be substituted at no charge, but requires Popular Equipment Discount Pkg.), cloth and vinyl upholstery, intermittent wipers, optical horn, left remote mirror, right visor mirror with map/reading light, 185/70R13 SBR tires.

Optional Equipment:

2.5-liter engine	279	237	257
Requires Basic or Popular Pkg.			
Power steering	240	204	221
Air conditioning	775	659	713
Requires tinted glass.			
Tinted glass	120	102	110
Basic Equipment Pkg	776	660	714
3-speed automatic transmission, power steering.			
Basic Radio Discount Pkg	929	790	855
Basic Pkg. plus AM & FM ST ET.			
Popular Equipment Pkg., w/bucket seats	1292	1098	1189
w/bench seat	1192	1013	1097
Basic Pkg. (including radio) plus tinted glass, remote mirrors, bodyside tape stripes, added sound insulation, floor console (with bucket seats), trunk dress up, 185/70R14 tires, wheel covers.			
Premium Pkg., 2-door w/bucket seats	1730	1471	1592
2-door w/bench seat	1630	1386	1500
4-door w/bucket seats	1780	1513	1638

Prices are accurate at time of printing; subject to manufacturer's change.

	Retail Price	Dealer Invoice	Low Price
4-door w/bench seat	1680	1428	1546
Popular Pkg. plus cruise control, tilt steering column, power door locks, luxury steering wheel, Light Group.			
500-amp battery, w/2.2	44	37	40
Rear defogger	145	123	133
California emissions pkg	100	85	92
AM & FM ST ET cassette	152	129	140
Requires Popular Pkg.			
Conventional spare tire, 13″	73	62	67
14″	83	71	76
185/70R14 WSW tires	68	58	63
Requires Popular Pkg.			

Dodge Caravan/ Plymouth Voyager

Dodge Grand Caravan

A turbocharged engine and a new 4-speed automatic transmission are newsmakers for Chrsyler's successful and nearly identical front-drive minivans. Both are again available in in base, SE and LE versions that hold five to seven passengers, depending on seating configuration. The extended-length "Grand" models come in SE and LE trim and seat up to eight. The new 150-horsepower turbo 2.5-liter 4-cylinder is optional on short-wheelbase SE and LE models with either a 5-speed manual transmission or a 3-speed automatic. Chrysler's new 4-speed automatic is available only

Prices are accurate at time of printing; subject to manufacturer's change.

with the Mitsubishi-made 3.0-liter V-6. It's standard on the Grand LE models, optional on V-6-equipped Grand SEs. Among other Caravan additions for '89, the ride is supposed to improve through use of some front suspension components from the luxury Chrysler New Yorker. SE models have improved interior space thanks to thinner high-back front bucket seats. Leather seating is a new option on LEs and power rear-quarter vent windows are a new option for SEs and LEs. A tachometer is now included in the optional gauge package, air conditioning is standard on LE models, and a power liftgate release is now standard on SE and LE

Specifications

	4-door van	4-door van
Wheelbase, in.	112.0	119.1
Overall length, in.	179.5	190.5
Overall width, in.	69.6	69.6
Overall height, in.	64.2	65.0
Turn diameter, ft.	41.0	43.2
Curb weight, lbs.	3003	3304
Cargo vol., cu. ft.	125.0	150.0
Fuel capacity, gal.	15.0^1	15.0^1
Seating capacity	7	8
Front headroom, in.	39.0	39.0
Front shoulder room, in.	58.4	58.4
Front legroom, max., in.	38.2	38.2
Rear headroom, in.	37.7	37.6
Rear shoulder room, in.	61.3	61.3
Rear legroom, min., in.	37.7	37.8

1. 20.0 gal opt.

Engines	ohc I-4	Turbo ohc I-4	ohc V-6
Size, liters/cu. in.	2.5/153	2.5/153	3.0/181
Fuel delivery	TBI	PFI	PFI
Horsepower @ rpm	100 @ 4800	150 @ 4800	141 @ 5000
Torque (lbs./ft.) @ rpm	135 @ 2800	180 @ 2000	171 @ 2800
Availability	S	O	O^1

EPA city/highway mpg

	ohc I-4	Turbo ohc I-4	ohc V-6
5-speed OD manual	21/28	18/25	
3-speed automatic	21/23	18/21	18/22
4-speed OD automatic			18/23

1. Standard, Grand Caravan LE

models. An optional power sunroof is due later in the model year. The turbo 2.5 is somewhat mismatched to minivan duty. It's quick off the line and in highway passing, but turbo lag causes it to deliver power in bursts more suited to sporty cars. It might be more fuel efficient than the V-6, but the turbo four won't be as quiet or as smooth-running. The V-6 is the best choice, with the power and flexibility to justify its extra cost over the base 2.5-liter four. The new automatic transmission's principal benefit is its overdrive fourth gear, which should make for more relaxed and economical highway driving. Chrysler has wisely done little else to alter the character of its front-drive minivans, which remain our favorites for passenger duty.

Prices

Dodge Caravan/ Plymouth Voyager	Retail Price	Dealer Invoice	Low Price
Base SWB 4-door van	$11312	$10105	$10909
SE SWB 4-door van	12039	10744	11592
LE SWB 4-door van	13987	12459	13423
Grand SE 4-door van	13061	11644	12553
Grand LE 4-door van	16362	14549	15656
Destination charge	500	500	500

SWB denotes short-wheelbase models.

Standard Equipment:

2.5-liter TBI engine, 5-speed manual transmission, power steering, power brakes, liftgate wiper/washer, headlamps-on tone, 5-passenger seating, variable intermittent wipers, tinted glass, left remote mirror, AM & FM ST ET, P185/75R14 SBR tires. **SE** adds: highback reclining front seats, rear seat (Grand), front folding center armrests, upgraded door panels, power liftgate release. **LE** adds: front air conditioning, added sound insulation, remote mirrors, bodyside moldings, woodgrain exterior applique, upgraded steering wheel. **Grand LE** adds: 3.0-liter PFI V-6, 4-speed automatic transmission.

Optional Equipment:

2.5-liter turbo engine, SWB	680	578	626
3.0-liter V-6, SE & LE SWB	680	578	628
3-speed automatic transmission (NA 7-pass.)	565	480	520
4-speed automatic, Grand SE	735	625	676
Requires 3.0 V-6.			
Front air conditioning, base & SE	840	714	773

Prices are accurate at time of printing; subject to manufacturer's change.

	Retail Price	Dealer Invoice	Low Price
Rear air conditioning w/heater, Grand . . .	560	476	515
Cloth lowback seats, base	45	38	41
Leather highback seats, LE	671	570	617
Requires Luxury Equipment or LE Decor Pkg.			
7-pass. seating, SWB	389	331	358
8-pass. seating, SE Grand	120	102	110
SE Grand w/Popular Pkg	5	4	5
Converta-Bed, SWB (NA base)	542	461	499
Value Wagon Pkg., base w/5-speed	1045	888	961
Base incl. automatic	1283	1091	1180
SE SWB w/5-speed	994	845	914
SE SWB incl. automatic	1232	1047	1133
Front air conditioning, rear defogger, dual horns, deluxe sound insulation, Light Group, high-back cloth reclining front seats.			
Popular Equipment Discount Pkg., SE SWB	1661	1412	1528
SE SWB w/Value Wgn Pkg	743	632	684
SE SWB w/7/8-pass	1683	1431	1548
SE SWB w/7/8-pass. & Value Wgn Pkg .	765	650	704
SE Grand	1683	1431	1548
LE SWB	981	834	903
LE SWB w/7-pass, LE Grand	1003	853	923
SE: front air conditioning, forward storage console, overhead console, floormats, gauges, deluxe sound insulation, Light Group, power rear quarter vent windows, conventional spare tire, cruise control, tilt steering column. LE adds: lighted visor mirror, power door locks.			
Luxury Equipment Discount Pkg., SE SWB .	2348	1996	2160
SE SWB w/Value Wgn Pkg	1485	1262	1366
SE SWB w/7/8-pass., SE Grand	2371	2015	2181
SE SWB w/7-pass. & Value Wgn Pkg . .	1507	1281	1386
LE SWB	1603	1363	1475
LE SWB w/7-pass, LE Grand	1626	1382	1496
SE: Popular Pkg. plus lighted visor mirror, power door locks, power mirrors, power front windows, AM & FM ST ET cassette, Eurosport steering wheel. LE adds: power driver's seat.			
Turbo Sport Pkg., SE SWB	1073	912	987
2.5-liter turbo engine, gauges, 205/70R15 all-season tires on alloy wheels.			
HD Trailer Tow Pkg., SE Grand	392	333	361
HD suspension, 120-amp alternator, conventional spare tire, trailer wiring harness, 205/70R15 all-season tires on styled steel wheels.			
LE Decor Pkg., LE SWB	1449	1232	1333
2.5-liter turbo engine, warm silver fascia, moldings, 7-passenger seating, tape stripes, 205/70R15 all-season tires on alloy wheels.			
Rear defogger	165	140	152
California emissions pkg	99	84	91
Sunscreen glass	406	345	374
Rear heater, SE & LE SWB	329	280	303
120-amp alternator, Grand	62	53	57

Prices are accurate at time of printing; subject to manufacturer's change.

	Retail Price	Dealer Invoice	Low Price
Luggage rack, base & SE	144	122	132
Power door locks	203	173	187
Requires Value Wgn or Popular Pkg.			
AM & FM ST ET cassette, base & SE . . .	152	129	140
Requires Value Wagon or Popular Pkg.			
Ultimate Sound stereo	214	182	197
Requires Luxury or LE Decor Pkg.			
AM & FM ST ET delete (credit)	(136)	(116)	(116)
Cruise control, base	207	176	190
Requires tilt steering column and Value Wgn Pkg.			
Tilt steering column, base	122	104	112
Requires cruise control and Value Wgn Pkg.			
HD suspension	68	58	63
Conventional spare tire	104	88	96
Wire wheel covers, LE (Luxury Pkg. req.) .	239	203	220
Sport road wheels (NA base)	415	353	382
Pearl coat paint	46	39	42
Two-tone paint, SE	236	201	217

Dodge/Plymouth Colt

Dodge Colt 3-door

An all-new 3-door hatchback and a full-time 4-wheel drive version of the carried-over 5-door station wagon mark the subcompact Colt line. The 4-door body style has been dropped. Colts are built by Chrysler's Japanese partner, Mitsubishi, and sold in identical form under Dodge and Plymouth nameplates. Mitsubishi will sell the hatchback under the Mirage name. The new front-drive 3-door has more rounded styling than the previous version. Its wheelbase is

Prices are accurate at time of printing; subject to manufacturer's change.

virtually unchanged, though its body is longer, wider and taller. Rear-seat leg room is up by nearly two inches and there's more cargo room. The hatchbacks range from an entry-level model with a 4-speed manual transmission and manual steering through the Colt E and sporty GT models that offer a choice of a 5-speed manual or a 4-speed automatic. All three use a fuel-injected 1.5-liter 4-cylinder engine rated at 81 horsepower, 13 more than the carbureted 1.5 in the previous Colt. Top of the line is the GT DOHC Turbo with a turbocharged 16-valve 1.6-liter four making 135 horsepower—30 more than its '88 counterpart. A 5-speed, power steering, sport suspension, aero body add-ons, a tachometer

Specifications	3-door hatchback	5-door wagon
Wheelbase, in.	93.9	93.7
Overall length, in.	158.7	169.3
Overall width, in.	65.5	64.4
Overall height, in.	54.1	55.9
Turn diameter, ft.	32.4	32.4
Curb weight, lbs.	2195	2271[1]
Cargo vol., cu. ft.	34.7	60.4
Fuel capacity, gal.	12.4	12.4
Seating capacity	5	5
Front headroom, in.	38.3	37.7
Front shoulder room, in.	53.5	52.8
Front legroom, max., in.	41.9	40.6
Rear headroom, in.	36.9	38.2
Rear shoulder room, in.	52.1	52.8
Rear legroom, min., in.	32.5	34.1

1. 2568 lbs., 4WD wagon.

Engines	ohc I-4	Turbo dohc I-4	ohc I-4
Size, liters/cu. in.	1.5/90	1.6/97	1.8/110
Fuel delivery	PFI	PFI	PFI
Horsepower @ rpm	81 @ 5500	135 @ 6000	87 @ 5000
Torque (lbs./ft.) @ rpm	91 @ 3000	141 @ 3000	102 @ 3000
Availability	S	O	S[1]

EPA city/highway mpg

5-speed OD manual	30/35	23/29	23/28
3-speed automatic	27/29		

1. Colt DL 4WD wagon.

and a tilt and telescope steering column are Turbo standards. The front-drive, 5-passenger, 5-door wagon gets the hatchback's 1.5-liter four and new interior trim. The 4-wheel-drive wagon gets a 1.8-liter four and a permanently engaged 4WD system that can automatically send power to the wheels that need traction. Initial test-track test drives reveal the hatchbacks to be vastly improved over the previous generation, which was introduced for 1985. Their trim, aero-shapes, build quality and over-the-road feel all recall the pace-setting Honda Civic hatchbacks. The base model with the 4-speed and manual steering has a pleasing, no-nonsense manner. The GT DOHC Turbo is slick and quick.

Prices

Dodge/Plymouth Colt	Retail Price	Dealer Invoice	Low Price
3-door hatchback	$6678	$6110	$6494
E 3-door hatchback	7505	6822	7164
GT 3-door hatchback	8863	7711	8287
Destination charge	255	217	235

Standard Equipment:

1.5-liter PFI 4-cylinder engine, 4-speed manual transmission, power brakes, vinyl bucket seats, center console with storage, split folding rear seatback, coolant temperature gauge, trip odometer, motorized front shoulder belts and manual lap belts, outboard rear lap/shoulder belts, locking fuel-filler door, 145/80R13 SBR tires. **E** adds: 5-speed manual transmission, rear defogger, cloth seat inserts, bodyside moldings, 155/80R13 tires. **GT** adds: wide bodyside moldings, remote left mirror, assist grips, cloth upholstery, rear security panel.

Optional Equipment:

3-speed automatic transmission, GT	499	414	459
Power steering, E & GT	259	215	238
Air conditioning	739	613	680
Turbo Pkg., GT	2819	2340	2593

    1.6-liter DOHC turbo engine, power steering, 4-wheel disc brakes, 195/60R14 tires, tachometer, low washer fluid light, sport steering wheel, sport suspension, upgraded seat trim, tilt/telescopic steering column, power mirrors, intermittent wipers, remote fuel door and hatch releases, foot rest, cargo lamp, digital clock, rear wiper/washer, front air dam, sill extensions, rear spoiler.

Prices are accurate at time of printing; subject to manufacturer's change.

	Retail Price	Dealer Invoice	Low Price
AM/FM ST ET, base & E	273	227	251
GT	298	247	274
AM/FM ST ET cassette, E & GT	465	386	428
AM/FM ST ET cassette w/EQ, GT w/Turbo Pkg	734	609	675
Carpet protectors, E & GT	28	23	26
Digital clock, GT	54	45	50
Cruise control & intermittent wipers, GT . .	208	173	191
Tinted glass	63	52	58
Power mirrors, GT	87	72	80
Power windows, GT	211	175	194
Rear shelf, base & E	51	42	47
Rear defogger, base	66	55	61
Rear wiper/washer, E & GT	133	110	122
Wheel trim rings, E	55	46	51
Intermittent wipers, GT	28	23	26
13"alloy wheels, GT	293	243	270
14"alloy wheels, GT w/Turbo Pkg	275	228	253
Two-tone paint	157	130	144

Dodge/Plymouth Colt DL Wagon

	Retail Price	Dealer Invoice	Low Price
5-door wagon, 2WD	$9316	$8105	$8711
5-door wagon, 4WD	11145	9696	10421
Destination charge	255	255	255

Standard Equipment:

1.5-liter PFI 4-cylinder engine, 5-speed manual transmission, power brakes, cloth reclining front bucket seats, outboard rear lap/shoulder belts, trip odometer, coolant temperature gauge, rear defogger, locking fuel-filler door, rear wiper/washer, 175/70R13 SBR tires. **4WD** adds: 1.8-liter engine, permanent, full-time 4WD, power steering, 185/70R14 tires.

Optional Equipment:

	Retail Price	Dealer Invoice	Low Price
3-speed automatic transmission, 2WD . . .	499	414	459
Power steering	259	215	238
Air conditioning	739	613	680
Tinted glass	63	52	58
AM/FM ST ET	273	227	251
AM/FM ST ET cassette	424	352	390
Digital clock	54	45	50
Power mirrors	81	67	75
Intermittent wipers	52	43	48
Alloy wheels	299	248	275
Custom Pkg	516	428	475

Velour sport seats, power mirrors, intermittent wipers, rear heat ducts, remote fuel and liftgate releases, tape stripes.

Prices are accurate at time of printing; subject to manufacturer's change.

	Retail Price	Dealer Invoice	Low Price
Limited-slip differential, 4WD	218	181	201
Driver's seat height control	19	16	17
Carpet protectors	28	23	26
Luggage rack	128	106	118

Dodge/Plymouth Colt Vista

Dodge Colt Vista 2WD

The only changes to these 7-passenger front-drive and 4-wheel-drive wagons is the addition of shoulder belts for rear outboard passengers and an auto-down control for the optional power driver's window. Vista is made by Chrysler's Japanese partner, Mitsubishi. The front-drive version comes standard with a 5-speed manual transmission; a 3-speed automatic is optional. It also has 13-inch tires. The optional 4WD system can be engaged while underway and can be used on smooth, dry pavement. The 4WD model comes with a 5-speed manual transmission only, 14-inch tires and a torsion-bar rear suspension. Both have front bucket seats and two sets of 50/50 split folding rear seats, for a capacity of seven passengers. With the second and third rear seats folded forward, a carpeted cargo area of 78 cubic feet is formed. Fold them back and their cushions form a single or double bed. The 2-place rear seat is cramped, though, so it's better suited to children than adults, and there isn't much room for climbing in or out of the middle or rear seats. With only 96 horsepower for nearly 2600 pounds

Prices are accurate at time of printing; subject to manufacturer's change.

of curb weight on the front-drive model (and nearly 2900 on the 4WD model), there's little power to climb hills or to accelerate briskly. Add four or five people and the engine is overmatched, especially with automatic transmission. The convenient 4WD system is engaged with the push of a button to give you extra traction without having to stop or shift a transfer case lever. Trailer towing is limited to 1500 pounds on the front-drive model and 2000 pounds on the 4x4.

Specifications

	5-door wagon	5-door 4WD wagon
Wheelbase, in.	103.3	103.3
Overall length, in.	174.6	174.6
Overall width, in.	64.6	64.6
Overall height, in.	57.3	59.4
Turn diameter, ft.	34.8	34.8
Curb weight, lbs.	2557	2888
Cargo vol., cu. ft.	63.9	63.9
Fuel capacity, gal.	13.2	14.5
Seating capacity	7	7
Front headroom, in.	38.3	38.3
Front shoulder room, in.	53.1	53.1
Front legroom, max., in.	38.8	38.8
Rear headroom, in.	38.3	38.3
Rear shoulder room, in.	53.2	53.2
Rear legroom, min., in.	36.5	36.5

Engines

	ohc I-4
Size, liters/cu. in.	2.0/122
Fuel delivery	PFI
Horsepower @ rpm	96 @ 5000
Torque (lbs./ft.) @ rpm	113 @ 3500
Availability	S

EPA city/highway mpg

5-speed OD manual	22/28
3-speed automatic	22/23

Prices

Dodge/Plymouth Colt Vista	Retail Price	Dealer Invoice	Low Price
5-door wagon, 2WD	$11518	$9790	$10654
5-door wagon, 4WD	12828	10904	11866
Destination charge	255	255	255

Prices are accurate at time of printing; subject to manufacturer's change.

Standard Equipment:

2.0-liter PFI 4-cylinder engine, 5-speed manual transmission, power steering (4WD), power brakes, reclining front bucket seats, cloth and vinyl upholstery, trip odometer, coolant temperature gauge, left remote mirror, variable intermittent wipers, outboard rear lap/shoulder belts, rear defogger, remote fuel filler release, tinted glass, optical horn, rear seat heat ducts, wide bodyside moldings, 165/80R13 SBR tires (2WD), 185/70R14 SBR tires (4WD).

Optional Equipment:	Retail Price	Dealer Invoice	Low Price
3-speed automatic transmission, 2WD . . .	499	414	459
Air conditioning	739	613	680
Limited-slip differential, 4WD	218	181	201
Power steering, 2WD	259	215	238
AM/FM ST ET	273	227	251
AM/FM ST ET cassette	431	358	397
Cruise control	183	152	168
Rear wiper/washer	152	126	140
Power windows	260	216	239
Power door locks	173	144	159
Alloy wheels, 2WD w/o Custom Pkg	311	258	286
2WD w/Custom Pkg	269	223	247
4WD	299	248	275
Custom Pkg., 2WD	445	369	409
4WD	365	303	336

Power mirrors, velour upholstery, visor mirrors, digital clock, map lights, remote liftgate release, tachometer, courtesy lights, tape stripes, 185/ 70R13 SBR tires (2WD), wheel covers (2WD).

Luggage rack	128	106	118
Carpet protectors	28	23	26
Two-tone paint, w/o Custom Pkg	305	253	281
w/Custom Pkg	252	209	232

Dodge Daytona

Dodge turns up the performance wick on its front-drive sport coupes and freshens their styling with a new front fascia and wraparound taillights. Last year's Pacifica model is gone, replaced by an ES model. Daytona gained a standard driver's-side air bag late in 1988, and this year, all versions—base, ES, ES Turbo and Daytona Shelby—get standard 4-wheel disc brakes. ES Turbos have as standard a new 150-horsepower turbocharged 2.5-liter four known as the

Prices are accurate at time of printing; subject to manufacturer's change.

Dodge Daytona

Specifications

	3-door hatchback
Wheelbase, in.	97.0
Overall length, in.	175.0
Overall width, in.	69.3
Overall height, in.	50.4
Turn diameter, ft.	34.3
Curb weight, lbs.	2676
Cargo vol., cu. ft.	33.0
Fuel capacity, gal.	14.0
Seating capacity	4
Front headroom, in.	37.1
Front shoulder room, in.	55.9
Front legroom, max., in.	42.4
Rear headroom, in.	34.3
Rear shoulder room, in.	53.6
Rear legroom, min., in.	30.0

Engines	ohc I-4	Turbo ohc I-4	Turbo ohc I-4
Size, liters/cu. in.	2.5/153	2.5/153	2.2/135
Fuel delivery	TBI	PFI	PFI
Horsepower @ rpm	100 @ 4800	150 @ 4800	174 @ 5200
Torque (lbs./ft.) @ rpm	135 @ 2800	180 @ 2000	200 @ 2400
Availability	S	O	S[1]
EPA city/highway mpg			
5-speed OD manual	24/34	20/29	20/28
3-speed automatic	23/29	18/23	

1. *Daytona Shelby with 5-speed manual trans.*

Turbo I. Last year's Turbo I was a 146-horsepower 2.2-liter four. Daytona Shelby loses its previous "Z" suffix, but keeps its Turbo II engine, a turbocharged and intercooled 174-horsepower 2.2-liter four. Shelbys this year get a unique paint treatment that graduates from charcoal in the lower panels to body color in the upper panels. They also get new-style "pumper" alloy wheels and 205/55VR16 unidirectional performance tires (last year's were 225/50VR15). Shelbys ordered with automatic transmission must use the Turbo I engine. A removable interior sunshade is furnished this year with the optional T-bar roof. A new C/S Competition Package, available on base models only, includes many of the Shelby's mechanicals, but cuts about 200 pounds from the weight of a Shelby. The C/S package includes the Turbo II engine, 225/50VR15 tires and the Shelby's upgraded brakes, suspension, special bucket seats and rear spoiler. A tilt steering column is standard, but the only option available with the C/S package is a premium cassette radio. Dodge's interpretation of the front-drive sport coupe has improved each year since its 1984 introduction.

Prices

Dodge Daytona	Retail Price	Dealer Invoice	Low Price
3-door hatchback	$9295	$8423	$8859
ES 3-door hatchback	10395	9402	9899
ES Turbo 3-door hatchback	11995	10826	11411
Shelby 3-door hatchback	13295	11983	12639
Destination charge	439	439	439

Standard Equipment:

2.5-liter TBI 4-cylinder engine, 5-speed manual transmission, power steering, power 4-wheel disc brakes, driver's side air bag, passenger side motorized shoulder belt and manual lap belt, center console with armrest and storage compartment, rear defogger, remote fuel filler and liftgate releases, tinted glass, trip odometer, tachometer, gauges (coolant temperature, oil pressure, voltmeter), message center with warning lights, headlamps-on tone, variable intermittent wipers, visor mirrors, remote mirrors, bodyside moldings, AM & FM ST ET, reclining front seats, cloth and vinyl upholstery, folding rear seats, P185/70R14 SBR tires. **ES** adds: front air dam with fog lights, sill extensions, rear spoiler, 205/60HR15 tires on alloy wheels. **ES Turbo** adds: 2.5-liter turbocharged engine, Light Group, tilt

Prices are accurate at time of printing; subject to manufacturer's change.

steering column, cloth performance seats, AM & FM ST ET cassette, tonneau cover. **Shelby** adds: 2.2-liter intercooled Turbo II engine, P205/55VR16 SBR tires on alloy wheels.

Optional Equipment:

	Retail Price	Dealer Invoice	Low Price
3-speed automatic transmission	536	456	493
Popular Equipment Discount Pkg., base & ES	907	771	834
ES Turbo & Shelby	900	765	828
w/o A/C, base	322	274	296

Base & ES: air conditioning, front floormats, Light Group, heated power mirrors, tilt steering column. ES Turbo and Shelby add: power windows and locks.

Lights & Locks Discount Pkg., base & ES	287	244	264

Headlight extinguish delay, illuminated entry, power door locks, lighted visor mirrors; requires Popular Pkg.

C/S Performance Discount Pkg., base . . .	1443	1227	1328

2.5-liter turbo engine, rear spoiler, performance handling suspension, 205/60R15 SBR performance tires on alloy wheels, uprated brakes.

C/S Competition Pkg., base	2874	2443	2644

2.2-liter Turbo II engine, performance front seats, rear spoiler, tilt steering column, maximum performance suspension, 225/50VR15 SBR unidirectional tires on alloy wheels, uprated transmission and brakes.

Electronic Equipment Pkg., ES Turbo & Shelby	579	492	533
w/sunroof	404	343	372
w/T-Bar Roof Pkg	333	283	306

Overhead console with compass and outside temperature readouts, Electronic Navigator, headlight extinguish delay, illuminated entry, lighted visor mirrors; requires Popular Pkg.

T-Bar Roof Pkg., base & ES	1508	1282	1387
ES Turbo & Shelby	1324	1125	1218

T-bar roof and sunshades, lighted visor mirrors, power windows; requires Popular Pkg.

Automatic Transmission Pkg., Shelby . . .	NC	NC	NC

2.5-liter Turbo I engine, 3-speed automatic transmission, cruise control.

Performance seats, base	305	259	281
Enthusiast seats, ES Turbo & Shelby	391	332	360

Requires Popular Pkg.

Leather enthusiast seats, Shelby	879	747	809
ES Turbo	938	797	863

Requires Popular Pkg. on ES Turbo.

Electronic instruments, ES Turbo & Shelby .	311	264	286

Requires Electronic Equipment Pkg.

Power windows, base & ES	210	179	193

Requires Popular Pkg.

AM/FM ST ET cassette, base & ES	152	129	140
w/EQ, ES	632	537	581
w/EQ, ES Turbo & Shelby	210	179	193

Prices are accurate at time of printing; subject to manufacturer's change.

CONSUMER GUIDE®   **145**

	Retail Price	Dealer Invoice	Low Price
CD player, ES Turbo & Shelby	400	340	368
Requires factory cassette stereo.			
Cruise control (Popular Pkg. req)	175	149	161
Rear-window sun louver	210	179	193
Removable sunroof	384	326	353
Requires Popular Pkg. on base & ES.			
Tonneau cover, base & ES	69	59	63
Requires Popular Pkg.			
Rear wiper/washer	126	107	116
Alloy wheels, base	322	274	296

Dodge Dynasty

Dodge Dynasty

This is Dodge's version of the Chrysler New Yorker. Introduced last year, both are front-drive, 6-passenger 4-door notchback sedans. Both are back for 1989 with slightly more power and a newly available 4-speed automatic transmission. Dynasty comes in base and LE trim levels. The base car's 2.5-liter 4-cylinder engine goes to 100 horsepower, up from 96 last year, and is available only with a 3-speed automatic transmission. The top-line LE comes standard with a Mitsubishi-made 3.0-liter V-6. Its horsepower is up from 136 to 141. The V-6 is available only with Chrysler's new 4-speed overdrive automatic transmission. The V-6 powertrain is optional on the base Dynasty. Four-wheel disc brakes with an anti-lock feature are optional in place of the standard front disc/rear drum setup. Among 1989's new options are a 6-way power driver's seat with memory and an anti-theft system. Dynasty feels underpowered with the 2.5 but it's sufficiently peppy with the V-6. Its ride is soft and generally quite comfortable. Handling is a different story. The body leans heavily in turns and the all-season tires roll onto their sidewalls, scrubbing off speed with noticeable squealing. A redeeming feature is the anti-lock brake option, and we strongly recommend it, even if you have to sacrifice another expensive option. Dynasty's functional design provides plenty of leg room in the rear seat and adequate head room. It holds six adults without excessive crowding. Cargo space also is more than adequate. Overall, this is a well-designed family sedan.

Specifications

	4-door notchback
Wheelbase, in.	104.3
Overall length, in.	192.0
Overall width, in.	68.5
Overall height, in.	53.5
Turn diameter, ft.	40.5
Curb weight, lbs.	3000
Cargo vol., cu. ft.	16.0
Fuel capacity, gal.	16.0
Seating capacity	6
Front headroom, in.	37.6
Front shoulder room, in.	56.4
Front legroom, max., in.	41.9
Rear headroom, in.	37.5
Rear shoulder room, in.	55.9
Rear legroom, min., in.	37.9

Engines

	ohc I-4	ohc V-6
Size, liters/cu. in.	2.5/153	3.0/181
Fuel delivery	TBI	PFI
Horsepower @ rpm	100 @ 4800	141 @ 5000
Torque (lbs./ft.) @ rpm	135 @ 2800	171 @ 2800
Availability	S	O

EPA city/highway mpg

3-speed automatic	22/28	
4-speed OD automatic		18/26

Prices

Dodge Dynasty	Retail Price	Dealer Invoice	Low Price
4-door notchback	$12295	$10601	$11548
LE 4-door notchback	13595	11706	12751
Destination charge	505	505	505

Standard Equipment:

2.5-liter TBI 4-cylinder engine, 3-speed automatic transmission, power steering and brakes, bench seat, cloth upholstery, headlamps-on tone, front cup holder, rear defogger, optical horn, trip odometer, voltmeter, coolant temperature and oil pressure gauges, intermittent wipers, tinted glass, dual remote mirrors, visor mirrors, bodyside moldings, AM/FM ST ET, remote decklid and fuel filler releases, P195/75R14 SBR tires. **LE** adds: 3.0-liter PFI V-6, 4-speed automatic transmission, 50/50 bench seat, leather-wrapped steering wheel, upgraded wheel covers.

Optional Equipment:

3.0-liter V-6 & 4-speed auto trans, base . .	771	655	709
Anti-lock 4-wheel disc brakes, LE	926	787	852
Requires Popular Pkg.			
Air conditioning	775	659	713
Power Convenience Pkg., base	338	287	311
Power windows and mirrors; requires Popular Pkg.			
Popular Equipment Discount Pkg., base . .	1023	870	941
LE	1349	1147	1241
Base: air conditioning, cruise control, floormats, power locks, tilt steering column, undercoating. LE adds: heated power mirrors, power windows.			
Interior Illumination Pkg	192	163	177
Illuminated entry, lighted visor mirrors; requires Popular Pkg.			
Luxury Equipment Discount Pkg., LE	2380	2023	2190
Popular Pkg. plus illuminated entry, lighted visor mirrors, power front seats, security alarm, wire wheel covers, leather-wrapped steering wheel.			
Deluxe Convenience Pkg., LE	300	255	276
Cruise control, tilt steering column.			
Power locks	285	242	262
AM & FM ST ET cassette, base	152	129	140
w/seek & scan, LE	254	216	234
Sound Pkg	552	469	508
w/EQ, LE	762	648	701
AM & FM ST ET cassette, six Infinity speakers, power antenna; base requires Popular Pkg., Premium requires Luxury Pkg.			
Power driver's seat, LE	240	204	221
Memory power seats, LE w/Luxury Pkg . .	341	290	314

Prices are accurate at time of printing; subject to manufacturer's change.

CONSUMER GUIDE®

	Retail Price	Dealer Invoice	Low Price
Security alarm	146	124	134
Requires power locks.			
Conventional spare tire	83	71	76
Power sunroof, LE	776	660	714
Requires Popular Pkg.			
Auto load leveling suspension	180	153	166
Wire wheel covers	224	190	206
Requires Popular Pkg.			

Dodge Lancer

Dodge Lancer Shelby

Chrysler says it will stop building the slow-selling Lancer in March, though inventories of unsold cars mean dealers are likely to have them available though most of the '89 model year. Lancer shares its front-drive 5-door hatchback design with the Chrysler LeBaron hatchback, which also has been discontinued. For 1989, the high-performance Shelby package becomes a distinct Lancer model and a new turbocharged engine joins the line. Standard on base Lancers is a 2.2-liter 4-cylinder. A naturally aspirated 2.5-liter four is optional, as is the Turbo I engine, a 150-horsepower turbocharged 2.5. It replaces the previous Turbo I, a 146-horsepower 2.2 four. The Turbo I engine is standard on Lancer ES; the naturally aspirated 2.5 is optional. Shelbys have the 176-horsepower 2.2-liter Turbo II engine, a special sport-handling suspension, aero body add-ons and monochrome paint schemes. Turbo II Shelbys are available only with the 5-

Prices are accurate at time of printing; subject to manufacturer's change.

speed; ordering the automatic as a no-cost option mandates the Turbo I engine. All Lancers have front-disc and rear-drum brakes. The Shelby handles quite well and has great acceleration, but suffers a stiff ride and too much engine, road and exhaust noise. The turbocharged ES is a little tamer, but not a whole lot quieter. If you can live with less performance, opt for the quieter and smoother naturally aspirated 2.5. We also prefer the 3-speed automatic to the poor-shifting 5-speed manual. Lancer was born of the K-car platform in 1985 and remains a versatile hatchback that carries five in reasonable comfort with ample room for their luggage. It's always been short on refinement, long on practicality and now is sure to be available at fairly low prices.

Specifications

	5-door hatchback
Wheelbase, in.	103.1
Overall length, in.	180.4
Overall width, in.	68.3
Overall height, in.	53.0
Turn diameter, ft.	36.2
Curb weight, lbs.	2643
Cargo vol., cu. ft.	42.6
Fuel capacity, gal.	14.0
Seating capacity	5
Front headroom, in.	38.3
Front shoulder room, in.	55.8
Front legroom, max., in.	41.1
Rear headroom, in.	37.9
Rear shoulder room, in.	55.9
Rear legroom, min., in.	36.5

Engines	ohc I-4	ohc I-4	Turbo ohc I-4	Turbo ohc I-4
Size, liters/cu. in.	2.2/135	2.5/153	2.5/153	2.2/135
Fuel delivery	TBI	TBI	PFI	PFI
Horsepower @ rpm	93 @ 4800	100 @ 4800	150 @ 4800	174 @ 5200
Torque (lbs./ft.) @ rpm	122 @ 3200	135 @ 2800	180 @ 2000	200 @ 2400
Availability	S	O	S[1]	S[2]

EPA city/highway mpg

	ohc I-4	ohc I-4	Turbo ohc I-4	Turbo ohc I-4
5-speed OD manual	24/34	24/34	20/29	20/28
3-speed automatic	24/28	23/29	19/24	

1. ES.   2. Shelby with 5-speed manual trans.

Prices

Dodge Lancer	Retail Price	Dealer Invoice	Low Price
5-door hatchback	$11195	$10002	$10499
ES 5-door hatchback	13695	12202	12849
Shelby 5-door hatchback	17395	15458	16327
Destination charge	450	450	450

Standard Equipment:

2.2-liter TBI 4-cylinder engine, 5-speed manual transmission, power steering
and brakes, reclining front bucket seats, cloth and vinyl upholstery, mini
console, cup holder, rear defogger, remote mirrors, remote fuel filler and
liftgate releases, tinted glass, intermittent wipers, headlamps-on reminder,
optical horn, trip odometer, tachometer, coolant temperature and oil pressure
gauges, voltmeter, message center with warning lights, wide bodyside moldings, AM/FM ST ET, removable shelf panel, P195/70R14 SBR tires. **ES**
adds: 2.5-liter turbo engine, air conditioning, power door locks, heated
power mirrors, leather-wrapped steering wheel, alloy wheels. **Shelby** adds:
2.2-liter intercooled Turbo II engine, front and rear air dams, monochrome
exterior treatment, fog lights, overhead console with compass and outside
temperature readouts, map lights, premium leather bucket seats, power
driver's seat, power windows, AM & FM ST ET cassette w/EQ, 205/60R15
SBR tires on alloy wheels.

Optional Equipment:

2.5-liter engine, base (Basic Pkg. req.) . .	279	237	257
ES (credit)	(536)	(456)	(456)
2.5-liter turbo engine, base	536	456	493
Requires Popular or Luxury Pkg.			
3-speed automatic transmission, base & ES .	536	456	493
Shelby (credit; incl. 2.5-liter Turbo I) . .	(175)	(149)	(149)
Air conditioning, base	775	659	713
Basic Equipment Discount Pkg., base . . .	873	742	803
Air conditioning, console extension with armrest, Light Group.			
Popular Equipment Discount Pkg., base . .	1443	1227	1328
Base incl. automatic or turbo	1879	1597	1729
Base incl. automatic & turbo	2315	1968	2130
2.5-liter engine, air conditioning, console extension with armrest, cruise control, floormats, Light Group, illuminated entry, AM & FM ST ET cassette, tilt steering column, undercoating.			
Luxury Equipment Discount Pkg., base . .	2064	1754	1899
ES	1394	1185	1282
Base: Popular Pkg. plus power windows and locks, heated power mirrors, leather-wrapped steering wheel, lighted visor mirrors. ES adds: console with compass and outside temperature readout, fog lamps, AM & FM ST ET cassette with Infinity speakers, power driver's seat.			

Prices are accurate at time of printing; subject to manufacturer's change.

	Retail Price	Dealer Invoice	Low Price
Sport Appearance Discount Pkg., base . . .	1200	1020	1104
ES	1693	1439	1558

Base: 2.5-liter turbo engine, ground effects addenda, precision-feel steering, 205/60R15 tires on alloy wheels; requires Popular or Luxury Pkg. ES adds fog lamps, illuminated entry, AM & FM ST ET cassette with Infinity speakers, power sunroof.

Power Convenience Discount Pkg., base .	514	437	473

Power windows and locks, heated power mirrors; requires Popular Pkg.

Sport Handling Pkg., base	153	130	141
Base or ES w/Luxury Pkg	94	80	86

Leather-wrapped steering wheel, sport handling suspension, 195/70R14 all-season performance tires; base requires Popular or Luxury Pkg.; ES requires Luxury Pkg.

Deluxe Convenience Pkg., base & ES . . .	300	255	276

Cruise control, tilt steering column; base requires Basic Pkg.

Power locks, base	195	166	179

Requires Basic Pkg.

Electronic instruments, ES	299	254	275

Requires Electronic Navigator.

California emissions pkg	100	85	92
Electronic Navigator	272	231	250
Power driver's seat, base & ES	240	204	221

Requires Basic, Popular or Luxury Pkg. on base.

Power windows, ES	285	242	262
AM & FM ST ET cassette, base	152	129	140

Requires Basic, Popular or Luxury Pkg.

AM & FM ST ET cassette w/seek & scan, ES .	458	389	421
Base w/Popular or Luxury Pkg	306	260	282
AM & FM ST ET cassette w/EQ, ES	210	179	193

Requires Sport Appearance or Luxury Pkg.

Power sunroof, base & ES	776	660	714
ES w/Luxury Pkg	601	511	553

Base requires Luxury Pkg.

Rear wiper/washer, base & ES	126	107	116

Base requires Basic, Popular or Luxury Pkg.

Dodge Omni America/ Plymouth Horizon America

These twin front-drive subcompacts enter their 12th model year largely unchanged. The 5-door hatchbacks are equipped and priced identically. They earned the "America" suffix in 1987 when a cost-cutting program consolidated

Prices are accurate at time of printing; subject to manufacturer's change.

Dodge Omni

Specifications

	5-door hatchback
Wheelbase, in.	99.1
Overall length, in.	163.2
Overall width, in.	66.8
Overall height, in.	53.0
Turn diameter, ft.	38.1
Curb weight, lbs.	2237
Cargo vol., cu. ft.	33.0
Fuel capacity, gal.	13.0
Seating capacity	5
Front headroom, in.	38.1
Front shoulder room, in.	51.7
Front legroom, max., in.	42.1
Rear headroom, in.	36.9
Rear shoulder room, in.	51.5
Rear legroom, min., in.	33.3

Engines

	ohc I-4
Size, liters/cu. in.	2.2/135
Fuel delivery	TBI
Horsepower @ rpm	93 @ 4800
Torque (lbs./ft.) @ rpm	122 @ 3200
Availability	S

EPA city/highway mpg

5-speed OD manual	26/35
3-speed automatic	24/30

their lines into a single trim level with limited options. For
'89, the 2.2-liter 4-cylinder engine gets slight internal modifications intended to make it run quieter. Engine-bay service
items such as the power-steering reservoir cap get high-
lighted with paint for easier identification. Shop for a new
car and you'll find you don't get much equipment for less
than $10,000. The Omni and Horizon are exceptions. For
about $9000, they can be equipped with automatic transmis-
sion, power steering, rear window defogger, reclining cloth
bucket seats, a center console, rear window wiper/washer
and an AM/FM stereo radio. Among comparable cars, only
the Hyundai Excel/Mitsubishi Precis can compete with that
kind of value. Those Korean imports fall short in some key
areas, however. Omni/Horizon's 93-horsepower engine
gives adequate acceleration with automatic transmission,
even with the air conditioner on. The Excel/Precis 68-horse-
power 1.5-liter is sluggish with automatic and anemic with
the air conditioner on. Omni/Horizon's cabin is cramped
and its interior is decidedly dated next to contemporary
rivals such as the Mazda 323 and Toyota Tercel. The driving position is awkward, with the steering wheel too low,
the pedals too close and the seatback too reclined. The handling is unsporting, the ride is sometimes harsh.

Prices

Dodge Omni/Plymouth Horizon	Retail Price	Dealer Invoice	Low Price
5-door hatchback	$6595	$6001	$6350
Destination charge	348	348	348

Standard Equipment:

2.2-liter 4-cylinder TBI engine, 5-speed manual transmission, power brakes,
rear defogger, rear wiper/washer, trip odometer, tachometer, coolant temperature, oil pressure and voltage gauges, luggage compartment light, black
bodyside moldings, left remote mirror, right visor mirror, folding shelf panel,
intermittent wipers, cloth and vinyl upholstery, P165/80R13 tires on styled
steel wheels.

Optional Equipment:

Basic Pkg	776	660	714
3-speed automatic transmission, power steering.			

Prices are accurate at time of printing; subject to manufacturer's change.

	Retail Price	Dealer Invoice	Low Price
Manual Transmission Discount Pkg	705	599	648
Console, power steering, AM & FM ST ET, cloth reclining sport seats, trunk dress-up.			
Automatic Transmission Discount Pkg . . .	1186	1008	1091
Adds 3-speed automatic transmission to Manual Transmission Pkg.			
Air conditioning	694	590	638
Requires Transmission Discount Pkg. and conventional spare tire.			
California emissions pkg	100	85	92
AM & FM ST ET cassette	152	129	140
Requires Transmission Discount Pkg.			
Conventional spare tire	73	62	67
Tinted glass	105	89	97

Dodge Shadow/ Plymouth Sundance

Dodge Shadow 3-door

A new performance engine and a subtle facelift mark these front-drive subcompact cousins. They share 3- and 5-door hatchback body styles and most mechanicals, but the Dodge is marketed as the sportier car. Both get slightly revised grilles and near-flush aero-style headlamps for '89. The Sundance also gets new taillamps. New front bucket seats have thinner backs that increase rear-seat knee room slightly and outboard rear-seat passengers now have shoulder belts. To the Shadow/Sundance lineup of naturally aspirated 2.2- and 2.5-liter 4 cylinder engines comes Chrysler's new Turbo I, a 150-horsepower turbocharged 2.5 four. It replaces the pre-

Prices are accurate at time of printing; subject to manufacturer's change.

vious Turbo I, a 146-horsepower 2.2-liter four, and is available on Shadows and Sundances with the optional turbo and RS and ES sport-trim option groups. New to the Shadow options list are "pumper"-style alloy wheels. Dodge says Shadow's optional sport suspension is improved for '89 with stiffer front and rear springs and performance-tuned rear shock absorbers and front struts. Front jounce bumpers designed to provide a soft stop for the suspension on severe bumps also are added. A new Shadow competition package is available only on 3-door models and basically adds the ES tires, suspension components and spoilers and the Turbo I engine to a base Shadow. These cars have nicely packaged interiors. Rear-seat room is subpar, but the seatback folds to create a generous cargo hold. The standard suspension is

Specifications

	3-door hatchback	5-door hatchback
Wheelbase, in.	97.0	97.0
Overall length, in.	171.7	171.7
Overall width, in.	67.3	67.3
Overall height, in.	52.7	52.7
Turn diameter, ft.	36.2	36.2
Curb weight, lbs.	2520	2558
Cargo vol., cu. ft.	33.3	33.0
Fuel capacity, gal.	14.0	14.0
Seating capacity	5	5
Front headroom, in.	38.3	38.3
Front shoulder room, in.	54.4	54.7
Front legroom, max., in.	41.5	41.5
Rear headroom, in.	37.4	37.4
Rear shoulder room, in.	52.5	54.5
Rear legroom, min., in.	20.1	20.1

Engines	ohc I-4	ohc I-4	Turbo ohc I-4
Size, liters/cu. in.	2.2/135	2.5/153	2.5/153
Fuel delivery	TBI	TBI	TBI
Horsepower @ rpm	93 @ 4800	100 @ 4800	30 @ 4800
Torque (lbs./ft.) @ rpm	122 @ 3200	135 @ 2800	180 @ 2000
Availability	S	O	O
EPA city/highway mpg			
5-speed OD manual	24/34	24/34	20/29
3-speed automatic	24/28	23/29	19/24

firm for a domestic car and gives competent handling and a stable highway ride. The naturally aspirated 2.5 and automatic transmission is the best-balanced powertrain. With automatic, air conditioning, stereo and other options, the price is around $11,000.

Prices

Dodge Shadow	Retail Price	Dealer Invoice	Low Price
3-door hatchback	$8395	$7656	$8101
5-door hatchback	8595	7836	8291
Destination charge	425	425	425

Standard Equipment:

2.2-liter TBI 4-cylinder engine, 5-speed manual transmission, power steering and brakes, reclining front bucket seats, cloth upholstery, motorized front shoulder belts and manual lap belts, outboard rear lap/shoulder belts, one-piece folding rear seatback, removable shelf panel, dual remote mirrors, intermittent wipers, trip odometer, tachometer, coolant temperature gauge, voltmeter, headlamps-on tone, optical horn, mini console with storage bin, remote liftgate release, bodyside moldings, AM & FM ST ET, 185/70R14 SBR tires.

Optional Equipment:

2.5-liter engine	279	237	257
w/ES or Turbo Engine Pkg. (credit) . . .	(536)	(456)	(456)
Requires Popular Pkg.			
3-speed automatic transmission	536	456	493
Air conditioning	694	590	638
Requires tinted glass.			
Tinted glass	105	89	97
Popular Equipment Discount Pkg., 3-door .	253	215	233
5-door	265	225	244
Full console, rear defogger, Light Group, four speakers.			
Deluxe Convenience Pkg	203	173	187
w/ES Pkg	290	247	267
Conventional spare tire, floormats, cruise control, tilt steering column; requires Popular or ES Pkg.			
Power Assist Pkg. I, 3-door	174	148	160
5-door	219	186	201
w/ES Pkg	48	41	44
Power locks and mirrors; requires Popular or ES Pkg.			
Power Assist Pkg. II, 3-door	405	344	373
5-door	472	401	434
Power windows, power driver's seat; requires Pkg. I, Popular or ES Pkg.			

Prices are accurate at time of printing; subject to manufacturer's change.

	Retail Price	Dealer Invoice	Low Price
ES Pkg., 3-door	1972	1676	1814
5-door	2034	1729	1871

2.5-liter turbo engine (non-turbo 2.5 may be substituted for credit), AM & FM ST ET cassette, performance front seats, full console, rear defogger, fog lights, Light Group, power locks, premium interior, 195/60HR15 all-season performance tires on alloy wheels, message center with warning lights, sill moldings, front fender flares, tape stripes, four speakers, rear spoiler, sport suspension, leather-wrapped steering wheel, 125-mph speedometer, turbo boost gauge.

Turbo Engine Pkg	923	785	849

2.5-liter turbo engine, 185/70R14 all-season performance tires, message center with warning lights, turbo boost gauge, 125-mph speedometer; requires Popular Pkg.

Competition Pkg., 3-door	1515	1288	1394

2.5-liter turbo engine, engine dress-up, heel/toe pedals (w/5-speed), 195/60R15 all-season performance tires on alloy wheels, four speakers, rear spoiler, sport suspension, turbo boost gauge, message center with warning lights.

Rear defogger	145	123	133
Power locks, 3-door	145	123	133
5-door	195	166	179
AM & FM ST ET cassette	201	171	185
w/Popular or Competition Pkg	152	129	140
AM & FM ST ET cassette w/seek/scan . . .	254	216	234
Requires Popular Pkg.			
Removable sunroof	372	316	342
Requires Popular or ES Pkg.			

Plymouth Sundance

3-door hatchback	$8395	$7656	$8026
5-door hatchback	8595	7835	8215
Destination charge	425	425	425

Standard Equipment:

2.2-liter TBI 4-cylinder engine, 5-speed manual transmission, power steering and brakes, mini-console, tinted glass, cloth reclining front bucket seats, split folding rear seatback, headlamps-on tone, tachometer, coolant temperature gauge, voltmeter, trip odometer, optical horn, trip odometer, intermittent wipers, remote liftgate release, remote mirrors, visor mirrors, bodyside moldings, AM/FM ST ET, removable shelf panel, 185/70R14 SBR tires.

Optional Equipment:

2.5-liter 4-cylinder engine	279	237	257
Requires Popular or RS Pkg.			

Prices are accurate at time of printing; subject to manufacturer's change

	Retail Price	Dealer Invoice	Low Price
3-speed automatic transmission	536	456	493
Air conditioning	694	590	638
Requires tinted glass.			
Tinted glass	105	89	97
Popular Equipment Pkg., 3-door	353	300	325
5-door	365	310	336
Full console, rear defogger, Light Group, four speakers.			
Deluxe Convenience Pkg	203	173	187
Cruise control, tilt steering column, conventional spare tire, floormats; requires Popular or RS Pkg.			
Power Assist Pkg. I, 3-door w/Popular Pkg. .	174	148	160
5-door w/Popular Pkg.	219	186	201
3- & 5-door w/RS	48	41	44
Power locks and mirrors.			
Power Assist Pkg. II, 3-door	405	344	373
5-door	472	401	434
Power windows and driver's seat; requires Pkg. I.			
RS Pkg., 3-door	1193	1014	1098
5-door	1255	1067	1155
Popular Pkg. plus 2.5-liter engine, performance front seats, fog lights, liftgate luggage rack, power locks, AM/FM ST ET cassette, leather-wrapped steering wheel, two-tone paint, message center, 125-mph speedometer.			
Turbo Sport Pkg., w/Popular Pkg	923	785	849
w/RS	610	519	561
2.5-liter turbo engine, boost gauge, message center, 185/70R14 SBR performance tires, 125-mph speedometer.			
Rear defogger	145	123	133
Power locks, 3-door	145	123	133
5-door	195	166	179
Requires Power Assist I or Popular Pkg.			
AM/FM ST ET cassette	201	171	185
w/seek/scan, w/Popular Pkg.	152	129	140
Removable glass sunroof	372	316	342

h)
Requires Popular or RS Pkg.

Dodge Spirit/ Plymouth Acclaim

These near twins are Chrysler's new front-drive, 4-door notchback sedans. Set to go on sale in January, their conservative design is bigger than the compact Dodge Aries and Plymouth Reliant, and about the same size as the mid-size

Dodge Spirit

Plymouth Caravelle and Dodge 600, which they replace. Both come as 4-door notchbacks only. Spirit tilts more toward the sporty, Acclaim toward family transportation. Base and mid-line versions have a 2.5-liter 4-cylinder engine standard, with a more powerful turbocharged version optional. A 5-speed manual is standard; a 3-speed automatic is optional with either 2.5. The sporty Spirit ES has the turbo engine as standard, while a Mitsubishi-made 141-horsepower 3.0-liter V-6 mated to Chrysler's new 4-speed automatic transmission is optional. That V-6 powertrain is the only one offered on the top-line Acclaim LX. All models have analog instruments, including a tachometer. Base models come with front bucket seats, outboard rear-seat shoulder belts, remote trunk and fuel-door releases and 14-inch tires. A front bench seat and a folding split-back rear seat are optional. Mid- and top-range versions make more comfort and convenience equipment available. All Spirits have a firmer-riding suspension than base Acclaims, though a handling package and wider tires are optional on the Plymouths. All models have front disc and rear drum brakes. Spirit ES is the sportiest of the flock, with sport bucket seats, aero body panels, fog lamps and a monochromatic paint scheme in red, black, silver or white; its standard 15-inch alloy wheels are painted to match white cars. Neither of these cars breaks new ground, but both are vast improvements over Chrysler's recent bread-and-butter sedans. They're more solid, more sensibly designed, more comfortable and more competent on the road. The cabins are airy, the trunks usefully large. Brief test-track drives showed the Spirit was indeed firmer riding than Acclaim. It had an edge in handling, too, but Acclaim wasn't ill at ease in the corners. The V-6 is the most desirable engine.

Specifications

	4-door notchback
Wheelbase, in.	103.3
Overall length, in.	181.2
Overall width, in.	68.1
Overall height, in.	55.5
Turn diameter, ft.	37.6
Curb weight, lbs.	2770
Cargo vol., cu. ft.	14.4
Fuel capacity, gal.	16.0
Seating capacity	6
Front headroom, in.	38.4
Front shoulder room, in.	54.3
Front legroom, max., in.	41.8
Rear headroom, in.	37.9
Rear shoulder room, in.	54.9
Rear legroom, min., in.	38.5

Engines	ohc I-4	Turbo ohc I-4	ohc V-6
Size, liters/cu. in.	2.5/153	2.5/153	3.0/181
Fuel delivery	TBI	PFI	PFI
Horsepower @ rpm	100 @ 4800	150 @ 4800	141 @ 5000
Torque (lbs./ft.) @ rpm	135 @ 2800	180 @ 2000	171 @ 2800
Availability	S	O[1]	O[2]

EPA city/highway mpg			
5-speed OD manual	24/34	20/29	
3-speed automatic	23/29	19/24	
4-speed OD automatic			18/26

1. Standard, ES.   2. ES only.

Equipment Summary

Dodge Spirit
(prices not available at time of publication)

Standard Equipment:

2.5-liter TBI 4-cylinder engine, 5-speed manual transmission, power steering and brakes, cloth reclining front bucket seats, visor mirrors, AM & FM ST

ET, remote fuel filler and decklid releases, 195/70R14 all-season SBR tires. **LE** adds: tinted glass, driver's seat lumbar support adjustment, split folding rear seatback, dual remote mirrors, rear defogger, cruise control, tilt steering column, message center. **ES** adds: 2.5-liter turbo engine, AM & FM ST ET cassette, lighted visor mirrors, sill extensions, front air dam with fog lights, trip computer, 205/60R14 Goodyear Eagle GT all-season tires on alloy wheels.

Plymouth Acclaim
(prices not available at time of publication):

Standard Equipment:

2.5-liter TBI 4-cylinder engine, 5-speed manual transmission, power steering, cloth reclining front bucket seats, tachometer, coolant temperature and oil pressure gauges, voltmeter, trip odometer, intermittent wipers, AM/FM ST ET, remote fuel door and decklid releases, 185/70R14 all-season SBR tires. **LE** adds: cruise control, tilt steering column, driver's seat lumbar support adjustment, lighted visor mirrors, rear defogger, message center, 55/45 folding rear seat, armrest with dual cupholders, 195/70R14 tires. **LX** adds: 3.0-liter PFI V-6, 4-speed automatic transmission, sport suspension, decklid luggage rack, trip computer, AM/FM ST ET cassette, leather-wrapped steering wheel, 205/60R15 performance tires on alloy wheels.

Eagle Medallion

Eagle Medallion LX 4-door

A redesigned instrument panel and the prospect of a V-6 engine option are news for these French-built 4-door sedans and 5-door wagons. Chrysler Motors acquired the Medallion in August 1987 when it purchased AMC, which had been importing the Renault-made car. Chrysler dumped the Renault badge and now sells Medallion through its Jeep-Eagle division. The redesigned instrument panel places controls closer to the driver, but it has no glove compartment. The anticipated V-6 option will bring the same 150-horsepower 3.0-liter and 4-speed automatic transmission that's used in the larger Eagle Premier. For now, Medallions have a Renault-built 2.2-liter four mounted longitudinally. Wagons come only with automatic transmission. They have 5-passenger seating standard and room for seven with an optional third seat. Motorized front shoulder belts are standard. Medallion is comfortable, roomy and generally fun to drive. Its performance is anemic with automatic transmission, however, especially with several people aboard and the air conditioner on. Handling is above average for this class.

Specifications

	4-door notchback	5-door wagon
Wheelbase, in.	102.3	108.2
Overall length, in.	183.2	189.7
Overall width, in.	67.5	67.5
Overall height, in.	55.7	56.3
Turn diameter, ft.	NA	NA
Curb weight, lbs.	2588	2736
Cargo vol., cu. ft.	15.2	89.5
Fuel capacity, gal.	17.4	17.4
Seating capacity	5	5
Front headroom, in.	37.8	37.8
Front shoulder room, in.	55.1	55.1
Front legroom, max., in.	42.2	42.2
Rear headroom, in.	37.5	37.4
Rear shoulder room, in.	54.5	54.5
Rear legroom, min., in.	40.8	40.8

Engines

	ohc I-4
Size, liters/cu. in.	2.2/132
Fuel delivery	PFI
Horsepower @ rpm	103 @ 5000
Torque (lbs./ft.) @ rpm	124 @ 2500
Availability	S

EPA city/highway mpg

5-speed OD manual	23/31
3-speed automatic	21/27

a comfortable driving position are a plus. The sedan has ample room for four adults, and a fifth can fit with a little squeezing. Trunk volume is good for a compact. The longer wagon has more passenger room and a roomy cargo area with a flat floor. Poorly designed heat/vent controls and flimsy-feeling plastic trim detract from the cabin. Reliability woes helped doom previous Renault products in America, and that remains a concern. Plus, both Chrysler and Renault have indicated a possibility that the Medallion will no longer be exported to the U.S. after the 1989 model year.

Prices

Eagle Medallion	Retail Price	Dealer Invoice	Low Price
DL 4-door notchback	$10405	$8944	$9675
DL 5-door wagon	11649	10002	10826
LX 4-door notchback	10938	9397	10168
LX 4-door notchback	12275	10534	11405
Destination charge	425	425	425

Standard Equipment:

DL: 2.2-liter PFI 4-cylinder engine, 5-speed manual transmission (4-doors; wagons have 3-speed automatic), power steering and brakes, reclining front bucket seats, cloth upholstery, driver's seat height adjustment, passive front seatbelts, outboard rear lap/shoulder belts, intermittent wipers, tilt steering column, rear wiper/washer (wagon), tachometer, coolant temperature gauge, trip odometer, digital clock, rear defogger, tinted glass, door pockets, floormats, power mirrors, AM/FM ST ET, roof rack (wagon), 185/65R14 all-season SBR tires. **LX** adds: rear head restraints and courtesy lamps, rocker passenger seat, upgraded upholstery, split folding rear seat with center armrest.

Optional Equipment:

3-speed automatic transmission, 4-doors .	490	402	446
Air conditioning	799	655	727
Driving Group, LX	404	331	368
Leather-wrapped steering wheel, 195/60HR14 tires on alloy wheels.			
Power Windows and Door Locks Pkg., LX .	758	622	690
Power windows and locks, heated power mirrors, remote trunk release or tailgate lock, lighted right visor mirror, locking fuel door.			
Premium Audio Group, LX	515	422	469
AM/FM ST ET cassette with graphic EQ and six speakers, power antenna.			
Cargo cover, DL wagon	72	59	66

Prices are accurate at time of printing; subject to manufacturer's change.

	Retail Price	Dealer Invoice	Low Price
Cruise control	175	144	160
Power locks	366	300	333
Includes power trunk release or tailgate lock, locking fuel door			
AM/FM ST ET cassette	360	295	328
Power sunroof	599	491	545
Third seat, DL wagon	280	230	255
LX wagon	208	171	190

Eagle Premier

Eagle Premier LX

A sporty ES Limited model is due in April, but this front-drive 4-door sedan is otherwise carried over with only minor changes. Designed by AMC and French automaker Renault, Premier is built in Toronto and sold through Chrysler Motors' Jeep-Eagle division, which Chrysler formed after buying AMC. An AMC 2.5-liter 4-cylinder is standard in the base LX. Optional on LX and standard on ES is a 3.0-liter V-6. A 4-speed automatic is the only transmission. Both models have all-independent suspensions, though ES's is set for a firmer ride. Six-passenger seating with a 55/45 reclining front-bench is standard. Models with optional 5-passenger seating have front buckets and a center console, and they are set to get a floor-mounted shift lever during the model year. Premier's electronic turn-signal beep has been

Prices are accurate at time of printing; subject to manufacturer's change.

Specifications

	4-door notchback
Wheelbase, in.	105.5
Overall length, in.	192.7
Overall width, in.	69.8
Overall height, in.	55.9
Turn diameter, ft.	36.9
Curb weight, lbs.	2862
Cargo vol., cu. ft.	16.3
Fuel capacity, gal.	17.0
Seating capacity	5
Front headroom, in.	38.5
Front shoulder room, in.	57.8
Front legroom, max., in.	43.7
Rear headroom, in.	37.5
Rear shoulder room, in.	56.9
Rear legroom, min., in.	39.4

Engines

	ohv I-4	ohc V-6
Size, liters/cu. in.	2.5/150	3.0/182
Fuel delivery	TBI	PFI
Horsepower @ rpm	111 @ 4750	150 @ 5000
Torque (lbs./ft.) @ rpm	142 @ 2500	171 @ 3750
Availability	S	S[1]

EPA city/highway mpg

4-speed OD automatic	22/31	18/27

1. ES; optional, LX

changed to a chime tone, and the standard power steering gets increased assist. Previously optional, a rear-window defogger is now standard, while the LX gains the rallye instrument package as standard. The ES Limited model will feature a white monochromatic exterior, leather seat trim, V-6 engine, floor-shift automatic and will be the first Premier with 4-wheel disc brakes. A V-6 Premier is the best driving sedan in the Chrysler stable, with a smooth and responsive powertrain, well-controlled ride and sharp steering. Supportive seats and room for six highlight an airy cabin of pleasing and contemporary design. The trunk is roomy, and prices are reasonable. The quirkiness of some of the controls compromises their function, however, and the new floor-mounted shifter is welcome in place of the snakelike column stalk.

Prices

Eagle Premier	Retail Price	Dealer Invoice	Low Price
LX 4-door notchback	$13276	$11435	$12356
ES 4-door notchback	15259	13120	14190
Destination charge	440	440	440

Standard Equipment:

LX: 2.5-liter TBI 4-cylinder engine, 4-speed automatic transmission, power steering and brakes, 55/45 reclining front seats, rear armrest, AM/FM ST ET, tachometer, coolant temperature and oil pressure gauges, voltmeter, trip odometer, intermittent wipers, rear defogger, tinted glass, digital clock, door and seatback pockets, map lights, right visor mirror, leather-wrapped steering wheel, remote mirrors, 195/70R14 tires. **ES** adds: 3.0-liter PFI V-6, touring suspension, 45/45 velour front seats, full-length console with armrest, trip computer/vehicle maintenance monitor, 8 Jensen speakers, 205/70HR14 tires on polycast wheels.

Optional Equipment:

3.0-liter PFI V-6, LX	680	578	626
Air conditioning	855	727	787
Popular Option Group	1339	1138	1232
Air conditioning, cruise control, tilt steering column.			
Luxury Option Group, LX	2261	1922	2080
ES	2014	1712	1853
Popular Group plus power mirrors, lighted visor mirrors, power windows, premium audio system.			
Electronic Information Pkg., LX	309	263	284
Trip computer, vehicle maintenance monitor; requires Popular or Luxury Group.			
Enthusiast Group, LX	648	551	596
Velour bucket seats, touring suspension, 205/70HR14 tires on alloy wheels; requires Popular or Luxury Group.			
Convenience Group	309	263	284
Cruise control, tilt steering column.			
Decklid luggage rack	118	100	109
Power Lock Group	415	353	382
Power locks with remote control and illuminated entry, power decklid release, remote fuel door release.			
Power windows	294	250	270
Requires Power Lock Group.			
Power front seats	494	420	454
Requires Popular or Luxury Group.			
Velour bucket seats, LX	103	88	95

Prices are accurate at time of printing; subject to manufacturer's change.

	Retail Price	Dealer Invoice	Low Price
Leather/vinyl bucket seats, ES	583	496	536

Bucket seats include console and passive restraints (motorized shoulder belts/manual lap belts).

	Retail Price	Dealer Invoice	Low Price
AM/FM ST ET cassette	241	205	222
Premium audio system, LX	620	527	570
ES	447	380	411

AM/FM ST ET cassette w/EQ, eight Accusound by Jensen speakers, power antenna.

	Retail Price	Dealer Invoice	Low Price
Conventional spare tire	85	72	78
Alloy wheels, base	370	315	340
ES	295	251	271

Air conditioning, rear defogger.

Eagle Summit

Eagle Summit DL

This front-drive, 4-door subcompact sedan debuts for 1989 as the entry-level Eagle. Designed by Mitsubishi Motors Corporation, Chrysler's Japanese partner, Summit is a 4-door version of the Mitsubishi hatchback that Dodge and Plymouth dealers sell as the Colt. Mitsubishi dealers market a similar 4-door sedan as the Mirage. Summit is offered in two trim levels, DL and LX, with a performance package available on the LX version. A 1.5-liter 4-cylinder is the base engine. A 5-speed manual transmission is standard; a 3-speed automatic is optional. LXs upgrade DL equipment with velour seats, a height-adjustable driver's seat, split

Prices are accurate at time of printing; subject to manufacturer's change.

fold-down rear seat, power steering and a tilt and telescope steering column. The LX DOHC is built around a double-overhead-cam, 16-valve 1.6-liter four. A sport suspension, 4-wheel disc brakes and sport front bucket seats are standard, a 4-speed automatic is optional. All Summits have motorized front shoulder belts, as well as shoulder belts for outboard rear passengers. Summits are now built in Japan, but eventually will be assembled at the Chrysler-Mitsubishi joint-venture Diamond-Star Motors plant in Illinois. The car is a pleasant contemporary Japanese subcompact. Its main rivals are the Toyota Corolla and Honda Civic, and the Summits we drove at Chrysler's test track stacked up well against both. Construction is solid, road manners compe-

Specifications

	4-door notchback
Wheelbase, in.	96.7
Overall length, in.	170.1
Overall width, in.	65.7
Overall height, in.	52.8
Turn diameter, ft.	30.8
Curb weight, lbs.	2271
Cargo vol., cu. ft.	10.3
Fuel capacity, gal.	13.2
Seating capacity	5
Front headroom, in.	39.1
Front shoulder room, in.	53.5
Front legroom, max., in.	41.9
Rear headroom, in.	37.5
Rear shoulder room, in.	53.1
Rear legroom, min., in.	34.3

Engines

	ohc I-4	dohc I-4
Size, liters/cu. in.	1.5/90	1.6/97
Fuel delivery	PFI	PFI
Horsepower @ rpm	81 @ 5500	113 @ 6500
Torque (lbs./ft.) @ rpm	91 @ 3000	99 @ 5000
Availability	S	O[1]

EPA city/highway mpg

5-speed OD manual	29/35	23/28
3-speed automatic	27/30	
4-speed OD automatic		23/28

1. LX

tent. The cabins are relatively roomy, with bins and pockets placed thoughtfully. Trunk space is above average for the class. Blemishes include a noisy highway ride, and the base engine with automatic transmission runs at a buzzy 3400 rpm at 65 mph. You'll get quieter cruising and better fuel economy with the 5-speed. The LX DOHC is worth considering, but order the 5-speed to exact the full measure of its high-revving engine.

Prices

Eagle Summit	Retail Price	Dealer Invoice	Low Price
DL 4-door notchback	$9347	$8419	$8883
w/Pkg. IFB	10028	8998	9513
w/Pkg. IFC	10247	9184	9716
w/Pkg.IFD	10549	9441	9995
LX 4-door notchback	10364	9324	9844
w/Pkg. IFB	10714	9621	10168
w/Pkg. IFC	11324	10140	10732
w/Pkg. IFF	11596	10372	10984
w/DOHC Pkg. IFD	11695	10455	11075
w/DOHC Pkg. IFE	12920	11497	12209
Destination charge	255	255	255

Standard Equipment:

DL: 1.5-liter PFI 4-cylinder engine, 5-speed manual transmission, power brakes, cloth bucket seats, trip odometer, coolant temperature gauge, motorized front shoulder belts and manual lap belts, outboard rear lap/shoulder belts, locking fuel filler door, remote mirrors, rear defogger, intermittent wipers, 155/80R13 all-season SBR tires. **DL Pkg. IFB** adds: power steering, digital clock, tinted glass, AM/FM ST ET. **DL Pkg. IFC** adds: AM/FM ST ET cassette, power mirrors. **DL Pkg. IFD** adds: alloy wheels. **LX** adds to base DL: power steering, velour seats with driver's side height adjustment, split folding rear seat with center armrest, digital clock, remote fuel door and decklid releases, tachometer, tinted glass, full wheel covers, 175/70R13 tires. **LX Pkg. IFB** adds: power mirrors, AM/FM ST ET. **LX Pkg. ISC** adds: AM/FM ST ET cassette, power windows and locks. **LX Pkg. IFF** adds: alloy wheels. **LX DOHC Pkg. IFD** adds to base LX: DOHC Pkg., power mirrors, AM/FM ST ET cassette. **LX DOHC Pkg. IFE** adds: premium audio system w/EQ, power windows and locks, cruise control, alloy wheels.

Optional Equipment:

3-speed automatic transmission, DL & LX .	505	429	465
4-speed automatic transmission, LX w/DOHC	682	580	627

Prices are accurate at time of printing; subject to manufacturer's change.

	Retail Price	Dealer Invoice	Low Price
Power steering, DL	262	223	241
DOHC Pkg., LX	805	684	741
DOHC 16-valve engine, 4-wheel disc brakes, sport suspension, 195/60R14 tires, driver's footrest, sport seats, sport steering wheel, blackout exterior treatment.			
Air conditioning	748	636	688
Decklid luggage rack	94	80	86
Front floormats	28	24	26
Cruise control & variable int. wipers, LX .	211	179	194
Digital clock, DL	55	47	51
Power mirrors, DL & LX	49	42	45
LX w/DOHC	55	47	51
Power windows and locks, LX	440	374	405
AM/FM ST ET	301	256	277
AM/FM ST ET cassette	471	400	433
Premium audio system w/EQ, LX	743	632	684
Tinted glass, DL	63	54	58
Euro Cast alloy wheels	272	231	250
Sport alloy wheels, LX w/DOHC	302	257	278
Two-tone paint, LX	159	135	146

Ford Aerostar

An extended-length version of Ford's rear-drive compact van is to go on sale by the end of December. It rides the 118.9-inch wheelbase of the regular models, but 15.4 inches added to its rear cargo area boosts cargo volume by 28 cubic feet. It also gains one inch of leg room for the second-row seats and two inches for the third-row seats. Also new for '89 is a sporty body-trim package under the XL Sport Wagon badge. It features front and rear bumper cladding, lower rocker-panel moldings and a monochromatic paint scheme. Aerostar is available as a 2-seat cargo hauler, called the Aerostar Van, or as the Wagon, a passenger model with standard seating for five and optional seating for seven. All are powered by a 3.0-liter V-6. A 5-speed manual transmission is standard, a 4-speed automatic is optional. Among other changes for '89 are a slightly redesigned grille and a new front bumper with an air intake slot. The fuel tank grows from 17 to 21 gallons. Later in the year, the Wagon's second- and third-row bench seats will get seatbacks that

Prices are accurate at time of printing; subject to manufacturer's change.

Ford Aerostar Eddie Bauer

Specifications

	4-door van	4-door van
Wheelbase, in.	118.9	118.9
Overall length, in.	174.9	190.3
Overall width, in.	71.7	72.0
Overall height, in.	72.9	73.2
Turn diameter, ft.	39.8	39.8
Curb weight, lbs.	3500	NA
Cargo vol., cu. ft.	140.4	168.4
Fuel capacity, gal.	21.0	21.0
Seating capacity	7	7
Front headroom, in.	39.5	39.5
Front shoulder room, in.	60.0	60.0
Front legroom, max., in.	41.4	41.4
Rear headroom, in.	38.1	38.3
Rear shoulder room, in.	NA	NA
Rear legroom, min., in.	37.9	38.8

Engines

	ohv V-6
Size, liters/cu. in.	3.0/182
Fuel delivery	PFI
Horsepower @ rpm	145 @ 4800
Torque (lbs./ft.) @ rpm	165 @ 3600
Availability	S

EPA city/highway mpg

5-speed OD manual	16/23
4-speed OD automatic	17/22

fold flat and will unlatch more easily to improve cargo carrying. Aerostar is better suited to heavy-duty work and towing trailers than the front-drive Chrysler minivans, an advantage shared with the rear-drive Chevrolet Astro/GMC Safari. Now it joins the Dodge Grand Caravan and Plymouth Grand Voyager in the stretched-minivan arena. Aerostar has plenty of power, though it suffers poor fuel economy and a rough ride over bad pavement. Cabins are roomy and the XLT and Eddie Bauer interiors are plush and comfortable. Getting into the front seats requires a high step up compared to Caravan/Voyager. The standard-size model's cargo space is unimpressive with all seats in place and removing the heavy rear seat is a chore. We like Aerostar more than the rear-drive Japanese minivans, and a little better than the GM offerings. Caravan and Voyager are tops for passenger use, but Aerostar has the edge in brawn.

Prices

Ford Aerostar Wagon	Retail Price	Dealer Invoice	Low Price
4-door van	$11567	$10324	$11046
Destination charge	450	450	450

Standard Equipment:

XL: 3.0-liter PFI V-6, 5-speed manual transmission, power steering and brakes, lowback front bucket seats, 3-passenger middle seat, remote fuel door release, tinted glass, dual outside mirrors, visor mirrors, AM ET, 215/70R14SL tires. **XL Plus** trim adds: front air conditioning, intermittent wipers, electronic instrument cluster, front captain's chairs, cruise control, tilt steering column. **XLT Plus** trim adds: front captain's chairs with power lumbar support and seatback pockets, 2-passenger middle seat, 3-passenger rear seat, power windows and locks, leather-wrapped steering wheel, luggage rack, power mirrors, nylon liftgate net, Light Group, AM/FM ST ET cassette, overhead console with electronic day/night mirror, lighted visor mirrors, full wheel covers. **Eddie Bauer** trim adds: front and rear air conditioning with high-capacity heater, upgraded upholstery, middle and rear seat/bed, two-tone paint, alloy wheels.

Optional Equipment:

4-speed automatic transmission	607	516	558
Limited-slip axle	248	210	228

Prices are accurate at time of printing; subject to manufacturer's change.

	Retail Price	Dealer Invoice	Low Price
Air conditioning	846	719	778
High-capacity A/C & aux. heater, base . . .	1422	1209	1308
w/any Preferred Pkg	576	489	530
XL Plus Preferred Pkg. 401A	2084	1771	1917
XLT Preferred Pkg. 402A	3162	2688	2909
XLT Plus Preferred Pkg. 403A	4543	3861	4180
Eddie Bauer Preferred Pkg. 404A	6503	5527	5983
California emissions pkg	99	84	91
WSW tires	72	61	66
7-pass. seating w/bucket seats	296	252	272
5-pass. seating w/2 captain's chairs	480	408	442
7-pass. seating w/2 captain's chairs &			
2- & 3-pass. seat/bed, base	1366	1161	1257
XL Plus	539	458	496
7-pass. seating w/2 captain's chairs	827	723	761
w/4 captain's chairs, XLT	585	498	538
w/4 captain's chairs, Eddie Bauer	NC	NC	NC
Rear defogger, base	224	191	206
XL Plus	166	141	153
Electronics Group, base	1027	873	945
w/XLT Pkg. 402A	745	633	685
Overhead console with trip computer, electronic day/night mirror and map lights, electronic instruments, Super Sound System.			
Exterior Appearance Group, base	632	537	581
w/XL Plus Pkg. 401A	263	224	242
w/XLT Pkg. 402A or 403A	184	157	169
Privacy glass, two-tone paint.			
Engine block heater	33	28	30
Light Group	159	135	146
Luggage rack	141	120	130
Black swing-away mirrors	52	45	48
Bodyside moldings, w/XL trim	63	54	58
w/XLT or Eddie Bauer	35	30	32
Power Convenience Group	501	426	461
Power windows, locks and mirrors.			
Cruise control & tilt steering column	296	252	272
Trailer Towing Pkg	282	239	259
Class I wiring harness, HD turn signal flasher, limited-slip axle.			
Rear wiper/washer, w/rear defogger	139	118	128
w/o rear defogger	198	168	182
Forged aluminum wheels, w/XL trim	309	262	284
w/XLT or Exterior Appearance Group . .	270	229	248
Intermittent wipers	59	50	54
AM/FM ST ET	211	179	194
AM/FM ST ET cassette	313	266	288
AM radio delete (credit)	(61)	(52)	(52)

Prices are accurate at time of printing; subject to manufacturer's change.

Ford Escort

Ford Escort GT

One of America's top-selling cars is carried over virtually unaltered, save for discontinuation of the slow-selling EXP 2-seat hatchback. Its demise leaves the stripper Escort Pony and sporty Escort GT, both 3-door hatchbacks, and the Escort LX 3- and 5-door hatchbacks and 5-door wagon. Retained is the moderate facelift bestowed in mid-1988. The hatchback and wagon got plastic bumpers and new fenders, taillamps and quarter panels and 14-inch wheels in place of 13s. The GT got a new grille and rear spoiler. Added to all models this fall is an engine malfunctioning light and gas-pressurized struts. Escort Ponys and LXs have a 90-horsepower 1.9-liter 4-cylinder, GTs a 115-horsepower version. GTs also have wider tires on 15-inch alloy wheels and a firmer suspension. All Escorts have motorized automatic front shoulder belts with manual lap belts. Escort is average in most ways, but its fairly low price and good warranties qualify it as a pretty good value. It's still more expensive than the Dodge Omni/Plymouth Horizon subcompacts, although most options are available in money-saving packages and direct dealer discounts and factory incentives abound. Like the Omni/Horizon, Escort shows its age primarily with an interior that's cramped compared to newer Japanese designs. The engine has adequate power and is economical, but it's not nearly as strong as Chrysler's 2.2 or the smaller, multi-valve engines in Toyota and Honda subcompacts. Plus, the 3-speed automatic robs it of most of its response. The 4- and 5-speed manual transmissions are cheaper, faster and more economical.

Specifications

	3-door hatchback	5-door hatchback	5-door wagon
Wheelbase, in.	94.2	94.2	94.2
Overall length, in.	166.9	166.9	168.0
Overall width, in.	65.9	65.9	65.9
Overall height, in.	53.5	53.5	53.3
Turn diameter, ft.	35.7	35.7	35.7
Curb weight, lbs.	2180	2222	2274
Cargo vol., cu. ft.	38.5	38.5	58.8
Fuel capacity, gal.	13.0	13.0	13.0
Seating capacity	5	5	5
Front headroom, in.	37.9	37.9	37.9
Front shoulder room, in.	51.3	51.3	51.3
Front legroom, max., in.	41.5	41.5	41.5
Rear headroom, in.	37.3	37.3	38.2
Rear shoulder room, in.	51.6	51.4	51.6
Rear legroom, min., in.	35.1	35.1	35.1

Engines

	ohc I-4	ohc I-4
Size, liters/cu. in.	1.9/114	1.9/114
Fuel delivery	TBI	PFI
Horsepower @ rpm	90 @ 4600	115 @ 5200
Torque (lbs./ft.) @ rpm	106 @ 3400	120 @ 4400
Availability	S	S[1]

EPA city/highway mpg

4-speed OD manual	32/42	
5-speed OD manual	27/36	25/32
3-speed automatic	26/31	

1. Escort GT

Prices

Ford Escort	Retail Price	Dealer Invoice	Low Price
Pony 3-door hatchback	$6964	$6418	$6691
LX 3-door hatchback	7349	6621	6985
LX 5-door hatchback	7679	6915	7297
LX 5-door wagon	8280	7450	7865
GT 3-door hatchback	9315	8371	8843
Destination charge	335	335	335

Prices are accurate at time of printing; subject to manufacturer's change.

Standard Equipment:

Pony: 1.9-liter TBI 4-cylinder engine, 4-speed manual transmission, power brakes, cloth and vinyl reclining front bucket seats, folding rear seat, motorized front shoulder belts with manual lap belts, removable cargo cover, 175/70R14 tires. **LX** adds: AM ET radio, full cloth upholstery, door pockets; wagon has 5-speed manual transmission and retractable cargo cover. **GT** adds: PFI engine, 5-speed manual transmission, handling suspension, sport seats, remote fuel door and liftgate releases, power mirrors, tachometer, coolant temperature gauge, trip odometer, visor mirrors, overhead console with digital clock and stopwatch, map lights, center console with graphic monitor and folding armrest, AM/FM ST ET, split folding rear seatback, 195/60HR15 tires on alloy wheels.

Optional Equipment:

	Retail Price	Dealer Invoice	Low Price
5-speed manual trans, LX exc. wagon . . .	76	64	70
3-speed auto trans, Pony, LX exc. wagon .	490	417	451
LX wagon	415	352	382
Air conditioning	688	585	633
Power steering	235	200	216
WSW tires, LX	73	62	67
HD battery	27	23	25
Digital clock/overhead console	82	69	75
Rear defogger	145	123	133
Tinted glass	105	89	97
Instrumentation Group	87	74	80
Tachometer, coolant temperature gauge, trip odometer.			
Light/Security Group, LX	91	78	84
GT	67	57	62
Misc. lights, remote fuel door and liftgate releases.			
Luggage rack	115	97	106
Power mirrors (std. GT)	88	75	81
Wide bodyside moldings	50	43	46
Clearcoat paint, LX	91	78	84
GT (incl. two-tone paint)	183	155	168
Two-tone paint	91	78	84
AM ET radio, Pony	54	46	50
AM/FM ST ET, Pony	206	175	190
LX	152	130	140
AM/FM ST ET cassette, Pony	343	291	316
LX	289	246	266
GT	137	116	126
Premium sound system	138	117	127
AM delete, LX (credit)	(54)	(46)	(46)
AM/FM ST ET delete, GT (credit)	(206)	(175)	(175
Cruise control	182	154	167
Split folding rear seat	50	42	46
Tilt steering column	124	106	114

Prices are accurate at time of printing; subject to manufacturer's change.

	Retail Price	Dealer Invoice	Low Price
Luxury wheel covers	71	60	65
Vinyl trim	37	31	34
Polycast wheels	162	138	149
Intermittent wipers	55	47	51
Rear wiper/washer	126	107	116
Conventional spare tire	73	62	67
Special Value Pkg. 330A, GT	815	692	750
Manual Transaxle Pkg., LX exc. wagon . .	560	476	515
LX wagon	484	412	445

5-speed manual transmission, digital clock/overhead console, rear defogger, tinted glass, Instrumentation Group, Light/Security Group, power mirrors, wide bodyside moldings, AM/FM ST ET, power steering, luxury wheel covers, intermittent wipers.

Automatic Transaxle Pkg., LX exc. wagon .	938	798	863
LX wagon	863	733	794

Manual Transmission Pkg. plus 3-speed automatic transmission.

Ford Festiva

Ford Festiva L Plus

Built for Ford in South Korea by Kia Motors, this diminutive front-driver is available with automatic transmission for the first time. Festiva, entering its first model year in national distribution, is a 3-door hatchback based on a design by Mazda, which is owned partly by Ford Motor Co. Its 1.3-liter 4-cylinder engine has a 2-barrel carburetor and is

Prices are accurate at time of printing; subject to manufacturer's change.

rated at 58 horsepower with manual transmission. Order the optional 3-speed automatic transmission and the engine gains fuel injection and five additional horsepower. The automatic is unavailable on the base L model. A 4-speed manual is standard on L and L Plus; LXs get a 5-speed. Air conditioning and aluminum wheels are among the few options. Among cars sold in the U.S., only the Suzuki-built Geo Metro and the Subaru Justy have base curb weights lower than Festiva's 1713 pounds. A quick-shifting manual helps get the most from the 1.3 liter, which produces little power at low engine speeds, yet thrashes above 4000 rpm. Fuel economy compensates some for the shortage of performance and refinement. We haven't tested an automatic transmis-

Specifications

	3-door hatchback
Wheelbase, in.	90.2
Overall length, in.	140.5
Overall width, in.	63.2
Overall height, in.	55.3
Turn diameter, ft.	28.2
Curb weight, lbs.	1713
Cargo vol., cu. ft.	26.5
Fuel capacity, gal.	10.0
Seating capacity	4
Front headroom, in.	38.8
Front shoulder room, in.	51.9
Front legroom, max., in.	40.6
Rear headroom, in.	37.7
Rear shoulder room, in.	50.9
Rear legroom, min., in.	35.7

Engines

	ohc I-4	ohc I-4
Size, liters/cu. in.	1.3/81	1.3/81
Fuel delivery	2 bbl.	PFI
Horsepower @ rpm	58 @ 5000	63 @ 5000
Torque (lbs./ft.) @ rpm	73 @ 3500	73 @ 3000
Availability	S	S[1]

EPA city/highway mpg

4-speed OD manual	38/40	
5-speed OD manual	39/43	
3-speed automatic		30/31

1. With automatic transmission

sion model, but expect it to take a toll on power and economy. The manual steering is heavy at low speeds and you have to fight the wheel in bumpy corners to stay on course. Turns bring on body roll and cause the front end to plow, with little help from the skinny 12-inch tires. Head room is adequate, but don't sentence adults to the back seat for very long. Ride comfort is good, all things considered, though even with the LX's added sound insulation, Festiva is plenty noisy.

Prices

Ford Festiva	Retail Price	Dealer Invoice	Low Price
L 3-door hatchback	$5699	$5300	$5550
L Plus 3-door hatchback	6372	5926	6149
LX 3-door hatchback	7101	6604	6853
Destination charge	255	255	255

Standard Equipment:

L: 1.3-liter 2bbl. 4-cylinder engine, 4-speed manual transmission, power brakes, locking fuel filler door, tethered fuel cap, composite halogen headlamps, wide bodyside moldings, reclining high-back front bucket seats, folding rear seat, cloth upholstery, coolant temperature gauge, rear passenger walk-in device, instrument panel coin bin, shift indicator light, 145/SR12 SBR tires on styled steel wheels. **L Plus** adds: rear defogger, AM/FM ST ET. **LX** adds: 5-speed manual transmission, tachometer, trip odometer, intermittent wipers, rear defogger, tilt steering column, sound insulation package, dual horns, tinted glass, dual power mirrors, low-back reclining front bucket seats, upgraded cloth upholstery, split fold-down rear seat, consolette, full door trim with cloth inserts, door map pockets, underseat stowage, urethane soft-feel steering wheel, package tray, headlamps-on alert, cargo area lamp, driver's side coat hook, 165/70SR12 SBR tires.

Optional Equipment:

3-speed automatic transmission (NA L) ..	515	437	476
Includes PFI engine.			
Air conditioning, L Plus	793	674	734
LX	688	585	637
Rear defogger, L	267	227	247
AM ET radio, L	162	138	150
AM/FM ST ET cassette, L & L Plus	137	116	127
Alloy wheels, L Plus	421	358	390
LX	396	337	367

Prices are accurate at time of printing; subject to manufacturer's change.

Ford LTD Crown Victoria/ Mercury Grand Marquis

Ford LTD Crown Victoria LX 4-door

Ford's conservative full-size cars return nearly unaltered for an 11th model year on their current rear-drive platform. Mercury's Grand Marquis is slightly plusher and the division is celebrating its 50th year in '89 with an Anniversary Edition. It's set to arrive mid-year as a limited-volume sedan with unique body striping, lacy spoke alloy wheels, premium sound system, luxury cloth and leather interior trim, 6-way power front seats, and a leather-wrapped 4-spoke steering wheel. It deletes the drip moldings standard on other models. Both the Crown Vic and Grand Marquis are available as 6-passenger 4-door sedans or as 5-door wagons that seat eight with an optional rear-facing third seat. A fuel-injected 5.0-liter V-8 and a 4-speed automatic transmission comprise the sole powertrain. A heated windshield is optional. An engine-systems warning light replaces the dashboard's low-oil warning light as the only change on the Ford. On the Grand Marquis, clear-coat metallic paint is a new option, cast aluminum wheels are a required option on all LS models and bumper guards, previously standard on sedans, are now optional. These are among the few cars still using body-on-frame construction. Chevrolet's Caprice is comparable in most ways, but we prefer the Ford products for their more responsive powertrain. Virtues include true 6-passenger room, good cargo space, trailer-towing ability, a quiet ride, and high marks on insurance-industry safety surveys. Vices are low fuel economy, poor maneuverability, a floaty high-speed ride and generally cumbersome handling. In today's market, however, compacts such as the 4-cylinder Honda Accord LXi or a V-6 Toyota Camry LE cost as much as these full-size Americans. It's a choice between size and sophistication.

Specifications

	4-door notchback	5-door wagon
Wheelbase, in.	114.3	114.3
Overall length, in.	211.0	216.0
Overall width, in.	77.5	79.3
Overall height, in.	55.5	57.0
Turn diameter, ft.	39.1	39.1
Curb weight, lbs.	3779	3991
Cargo vol., cu. ft.	22.4	88.2
Fuel capacity, gal.	18.0	18.0
Seating capacity	6	8
Front headroom, in.	37.9	38.8
Front shoulder room, in.	61.6	61.6
Front legroom, max., in.	43.5	43.5
Rear headroom, in.	37.2	39.1
Rear shoulder room, in.	61.6	61.6
Rear legroom, min., in.	39.3	37.9

Engines

	ohv V-8
Size, liters/cu. in.	5.0/302
Fuel delivery	PFI
Horsepower @ rpm	150 @ 3200
Torque (lbs./ft.) @ rpm	270 @ 2000
Availability	S

EPA city/highway mpg

4-speed OD automatic	17/24

Prices

Ford LTD Crown Victoria	Retail Price	Dealer Invoice	Low Price
4-door notchback	$15851	$13633	$14842
LX 4-door notchback	16767	14441	15704
5-door wagon	16209	13936	15173
Country Squire 5-door wagon	16527	14207	15467
LX 5-door wagon	17238	14811	16125

Prices are accurate at time of printing; subject to manufacturer's change

	Retail Price	Dealer Invoice	Low Price
LX Country Squire 5-door wagon	17556	15082	16419
Destination charge	480	480	480

Standard Equipment:

5.0-liter PFI V-8 engine, 4-speed automatic transmission, power steering and brakes, air conditioning, Autolamp on/off/delay system, split bench seat with reclining backrests and two center armrests, cloth and vinyl upholstery, automatic parking brake release, trip odometer, intermittent wipers, remote mirrors, padded rear half vinyl roof, digital clock, AM/FM ST ET, front door map pockets, right visor mirror, P215/70R15 all-season SBR WSW tires. Wagons have vinyl upholstery, HD rear brakes, three-way doorgate with power window, locking side and underfloor storage compartments. **LX** adds: power windows, velour upholstery, dual-facing rear seats (wagon), upgraded door panels with curb lights, Light Group, pivoting front head restraints, lighted visor mirrors, rear center armrest, seatback map pockets. **Country Squire** adds to base wagon: luggage rack, woodtone exterior applique.

Optional Equipment:

Traction-Lok axle	100	85	92
Automatic air conditioning, w/Pkg.			
111A, 112A, 131A or 132A	66	56	61
Others	211	179	194
Pkg. 111A, LX 4-door	383	325	352
Pkg. 112A, LX 4-door	938	796	863
Pkg. 113A, LX 4-door	1514	1285	1393
Pkg. 131A, base 4-door & Country Squire .	1280	1088	1178
Pkg. 132A, LX 4-door & wagon	688	584	633
Pkg. 133A, LX 4-door & wagon	1191	1011	1096
High Level Audio System, w/Pkg.			
112A or 132A	335	285	308
w/Pkg. 133A or 133A	167	142	154
Others	472	401	434
HD battery	27	23	25
Bumper guards	62	53	57
Front cornering lamps	68	58	63
Rear defogger	145	123	133
Floormats	43	36	40
Engine block heater	18	16	17
Illuminated entry	82	69	75
Light Group	59	50	54
Power Lock Group	245	208	225
Power locks, remote decklid or tailgate release.			
Bodyside moldings	66	56	61
Clearcoat paint	226	192	208
Two-tone paint/tape treatment	159	135	146

Prices are accurate at time of printing; subject to manufacturer's change

	Retail Price	Dealer Invoice	Low Price
AM/FM ST ET cassette	137	116	126
Power antenna	76	64	70
AM/FM ST ET delete (credit)	(206)	(175)	(175)
Premium Sound System	168	143	155
Power driver's seat	251	214	231
Power front seats, w/Pkg. 112A, 131A or 132A	251	214	231
Others	502	427	462
Dual-facing rear seats, wagon	173	147	159
Cruise control	182	154	167
Leather-wrapped steering wheel	59	50	54
Tilt steering column	124	106	114
Automatic load-leveling suspension	195	166	179
HD/handling suspension	26	22	24
HD Trailer Towing Pkg., 4-doors	387	329	356
Wagons	399	339	367

3.55 Traction-Lok axle, HD battery, trailer wiring harness, power steering and transmission fluid oil coolers, HD flasher, conventional spare tire, HD rear brakes (4-doors), HD U-joint, HD radiator, dual exhaust system; for 5000-lb. capacity/750-lb. tongue load.

	Retail Price	Dealer Invoice	Low Price
Tripminder computer	215	182	198
Pivoting front vent windows	79	67	73
Vinyl roof delete (credit)	(200)	(170)	(170)
Alloy wheels (4)	390	332	359
Power windows & mirrors	379	322	349
Insta-Clear windshield	250	213	230
Brougham half roof treatment	665	565	612
California emissions pkg	99	84	91
All-vinyl seat trim	37	31	34
Duraweave vinyl seat trim	96	82	88
Leather seat trim	415	352	382

Mercury Grand Marquis

	Retail Price	Dealer Invoice	Low Price
GS 4-door notchback	$16701	$14366	$15534
LS 4-door notchback	17213	14801	16007
GS Colony Park 5-door wagon	17338	14907	16123
LS Colony Park 5-door wagon	17922	15404	16663
Destination charge	480	480	480

Standard Equipment:

GS: 5.0-liter PFI V-8 engine, 4-speed automatic transmission, power steering and brakes, air conditioning, tinted glass, reclining front seats, cloth trim (vinyl on wagon), power windows, intermittent wipers, digital clock, trip odometer, Autolamp system, optical horn, padded half vinyl roof, right visor mirror, AM/FM ST ET, power 3-way tailgate (wagon), lockable storage com-

Prices are accurate at time of printing; subject to manufacturer's change

partments (wagon), simulated woodgrain exterior applique (wagon), 215/70R15 WSW SBR tires. **LS** adds: rear armrest (4-door), front seatback map pockets, Light Group.

Optional Equipment:

	Retail Price	Dealer Invoice	Low Price
Preferred Pkg. 156A, GS 4-door	974	829	896
Preferred Pkg. 157A, GS 4-door	1200	1019	1104
Preferred Pkg. 171A, LS 4-door	1126	957	1036
Preferred Pkg. 172B, LS 4-door	1216	1031	1119
Preferred Pkg. 192A, GS wagon	1143	971	1052
LS wagon	1097	932	1009
Preferred Pkg. 193A, GS wagon	1392	1181	1281
LS wagon	1346	1142	1238
Conventional spare tire	73	62	67
Automatic climate control	211	179	194
w/any Preferred Pkg.	66	56	61
Rear defogger	145	123	133
Insta-Clear heated windshield	250	213	230
HD battery	27	23	25
Power Lock Group	245	208	225
Power locks, power decklid or tailgate release.			
Power decklid release	50	43	46
Power driver's seat	251	214	231
Power front seats	502	427	462
AM/FM ST ET cassette	137	116	126
High Level Audio System	472	401	434
w/Pkg. 157A	335	286	308
w/Pkg. 172A or 193A	167	142	154
AM/FM ST ET delete (credit)	(206)	(175)	(175)
Premium sound system	168	143	155
Power antenna	76	64	70
Cornering lamps	68	58	63
Bodyside moldings	66	56	61
Two-tone paint	159	135	146
Formal coach roof	665	563	612
Clearcoat paint	226	192	208
Leather-wrapped steering wheel	59	50	54
Floormats	43	37	40

Ford Mustang

The original pony car is celebrating its 25th anniversary, but whatever commemorative plans Ford may have had not been announced at publication time. Rumors abound about a possible anniversary Mustang with special performance

Prices are accurate at time of printing; subject to manufacturer's change

Ford Mustang GT

Specifications

	2-door notchback	3-door hatchback	2-door conv.
Wheelbase, in.	100.5	100.5	100.5
Overall length, in.	179.6	179.6	179.6
Overall width, in.	69.1	69.1	69.1
Overall height, in.	52.1	52.1	51.9
Turn diameter, ft.	37.4	37.4	37.4
Curb weight, lbs.	2724	2782	3214
Cargo vol., cu. ft.	12.2	30.0	6.4
Fuel capacity, gal.	15.4	15.4	15.4
Seating capacity	4	4	4
Front headroom, in.	37.0	37.0	37.6
Front shoulder room, in.	55.4	55.4	55.4
Front legroom, max., in.	41.7	41.7	41.7
Rear headroom, in.	35.9	35.6	37.0
Rear shoulder room, in.	54.3	54.3	48.9
Rear legroom, min., in.	30.7	30.7	30.7

Engines

	ohc I-4	ohv V-8
Size, liters/cu. in.	2.3/140	5.0/302
Fuel delivery	PFI	PFI
Horsepower @ rpm	90 @ 3800	225 @ 4200
Torque (lbs./ft.) @ rpm	130 @ 2800	300 @ 3200
Availability	S[1]	S[2]

EPA city/highway mpg

5-speed OD manual	23/29	17/24
4-speed OD automatic	NA	17/25

1. LX   2. GT, LX 5.0L Sport

or styling features. One certainty is that Mustang returns for '89 with the same basic front-engine, rear-drive platform introduced in 1978. It continues in LX and GT trim, though LXs ordered with the 5.0-liter V-8 engine now get their own model designation: LX 5.0L Sport. The LX comes standard with a 2.3-liter 4-cylinder and is available as a 2-door coupe, 3-door hatchback or 2-door convertible. GTs are 5.0-liter hatchbacks or convertibles. LX 5.0L Sports get the GT's articulated sports seats, beefed-up suspension, wider tires and alloy wheels, but not its body spoilers and air dams. A 5-speed manual transmission or a 4-speed overdrive automatic can be had with either engine. Power windows and locks are now standard on convertibles. The 4-cylinder is too weak for this 2800-pound car, so if you want a Mustang, order a V-8. You'll get blistering acceleration, acceptable handling and a fine-shifting manual transmission—all at a reasonable price. Our major performance concern is that the mandatory front disc/rear drum brakes are not up to the 5.0 liter's speed potential. We realize a high-powered, rear-drive car with a small interior and a rough ride isn't everyone's cup of tea, but for performance-minded buyers on a budget, nothing delivers so much bang for so few bucks. On the practical side, Mustang's cabin and ride quality are more livable than the arch-rival Chevrolet Camaro's, though traction on wet pavement can be treacherous. V-8 Mustangs are good bets as future collectible cars.

Prices

Ford Mustang	Retail Price	Dealer Invoice	Low Price
LX 2-door notchback	$9050	$8178	$8714
LX 3-door hatchback	9556	8628	9192
LX 2-door convertible	14140	12707	13524
LX 5.0L Sport 2-door notchback	11410	10278	10944
LX 5.0L Sport 3-door hatchback	12265	11039	11752
LX 5.0L Sport 2-door convertible	17001	15254	16228
GT 3-door hatchback	13272	11935	12704
GT 2-door convertible	17512	15708	16710
Destination charge	374	374	374

Standard Equipment:

LX: 2.3-liter PFI 4-cylinder engine, 5-speed manual transmission, power steering and brakes, cloth reclining bucket seats, tinted glass, tachometer, trip odometer, coolant temperature and oil pressure gauges, voltmeter, intermittent wipers, remote mirrors, console with armrest, cargo area cover (3-door), AM/FM ST ET, 195/70R14 tires. **LX 5.0L Sport** adds: 5.0-liter PFI V-8, Traction-Lok axle, articulated sport seats (hatchback and convertible), 225/60VR15 tires on alloy wheels. **GT** adds: power windows and locks, remote hatch release, tilt steering column, fog lights, driver's foot rest, pivoting map light. Convertibles have power top, power windows and locks, remote decklid release, luggage rack, footwell lights.

Optional Equipment:

	Retail Price	Dealer Invoice	Low Price
4-speed automatic transmission	515	437	474
Custom Equipment Group, LX exc. conv .	1180	1004	1086
LX conv	1080	919	994
Air conditioning, premium sound system, tilt steering column, lighted visor mirrors.			
Pkg. 245B (LX 5.0), 249B (GT), exc. conv. .	1006	854	926
LX 5.0L & GT conv.	487	413	448
WSW tires, LX 2.3	82	69	75
Bodyside molding insert stripe	61	52	56
Rear defogger	145	123	133
AM/FM ST ET delete (credit)	(206)	(175)	(175)
Flip-up sunroof	355	302	327
Premium Sound System	168	143	155
Wire wheel covers, LX 2.3	178	151	164
California emissions pkg	99	84	91
Leather articulated sport seats, LX conv . .	780	663	718
GT conv	415	352	382
Vinyl seat trim	37	31	34

Ford Probe

Ford's front-drive sporty coupe was introduced in May 1988 as an '89 model and continues unchanged. It shares its chassis and powertrains with Mazda's new MX-6 coupe; both are built at Mazda's plant in Flat Rock, Michigan. Base GL and luxury LX models use a 2.2-liter 12-valve 4-cylinder engine. Probe GT comes with a turbocharged and intercooled version. The GT has rear disc brakes instead of drums, a firmer suspension, alloy wheels, unique front and rear fascias and lower-body cladding. Anti-lock brakes are optional only on the GT. A 5-speed manual transmission is standard on all three models; a 4-speed automatic is optional on the GL and LX. Ford stylists threw out the MX-6's upright styling for a

Ford Probe LX

Specifications

	3-door hatchback
Wheelbase, in.	99.0
Overall length, in.	177.0
Overall width, in.	67.9
Overall height, in.	51.8
Turn diameter, ft.	34.8
Curb weight, lbs.	2720
Cargo vol., cu. ft.	40.7
Fuel capacity, gal.	15.1
Seating capacity	5
Front headroom, in.	37.3
Front shoulder room, in.	54.7
Front legroom, max., in.	42.5
Rear headroom, in.	35.0
Rear shoulder room, in.	53.7
Rear legroom, min., in.	29.9

Engines

	ohc I-4	Turbo ohc I-4
Size, liters/cu. in.	2.2/133	2.2/133
Fuel delivery	PFI	PFI
Horsepower @ rpm	110 @ 4700	145 @ 4300
Torque (lbs./ft.) @ rpm	130 @ 3000	190 @ 3500
Availability	S[1]	S[2]

EPA city/highway mpg

5-speed OD manual	24/31	21/27
4-speed OD automatic	22/29	

1. GL/LX   2. GT

strong aero look on the Probe's exterior. Their interior design borrows liberally from the Mazda, however, including a main instrument binnacle that tilts along with the steering wheel. GL and LX Probes have a vastly different personality than the turbocharged GT. With 110 horsepower moving 2720 pounds, they're unsporting, especially with automatic transmission. They ride well for small coupes, but handling, braking and roadholding are average for the class. The GT is quite fast, but it can be an unpredictable handful under power because of excessive torque steer. At low speeds, turbo boost comes on abruptly with a rush of power that wrenches the front wheels off course, even in second gear. The GT has good cornering grip, but quick driving on twisty roads is marred by steering that's artificially heavy off center. Automatic transmission is unavailable for the GT, and the 5-speed favors a firm hand through the gears. All Probes have ample cargo space, even with the rear seatback up, though the liftover is high. The tiny back seat is suitable only for children.

Prices

Ford Probe	Retail Price	Dealer Invoice	Low Price
GL 3-door hatchback	$10943	$9864	$10604
LX 3-door hatchback	11769	10599	11384
GT 3-door hatchback	14077	12653	13565
Destination charge	290	290	290

Standard Equipment:

GL: 2.2-liter PFI 4-cylinder engine, 5-speed manual transmission, power steering and brakes, cloth reclining front bucket seats with driver's seat height adjustment, tachometer, coolant temperature and oil pressure gauges, ammeter, AM/FM ST ET, tinted backlight and quarter windows, cargo cover, full console with storage, split folding rear seatbacks, right visor mirror, digital clock, 185/70SR14 tires. **LX adds:** remote fuel door and liftgate releases, intermittent wipers, rear defogger, full tinted glass, tilt steering column and instrument cluster, power mirrors, overhead console with map light, upgraded carpet and upholstery, door pockets, left visor mirror, folding armrest, driver's seat lumbar and side bolster adjustments. **GT adds:** turbocharged engine, 4-wheel disc brakes, performance suspension with automatic adjustment, passenger lumbar support adjustment, fog lights, 195/60VR15 tires on alloy wheels.

Prices are accurate at time of printing; subject to manufacturer's change

Optional Equipment:

	Retail Price	Dealer Invoice	Low Price
4-speed automatic transmission	515	437	476
Air conditioning	907	771	839
w/option pkg	788	670	729
Pkg. 251A, GL	334	285	310
Tinted glass, intermittent wipers, Light Group, power mirrors, tilt steering column and instrument cluster, rear defogger.			
Pkg. 253A, LX	2214	1880	2047
Electronic instrument cluster, electronic air conditioning, illuminated entry, leather-wrapped steering wheel and shift knob, power driver's seat, trip computer, rear wiper/washer, walk-in passenger seat, power windows and locks, cruise control, AM/FM ST ET cassette with power antenna.			
Pkg. 261A, GT	2621	2226	2424
Pkg. 253A plus anti-lock braking system, analog instruments.			
Rear defogger	145	123	134
Power locks	145	123	134
Cruise control	182	154	168
Flip-up sunroof	355	302	329
Alloy wheels, GL	306	260	283
LX	245	208	227
AM/FM ST ET	168	143	156
w/cassette	344	292	318
w/cassette & CD, w/Pkg. 251A, 252A or 260A	1052	895	974
w/cassette & CD, w/Pkg. 253A or 261A .	708	602	655
Cassette stereos include power antenna.			
AM/FM ST ET delete (credit)	(245)	(208)	(208)
Engine block heater	20	17	19

Ford Taurus/Mercury Sable

These hot-selling front-drive family cars get subtle grille and taillamp revisions, but the big news is the Taurus SHO. It's powered by a "Super High Output" 3.0-liter, double-overhead cam, 32-valve V-6 developed and built in Japan by Yamaha. Exclusive to SHO is a special handling suspension and the first 4-wheel disc brake system available on any Taurus. Optional on other models but standard on SHO are 15-inch performance tires on aluminum wheels. The only available SHO transmission is a 5-speed manual designed by Ford but built by Mazda, which is partly owned by Ford. The SHO is available only as a 4-door sedan and is set apart visually from other Tauruses by its modest ground-effects

Ford Taurus SHO

body panels. Inside, SHO has unique power front sports seats, power windows, a leather-wrapped steering wheel and analog gauges. Taurus's other major news is the discontinuation of the MT-5 model, which was previously the only Taurus available with a manual transmission. Both Sable and Taurus come in 4-door sedan and 5-door wagon body styles. Minor alterations have been made to the grille, headlamps and taillamp lenses of each, including the illumination of the entire width between Sable's headlights. Inside, all have revised door trim panels. Base Taurus sedans have a 2.5-liter 4-cylinder and a 3-speed automatic. Other Tauruses (except SHO) and all Sables come standard with a 3.0-liter V-6 (unrelated to the SHO engine) and a 4-speed automatic. Optional on all but the base Taurus sedan and SHO is a 3.8-liter V-6. These sedans and wagons are roomy, stylish and well built. Their ride is taut for a midrange American sedan, but strong sales suggest most buyers like the attendant European-style handling. Taurus and Sable work best with a V-6, though the 3.8 is not notable for its fuel economy. The SHO is startlingly fast, with a silken engine that rushes to its 7000-rpm redline. With good steering, great brakes, fine seats and a retail price of around $20,000 fully equipped, SHO shapes up as a solid threat to performance-oriented import sedans costing far more.

Specifications

	4-door notchback	5-door wagon
Wheelbase, in.	106.0	106.0
Overall length, in.	188.4	191.9
Overall width, in.	70.6	70.6
Overall height, in.	54.3	55.1
Turn diameter, ft.	39.8	39.8
Curb weight, lbs.	2982	3186
Cargo vol., cu. ft.	17.0	80.7
Fuel capacity, gal.	16.0	16.0
Seating capacity	6	8
Front headroom, in.	38.3	38.6
Front shoulder room, in.	57.5	57.5
Front legroom, max., in.	41.7	41.7
Rear headroom, in.	37.6	38.3
Rear shoulder room, in.	57.5	57.5
Rear legroom, min., in.	37.5	36.6

Engines

	ohv I-4	ohv V-6	ohv V-6	dohc V-6
Size, liters/cu. in.	2.5/153	3.0/182	3.8/232	3.0/182
Fuel delivery	TBI	PFI	PFI	PFI
Horsepower @ rpm	90 @ 4400	140 @ 4800	140 @ 3800	220 @ 6000
Torque (lbs./ft.) @ rpm	130 @ 2600	160 @ 3000	215 @ 2200	200 @ 4800
Availability	S	O[1]	O	S[2]

EPA city/highway mpg

	ohv I-4	ohv V-6	ohv V-6	dohc V-6
5-speed OD manual				NA
3-speed automatic	21/27			
4-speed OD automatic		21/29	19/28	

1. Standard on Taurus LX and Tarus wagons.   2. Taurus SHO

Prices

Ford Taurus	Retail Price	Dealer Invoice	Low Price
L 4-door notchback	$11778	$10152	$10965
L 5-door wagon	13143	11312	12228
GL 4-door notchback	12202	10513	11358
GL 5-door wagon	13544	11653	12599
SHO 4-door notchback	19739	16919	NA
LX 4-door notchback	15282	13130	14206
LX 5-door wagon	16524	14187	15356
Destination charge	450	450	450

Prices are accurate at time of printing; subject to manufacturer's change

Standard Equipment:

L: 2.5-liter TBI 4-cylinder engine, 3-speed automatic transmission (wagon has 3.0-liter PFI V-6 and 4-speed automatic), power steering and brakes, power mirrors, reclining split bench seat, cloth upholstery, outboard rear lap/shoulder belts, 60/40 folding rear seatbacks (wagon), cargo tiedowns (wagon), intermittent wipers, trip odometer, coolant temperature gauge, AM/FM ST ET, tinted glass, luggage rack (wagon), P195/70R14 SBR tires. **GL** adds: split bench or bucket seats with console and recliners, front seatback map pockets, digital clock, rear armrest, rear head restraints (4-door), cargo net (4-door). **LX** adds: 3.0-liter V-6 (4-door; wagon has 3.8-liter V-6), air conditioning, power windows and door locks, power lumbar support, diagnostic alert lights, tilt steering column, remote fuel filler and decklid/liftgate releases, Light Group, automatic parking brake release, lower bodyside cladding, cornering lights, upgraded door panels, lighted visor mirrors, P205/70R14 SBR tires. **SHO** adds: 3.0-liter DOHC 24-valve PFI V-6, 5-speed manual transmission, 4-wheel disc brakes, handling suspension, dual exhausts, sport seats with power lumbar, 8000-rpm tachometer, 140-mph speedometer, fog lamps, special bodyside cladding, wheel spats, rear defogger, cruise control, console with armrest and cup holders, leather-wrapped steering wheel, 215/65R15 performance tires on alloy wheels.

Optional Equipment:

	Retail Price	Dealer Invoice	Low Price
3.0-liter V-6, L & GL 4-doors	672	571	618
3.8-liter V-6, GL wagon	400	340	368
Others exc. LX wagon	1072	911	986
205/70R14 WSW tires	82	69	75
205/65R15 tires	65	55	60
205/65R15 WSW tires	146	124	134
Conventional spare tire	73	62	67
Automatic air conditioning, w/Pkg. 202A .	971	825	893
SHO, LX or w/Pkg. 204A	183	155	168
Manual air conditioning	788	670	725
Autolamp system	73	62	67
HD battery	27	23	25
Cargo area cover, wagons	66	56	61
Cornering lamps	68	58	63
Rear defogger	145	123	133
Engine block heater	18	16	17
Floormats	43	36	40
Remote fuel door & decklid/liftgate release .	91	78	84
Extended-range fuel tank	46	39	42
Illuminated entry	82	69	75
Diagnostic instrument cluster	89	76	82
Electronic instruments, LX	239	203	220
GL	351	299	323
Keyless entry, w/Pkg. 207A or 211A	121	103	111
Others	202	172	186

Prices are accurate at time of printing; subject to manufacturer's change

	Retail Price	Dealer Invoice	Low Price
Picnic table load floor extension, wagons .	66	56	61
Power locks	195	166	179
Lighted visor mirrors	100	85	92
Rocker panel moldings	55	47	51
Power moonroof	741	630	682
Clearcoat paint	183	155	168
Automatic parking brake release	12	10	11
High Level Audio System, w/Pkg. 204A . .	335	285	308
w/Pkg. 207A	167	142	154
Others	472	401	434
AM/FM ST ET cassette	137	116	126
Premium sound system	168	143	155
Power antenna	76	64	70
Rear-facing third seat, wagons	155	132	143
Power driver's seat	251	214	231
Dual power seats, w/Pkg. 204A or 211A .	251	214	231
Others	502	427	462
Cruise control	182	154	167
Tilt steering column	124	106	114
Leather-wrapped steering wheel	59	50	54
HD suspension	26	22	24
Rear wiper/washer, wagons	126	107	116
Locking wheel covers, w/Pkg. 202A	212	180	195
w/Pkg. 204A	148	125	136
Alloy wheels, GL	227	193	209
w/Pkg. 204A	162	138	149
Styled road wheels, GL	178	151	164
LX or w/Pkg. 204A	113	96	104
Power windows	296	252	272
Insta-Clear heated windshield	250	213	230
Leather seat trim, LX & SHO	415	352	382
GL	518	441	477
Vinyl seat trim, L	51	41	47
GL	37	31	34
Preferred Pkg. 204A, GL	1749	1488	1609
Preferred Pkg. 207A, LX	777	658	715
Preferred Pkg. 208A, LX 4-door	1913	1624	1760
LX wagon	1513	1284	1392
Preferred Pkg. 211A, SHO	533	453	490

Mercury Sable

	Retail Price	Dealer Invoice	Low Price
GS 4-door notchback	$14101	$12134	$13118
LS 4-door notchback	15094	12978	14036
GS 5-door wagon	14804	12731	13768
LS 5-door wagon	15872	13639	14756
Destination charge	450	450	450

Prices are accurate at time of printing; subject to manufacturer's change.

Standard Equipment:

GS: 3.0-liter PFI V-6 engine, 4-speed automatic transmission, power steering and brakes, air conditioning, 50/50 cloth reclining front seats with armrests, 60/40 split rear seatback (wagons), outboard rear lap/shoulder belts, tinted glass, digital clock, intermittent wipers, tachometer, coolant temperature gauge, trip odometer, optical horn, tiedown hooks (wagon), front cornering lamps, power mirrors, luggage rack (wagon), AM/FM ST ET, front door map pockets, rear armrest (except wagons), covered package tray storage bin (4-doors), visor mirrors, 205/70R14 all-season SBR tires. **LS** adds: power windows, automatic parking brake release, warning lights (low fuel, washer fluid and oil, lamp outage, door ajar), Light Group, bodyside cladding, remote fuel door and liftgate releases, upgraded upholstery, power front lumbar support adjustments, front seatback map pockets, lighted visor mirrors.

Optional Equipment:	Retail Price	Dealer Invoice	Low Price
3.8-liter V-6	400	340	368
Automatic air conditioning	183	155	168
Air conditioning delete, GS (credit)	(788)	(670)	(670)
Preferred Pkg. 450A	547	464	503
Preferred Pkg. 451A	1018	865	937
Preferred Pkg. 460A	462	393	425
Preferred Pkg. 461A	978	830	900
Preferred Pkg. 462A	2054	1745	1890
205/70R14 WSW tires	82	69	75
205/65R15 tires	65	55	60
205/65R15 WSW tires	146	124	134
Conventional spare tire	73	62	67
Alloy wheels	172	146	158
Polycast wheels	123	105	113
Autolamp system	73	62	67
Automatic parking brake release	12	10	11
Lighted visor mirrors, GS	100	85	92
Electronic instrument cluster	351	299	323
Insta-Clear heated windshield	250	213	230
Keyless entry	202	172	186
Power moonroof	741	630	682
Rear defogger	145	123	133
Cruise control	182	154	167
Tilt steering column	124	106	114
Light Group, GS	59	50	54
HD battery	27	23	25
HD suspension	26	22	24
Extended-range fuel tank	46	39	42
Power Lock Group, GS	287	244	264
LS	195	166	179

Power locks, remote fuel door and decklid/liftgate releases.

Prices are accurate at time of printing; subject to manufacturer's change.

	Retail Price	Dealer Invoice	Low Price
Power driver's seat	251	214	231
Dual power seats	502	427	462
w/pkg. containing power driver's seat	251	214	231
Power windows, GS	296	252	272
AM/FM ST ET delete (credit)	(206)	(175)	(175)
AM/FM ST ET cassette	137	116	126
Premium sound system	168	143	155
High Level Audio System	472	401	434
w/Pkg. 450 or 451	335	285	308
w/Pkg. 461	167	142	154
Power antenna	76	64	70
Clearcoat paint	183	155	168
Paint stripe	61	52	56
Floormats	43	36	40
Leather-wrapped steering wheel	59	50	54
Leather seat trim	415	352	382
All-vinyl trim	37	31	34
Picnic tray, wagons	66	56	61
Rear-facing third seat, wagons	155	132	143
Liftgate wiper/washer, wagons	126	107	116
Cargo area cover, wagons	66	56	61
Engine block heater	18	16	17

Ford Tempo/Mercury Topaz

Ford Tempo LX 4-door

These near-twin compacts coast into 1989 little changed from the freshened appearance and power boost they received for '88. Both come as front-drive 2- or 4-door sedans in several trim levels. Each also is available with All Wheel

Prices are accurate at time of printing; subject to manufacturer's change.

Specifications

	2-door notchback	4-door notchback
Wheelbase, in.	99.9	99.9
Overall length, in.	176.5	176.5
Overall width, in.	68.3	68.3
Overall height, in.	52.7	52.7
Turn diameter, ft.	38.7	38.7
Curb weight, lbs.	2462[1]	2515[2]
Cargo vol., cu. ft.	13.2	13.2
Fuel capacity, gal.	15.4[3]	15.4[3]
Seating capacity	5	5
Front headroom, in.	37.5	37.5
Front shoulder room, in.	53.4	53.4
Front legroom, max., in.	41.5	41.5
Rear headroom, in.	36.9	36.9
Rear shoulder room, in.	54.0	53.4
Rear legroom, min., in.	36.0	36.0

1. 2667 with 4WD   2. 2720 with 4WD   3. 13.7 with 4WD

Engines

	ohv I-4	ohv I-4
Size, liters/cu. in.	2.3/141	2.3/141
Fuel delivery	PFI	PFI
Horsepower @ rpm	98 @ 4400	100 @ 4400
Torque (lbs./ft.) @ rpm	124 @ 2200	130 @ 2600
Availability	S	S[1]

EPA city/highway mpg

5-speed OD manual	23/32	21/28
3-speed automatic	22/26	22/27

1. Tempo GLS, Topaz XR5, LTS, 4WD.

Drive, a part-time 4-wheel-drive system not for use on dry pavement. Among the few changes, a cargo tiedown net is now standard in the luggage compartment of sedans starting with the midrange versions and including the 4WD models. A driver's-side air bag is optional on all two-wheel-drive automatic-transmission four doors. Motorized automatic front shoulder belts are standard on all Tempos and Topazes. The base 98-horsepower 2.3-liter 4-cylinder engine in the Tempo GL and Topaz GS and LS is supplanted by a 100-horsepower 2.3 in the other versions and in the All Wheel Drive models. Front-drive models have a 5-speed manual transmission standard and a 3-speed automatic optional; the automatic is mandatory with All Wheel Drive. Freshened styling in '88 brought a pleasing resemblance to the larger Ford Taurus/Mercury Sable, and a redesign inside gave these cars one of the most attractive and functional dashboards in any domestic auto. Performance was improved also, but only to the adequate level. It's still far behind that of, say, a Honda Accord or a V-6 Chevrolet Corsica. Either 2.3 generates more noise than useful power, and the 3-speed automatic is particularly ill-suited to brisk driving. Tempo/Topaz can be nicely equipped for a reasonable price; the refinement of an Accord or the power of a V-6 Corsica does cost more.

Prices

Ford Tempo	Retail Price	Dealer invoice	Low Price
GL 2-door notchback	$9057	$8160	$8609
GL 4-door notchback	9207	8293	8750
GLS 2-door notchback	9697	8729	9213
GLS 4-door notchback	9848	8863	9356
LX 4-door notchback	10156	9138	9647
All Wheel Drive 4-door notchback	10860	9765	10313
Destination charge	425	425	425

Standard Equipment:

GL: 2.3-liter PFI 4-cylinder engine, 5-speed manual transmission, power steering and brakes, cloth reclining front bucket seats, motorized front shoulder belts and manual lap belts, AM/FM ST ET, coolant temperature gauge, tinted glass, intermittent wipers, door pockets, 185/70R14 tires. **GLS adds:** high-output engine, light group, tachometer and trip odometer, leather-wrapped steering wheel, AM/FM cassette, power mirrors, sport seats, luggage tiedown, front center armrest, performance tires on alloy wheels. **LX adds** to GL: illuminated entry, power locks, remote fuel door and decklid releases, tilt steering column, front armrest, upgraded upholstery, seatback pockets, polycast wheels. **All Wheel Drive adds** to GL: high- output engine, 3-speed automatic transmission, part-time 4-wheel drive.

Optional Equipment:

3-speed automatic transmission (std. AWD)	515	437	474
Driver's side air bag, GL	815	692	750
LX	751	639	691
185/70R14 WSW tires	82	69	75
185/70R14 WSW performance tires	82	69	75

Prices are accurate at time of printing; subject to manufacturer's change.

	Retail Price	Dealer Invoice	Low Price
Air conditioning	788	670	725
Rear defogger	145	123	133
Sport instrument cluster GL	87	74	80
Tachometer, trip odometer.			
Decklid luggage rack	115	97	106
Power Lock Group, 2-doors	237	201	218
4-doors	287	244	264
Power locks, remote fuel door and decklid releases.			
Power mirrors, GL	111	94	102
AM/FM ST ET cassette (std. GLS)	137	116	126
AM/FM ST ET delete, GL, LX & AWD (credit)	(245)	(208)	(208)
AM/FM ST ET cassette delete, GLS (credit)	(382)	(324)	(324)
Power driver's seat	251	214	231
Premium sound system	138	117	127
Cruise control	182	154	167
Sports Appearance Group, GLS	1178	1001	1084
Includes bodyside cladding.			
Tilt steering column	124	106	114
Polycast wheels	178	151	164
Power windows, 4-doors	296	252	272
California emissions pkg.	100	85	92
Clearcoat metallic paint	91	78	84
Lower accent paint	159	135	146
All vinyl seat trim	37	31	34
Preferred Pkg. 226A, GL 2-door	449	381	413
GL 4-door	499	424	459
Preferred Pkg. 227A, GL 4-door	1250	1060	1150
Preferred Pkg. 229A, GLS 2-door	1220	1037	1122
GLS 4-door	1270	1079	1168
Preferred Pkg. 233A, LX	863	733	794
Preferred Pkg. 234A, LX	1099	934	1011
Preferred Pkg. 232A, AWD	352	300	324

Mercury Topaz

	Retail Price	Dealer Invoice	Low Price
GS 2-door notchback	$9577	$8626	$9102
GS 4-door notchback	9734	8766	9250
XR5 2-door notchback	10498	9446	9972
LS 4-door notchback	11030	9920	10475
LTS 4-door notchback	11980	10765	11373
Destination charge	425	425	425

Standard Equipment:

GS: 2.3-liter PFI 4-cylinder engine, 5-speed manual transmission, power steering and brakes, reclining cloth and vinyl front bucket seats, motorized

Prices are accurate at time of printing; subject to manufacturer's change.

front shoulder belts, manual lap belts, tachometer, coolant temperature gauge, trip odometer, tinted glass, intermittent wipers, AM/FM ST ET, diagnostic alert module, door pockets, map lights, 185/70R14 tires. **LS** adds: tilt steering column, power windows and locks, cruise control, all-cloth upholstery, rear defogger, remote decklid and fuel door releases, Light Group, cargo net, headlamps-on tone, front armrest, console cassette storage, touring suspension, performance tires. **XR5** adds to GS: high-output engine, 3.73 final drive ratio, performance suspension, leather-wrapped steering wheel, tilt steering column, sport seats with power lumbar, Light Group, cargo net, front armrest, remote decklid and fuel door releases, performance tires on alloy wheels. **LTS** adds to LS: high-output engine, 3.73 final drive ratio, performance suspension, air conditioning, cruise control, sport seats with power lumbar, cargo net, performance tires on alloy wheels.

Optional Equipment:

	Retail Price	Dealer Invoice	Low Price
3-speed automatic transmission	515	437	474
All Wheel Drive, GS	1441	1229	1326
GS w/Pkg. 363A	927	788	853
LTS	1352	1132	1244
LS	1424	1215	1310
LS w/Pkg. 365A	915	777	842
Driver's side air bag, GS	815	692	750
LS & LTS	622	529	572
Air conditioning	788	670	725
Special Value Pkg. 361A, GS	436	371	401
Special Value Pkg. 363A, GS	751	639	691
Supplemental Restraint Pkg. 362A, GS 4-door	1124	954	1034
Special Value Pkg. 371A, XR5	427	363	393
Special Value Pkg. 365A, LS	NC	NC	NC
Supplemental Restraint Pkg. 366A, LS . . .	896	761	824
Supplemental Restraint Pkg. 376A, LTS . .	622	529	572
185/70R14 WSW tires	82	69	75
185/70R14 performance tires	82	69	75
Comfort/Convenience Group, GS	179	152	165
Folding center armrest, Light Group, remote fuel door and decklid releases.			
Rear defogger	145	123	133
Power Lock Group, GS 2-door	237	201	218
XR5	156	133	144
GS 4-door	288	245	265
GS 2-door w/Comfort/Convenience	156	133	144
GS 4-door w/Comfort/Convenience	207	176	190
Power locks, remote fuel door and decklid releases.			
Clearcoat metallic paint	91	78	84
Premium sound system	138	117	127
Speed control	182	154	167
Tilt steering column	124	106	114
Polycast wheels	178	151	164

Prices are accurate at time of printing; subject to manufacturer's change.

	Retail Price	Dealer Invoice	Low Price
Decklid luggage rack	115	97	106
Power windows, 4-doors	296	252	272
AM/FM ST ET cassette, GS	137	116	126
AM/FM ST ET delete, GS (credit)	(245)	(208)	(208)
AM/FM cassette delete, XR5, LS, LTS . . .	(382)	(324)	(324)
Power driver's seat	251	214	231
Locking spoke wheel covers	212	180	195
California emissions pkg.	100	85	92

Ford Thunderbird/
Mercury Cougar

Ford Thunderbird LX

Ford's mid-size 2-door coupes are fully redesigned for 1989. They retain their rear-drive layout, but get an all-new body that's 3.4 inches shorter, 1.6 inches wider and almost an inch lower than its predecessor. The wheelbase has been stretched nine inches, and every cabin measurement has been increased versus the '88 model. Underneath is the T-Bird and Cougar's first all-independent suspension. No V-8 or 4-cylinder engines are offered this year. A 3.8-liter V-6 with a 4-speed automatic transmission is the only power-train available in base and LX Thunderbirds and in base (LS) Cougars. The new performance engine is a super-charged and intercooled version of the 3.8 V-6. It's available only in the T-Bird Super Coupe and Cougar XR7. Those models come standard with aero body flares and 4-wheel,

Prices are accurate at time of printing; subject to manufacturer's change.

Specifications

	2-door notchback
Wheelbase, in.	113.0
Overall length, in.	198.7
Overall width, in.	72.7
Overall height, in.	52.7
Turn diameter, ft.	35.6
Curb weight, lbs.	3542
Cargo vol., cu. ft.	14.7
Fuel capacity, gal.	19.0
Seating capacity	5
Front headroom, in.	38.1
Front shoulder room, in.	59.1
Front legroom, max., in.	42.5
Rear headroom, in.	37.5
Rear shoulder room, in.	59.1
Rear legroom, min., in.	35.9

Engines

	ohv V-6	Supercharged ohv V-6
Size, liters/cu. in.	3.8/232	3.8/232
Fuel delivery	PFI	PFI
Horsepower @ rpm	140 @ 3800	210 @ 4000
Torque (lbs./ft.) @ rpm	215 @ 2400	315 @ 2600
Availability	S	S[1]

EPA city/highway mpg

5-speed OD manual		NA
4-speed OD automatic	NA	NA

1. *Thunderbird Super Coupe, Cougar XR-7*

anti-lock disc brakes. Those brakes are optional on other Thunderbirds and Cougars in place of the standard front disc/rear drum set up. Wheels on base and performance models increase one inch in diameter, to 15- and 16-inches, respectively. Standard on the supercharged models is the Automatic Adjustable Suspension that allows the driver to adjust shock absorber damping for a soft or a firm ride. Speed-sensitive variable-assist power steering is standard on all but the base T-Bird. LS T-Birds and LX Cougars get digital instruments, including a tachometer; all others get analog gauges. SCs and XR7s have power front seats with adjustable backrest wings and inflatable lumbar bolsters. All models have air conditioning and power windows standard. Safety features include automatic front shoulder belts and shoulder belts for outboard rear-seat passengers. The SCs and XR7s also have split, folding rear seatbacks that open to the trunk for added cargo capacity. Ford separates its personal coupes from the Buick Regal, Oldsmobile Cutlass Supreme and Pontiac Grand Prix competitors via rear-drive layouts, lower and wider bodies and more powerful top-rung engines. Brief test-track drives showed the supercharged models to be quite fast. They suffered little of the power lag associated with turbocharged engines, though automatic transmission tended to dampen their responsiveness. Naturally aspirated versions were capable but sedate by comparison, and were far less at home in the corners. Inside, the added width and wheelbase is clearly evident, especially in the rear seat, which is now comfortable for three adults. The new Thunderbird and Cougar are scheduled to go on sale December 26, 1988. Our initial impressions are that styling and packaging make these cars more attractive than GM's front-drive rivals.

Equipment Summary

Ford Thunderbird
(prices not available at time of publication):

Standard Equipment:

3.8-liter PFI V-6, 4-speed automatic transmission, power steering and brakes, air conditioning, cloth reclining front bucket seats, tinted glass, power windows, intermittent wipers, dual remote mirrors, full-length console with armrest and storage bin, coolant temperature gauge, trip odometer, visor mirrors, AM/FM ST ET, 205/70R15 all-season tires. **LX** adds: power driver's seat, illuminated entry, remote fuel door and decklid releases, power locks, cruise control, maintenance monitor, power mirrors, folding rear armrest, electronic instruments, Light Group, lighted visor mirrors, AM/FM ST ET cassette, leather-wrapped steering wheel, tilt steering column, instrument panel storage compartment. **Super Coupe** adds to base: supercharged engine with dual exhaust, 5-speed manual transmission, 4-wheel disc brakes, anti-lock braking system, handling suspension, articulated sport seats, lower bodyside cladding, fog lights, analog instruments with tachometer, soft-feel steering wheel, remote fuel door release, maintenance monitor, power mirrors, folding rear armrest, Light Group, instrument panel storage compartment, 225/60VR16 tires on alloy wheels.

Mercury Cougar
(prices not available at time of publication):

Standard Equipment:

LS: 3.8-liter PFI V-6, 4-speed automatic transmission, power steering and brakes, air conditioning, cloth reclining front bucket seats, tinted glass, intermittent wipers, electronic instruments (tachometer, coolant temperature, oil pressure, voltmeter, trip computer, service interval reminder), power windows and mirrors, visor mirrors, AM/FM ST ET, motorized front shoulder belts with manual lap belts, outboard rear lap/shoulder belts, 205/70R15 tires. **XR7** adds: supercharged engine with dual exhaust, 5-speed manual transmission, 4-wheel disc brakes, anti-lock braking system, handling suspension, Traction-Lok axle, sport seats with power lumbar and side bolsters, analog instruments (tachometer, coolant temperature, oil pressure, boost/vacuum), maintenance monitor, 225/60VR16 tires on alloy wheels.

Geo Metro

Geo Metro LSi

The front-drive minicompact previously known as the Chevrolet Sprint has been restyled, renamed, and repositioned as part of Chevrolet's new Geo program. Geo models are either imported from Japan or built in North America from a Japanese design, and are sold through Chevy dealers with Geo franchises. Metro's styling now echoes that of the Honda Civic 3-door hatchback. Body styles include a 3-door and longer 5-door hatchback, though wheelbases and overall length are slightly longer. The base 3-door is the price- and fuel-economy leader, available only with a 5-speed manual transmission. Upscale LSi trim is available on both body styles with a choice of 5-speed manual or 3-speed automatic transmission. A revised 1.0-liter 3-cylinder engine with fuel injection instead of a carburetor produces 55 horsepower, seven more than last year's 1.0. The turbocharged model of previous years has been dropped. Other than the new name and a few more horses under the hood, Metro's main difference from Sprint is its attractive new styling, which should greatly enhance showroom appeal. Metro's main virtue is still fuel economy, which should stay around 40 mpg or above for most drivers. With the 5-speed, Metro is lively in the lower gears and easily keeps pace with traffic. Road noise and engine thrashing are very intrusive, however, and

Specifications

	3-door hatchback	5-door hatchback
Wheelbase, in.	89.2	93.2
Overall length, in.	146.3	150.4
Overall width, in.	62.0	62.7
Overall height, in.	52.4	53.5
Turn diameter, ft.	30.2	31.5
Curb weight, lbs.	1591	1640
Cargo vol., cu. ft.	29.1	31.4
Fuel capacity, gal.	10.6	10.6
Seating capacity	4	4
Front headroom, in.	37.8	38.8
Front shoulder room, in.	51.6	51.6
Front legroom, max., in.	42.5	42.5
Rear headroom, in.	36.6	38.0
Rear shoulder room, in.	50.5	50.6
Rear legroom, min., in.	29.8	32.6

Engines

	ohc I-3
Size, liters/cu. in.	1.0/61
Fuel delivery	TBI
Horsepower @ rpm	55 @ 5700
Torque (lbs./ft.) @ rpm	58 @ 3300
Availability	S

EPA city/highway mpg

5-speed OD manual	NA
3-speed automatic	NA

a short wheelbase and light curb weight puts ride comfort at the mercy of bumpy pavement. We're also leery of the crash protection cars this small provide. However, if low prices and high fuel economy are important to you, this is a good place to look.

Prices

Geo Metro	Retail Price	Dealer Invoice	Low Price
3-door hatchback	$5995	$5755	$5875
LSi 3-door hatchback	6895	6481	6688
LSi 5-door hatchback	7195	6763	6979
Destination charge	255	255	255

Standard Equipment:

1.0-liter TBI 3-cylinder engine, 5-speed manual transmission, power brakes, cloth/vinyl reclining bucket seats, rear lap/shoulder belts, coolant temperature gauge, 145/80R12 SBR tires. **LSi** adds: flush headlights, full cloth upholstery, bodyside molding, dual outside mirrors, full wheel covers.

Optional Equipment:

Air conditioning	655	576	616
AM/FM ST ET	301	265	283
AM/FM ST ET cassette	423	372	398
w/LSi w/Group 2 or 3	122	107	115
Preferred Group 2, base	140	123	132
Rear defogger.			
Preferred Group 2, LSi	476	419	447
Rear defogger, AM/FM ST ET cassette, intermittent wipers, rear wiper/washer.			
Preferred Group 3, LSi	896	788	842
Group 2 plus 3-speed automatic transmission.			
Console	25	22	24
Left remote and right manual mirrors . . .	20	18	19
Removable sunroof	250	220	235

Geo Spectrum

Last year's Chevrolet Spectrum line is trimmed to a single price series in front-drive 3-door hatchback and 4-door sedan guise. Other than the new Geo badging, the subcompact Spectrum is unchanged. It's sold through Chevrolet dealers

Prices are accurate at time of printing; subject to manufacturer's change.

Geo Spectrum

who have joined GM's new Geo program for marketing imports. Standard equipment is similar to that of last year's entry-level Express model. The turbocharged engine has been dropped, leaving a 1.5-liter 4-cylinder with a 2-barrel carburetor. A 5-speed manual is standard and a 3-speed automatic optional. Spectrum is built in Japan by Isuzu, which is partly owned by GM. Isuzu dealers sell a similar model as the I-Mark, which is offered with more engine choices. Spectrum and I-Mark will be redesigned for 1990; the Geo version will be renamed Storm and a sport model with I-Mark's optional 1.6-liter double-overhead cam engine will likely be added. Spectrum was supposed to give Chevy dealers a low-cost rival to the subcompacts offered by Nissan, Toyota and other Japanese dealers. But once you add options such as air conditioning, a stereo and automatic transmission, the cost is no longer low: nearly $10,000 for a Spectrum 4-door. At that price, Spectrum's weak, noisy engine and sluggish performance stand out as glaring drawbacks. For the same money, you can get a Mazda 323 with spunkier acceleration and comparable fuel economy, or for less money you can get a Dodge Omni/Plymouth Horizon or a Hyundai Excel. The new Geo program doesn't improve Spectrum's pricing, the performance and refinement are mediocre, and interior room and accommodations are nothing special. You can do better elsewhere.

Specifications

	3-door hatchback	4-door notchback
Wheelbase, in.	94.5	94.5
Overall length, in.	157.4	160.2
Overall width, in.	63.6	63.6
Overall height, in.	52.0	52.0
Turn diameter, ft.	34.8	34.8
Curb weight, lbs.	1947	1989
Cargo vol., cu. ft.	29.7	11.4
Fuel capacity, gal.	11.1	11.1
Seating capacity	5	5
Front headroom, in.	38.0	37.7
Front shoulder room, in.	52.8	52.8
Front legroom, max., in.	41.7	41.7
Rear headroom, in.	37.1	37.6
Rear shoulder room, in.	52.8	53.8
Rear legroom, min., in.	33.0	33.5

Engines

	ohc I-4
Size, liters/cu. in.	1.5/90
Fuel delivery	2 bbl.
Horsepower @ rpm	70 @ 5400
Torque (lbs./ft.) @ rpm	87 @ 3400
Availability	S

EPA city/highway mpg

5-speed OD manual	37/41
3-speed automatic	31/33

Prices

Geo Spectrum	Retail Price	Dealer Invoice	Low Price
4-door notchback	$7795	$7327	$7561
3-door hatchback	7295	6857	7076
Destination charge	315	315	315

Standard Equipment:

1.5-liter 2bbl. 4-cylinder engine, 5-speed manual transmission, power brakes, cloth/vinyl reclining front bucket seats, split folding rear seatback (hatchback), left remote mirror, center console with storage, headlamps-on tone, coolant temperature gauge, 155/80R13 SBR tires.

Optional Equipment:

Air conditioning	660	614	637
AM/FM ST ET	301	280	290

Prices are accurate at time of printing; subject to manufacturer's change.

	Retail Price	Dealer Invoice	Low Price
AM/FM ST ET cassette	423	393	408
Sound system prices vary with option package content.			
Preferred Group 2	421	392	406
Floormats, remote mirrors, AM/FM ST ET, full wheel covers.			
Preferred Group 3	634	590	612
Power steering, 3-speed automatic transmission.			
Preferred Group 4	1055	981	1018
Group 3 plus floormats, remote mirrors, AM/FM ST ET, full wheel covers.			
Cargo area cover	69	64	67
Floormats	25	23	24
Remote mirrors	43	40	41
Cruise control	175	163	169
Bodyside striping	53	49	51

Honda Accord

Honda Accord DX Coupe

The SEi, a luxury version of the Accord sedan, is the only addition to Honda's line of front-drive compacts, which are due for a full redesign for 1990. The '89 roster retains 2-door coupe, 3-door hatchback and 4-door sedan body styles. All coupes and some sedans are built at Honda's plant in Marysville, Ohio. DX and LX Accords use a carbureted 2.0-liter 4-cylinder engine. Plusher LXi and the new SEi variations get a fuel-injected version of the 2.0. A 5-speed manual transmission and a 4-speed automatic are available with either engine. The SEi has LXi equipment, plus the line's first 4-wheel disc brakes. Redesigned seats with leather trim, special alloy wheels and a high-power Bose stereo are among SEi features. All automatic-transmission Accords

Specifications

	2-door notchback	3-door hatchback	4-door notchback
Wheelbase, in.	102.4	102.4	102.4
Overall length, in.	179.1	174.8	179.7
Overall width, in.	66.7	66.7	67.4
Overall height, in.	52.6	52.6	53.4
Turn diameter, ft.	34.1	34.8	34.8
Curb weight, lbs.	2493	2513	2482
Cargo vol., cu. ft.	14.3	18.9	13.7
Fuel capacity, gal.	15.9	15.9	15.9
Seating capacity	5	5	5
Front headroom, in.	37.9	38.0	38.7
Front shoulder room, in.	54.5	54.5	54.9
Front legroom, max., in.	42.9	42.8	42.8
Rear headroom, in.	36.6	36.6	37.1
Rear shoulder room, in.	53.3	53.1	54.5
Rear legroom, min., in.	30.9	30.2	32.4

Engines

	ohc I-4	ohc I-4
Size, liters/cu. in.	2.0/119	2.0/119
Fuel delivery	2 bbl.	PFI
Horsepower @ rpm	98 @ 5500	120 @ 5800
Torque (lbs./ft.) @ rpm	109 @ 3500	122 @ 4000
Availability	S[1]	S[2]

EPA city/highway mpg

5-speed OD manual	27/34	25/30
4-speed OD automatic	23/30	22/28

1. DX, LX   2. LXi

get a shift-lock mechanism for '89. It requires the driver to apply the brakes when shifting from park into drive or reverse. And all Hondas get a rear-defroster timer this year and a basic warranty upped from 12 months/12,000 miles to 36 months/36,000 miles. The '90 Accord will be about six inches longer and somewhat wider than the present model, and may have an optional V-6 engine. A sales winner since its 1986 debut, the third-generation Accord is the class of the compact class, though some rivals, notably the Mazda 626 and Toyota Camry, are closing the gap. Still, Accord is an outstanding all-around family car buy. Attractions include decent room for four, adequate cargo space, a comfortable driving position, superb outward vision, exemplary workmanship and good fuel economy.

Prices

Honda Accord	Retail Price	Dealer Invoice	Low Price
DX 3-door hatchback, 5-speed	$11230	$9433	$10730
DX 3-door hatchback, automatic	11840	9945	11340
LXi 3-door hatchback, 5-speed	14530	12205	14030
LXi 3-door hatchback, automatic	15140	12717	14640
DX 2-door notchback, 5-speed	11650	9786	11450
DX 2-door notchback, automatic	12260	10298	12060
LXi 2-door notchback, 5-speed	14690	12339	14490
LXi 2-door notchback, automatic	15300	12852	15100
DX 4-door notchback, 5-speed	11770	9886	11570
DX 4-door notchback, automatic	12380	10399	12180
LX 4-door notchback, 5-speed	14180	11911	13980
LX 4-door notchback, automatic	14790	12423	14590
LXi 4-door notchback, 5-speed	15920	13372	15720
LXi 4-door notchback, automatic	16530	13885	16330
SEi 4-door notchback, 5-speed	NA	NA	NA
SEi 4-door notchback, automatic	NA	NA	NA
Destination charge	245	245	245

Standard Equipment:

DX: 2.0-liter 2bbl. 4-cylinder engine, 5-speed manual or 4-speed automatic transmission, power steering, cloth reclining front bucket seats, tilt steering column, digital clock, remote fuel door and trunk/hatch releases, cruise control (4-door), tinted glass, rear wiper/washer (3-door), bodyside molding, 185/70R14 tires. **LX** adds: air conditioning, power windows and locks, power mirrors, AM/FM ST ET cassette, one-piece folding rear seatback. **LXi** adds: PFI engine, driver's seat lumbar support adjustment, power moonroof, 50/50 folding rear seatbacks, Michelin MXV 195/60R14 tires on alloy wheels; 2- and 3-door delete power locks. **SEi** adds: 4-wheel disc brakes, leather upholstery, bronze tinted glass, front center armrest, cup holder.

OPTIONS are available as dealer-installed accessories.

Honda Civic

Completely redesigned for 1988, these slick subcompacts return largely unchanged for '89, though the sporty Si hatchback is reintroduced. Front-drive Civics come as 3-door hatchbacks, 4-door sedans and 5-door wagons; Honda's auto-

Prices are accurate at time of printing; subject to manufacturer's change.

Honda Civic Si

matically engaged 4WD system is available on the wagon. The Si hatchback, which sat out the '88 model year, returns with the 108-horsepower 16-valve 1.6-liter 4-cylinder engine that's used in the 2-seat CRX Si. It has sports seats, gas-filled shock absorbers, a power sunroof and a mandatory 5-speed manual transmission. It's the only Civic with 14-inch tires (others have 13s) and the only hatchback with a tachometer. The base Civic hatchback comes with a 70-horsepower 1.5-liter four and 4-speed manual transmission only. A 92-horsepower 1.5-liter four is standard on the DX hatchbacks, DX and LX sedans, and the 2WD wagon. It's teamed with either a 5-speed manual or a 4-speed automatic. The 4WD wagon uses the Civic Si engine and comes with either a 6-speed manual transmission or, for the first time, a 4-speed automatic. Power steering is standard on LX sedans and 4WD wagons and on automatic-transmission DX models and the 2WD wagon. Honda warranties increase from 12 months/12,000 miles to 36 months/36,000 miles this year. Civics blend thoughtful design, inside and out, with precision workmanship. They're not fast—though the new Si should be quick—but their spunky engines rev willingly and, when equipped with the fine 5-speed, they're downright fun to drive. The automatic robs the engine of much of its responsiveness. The cabins accommodate four adults, but the ride can be harsh over bumps and the manual steering a chore for parking. Demand is high so prices are steep, but some dealers may be willing to part with base and DX hatchbacks and sedans at reasonable sums.

Specifications

	3-door hatchback	4-door notchback	5-door wagon
Wheelbase, in.	98.4	98.4	98.4
Overall length, in.	156.1	166.5	161.6
Overall width, in.	65.6	65.9	66.1
Overall height, in.	52.4	53.5	57.9
Turn diameter, ft.	31.5	31.5	31.5
Curb weight, lbs.	1933	2039	2130[1]
Cargo vol., cu. ft.	25.0	12.2	60.3
Fuel capacity, gal.	11.9	11.9	11.9
Seating capacity	5	5	5
Front headroom, in.	38.2	38.5	39.4
Front shoulder room, in.	53.5	53.5	53.5
Front legroom, max., in.	43.3	43.1	41.2
Rear headroom, in.	36.6	37.4	38.0
Rear shoulder room, in.	53.2	53.0	53.5
Rear legroom, min., in.	30.4	32.0	33.3

1. 2366 lbs., 4WD wagon

Engines

	ohc I-4	ohc I-4	ohc I-4
Size, liters/cu. in.	1.5/91	1.5/91	1.6/97
Fuel delivery	TBI	TBI	PFI
Horsepower @ rpm	70 @ 5500	92 @ 6000	108 @ 6000
Torque (lbs./ft.) @ rpm	83 @ 3000	89 @ 4500	100 @ 5000
Availability	S[1]	S[2]	S[3]

EPA city/highway mpg

4-speed OD manual	34/38		
5-speed OD manual		31/36	28/33
4-speed OD automatic		27/32	24/27

1. Civic Hatchback   2. DX, LX, 2WD wagon   3. Si, 4WD wagon

Prices

Honda Civic	Retail Price	Dealer Invoice	Low Price
3-door hatchback, 4-speed	$6385	$5746	$6035
DX 3-door hatchback, 5-speed	8445	7178	8095
DX 3-door hatchback, automatic	9295	7900	8945
Si 3-door hatchback, 5-speed	9980	8483	9630
DX 4-door notchback, 5-speed	9190	7811	8990
DX 4-door notchback, automatic	10090	8576	9890
LX 4-door notchback, 5-speed	10150	8627	9950
LX 4-door notchback, automatic	10720	9112	10520
5-door wagon, 5-speed	10125	8606	9775

Prices are accurate at time of printing; subject to manufacturer's change.

	Retail Price	Dealer Invoice	Low Price
5-door wagon, automatic	11140	9469	10790
4WD 5-door wagon, 6-speed	12210	10378	11860
4WD 5-door wagon, automatic	12810	10888	12460
Destination charge	245	245	245

Standard Equipment:

1.5-liter SOHC 16-valve PFI 4-cylinder engine, 4-speed manual transmission, reclining front bucket seats, left remote mirror, 50/50 folding rear seatbacks, trip odometer, coolant temperature gauge, rear defogger, remote fuel door and hatch releases, bodyside moldings, 165/70SR13 tires. **DX** adds: 5-speed manual or 4-speed automatic transmission, power steering (on 4-door with automatic transmission), rear wiper/washer (3-door), tilt steering column (3-door), tinted glass, remote hatch release (3-door), intermittent wipers (3-door), 175/70R13 tires; Si has 1.6-liter engine, uprated suspension, sport seats, power sunroof, tachometer, remote mirrors, 185/60R14 tires. **LX** adds to DX: power steering, tachometer, power mirrors, tilt steering column, power windows and locks, one-piece folding rear seatback, rear head restraints, remote trunklid release. **2WD wagon** has tilt steering column, 60/40 folding rear seatbacks, rear head restraints, rear wiper/washer, intermittent wipers, tinted glass, remote liftgate release, 175/70R13 tires. **4WD wagon** adds: 1.6-liter engine, 6-speed manual or 4-speed automatic transmission, storage drawer under passenger seat, 165SR13 tires. Si has higher-output engine, uprated suspension, sport seats, power sunroof.

OPTIONS are available as dealer-installed accessories.

Honda CRX

Like the related Civics, Honda's 2-seat CRX coupes were redesigned for '88 and return almost unchanged for '89. The redesign brought more horsepower, all-independent suspension and a longer, wider body. Three front-drive models continue. The HF (high fuel economy) uses an 8-valve, 63-horsepower 1.5-liter 4-cylinder engine. The midrange CRX gets a 16-valve, 92-horsepower 1.5 and is the only model available with automatic transmission. The CRX Si has a 16-valve 1.6-liter four that gets three additional horsepower this year, to 108. The Si also has a standard power sunroof, a stiffer suspension and 14-inch-diameter tires, versus 13s on other models. For '89, all CRXs except the HF get seat and shoulder belts that can be left buckled to wrap automatical-

Prices are accurate at time of printing; subject to manufacturer's change.

Honda CRX Si

Specifications

	3-door hatchback
Wheelbase, in.	90.6
Overall length, in.	147.8
Overall width, in.	65.7
Overall height, in.	50.0
Turn diameter, ft.	29.5
Curb weight, lbs.	1819[1]
Cargo vol., cu. ft.	23.2
Fuel capacity, gal.	11.9[2]
Seating capacity	2
Front headroom, in.	37.0
Front shoulder room, in.	53.5
Front legroom, max., in.	43.9
Rear headroom, in.	—
Rear shoulder room, in.	—
Rear legroom, min., in.	—

1. CRX HF; 1992 lbs., CRX; 2017 lbs. CRX Si.   2. 10.6 gals. CRX HF

Engines

	ohc I-4	ohc I-4	ohc I-4
Size, liters/cu. in.	1.5/91	1.5/91	1.6/97
Fuel delivery	PFI	TBI	PFI
Horsepower @ rpm	62 @ 4500	92 @ 6000	108 @ 6000
Torque (lbs./ft.) @ rpm	90 @ 2000	89 @ 4500	100 @ 5000
Availability	S[1]	S[2]	S[3]

EPA city/highway mpg

5-speed OD manual	45/52	34/41	28/33
4-speed OD automatic		29/36	

1. CRX HF   2. CRX   3. CRX Si

ly around front-seat occupants when the doors are closed. The mid-line CRX also gets a standard rear-window wiper. Warranties on all Hondas increase this year to 36 months/36,000 miles, up from last year's 12 months/12,000 miles. If a practical, sporty, low-cost, economical car is what you seek, and you don't need more than two seats, there's no better choice. The Si has true sports-car moves. The front tires spin too easily in hard acceleration and the ride is brutally stiff over bad pavement. But the slick 5-speed, precise steering and sharp handling are very rewarding. The mid-level CRX is only slightly less feisty and benefits from a ride that's not as stiff. The HF gets great fuel economy, but more practical designs come close to its mileage. Automatic transmission plain wastes the CRX's spirit.

Prices

Honda CRX	Retail Price	Dealer Invoice	Low Price
HF 3-door hatchback, 5-speed	$8895	$7560	$8395
3-door hatchback, 5-speed	9310	7913	8810
3-door hatchback, automatic	9880	8398	9380
Si 3-door hatchback, 5-speed	10930	9290	10430
Destination charge	245	245	245

Standard Equipment:

HF: 1.5-liter 8-valve PFI 4-cylinder engine, 5-speed manual transmission, reclining front bucket seats, left remote mirror, tinted glass, tachometer, coolant temperature gauge, trip odometer, intermittent wipers, rear defogger, remote fuel door and hatch releases, bodyside moldings, 165/70R13 tires. **CRX adds:** 1.5-liter SOHC 16-valve PFI engine (92 bhp), tilt steering column, dual remote mirrors, digital clock, cargo cover. **Si adds:** 105-bhp PFI engine, uprated suspension, rear wiper/washer, 185/60HR14 tires on alloy wheels.

OPTIONS are available as dealer-installed accessories.

Honda Prelude

Honda redesigned its Prelude last year and renews it with only minor changes for '89. The base S continues with a 104-horsepower 2.0-liter overhead-cam 4-cylinder engine with 12 valves and dual sidedraft carburetors. It gets cruise

Honda Prelude Si

Specifications

	2-door notchback
Wheelbase, in.	101.0
Overall length, in.	175.6
Overall width, in.	67.3
Overall height, in.	51.0
Turn diameter, ft.	34.8[1]
Curb weight, lbs.	2522
Cargo vol., cu. ft.	11.2
Fuel capacity, gal.	15.9
Seating capacity	4
Front headroom, in.	36.9
Front shoulder room, in.	53.1
Front legroom, max., in.	43.1
Rear headroom, in.	34.1
Rear shoulder room, in.	51.1
Rear legroom, min., in.	27.1

1. 31.4 ft. on 4WS

Engines

	ohc I-4	dohc I-4
Size, liters/cu. in.	2.0/119	2.0/119
Fuel delivery	2 × 1 bbl.	PFI
Horsepower @ rpm	104 @ 5800	135 @ 6200
Torque (lbs./ft.) @ rpm	111 @ 4000	127 @ 4500
Availability	S	S[1]

EPA city/highway mpg

	ohc I-4	dohc I-4
5-speed OD manual	23/28	23/26
4-speed OD automatic	20/26	21/26

1. Si

control and body-colored bumpers as standard for '89. The Si has a 135-horsepower 2.0-liter four with 16 valves, dual overhead camshafts and fuel injection. It has 14-inch wheels in place of the S's 13s. A 5-speed manual transmission is standard. Optional is a 4-speed automatic with a driver-selective "sport" mode for improved acceleration. Prelude is one of two cars offered in the U.S. with optional 4-wheel steering (the other is the Mazda MX-6 GT 4WS). Available only on the Si, Honda's 4WS mechanically links front and rear steering boxes. It steers the rear wheels a few degrees left or right depending on the angle of the steering wheel and is designed to improve handling and maneuverability. The turning diameter is 31.5 feet for the 4WS model, versus 34.8 feet for other Preludes. For '89, 4WS models get polished alloy wheels and a rear-deck spoiler. A top-notch car became subtly better with the '88 redesign, but the Prelude is close to being priced out of its league, which is still sporty coupe, not sports and GT. The flagship Si 4WS goes for more than $19,000 with automatic, while a 5-speed Prelude S is some $5000 cheaper. For our money, the S's carbureted engine is sufficient, and automatic transmission robs the car of much of its verve. And we don't believe the added maneuverability of 4WS justifies its extra cost, weight or complexity. Any Prelude is an somewhat rough-riding but agile coupe. The feel is typically Honda, and that means an efficiency of design and a pleasing mechanical smoothness.

Prices

Honda Prelude	Retail Price	Dealer Invoice	Low Price
S 2-door notchback, 5-speed	$13945	$11713	$13445
S 2-door notchback, automatic	14670	12322	14170
Si 2-door notchback, 5-speed	16965	14250	16465
Si 2-door notchback, automatic	17690	14859	17190
Si 4WS 2-door notchback, 5-speed	18450	15498	17950
Si 4WS 2-door notchback, automatic	19175	16107	18675
Destination charge	245	245	245

Standard Equipment:

S: 2.0-liter 12-valve carbureted 4-cylinder engine, 5-speed manual or 4-speed automatic transmission, power steering, power 4-wheel disc brakes, cloth reclining front bucket seats, cloth trim, tilt steering column, console, AM/FM ST ET cassette, power antenna, door-mounted passive lap and shoulder

Prices are accurate at time of printing; subject to manufacturer's change.

belts, tachometer, coolant temperature gauge, trip odometer, intermittent wipers, 185/70HR13 tires. **Si** adds: DOHC 16-valve PFI engine, air conditioning, cruise control, adjustable lumbar support and side bolsters, diversity antenna, 195/60HR14 tires. **Si 4WS** adds: 4-wheel steering, power door locks, bronze tinted glass, alloy wheels.

OPTIONS are available as dealer-installed accessories.

Hyundai Excel/ Mitsubishi Precis

Hyundai Excel GS 3-door

These front-drive subcompact siblings return with very minor alterations for '89. Hyundai, a South Korean firm, builds the Excel using an engine, transmission and mechanical design purchased from the Japanese automaker Mitsubishi. Excel's design is based on a previous-generation Mitsubishi Mirage (which was also sold through Dodge and Plymouth dealers as the Colt). With exterior and interior styling by Hyundai, Excel has become this country's best-selling import nameplate since its 1986 U.S. introduction. Mitsubishi added the car to its lineup in 1987. Importing Precis from Korea, where wages and production costs are lower than in Japan, allows Mitsubishi to offer a less-expensive alternative to its new Mirage. The Hyundai comes as a 3- or 5-door hatchback or as a 4-door notchback; Mitsubishi uses the hatchback body style only. Both are powered by a

68-horsepower 1.5-liter 4-cylinder engine. Transmission choices are 4- and 5-speed manuals and a 3-speed automatic. The major change for the Excel is a new 36-month/36,000-mile basic warranty in place of the previous 12-month/12,500-mile plan. For the Precis, an audible wear indicator warning has been added to the front disc brakes. And mirroring the interior furnishings of the Excel, all Precis except the base model gain a new center console, center armrest and velour upholstery. Hyundai's extraordinary success with the Excel is mainly because of its low base price, though astute marketing also has helped. About the only car that matches the Excel or Precis in price and value-per-dollar is the Dodge Omni/Plymouth Horizon.

Specifications

	3-door hatchback	4-door notchback	5-door hatchback
Wheelbase, in.	93.7	93.7	93.7
Overall length, in.	161.0	168.0	161.0
Overall width, in.	63.1	63.1	63.1
Overall height, in.	54.1	54.1	54.1
Turn diameter, ft.	33.8	33.8	33.8
Curb weight, lbs.	2156	2156	2178
Cargo vol., cu. ft.	26.6	11.2	26.0
Fuel capacity, gal.	10.6[1]	10.6[1]	10.6[1]
Seating capacity	5	5	5
Front headroom, in.	37.5	37.5	37.5
Front shoulder room, in.	52.1	52.1	52.1
Front legroom, max., in.	40.9	40.9	40.9
Rear headroom, in.	36.9	36.9	36.9
Rear shoulder room, in.	51.6	51.6	51.6
Rear legroom, min., in.	32.4	32.4	32.4

1. 13.2 gals. on GLS with automatic

Engines

	ohc I-4
Size, liters/cu. in.	1.5/90
Fuel delivery	2 bbl.
Horsepower @ rpm	68 @ 5500
Torque (lbs./ft.) @ rpm	82 @ 3500
Availability	S

EPA city/highway mpg

4-speed manual	27/33
5-speed OD manual	28/37
3-speed automatic	27/31

The Excel and Precis are little more than basic transportation, but at that they are competent. Among the pluses is a proven mechanical design; negatives include a small interior and dealers who routinely pile on options until these entry-level cars lose their entry-level price.

Prices

Hyundai Excel	Retail Price	Dealer Invoice	Low Price
3-door hatchback, 4-speed	$5499	—	—
GL 3-door hatchback, 5-speed	6699	—	—
GL 3-door hatchback, automatic	7184	—	—
GS 3-door hatchback, 5-speed	7699	—	—
GS 3-door hatchback, automatic	8184	—	—
GL 5-door hatchback, 5-speed	6949	—	—
GL 5-door hatchback, automatic	7434	—	—
GLS 5-door hatchback, 5-speed	7599	—	—
GLS 5-door hatchback, automatic	8084	—	—
4-door notchback, 4-speed	6199	—	—
GL 4-door notchback, 5-speed	7149	—	—
GL 4-door notchback, automatic	7634	—	—
GLS 4-door notchback, 5-speed	7749	—	—
GLS 4-door notchback, automatic	8234	—	—
Destination charge	255	255	255

Dealer invoice and low price not available at time of publication.

Standard Equipment:

1.5-liter 2bbl. 4-cylinder engine, 4-speed manual transmission, power brakes, cloth and vinyl reclining front bucket seats, variable intermittent wipers, coolant temperature gauge, graphic display, rear defogger, locking fuel filler door, split folding rear seat, rear-seat heat ducts, 155/80R13 all-season SBR tires with full-size spare. **GL** adds: 5-speed manual or 3-speed automatic transmission, cloth trim, dual remote mirrors, analog clock, tinted glass, rear wiper/washer (hatchbacks), remote fuel door and hatch/trunk releases, full center console, bodyside moldings, wheel covers. **GLS** adds: cloth headliner, windshield sunshade band, digital clock, driver's seat height and lumbar support adjustments, tachometer, underseat tray (4- and 5-doors), full cloth seats, AM/FM ST ET cassette, upgraded carpeting, visor mirror. **GS** adds: front sport seats, P175/70R13 tires on alloy wheels.

Optional Equipment:

Air conditioning	735	—	—
5 175/70R13 tires on alloy wheels	325	—	—

Prices are accurate at time of printing; subject to manufacturer's change.

	Retail Price	Dealer Invoice	Low Price
Excel Option Pkg.	175	—	—
Right outside mirror, tinted glass, bodyside molding.			
Passive restraint system	75	—	—
Power steering	260	—	—
AM/FM ST cassette (std. GLS)	295	—	—
Panasonic AM/FM ST ET cassette, GL . . .	430	—	—
GLS	135	—	—
Power sunroof	395	—	—
Two-tone paint	125	—	—

Mitsubishi Precis

	Retail Price	Dealer Invoice	Low Price
3-door hatchback, 4-speed	$5499	—	—
RS 3-door hatchback, 5-speed	6699	—	—
LS 3-door hatchback, 5-speed	7349	—	—
LS 3-door hatchback, automatic	7839	—	—
LS 5-door hatchback, 5-speed	7599	—	—
LS 5-door hatchback, automatic	8089	—	—
Destination charge	265	265	265

Dealer invoice and low price not available at time of publication.

Standard Equipment:

1.5-liter 2bbl. 4-cylinder engine, 4-speed manual transmission, power brakes, vinyl reclining front bucket seats, folding rear seatbacks, cargo cover, variable intermittent wipers, rear defogger, rear heat ducts, trip odometer, coolant temperature gauge, low fuel and door/hatch ajar warning lights, locking fuel door, 155/80R13 all-season tires with full-size spare. **RS** adds: 5-speed manual transmission, cloth trim, upgraded door panels with map pockets, console, analog clock, wide bodyside moldings, remote fuel door and hatch releases, rear wiper/washer, dual remote mirrors, tinted glass. **LS** adds: 5-speed manual or 3-speed automatic transmission, tachometer, digital clock, upgraded steering wheel, storage tray under front passenger seat (5-door), right visor mirror, AM/FM ST ET cassette, dark upper windshield band, roll-down rear windows (5-door), wheel covers, 175/70R13 all-season tires.

Optional Equipment:

Air conditioning (NA base)	735	—	—
AM/FM ST ET cassette, base & RS	295	—	—
High Power, LS	135	—	—
High Power, RS	565	—	—
Passive restraint, LS 5-door	75	—	—
Alloy Wheel Pkg., LS	295	—	—
Power steering, LS	260	—	—
Power sunroof, LS	395	—	—

Prices are accurate at time of printing; subject to manufacturer's change.

Hyundai Sonata

Hyundai Sonata

On the strength of just one model, the subcompact Excel,
Hyundai has become the fourth largest importer, behind
Toyota, Honda and Nissan. In November 1988, it adds a
larger car to its U.S. lineup, the Sonata. Like Excel, the
front-drive Sonata is built in Korea. At 184.3 inches overall,
Sonata is nearly two feet longer than Excel. Wheelbase is
104.3 inches, one to two inches longer than compacts such
as the Honda Accord, Toyota Camry and Chevrolet Corsica,
but an inch or two shorter than mid-size domestics such as
the Ford Taurus and Chevrolet Celebrity. At 68.9 inches
wide, Sonata also falls between contemporary compacts and
intermediates. Base curb weight is about 2750 pounds. Available only as a 4-door notchback sedan, Sonata was styled by
Italian designer Giorgio Giugiaro, who also did the Excel.
Unlike the Excel, which relies mainly on Mitsubishi mechanical components, Sonata's engineering is mostly by
Hyundai's own staff. An exception is the engine, which is
licensed by Mitsubishi. The U.S. Sonata will use a fuel-
injected 4-cylinder engine in the 2.0- to 2.4-liter range; this
engine likely will be related to the 2.4-liter engine used in the
1985-87 Mitsubishi Galant sedan and the current Mitsubishi Wagon/Van. An electronically controlled 4-speed overdrive automatic transmission will be offered. We haven't
driven Sonata, so we can't comment on its performance.

Specifications and prices not available at time of publication.

CONSUMER GUIDE®

Isuzu I-Mark

Isuzu I-Mark RS

Isuzu's front-drive subcompact gets a new double-overhead cam, 16-valve 1.6-liter engine. The new 4-cylinder produces 125 horsepower and comes only with a 5-speed manual transmission in sporty 3- and 5-door RS versions of I-Mark. The RS debuted last spring with a suspension tuned by Lotus, the British sports car company now owned by General Motors. The I-Mark LS 4-door also has the Lotus-tuned suspension, but uses a 110-horsepower, turbocharged 1.5-liter four, also available only with a 5-speed. Base I-Mark S and higher-priced XS hatchbacks and sedans return for 1989 with a 70-horsepower, carbureted 1.5-liter four and are available with either a 5-speed manual or 3-speed automatic transmission. GM owns part of Isuzu and sells a version of the I-Mark through Chevrolet dealers as the Geo Spectrum. While Isuzu is pushing ahead with a performance image this year for I-Mark, Chevrolet has dropped the turbocharged engine from Spectrum and will not get the new twin-cam engine for 1989. A new Sunsport option for the I-Mark S 3-door includes an electric canvas sunroof with built-in air deflector, body color mirrors, wheel covers and front bumper, and cloth sport seats. We haven't driven the RS with its new double-overhead-cam engine or tried the Lotus suspension, but both the I-Mark's turbocharged engine and its base engine generate too much noise for peaceful motoring, though the turbo justifies is racket with good power. The base engine is quite economical, but lags well behind the 1.5-liter engines offered by Honda and Toyota.

Specifications

	3-door hatchback	4-door notchback
Wheelbase, in.	94.5	94.5
Overall length, in.	157.9	160.7
Overall width, in.	63.6	63.6
Overall height, in.	54.1	54.1
Turn diameter, ft.	32.8	32.8
Curb weight, lbs.	1984	2011
Cargo vol., cu. ft.	29.7	11.4
Fuel capacity, gal.	11.1	11.1
Seating capacity	5	5
Front headroom, in.	38.0	37.7
Front shoulder room, in.	52.8	52.8
Front legroom, max., in.	41.7	41.7
Rear headroom, in.	37.1	37.6
Rear shoulder room, in.	52.8	52.8
Rear legroom, min., in.	33.3	33.5

Engines

	ohc I-4	Turbo ohc I-4	dohc I-4
Size, liters/cu. in.	1.5/90	1.5/90	1.6/97
Fuel delivery	2 bbl.	PFI	PFI
Horsepower @ rpm	70 @ 5400	110 @ 5400	125 @ 6800
Torque (lbs./ft.) @ rpm	87 @ 3400	120 @ 3500	102 @ 5400
Availability	S[1]	S[2]	S[3]

EPA city/highway mpg

5-speed OD manual	37/41	26/34	24/32
3-speed automatic	31/33		

1. S, XS   2. LS   3. RS

Prices

Isuzu I-Mark	Retail Price	Dealer Invoice	Low Price
S 4-door notchback, 5-speed	$8179	$7362	$7771
S 4-door notchback, automatic	8609	7732	8171
S 3-door hatchback, 5-speed	7779	7002	7391
S 3-door hatchback, automatic	8209	7372	7791
XS 4-door notchback, 5-speed	9379	8160	8770
XS 4-door notchback, automatic	9809	8530	9170
XS 3-door hatchback, 5-speed	9179	7986	8583
XS 3-door hatchback, automatic	9609	8356	8983
RS DOHC 4-door notchback, 5-speed	9559	8317	8938
RS DOHC 3-door hatchback, 5-speed	9359	8143	8751

Prices are accurate at time of printing; subject to manufacturer's change.

	Retail Price	Dealer Invoice	Low Price
LS Turbo 4-door notchback, 5-speed	11369	9892	10631
Destination charge	259	259	259

Standard Equipment:

S: 1.5-liter 2bbl. 4-cylinder engine, 5-speed manual or 3-speed automatic transmission, cloth reclining front bucket seats, split folding rear seat (3-door), rear defogger, console, tinted glass, left remote mirror, trip odometer, 155/80R13 all-season SBR tires. **XS** adds: power steering, tilt steering column, tachometer, cargo cover (3-door), digital clock, fog lights, remote fuel door and trunk/hatch releases, power mirrors, split folding rear seat (4-door), rear wiper/washer (3-door), 175/70R13 all-season SBR tires on alloy wheels. **RS DOHC** adds: 1.6-liter DOHC 16-valve PFI 4-cylinder engine, coolant temperature and oil pressure gauges, voltmeter, remote manual mirrors, AM/FM ST ET cassette, leather-wrapped steering wheel, 185/60R14 all-season SBR tires. **LS Turbo** adds: 1.5-liter turbocharged PFI 4-cylinder engine, removable sunroof, AM/FM ST ET cassette with EQ.

Optional Equipment:

Power steering, S	250	212	231
Air conditioning	680	578	629
Recaro Pkg., RS	1200	1044	1122
Recaro front seats, leather-wrapped steering wheel, oil pressure gauge, voltmeter, removable sunroof.			
Sunsport Pkg., S 3-door	1200	1080	1140
Power canvas sunroof, full wheel covers, right manual mirror, upgraded interior trim.			
Cruise control, XS	195	160	178
Carpet mats	50	35	43
AM/FM ST, S & XS	185	130	158
AM/FM ET cassette, XS	410	287	349
Sunroof, XS	300	240	270

Isuzu Impulse

The rear-drive Impulse sport coupe carries on for its final year with refinements and minor equipment changes, including new body-colored bumpers. Last year Impulse gained new suspension components and tires selected by Lotus, the British car company now owned by General Motors. Like this year's I-Mark, Impulse carries "Handling by Lotus" badges to note the British firm's influence. Base engine remains a 110-horsepower 2.3-liter 4-cylinder engine, while Turbo models have a 140-horsepower, turbocharged

Prices are accurate at time of printing; subject to manufacturer's change.

Isuzu Impulse Turbo

Specifications

	3-door hatchback
Wheelbase, in.	96.1
Overall length, in.	172.6
Overall width, in.	65.2
Overall height, in.	51.4
Turn diameter, ft.	31.5
Curb weight, lbs.	2727
Cargo vol., cu. ft.	29.4
Fuel capacity, gal.	15.1
Seating capacity	4
Front headroom, in.	36.9
Front shoulder room, in.	54.5
Front legroom, max., in.	41.9
Rear headroom, in.	35.8
Rear shoulder room, in.	54.0
Rear legroom, min., in.	28.1

Engines

	ohc I-4	Turbo ohc I-4
Size, liters/cu. in.	2.3/137	2.0/122
Fuel delivery	PFI	PFI
Horsepower @ rpm	110 @ 5000	140 @ 5400
Torque (lbs./ft.) @ rpm	127 @ 3000	166 @ 3000
Availability	S	S

EPA city/highway mpg

5-speed OD manual	20/26	21/27
4-speed OD automatic	20/26	20/26

2.0-liter 4-cylinder. Both are available with a 5-speed manual or a 4-speed overdrive automatic. Styled in Italy by Giorgio Giugiaro and built in Japan, Impulse debuted in the U.S. in 1983. The slow-selling coupe has humble origins: a chassis distantly related to that of the discontinued Chevrolet Chevette. It took a few years, but Isuzu has finally imbued Impulse with the performance to go with its good looks. The potent turbo engine's boost comes on smoothly and provides fine performance across a broad range of engine speeds. It sounds strained and thrashy above 3000 rpm, though, which discourages the higher revs needed to tap its full power potential. The Lotus-tuned suspension trades ride comfort for impressive cornering ability. The car feels jittery on rough pavement and the rear tires lose traction in bumpy turns. The cabin is well furnished, but sporty-coupe typical in its lack of head room and a token rear seat.

Prices

Isuzu Impulse	Retail Price	Dealer Invoice	Low Price
Standard 3-door hatchback, 5-speed	$14829	$12323	$13576
Standard 3-door hatchback, automatic . . .	14869	12787	13828
Turbo 3-door hatchback, 5-speed	16329	14043	15186
Turbo 3-door hatchback, automatic	16869	14507	15688
Destination charge	259	259	259

Standard Equipment:

Standard: 2.3-liter PFI 4-cylinder engine, 5-speed manual or 4-speed automatic transmission, power steering, 4-wheel disc brakes, cloth reclining front bucket seats, split folding rear seat with recliners, air conditioning, power windows and locks, cruise control, tachometer, trip odometer, digital clock, rear defogger and wiper/washer, remote fuel door and hatch releases, tinted glass, tilt steering column, power mirrors, right visor mirror, cargo cover, AM/FM ST ET, power antenna, removable sunroof, variable intermittent wipers, 205/60R14 all-season SBR tires on alloy wheels. **Turbo** adds: 2.0-liter turbocharged, intercooled engine, front air dam, AM/FM ST ET cassette with EQ, 7-way driver's seat, leather-wrapped steering wheel, theft deterrent system.

Optional Equipment:

Carpet mats	50	35	43

Prices are accurate at time of printing; subject to manufacturer's change.

Lincoln Continental

Lincoln Continental Signature Series

The all-new 1988 Continental was the first Lincoln with front-wheel drive and fewer than eight cylinders. For '89, it becomes the first U.S. car with air bags standard for both the driver and front-seat passenger. The driver's-side air bag is contained in the steering wheel hub; the passenger's is loaded above the glove compartment in a revamped dashboard. Available only as a 4-door, 6-passenger notchback, Continental is 4.4 inches longer but 170 pounds lighter and has more interior room than the rear-drive car it replaced. Standard and Signature Series trim levels are offered. Ford's 3.8-liter V-6 and 4-speed automatic transmission is the only powertrain. Power ratings are unchanged, but Lincoln says engine response is better thanks to higher wide-open-throttle shift speeds and a revised final-drive ratio. Continental's chassis has a computer-controlled damping system designed to maintain a smooth ride by adjusting in fractions of a second to changes in the road surface. Its power steering has speed-sensitive variable assist. Brakes are 4-wheel discs with anti-lock control. Lincoln says Continental's electronic gauges have enhanced contrast this year for improved readability. The door trim panels are also revised and front seat-track travel is increased. Also, ordering the optional Insta-Clear heated windshield brings a heavy-duty battery. Continental has been well accepted by luxury-car buyers, despite a V-6 that has adequate power, but falls short of the V-8s most shoppers in this class expect. In the car's favor is styling that's contemporary and aerodynamic, dimensions that are full-size inside and out, and a level of comfort and amenities demanded by domestic-luxury buyers. We applaud the air bags and anti-lock brakes.

Specifications

	4-door notchback
Wheelbase, in.	109.0
Overall length, in.	205.1
Overall width, in.	72.7
Overall height, in.	55.6
Turn diameter, ft.	38.0
Curb weight, lbs.	3628
Cargo vol., cu. ft.	19.0
Fuel capacity, gal.	18.6
Seating capacity	6
Front headroom, in.	38.7
Front shoulder room, in.	57.5
Front legroom, max., in.	41.7
Rear headroom, in.	38.4
Rear shoulder room, in.	57.5
Rear legroom, min., in.	39.2

Engines

	ohv V-6
Size, liters/cu. in.	3.8/232
Fuel delivery	PFI
Horsepower @ rpm	140 @ 3800
Torque (lbs./ft.) @ rpm	215 @ 2200
Availability	S

EPA city/highway mpg

4-speed OD automatic	19/28

Prices

Lincoln Continental	Retail Price	Dealer Invoice	Low Price
4-door notchback	$27468	$23305	$25587
Signature 4-door notchback	29334	24873	27304
Destination charge	524	524	524

Standard Equipment:

3.8-liter PFI V-6 engine, 4-speed automatic transmission, speed-sensitive power steering, power 4-wheel disc brakes, anti-lock braking system, dual front airbags, automatic climate control air conditioning, 50/50 front seats

Prices are accurate at time of printing; subject to manufacturer's change.

with recliners, leather upholstery (cloth is available at no cost), folding front and rear armrests, rear lap/shoulder belts, cruise control, automatic parking brake release, AM/FM cassette, tinted glass, heated power mirrors, rear defogger, remote fuel door and decklid releases, power windows and locks, intermittent wipers, tilt steering column, right visor mirror, electronic instruments with coolant temperature, oil pressure and voltage gauges, trip computer, service interval reminder, digital clock, vinyl bodyside moldings, bright rocker panel moldings, cornering lamps, 205/70R15 tires. **Signature** adds: power recliners, power passenger seat, power decklid pulldown, Autolamp on/off/delay, automatic headlamp dimmer, upgraded upholstery, lighted visor mirrors, alloy wheels.

Optional Equipment:

	Retail Price	Dealer Invoice	Low Price
Alloy wheels	478	401	440
Keyless illuminated entry	209	175	192
Anti-theft alarm	200	168	184
Power glass moonroof	1319	1108	1213
Memory seat w/power lumbar	301	253	277
Leather-wrapped steering wheel	115	96	106
Ford JBL Audio System	525	441	483
CD player	617	519	568
Insta-Clear heated windshield	253	213	233
Comfort/Convenience Group	819	688	753
Power decklid pulldown, power passenger seat, lighted visor mirrors, automatic headlamp dimmer, Autolamp on/off/delay, rear floormats, power passenger recliner.			
Overhead Console Group	226	190	208
Digital compass, automatic day/night mirror.			
Cloth seat trim	NC	NC	NC
California emissions pkg.	99	83	91

Lincoln Mark VII

Lincoln's premium coupe is carried over virtually unchanged after getting a more powerful engine, a better stereo and minor restyling for 1988. The only '89 alteration is the addition of an engine-management computer malfunction warning light to cars sold in all 50 states; the light previously was standard in California only. Two Mark VII models are offered at the same price: the sporty LSC and the luxury Bill Blass Designer Series. Both are rear-drive, 5-seat, 2-door coupes. They retain the 225-horsepower 5.0-liter V-8 acquired in '88. A 4-speed automatic transmission and

Prices are accurate at time of printing; subject to manufacturer's change.

Lincoln Mark VII LSC

Specifications

	2-door notchback
Wheelbase, in.	108.5
Overall length, in.	202.8
Overall width, in.	70.9
Overall height, in.	54.2
Turn diameter, ft.	40.0
Curb weight, lbs.	3722
Cargo vol., cu. ft.	14.2
Fuel capacity, gal.	22.1
Seating capacity	5
Front headroom, in.	37.8
Front shoulder room, in.	56.0
Front legroom, max., in.	42.0
Rear headroom, in.	37.1
Rear shoulder room, in.	57.8
Rear legroom, min., in.	36.9

Engines

	ohv V-8
Size, liters/cu. in.	5.0/302
Fuel delivery	PFI
Horsepower @ rpm	225 @ 4000
Torque (lbs./ft.) @ rpm	300 @ 3200
Availability	S

EPA city/highway mpg

4-speed OD automatic	17/24

anti-lock brakes are standard on both. The Designer Series gets whitewall tires, its own chrome exterior trim and a choice of leather or cloth seating. The LSC has wider black-sidewall high-performance tires on alloy wheels, quick-ratio power steering, a handling suspension and leather upholstery. There's plenty to recommend the Mark VII, especially in sporty LSC guise. Its V-8 delivers satisfying performance. Its firm suspension might turn off many traditional Lincoln buyers, but coupled with wide tires, it gives the LSC commendable handling and roadholding. The car can feel ponderous around town, however. Other drawbacks include a rear seat that has ample leg room for adults, but not much head room, and a driveline hump that discourages squeezing three people into the back. The trunk is poorly shaped and undersized and fuel economy is not a strong suit. On balance, the Mark VII LSC has much to offer, including a reasonable price for the class. Its strongest domestic competitor is the Cadillac Eldorado with the optional touring suspension. The front-drive Eldo feels a bit lighter on its feet, though its dashboard is less sporting and its price is slightly higher.

Prices

Lincoln Mark VII	Retail Price	Dealer Invoice	Low Price
Bill Blass 2-door notchback	$27218	$23087	$25053
LSC 2-door notchback	27218	23087	25053
Destination charge	524	524	524

Standard Equipment:

LSC: 5.0-liter PFI V-8, 4-speed automatic transmission, power steering, power 4-wheel disc brakes, anti-lock braking system, electronic air suspension with automatic level control, automatic climate control, overhead console with warning lights and reading lamps, power decklid release, defroster group, power windows and door locks, remote fuel door release, tinted glass, automatic headlamp dimmer, Autolamp on/off/delay, illuminated entry, analog instruments including tachometer and coolant temperature gauge, heated power mirrors, AM/FM ST ET cassette, power seats, cruise control, tilt steering column, intermittent wipers, full-length console with lockable compartment, leather interior trim including steering wheel, shift knob, and console, handling suspension, P225/60R16 tires on aluminum wheels. **Bill Blass** has electronic instrument cluster, prairie mist metallic

Prices are accurate at time of printing; subject to manufacturer's change.

clearcoat paint, bodyside and decklid paint stripes, choice of leather, UltraSuede or cloth/leather seat trim, P215/70R15 tires on wire-spoke aluminum wheels.

Optional Equipment:	Retail Price	Dealer Invoice	Low Price
Traction-Lok axle	101	85	93
Anti-theft alarm	200	168	184
Power glass moonroof	1319	1108	1213
Automatic day/night mirror	89	75	82
Ford JBL Audio System	525	441	483

Lincoln Town Car

Lincoln Town Car Signature Series

A Gucci Designer Series arrives for 1989 to top the Cartier Designer and Signature series as the ultimate expression of Lincoln's best-selling model, the Town Car. The full-size, rear-drive luxury car returns functionally unchanged. All models are 4-door sedans with 6-passenger seating. Power is from a fuel-injected 5.0-liter V-8 mated to a 4-speed automatic transmission. Town Car starts with the base sedan, which gets a new Frenched rear window for its standard full vinyl roof this year. The Signature Series upgrades interior appointments and supplants the base model's full vinyl top for a coach roof. The Cartier Designer Series adds platinum bodyside moldings, a new-for-'89 dual-shade paint treatment and other amenities. The new Gucci series features a full Cambria top and color-keyed bodyside accent stripes. An engine-computer management system malfunction warn-

Prices are accurate at time of printing; subject to manufacturer's change.

ing light has been added to all models. The current Town Car has its roots in the downsized model of 1980. A restyled but still-rear-drive Town Car is due for 1990. We prefer the Lincoln to its nearest competitor, the Cadillac Brougham, though neither makes our hearts sing. Both feel clumsy in tight maneuvers and their overall handling pales in comparison to European luxury sedans. The Town Car's V-8 is more powerful and responsive than the Brougham's, and both have expansive interiors and ample luggage space. But neither offers anti-lock brakes, an important safety feature that's either standard or optional on many smaller, less expensive sedans. The Town Car tops our short list of traditional American luxury cars, but we think buyers spending this much should also look at some newer, more roadworthy cars. They'll get more substance for their money.

Specifications

	4-door notchback
Wheelbase, in.	117.3
Overall length, in.	219.0
Overall width, in.	78.1
Overall height, in.	55.9
Turn diameter, ft.	40.0
Curb weight, lbs.	4051
Cargo vol., cu. ft.	22.4
Fuel capacity, gal.	18.0
Seating capacity	6
Front headroom, in.	39.0
Front shoulder room, in.	60.7
Front legroom, max., in.	43.5
Rear headroom, in.	38.2
Rear shoulder room, in.	60.7
Rear legroom, min., in.	42.1

Engines

	ohv V-8
Size, liters/cu. in.	5.0/302
Fuel delivery	PFI
Horsepower @ rpm	150 @ 3200
Torque (lbs./ft.) @ rpm	270 @ 2000
Availability	S

EPA city/highway mpg

4-speed OD automatic	17/24

Prices

Lincoln Town Car

	Retail Price	Dealer Invoice	Low Price
4-door notchback	$25205	$21395	$23300
Signature 4-door notchback	28206	23916	26061
Cartier 4-door notchback	29352	24879	27116
Gucci 4-door notchback	NA	NA	NA
Destination charge	524	524	524

Standard Equipment:

5.0-liter PFI V-8 engine, 4-speed automatic transmission, power steering and brakes, power vent and door windows, power locks, automatic climate control, tilt steering column, automatic parking brake release, tinted glass, front bumper guards, cornering lamps, coach lamps, power mirrors, variable intermittent wipers, cruise control, full vinyl roof with padded rear pillars, Twin-Comfort lounge front seats with six-way power driver's seat and dual fold-down center armrests, folding rear armrest, AM/FM ST ET cassette, Premium Sound System, passenger assist handles, electronic warning chimes, full interior courtesy lighting, rear defogger, P215/70R15 tires w/full-size spare. **Signature** adds: 3.27 axle ratio, coach roof, manual front passenger seatback recliner, pleat-pillow-style upholstery, seatback assist straps and map pockets, door and quarter trim woodtone accents. **Cartier** adds: two-tone paint, full textured-vinyl roof, platinum bodyside moldings, turbine-spoke aluminum wheels, leather-wrapped steering wheel. **Gucci** adds: full cambria roof.

Optional Equipment:

Traction-Lok axle	101	85	93
Wire wheel covers, base	341	286	314
Signature & Cartier (credit)	(137)	(115)	(115)
Lacy spoke alloy wheels, base	478	401	440
Signature & Cartier (credit)	(NC)	(NC)	(NC)
Wire spoke alloy wheels, base	873	733	803
Signature & Cartier	395	332	363
Electronic instrument panel	822	691	756
Keyless illuminated entry	209	175	192
Anti-theft alarm	200	168	184
Power glass moonroof	1319	1108	1213
Comfort/Convenience Group	694	583	638
Power decklid pulldown, lighted visor mirrors, automatic headlamp dimmer, Autolamp on/off/delay, power seats, rear floormats.			
Leather-wrapped steering wheel	115	96	106
Automatic day/night mirror	89	75	82
Automatic load leveling	202	170	186
Bodyside molding	70	59	64

Prices are accurate at time of printing; subject to manufacturer's change.

	Retail Price	Dealer Invoice	Low Price
Carriage roof, Signature	710	596	653
Others	1069	898	983
Valino luxury coach roof	359	302	330
Ford JBL Audio System	525	441	483
CD player	617	519	568
Leather seat trim, Signature	469	394	431
Others	531	446	489
California emissions pkg	99	83	91
Dual exhaust	83	70	76
Class III trailer tow pkg.	546	458	502

3.55 Traction-Lok axle, dual exhaust, trailer towing suspension and wiring harness, power steering and transmission oil coolers, HD U-joint and rear brakes, HD radiator, automatic load leveling, HD turn signals and flasher. For 5000-lb. capacity/750 lb. tongue load.

Mazda MPV

Mazda MPV

Called MPV, for "Multi-Purpose Vehicle," Mazda's first U.S. minivan is available as a rear-drive passenger model with seats for five or seven and as a 2-seat cargo model. A 4-wheel-drive passenger version is due in spring 1989. MPV is packaged for the same car-like comfort and driving feel that spelled success for the front-drive Chrysler minivans, though it's larger than the standard-size Caravan/Voyager in all dimensions except length. It also has a swing-open rear side door, rather than the minivan-traditional sliding door. Standard power is a new 121-horsepower fuel-injected 2.6-liter 4-cylinder engine. Optional with rear drive and standard with the planned 4WD is a 150-horsepower version of the Mazda 929's 3.0-liter V-6. A 5-speed manual transmission is standard, a 4-speed automatic is optional. Mazda says the rear-drive gives superior handling and towing capabilities compared to front drive, and makes the 4WD conversion easier. Indeed, the MPV is the most car-like minivan since the Caravan/Voyager. Entering the cabin through the front doors requires a slightly higher step-up than in the Cara-

---

Specifications

	4-door van
Wheelbase, in.	110.4
Overall length, in.	175.8
Overall width, in.	71.9
Overall height, in.	68.1
Turn diameter, ft.	36.1
Curb weight, lbs.	3463
Cargo vol., cu. ft.	37.5
Fuel capacity, gal.	15.9[1]
Seating capacity	7
Front headroom, in.	40.0
Front shoulder room, in.	57.5
Front legroom, max., in.	40.6
Rear headroom, in.	39.0
Rear shoulder room, in.	57.5
Rear legroom, min., in.	34.8

1. 19.6 with V-6

Engines

	ohc I-4	ohc V-6
Size, liters/cu. in.	2.6/159	3.0/180
Fuel delivery	PFI	PFI
Horsepower @ rpm	121 @ 4600	150 @ 5000
Torque (lbs./ft.) @ rpm	149 @ 3500	165 @ 4000
Availability	S	O

EPA city/highway mpg

	ohc I-4	ohc V-6
5-speed OD manual	20/24	18/23
4-speed OD automatic	19/24	17/22

van/Voyager, but there's a similarly car-like driving position. The MPV's middle seat has a reclining backrest and fore/aft movement; the recliner allows conversion of the middle and rear seats into a makeshift bed. Seven-passenger seating is arrayed 2/2/3, and passengers can move from front to rear without leaving the vehicle. The swing-out right-rear door is easier to open and close than most minivans' sliding type, and may prove less prone to rattles. On the road, our test V-6 automatic had fine acceleration and passing power. The MPV felt light on its feet, maneuverable in tight spots and had decent resistance to crosswinds on the highway. It cornered with more apparent body roll than the Chrysler products, but didn't feel tippy at moderate speeds. The V-6 was subdued except when pushed, but wind noise was prominent despite the low-drag styling. In all, the MPV is pleasant, practical and thoroughly professional. It lives up to its name by combining station wagon comfort and driving ease with minivan versatility in a compact package.

Prices

Mazda MPV	Retail Price	Dealer Invoice	Low Price
5-passenger, 2.6L, 5-speed	$12909	—	—
5-passenger, 2.6L, automatic	13609	—	—
7-passenger, 2.6L, 5-speed	13759	—	—
7-passenger, 2.6L, automatic	14459	—	—
7-passenger, 3.0L, 5-speed	14359	—	—
7-passenger, 3.0L, automatic	15109	—	—
Destination charge	269	269	269

Dealer invoice and low price not available at time of publication.

Standard Equipment:

2.6-liter PFI 4-cylinder or 3.0-liter PFI V-6 engine, 5-speed manual transmission, power steering and brakes, cloth reclining front bucket seats, 3-passenger middle seat (5-passenger), 2-passenger middle and 3-passenger rear seats (7-passenger), power mirrors, tachometer, coolant temperature gauge, trip odometer, tilt steering column, intermittent wipers, illuminated entry, rear wiper/washer, tinted glass, AM/FM ST ET cassette, lighted visor mirrors, floormats, rear defogger, remote fuel door release, 205/70R14 all-season tires.

Options prices not available at time of publication.

Prices are accurate at time of printing; subject to manufacturer's change.

Mazda RX-7

Mazda RX-7 SE

A facelifted RX-7 is due in January 1990, but until then Mazda dealers will be selling leftover '88 versions of the rotary-powered sports car. No information has been released about the facelifted edition. The second-generation RX-7 debuted for 1986 and the lineup at the end of '88 included base SE models in 2-seat and 2+2 configurations; performance-oriented GTU and Turbo 2-seaters; luxury 2-seat and 2+2 GXL models; and a 2-seat convertible. A 10th anniversary Turbo model went on sale during the '88 model year. All have a 1.3-liter, twin-rotor Wankel engine making 146 horsepower in naturally aspirated form and 182 with a turbocharger. Tenacious handling and terrific acceleration distinguish the Turbo. Naturally aspirated RX-7s are no slouches, but they lack the Turbo's knockout punch. The fine-shifting 5-speed manual transmission is critical to tapping either engine's high-rev horsepower. RX-7s have quick reflexes, good grip in fast turns and fine stability at high speed. Braking is sure and drama-free, and an anti-lock feature is optional on GXLs and Turbo. Now the bad news. The ride is punishingly harsh, especially on the Turbo, and it can compromise control if bumps or ruts surprise you in the middle of a fast turn. The tires roar constantly and boom over bumps, and have mediocre traction in the wet. Inside, taller people will likely wish for more foot room and a higher roof; the +2 seating is for small children only. And fuel economy is an RX-7 weak point. Such negatives plague most sports cars, so RX-7 isn't any worse than its rivals. It's better in many ways, so we still rate it highly. And if you're interested in a convertible, the RX-7's is one of the best.

1988 Specifications

	3-door hatchback	2+2 3-door hatchback	2-door conv.
Wheelbase, in.	95.7	95.7	95.7
Overall length, in.	168.9	168.9	168.9
Overall width, in.	66.5	66.5	66.5
Overall height, in.	49.8	49.8	49.8
Turn diameter, ft.	32.2	32.2	32.2
Curb weight, lbs.	2625[1]	2645	3003
Cargo vol., cu. ft.	19.5	20.9	4.1
Fuel capacity, gal.	16.6	16.6	16.6
Seating capacity	2	4	2
Front headroom, in.	37.2	37.2	36.5
Front shoulder room, in.	52.8	52.8	52.8
Front legroom, max., in.	43.7	43.7	43.7
Rear headroom, in.	—	33.0	—
Rear shoulder room, in.	—	NA	—
Rear legroom, min., in.	—	NA	—

1. 2850 lbs., Turbo

Engines

	2-rotor Wankel	Turbo 2-rotor Wankel
Size, liters/cu. in.	1.3/80	1.3/80
Fuel delivery	PFI	PFI
Horsepower @ rpm	146 @ 6500	182 @ 6500
Torque (lbs./ft.) @ rpm	138 @ 3500	183 @ 3500
Availability	S	S[1]

EPA city/highway mpg

5-speed OD manual	17/24	17/23
4-speed OD automatic	17/23	

1. Turbo

Prices

Mazda RX-7 (1988 Prices)	Retail Price	Dealer Invoice	Low Price
SE 3-door hatchback	$16150	$14030	$14940
SE 2+2 3-door hatchback	16650	14460	15405
GTU 3-door hatchback	18150	15569	16710
GXL 3-door hatchback	20050	16983	18367
GXL 2+2 3-door hatchback	20550	17403	18617

Prices are accurate at time of printing; subject to manufacturer's change.

	Retail Price	Dealer Invoice	Low Price
Turbo 3-door hatchback	22750	19251	20851
2-door convertible	21550	18243	19747
2-door convertible w/Option Pkg.	24050	20343	22047
10th Anniversary 3-door hatchback	24650	20897	22624
Destination charge	269	269	269

Standard Equipment:

SE: 1.3-liter PFI rotary engine, 5-speed manual transmission, power steering, power 4-wheel disc brakes, reclining front bucket seats, tachometer, trip odometer, coolant temperature and oil pressure gauges, voltmeter, remote liftgate and fuel door releases, AM/FM ST ET cassette, power antenna, digital clock, theft-deterrent system, 185/70HR14 SBR tires on alloy wheels. **GTU** adds: limited-slip differential, aerodynamic body addenda, sport-tuned suspension, sport seats, power mirrors. **GXL** adds to base: Auto Adjusting Suspension, air conditioning, cruise control, graphic EQ, power windows, power sunroof, rear wiper/washer, leather-wrapped steering wheel. **Turbo** adds to GTU: power sunroof, air conditioning, cruise control, power windows, graphic EQ, leather-wrapped steering wheel, 205/55VR16 tires. **Convertible** has GXL equipment plus upgraded stereo. **Convertible Option Package** adds leather trim, compact disc player, headrest speakers. **10th Anniversary** has Turbo equipment plus monochromatic exterior treatment, bronze tinted glass, headlamp washer.

Optional Equipment:

4-speed automatic transmission, SE &			
GXL	670	570	620
Anti-lock brakes, GXL & Turbo	1400	1190	1295
Air conditioning (std. GXL & Turbo)	859	688	774
Leather seats, GXL 2-seater	850	680	765
GXL 2+2	1075	860	968
Turbo	1000	800	900
Power sunroof, SE & GTU	595	506	551
Compact Disc player, GXL & Turbo	875	705	790
Cruise control, conv.	239	179	209
Graphic EQ, SE & GTU	149	112	131

Mazda 323

Mazda has trimmed its front-drive 323 subcompact line to five models for 1989. Gone are last year's 5-door station wagon, the turbocharged GT 4-door and the base 4-door. Returning unchanged are base, SE and GTX Turbo 3-door

Prices are accurate at time of printing; subject to manufacturer's change.

Mazda 323 SE 3-door

Specifications

	3-door hatchback	4-door notchback
Wheelbase, in.	94.5	94.5
Overall length, in.	161.8	169.7
Overall width, in.	64.8	64.8
Overall height, in.	54.7	54.7
Turn diameter, ft.	30.8	30.8
Curb weight, lbs.	2100[1]	2175
Cargo vol., cu. ft.	10.5	14.7
Fuel capacity, gal.	12.7[2]	12.7
Seating capacity	5	5
Front headroom, in.	38.3	38.3
Front shoulder room, in.	52.8	52.8
Front legroom, max., in.	41.5	41.5
Rear headroom, in.	37.0	37.4
Rear shoulder room, in.	52.8	52.8
Rear legroom, min., in.	34.7	34.7

1. 2600 lbs., GTX   2. 13.2 gals., GTX

Engines	ohc I-4	Turbo dohc I-4
Size, liters/cu. in.	1.6/97	1.6/97
Fuel delivery	PFI	PFI
Horsepower @ rpm	82 @ 5000	132 @ 6000
Torque (lbs./ft.) @ rpm	92 @ 2500	136 @ 3000
Availability	S	S[1]

EPA city/highway mpg

4-speed OD manual	26/30	
5-speed OD manual	28/33	21/24
4-speed OD automatic	24/30	

1.   GTX

hatchbacks, and SE and LX 4-door sedans. All have front-wheel drive except the GTX hatchback, which has full-time 4-wheel-drive. All except the GTX use an 82-horsepower 1.6-liter 4-cylinder engine; the GTX's turbocharged 1.6 has dual overhead cams and 132 horsepower. The base 3-door hatchback comes only with a 4-speed manual; the SE 3-door and both 4-door sedans come with either a 5-speed manual or 4-speed overdrive automatic; the GTX comes only with a 5-speed manual. There's nothing here that's unusual or trend-setting, except for the turbocharged, 4WD GTX, but there's still plenty to recommend about the 323. They're reasonably priced, well-built, economical subcompacts protected by a 3-year/50,000-mile "bumper-to-bumper" warranty. Their base engine provides sufficient power and good fuel economy. You'll get the best performance and highest mileage with the 5-speed manual transmission, but the optional automatic has an overdrive fourth gear, which helps highway fuel economy. Both the hatchback and the sedan have fairly roomy interiors, and both suffer from too much engine and road noise, plus flat, poorly padded seats. The hatchback benefits from a folding rear seat for increased cargo room, while the 4-door's deep, cavernous trunk holds a surprising amount of luggage. Figure on around $10,500 for a 323 with air conditioning, automatic transmission, power steering and a stereo radio. But shop around, you may find a Mazda dealer who's selling 323s for less than suggested retail.

Prices

Mazda 323	Retail Price	Dealer Invoice	Low Price
3-door hatchback	$6299	$5865	$6150
SE 3-door hatchback	7399	6892	7146
SE 4-door notchback	8299	7554	7927
LX 4-door notchback	9499	8349	8924
GTX 3-door hatchback	12999	11264	12132
Destination charge	269	269	269

Standard Equipment:

1.6-liter PFI 4-cylinder engine, 4-speed manual transmission, power brakes, vinyl reclining front bucket seats, one-piece folding rear seatback, trip odometer, coolant temperature gauge, intermittent wipers, cargo cover, rear

Prices are accurate at time of printing; subject to manufacturer's change.

defogger, tinted glass, map lights, left remote mirror, bodyside moldings, 155SR13 tires. **SE** adds: 5-speed manual transmission, cloth upholstery, 50/50 folding rear seatbacks, remote fuel door and liftgate/decklid releases, day/night mirror, center console. **LX** adds: power steering, folding rear armrest, illuminated entry, power mirrors, tilt steering column, tachometer, variable intermittent wipers. **GTX** adds: turbocharged DOHC 16-valve engine, permanent 4-wheel drive, 4-wheel disc brakes, sport seats, 185/60R14 tires on alloy wheels.

Optional Equipment:

	Retail Price	Dealer Invoice	Low Price
4-speed automatic transmission (NA GTX) .	700	630	665
Power steering, base & SE	250	213	232
Air conditioning	760	616	688
Manual sunroof, LX & GTX	350	298	324
Alloy wheels, LX	400	320	360
Cruise control, 4-doors	200	160	180
Power windows & locks, LX & GTX	300	240	270
AM/FM ST ET cassette, 4-doors & GTX . .	450	342	396
Floormats	55	39	47
Armrest	59	47	53
Rear spoiler, SE hatchback	199	159	179

Mazda 626/MX-6

Mazda MX-6 LX

Mazda wasn't selling many 4-door 626s with the 4-wheel steering option, so this year it moved the feature to the sporty 2-door MX-6. The decision gives Mazda a more direct competitor to Honda's 4WS Prelude. The major change for

Prices are accurate at time of printing; subject to manufacturer's change.

these front-drive compacts is that the anti-lock brake option has been reduced from $1400 to $1000. It's available only on turbocharged 626 and MX-6 models. Four-door 626s use a 110-horsepower 2.2-liter four; the 5-door Touring Sedan has a 145-horsepower turbocharged 2.2. All 626s are imported from Japan. The MX-6 coupe shares the 626's platform and engines, but some are built at Mazda's Michigan plant along side the Ford Probe, which is an MX-6 under the skin. DX and LX coupes use the 110-horsepower engine, while the MX-6 GT and GT 4WS use the turbo. A 5-speed manual transmission is standard on all models and a 4-speed automatic is optional for all except the MX-6 GT 4WS. The 626 is

Specifications

	MX-6 2-door notchback	626 4-door notchback	626 5-door hatchback
Wheelbase, in.	99.0	101.4	101.4
Overall length, in.	177.0	179.3	179.3
Overall width, in.	66.5	66.5	66.5
Overall height, in.	53.5	55.5	54.1
Turn diameter, ft.	35.3[1]	36.0	36.0
Curb weight, lbs.	2535[2]	2590	2680
Cargo vol., cu. ft.	15.4	15.9	22.0
Fuel capacity, gal.	15.9	15.9	15.9
Seating capacity	4	5	5
Front headroom, in.	38.4	39.0	38.7
Front shoulder room, in.	54.9	54.9	54.9
Front legroom, max., in.	43.6	43.7	43.6
Rear headroom, in.	37.8	37.8	37.2
Rear shoulder room, in.	53.3	54.9	54.9
Rear legroom, min., in.	31.8	36.6	32.9

1. 31.5 with 4WS   2. 2705 lbs., GT; 2888 lbs., GT 4WS

Engines	ohc I-4	Turbo ohc I-4
Size, liters/cu. in.	2.2/133	2.2/133
Fuel delivery	PFI	PFI
Horsepower @ rpm	110 @ 4700	145 @ 4300
Torque (lbs./ft.) @ rpm	130 @ 3000	190 @ 3500
Availability	S	S[1]
EPA city/highway mpg		
5-speed OD manual	24/31	21/28
4-speed OD automatic	22/28	19/25

1. 626 Turbo, MX-6 GT

just a notch below the compact-class-leading Honda Accord and Toyota Camry. But it is worth considering, especially since Mazda dealers are more likely than Honda or Toyota dealers to offer discounts. The same goes for the MX-6 versus the Honda Prelude or Toyota Celica. The MX-6 is distinguished from the sleeker Probe primarily by its upright stance. You have to buy one of the expensive turbocharged models to get anti-lock brakes, though these are still among the lowest-priced cars to offer that important safety feature. We don't find the 4WS worth the extra cost, weight or complexity. The 626 LX 4-door in our long-term test fleet has proven comfortable and capable, though its automatic transmission diminishes the driving pleasure because it balks at downshifting.

Prices

Mazda 626/MX-6	Retail Price	Dealer Invoice	Low Price
626 DX 4-door notchback	$11299	$9869	$10584
626 LX 4-door notchback	13199	11380	12290
626 LX 5-door Touring Sedan	13399	11551	12475
626 Turbo 5-door Touring Sedan	15049	12962	14006
MX-6 DX 2-door notchback	11399	9841	10620
MX-6 LX 2-door notchback	13299	11333	12316
MX-6 GT Turbo 2-door notchback	15499	13192	14346
MX-6 GT Turbo 4WS 2-door notchback	16699	NA	NA
Destination charge	269	269	269

Standard Equipment:

DX: 2.2-liter PFI 4-cylinder engine, 5-speed manual transmission, power steering and brakes, cloth reclining front bucket seats, tachometer, coolant temperature gauge, trip odometer, tilt steering column, tinted glass, intermittent wipers, digital clock, center console, rear defogger, remote fuel door and trunk/liftgate releases, remote mirrors, 185/70R14 SBR tires. **LX** adds: power windows and locks, cruise control, AM/FM ST ET cassette, power antenna, map lights, variable intermittent wipers; Touring Sedan has removable shelf panel and rear wiper/washer. **Turbo** models add: 2.2-liter intercooled turbocharged engine, 4-wheel disc brakes, Auto Adjusting Suspension (exc. MX-6 4WS), graphic EQ (MX-6), 195/60HR15 tires on alloy wheels.

Optional Equipment:

4-speed automatic transmission	720	634	677
Anti-lock brakes, Turbos	1000	850	925

Prices are accurate at time of printing; subject to manufacturer's change.

	Retail Price	Dealer Invoice	Low Price
Air conditioning	800	642	721
Sunroof (NA DX, MX-6 GT)	555	444	500
Alloy wheels, exc. Turbo	400	320	360
Cruise control, DX	220	176	198
AM/FM ST ET cassette, DX	450	342	396
Graphic EQ	149	112	131
Floormats	58	41	50
Armrest w/lid (NA DX)	57	44	51
Rear spoiler, MX-6 LX	375	300	338

Mazda 929

Mazda 929

Lackluster U.S. response to the rear-drive 929, introduced
for 1988, has sparked feverish efforts to give the staid but
capable luxury sedan some styling zip. A facelift has been
rumored for as early as mid-1989, but don't expect it before
model year 1990. Among the few changes for '89, the 5-speed
manual transmission, a no-cost option last year, has been
dropped, and all 929s now have a 4-speed overdrive automatic. Also, the power moonroof and power driver's seat are
moved from the options list to the standard-equipment
roster. The 158-horsepower 3.0-liter V-6 engine is unchanged. Anti-lock brakes (ABS) are optional: $1000 as an
individual item and $1355 with the electronic Auto Adjust-

Prices are accurate at time of printing; subject to manufacturer's change.

ing Suspension. Last year, ABS alone was $1400 and the auto suspension/ABS package was $1800. Despite its generic styling, there's a pretty good luxury sedan here at a reasonable price. On the road, the 929 feels about as bland as it looks. That's not all bad, especially if you like your driving peaceful and undemanding. The polished powertrain delivers sufficient power to get through traffic without strain. The transmission shifts smoothly and doesn't hunt in and out of overdrive on the expressway. The ride is controlled and supple, handling is unsporting but balanced, braking is strong, and ABS is cheaper this year. The cabin is spacious for up to five adults, though the driver's seat with the optional leather upholstery is too flat. The dashboard has a refreshing lack of gimmickry. In all, the 929 is a substantial, comfortable and competent car with a decidedly conserva-

Specifications

	4-door notchback
Wheelbase, in.	106.7
Overall length, in.	193.1
Overall width, in.	66.9
Overall height, in.	54.5
Turn diameter, ft.	35.4
Curb weight, lbs.	3373
Cargo vol., cu. ft.	15.1
Fuel capacity, gal.	18.5
Seating capacity	5
Front headroom, in.	37.8
Front shoulder room, in.	55.2
Front legroom, max., in.	43.3
Rear headroom, in.	37.4
Rear shoulder room, in.	55.2
Rear legroom, min., in.	37.0

Engines

	ohc V-6
Size, liters/cu. in.	3.0/180
Fuel delivery	PFI
Horsepower @ rpm	158 @ 4500
Torque (lbs./ft.) @ rpm	170 @ 4000
Availability	S

EPA city/highway mpg

4-speed OD automatic	19/23

tive nature. Add ABS and even a compact disc player and the price is still on the right side of $25,000, or some $5000 less than a top-line Acura Legend LS.

Prices

Mazda 929	Retail Price	Dealer Invoice	Low Price
4-door notchback	$21920	$18329	$20125
Destination charge	269	269	269

Standard Equipment:

3.0-liter PFI V-6 engine, 4-speed automatic transmission, power steering, power 4-wheel disc brakes, automatic air conditioning, cloth reclining front bucket seats, power driver's seat, power windows, locks and mirrors, power moonroof, rear armrest, tachometer, coolant temperature gauge, voltmeter, trip odometer, intermittent wipers, AM/FM ST ET cassette with EQ, P195/65R15 tires on alloy wheels.

Optional Equipment:

Anti-lock brakes	1000	850	925
Incl. Auto Adjusting Suspension	1355	1152	1254
Leather power seats	880	730	805
Digital instruments	530	451	491
Cold Pkg.	250	208	229
All-season tires, HD battery, semi-concealed wipers, heated driver's seat, larger washer fluid reservoir.			
Floormats	79	55	67
Armrest w/lid	79	55	67

Mercedes-Benz S-Class

A passenger-side air bag is a new option for all S-Class cars except the 2-seat 560SL. A driver's-side air bag has been standard since 1986. The passenger-side bag is mounted in the glove box space so models with that option get a lockable storage box in the center console. Mercedes names its six flagship models for their engine displacement and wheelbase. Hence, the 300SE rides a 115.6-inch wheelbase and has a 177-horsepower 3.0-liter inline 6-cylinder engine. Riding a

Prices are accurate at time of printing; subject to manufacturer's change.

Mercedes-Benz 300 SEL

Specifications

	560SL 2-door conv.	560SEC 2-door notchback	300SE 4-door notchback	SEL 4-door notchback
Wheelbase, in.	96.7	112.2	115.6	121.1
Overall length, in.	180.3	199.2	202.6	208.1
Overall width, in.	70.5	72.0	71.7	71.7
Overall height, in.	51.1	55.0	56.6	56.7
urn diameter, ft.	34.4	38.1	39.0	40.6
Curb weight, lbs.	3705	3915	3730	3770[1]
Cargo vol., cu. ft.	6.6	14.9	15.2	15.2
Fuel capacity, gal.	25.5	27.1	23.6	27.1
Seating capacity	2	4	5	5
Front headroom, in.	36.5	37.8	38.5	38.6
Front shoulder room, in. .	51.6	57.2	56.2	56.2
Front legroom, max., in. .	42.2	41.9	41.9	41.9
Rear headroom, in.	—	36.7	36.5	37.2
Rear shoulder room, in. .	—	54.2	55.7	55.7
Rear legroom, min., in. .	—	30.6	34.4	39.6

1. 300SEL; 3885 lbs.; 420SEL; 4080 lbs.; 560SEL

Engines

	ohc I-6	ohc V-8	ohc V-8
Size, liters/cu. in.	3.0/181	4.2/256	5.6/338
Fuel delivery	PFI	PFI	PFI
Horsepower @ rpm	177 @ 5700	201 @ 5200	238 @[1] 4800
Torque (lbs./ft.) @ rpm	188 @ 4400	228 @ 3600	287 @[1] 3500
Availability	S	S	S

EPA city/highway mpg

	ohc I-6	ohc V-8	ohc V-8
4-speed automatic	17/19	15/18	14/16

1. 227 horsepower and 279 lbs./ft. torque, 560SL.

longer 121.1-inch wheelbase but using the same 3.0 six is the 300SEL. On the long wheelbase is the 4.2-liter V-8 420SEL and the 5.6-liter V-8 560SEL. The larger V-8 also powers the 560SEC 4-seat coupe and the 560SL 2-seat convertible. Soft-leather upholstery is standard this year and there are some new exterior colors. All models also have revised first-and second-gear ratios (slightly shorter in first, slightly taller in second). The 300SE gains the 10-speaker, 100-watt stereo system found in the other S-Class sedans and in the 560SEC. All these cars are built from the finest materials and with excellent craftsmanship, and all offer commendable handling as well as the safety of anti-lock brakes and air bags. They ride stiffly compared to most luxury cars, but are unperturbed by bumps and high-speed dips. The question is how many seats do you want, how much performance do you crave and how much are you willing to pay? The 6-cylinder models have all the features of the V-8-powered cars but less power and lower prices. Acceleration isn't brisk but they do cruise at high speeds with minimal effort. The V-8 cars combine that impeccable workmanship and exceptional engineering with stellar performance.

Prices

Mercedes-Benz S-Class	Retail Price	Dealer Invoice	Low Price
300SE 4-door notchback	$51400	—	—
300SEL 4-door notchback	55100	—	—
420SEL 4-door notchback	61210	—	—
560SEL 4-door notchback	72280	—	—
560SEC 2-door notchback	79840	—	—
560SL 2-door convertible	64230	—	—
Destination charge	250	250	250
Gas Guzzler Tax, 300SE, SEL	650	650	650
420SEL	1050	1050	1050
560SL	1300	1300	1300
560SEL, SEC	1500	1500	1500

Dealer invoice and low price not available at time of publication.

Standard Equipment:

300SE, 300SEL, 420SEL: 3.0-liter PFI 6-cylinder or 4.2-liter PFI V-8 engine, 4-speed automatic transmission, power steering, anti-lock braking system, 4-wheel disc brakes, Supplemental Restraint System, outboard rear lap/shoulder belts, anti-theft alarm, central locking, power windows, air conditioning, automatic climate control, AM/FM ST ET cassette, leather power front seats with 2-position memory, power telescopic steering column, leather-wrapped steering wheel and shift handle, rear defogger, cruise control, headlight wipers and washers, heated power mirrors, outside temperature indicator, tachometer, coolant temperature and oil pressure gauges, lighted visor mirrors, 205/65VR15 SBR tires on alloy wheels. **560SEL and 560SEC** add: 5.6-liter PFI V-8, automatic rear level control, limited-slip differential. **560SL** has removable hardtop and folding convertible top.

OPTIONS prices not available at time of publication.

Mercedes-Benz 190

Mercedes-Benz 190E 2.6

Mercedes' compact sedan loses its 4-cylinder gasoline engine and gets a mild facelift for '89. Dropping the 130-horsepower 2.3-liter four leaves a 158-horsepower 2.6-liter inline six as the 190's only gasoline engine. Returning is the 190D 2.5, Mercedes' only diesel-powered North American model. Its 2.5-liter diesel 5-cylinder is rated at 90 horsepower, three less than last year. The 190D 2.5, which is unavailable in California, has a new glow-plug system and a revised exhaust gas-recirculation system for lower emissions. The addition of anti-lock brakes (ABS) to the 190D makes ABS standard on all of Mercedes' North American models. Wide body-side moldings, a deeper front air dam and restyled bumpers constitute the facelift. Inside, redesigned seats have softer upholstery and more side support and allow, Mercedes says, nearly an inch more rear knee room. Front seat shoulder belts now have height adjustments at their anchors on the center roof pillars. As the price of Mercedes' smallest sedan has crept up, sales have gone down. Mercedes lowered the base price of a 2.6 5-speed $1910 for '89, though the price of a diesel model has increased by $1020. The 190 sedans have the same high-level quality and engineering as the larger Mercedes models, but are much smaller inside and out. The rear seat is downright cramped and the trunk provides modest luggage space. High price and close quarters aside, the 190E 2.6 offers satisfying acceler-

Specifications

	4-door notchback
Wheelbase, in.	104.9
Overall length, in.	175.1
Overall width, in.	66.5
Overall height, in.	54.7
Turn diameter, ft.	34.8
Curb weight, lbs.	2955
Cargo vol., cu. ft.	11.7
Fuel capacity, gal.	16.5
Seating capacity	5
Front headroom, in.	38.0
Front shoulder room, in.	53.5
Front legroom, max., in.	41.9
Rear headroom, in.	36.7
Rear shoulder room, in.	53.2
Rear legroom, min., in.	30.9

Engines	ohc I-6	Diesel ohc I-5
Size, liters/cu. in.	2.6/159	2.5/152
Fuel delivery	PFI	PFI
Horsepower @ rpm	158 @ 5800	90 @ 4600
Torque (lbs./ft.) @ rpm	162 @ 4600	117 @ 2800
Availability	S	S
EPA city/highway mpg		
5-speed OD manual	19/27	
4-speed automatic	20/23	28/33

ation, capable handling, a taut and stable ride, excellent stopping ability and the added protection of a standard driver's-side air bag. Throw in a long list of comfort and convenience features, and this is a lot of car in a very compact package.

Prices

Mercedes-Benz 190	Retail Price	Dealer Invoice	Low Price
190D 2.5 4-door notchback, automatic . .	$30980	—	—
190E 2.6 4-door notchback, 5-speed	31590	—	—
190E 2.6 4-door notchback, automatic . . .	32500	—	—
Destination charge	250	250	250

Dealer invoice and low price not available at time of publication.

Standard Equipment:

2.6-liter PFI 6-cylinder engine (2.5-liter diesel on 190D 2.5), 5-speed manual or 4-speed automatic transmission, power steering, anti-lock braking system, 4-wheel disc brakes, Supplemental Restraint System, outboard rear lap/shoulder belts, automatic climate control, power windows and locks, cruise control, intermittent wipers, rear defogger, vinyl reclining front bucket seats, heated power mirrors, AM/FM ST ET cassette, tachometer, coolant temperature and oil pressure gauges, trip odometer, lighted visor mirrors, wide bodyside moldings, 185/65R15 (V-rated on 190E 2.6) SBR tires on alloy wheels.

OPTIONS prices not available at time of publication.

Mercedes-Benz 260/300

These mid-size rear-drive sedans lose their 5-speed manual transmission and gain a passenger-side air bag option for '89. As with Mercedes' S-Class cars, the passenger-side air bag in the 260/300 occupies the space usually devoted to the glove box. All Mercedes sold in North America come with a standard driver's-side air bag. This year's lineup duplicates 1988's: 260E and 300E sedans, 300CE coupe and 300TE station wagon. A 2.6-liter inline 6-cylinder is standard on the 260E. The others use a 3.0-liter six. The 5-speed manual

Mercedes-Benz 300 TE

Specifications

	300CE 2-door notchback	260E, 300E 4-door notchback	300TE 5-door wagon
Wheelbase, in.	106.9	110.2	110.2
Overall length, in.	183.9	187.2	188.2
Overall width, in.	68.5	68.5	68.5
Overall height, in.	55.5	56.9	59.8
Turn diameter, ft.	35.8	36.7	36.7
Curb weight, lbs.	3310	3210	3530
Cargo vol., cu. ft.	14.4	14.6	76.8
Fuel capacity, gal.	20.9	20.9	21.4
Seating capacity	4	5	5
Front headroom, in.	36.0	36.9	37.4
Front shoulder room, in.	55.7	55.9	55.9
Front legroom, max., in.	41.9	41.7	41.7
Rear headroom, in.	35.5	36.9	36.8
Rear shoulder room, in.	50.2	55.7	55.6
Rear legroom, min., in.	29.6	33.5	33.9

Engines

		ohc I-6	ohc I-6
Size, liters/cu. in.		2.6/159	3.0/181
Fuel delivery		PFI	PFI
Horsepower @ rpm		158 @ 5800	177 @ 5700
Torque (lbs./ft.) @ rpm		162 @ 4600	188 @ 4400
Availability		S	S

EPA city/highway mpg

4-speed automatic		20/24	18/22

standard last year on the sedans has been dropped, so all models now have a 4-speed automatic. They also get the heated windshield washer system from the S-Class. The 300CE gains eight more color choices for the bumpers and body-side moldings, for a total of 12. Far roomier than the compact 190, less costly than the larger S-Class, the 260/300 series is Mercedes' most practical and best-selling U.S. line, accounting for 40 percent of the German automaker's sales here. All models have ample room for five except the 300CE, which seats four. Acceleration is brisk with the 3.0 six, adequate with the 2.6. The automatic transmission doesn't always react promptly when you need a quick burst of power for passing, but driveability is otherwise flawless. The ride is taut and composed, if a bit stiff. The steering is direct and responsive, though it requires substantial effort. The athletic handling devours curves. The interior design nearly duplicates the S-Class's functional control layout. There are only a handful of comfort and convenience options to pad prices that most shoppers will find out of reach anyway. But if price is no obstacle, these excellent cars should top your shopping list.

Prices

Mercedes-Benz 260/300	Retail Price	Dealer Invoice	Low Price
260E 4-door notchback	$39200	—	—
300E 4-door notchback	44850	—	—
300CE 2-door notchback	53880	—	—
300TE 5-door wagon	48210	—	—
Destination charge	250	—	—
Gas Guzzler Tax, 300TE	650	650	650

Dealer invoice and low price not available at time of publication.

Standard Equipment:

260E: 2.6-liter PFI 6-cylinder engine, 4-speed automatic transmission, power steering, anti-lock braking system, 4-wheel disc brakes, Supplemental Restraint System, cruise control, rear headrests, outboard rear lap/shoulder belts, heated power mirrors, automatic climate control, power windows and locks, rear defogger, tachometer, coolant temperature and oil pressure gauges, trip odometer, intermittent wipers, heated windshield washer fluid reservoir and nozzles. 195/65VR15 SBR tires; power sunroof is available at no charge. **300E** adds: 3.0-liter engine, headlamp wipers and washers, anti-theft alarm system, power telescopic steering column, power front seat, outside temperature indicator (300CE has leather upholstery; velour is available at no charge). **300TE wagon** adds: automatic level control, roof rack, rear wiper/washer.

OPTIONS prices not available at time of publication.

Mercury Tracer

Mercury Tracer 3-door

Introduced in March 1987 as an '88 model, Tracer is a subcompact built in Hermosillo, Mexico, from the design for the Mazda 323. It's an upscale replacement for the Lynx, which was Mercury's version of the Ford Escort. It comes in 3- and 5-door hatchback and 5-door wagon body styles. All have folding rear seatbacks that enlarge the cargo hold. The sole '89 change is the addition of yellow paint to mark service points in the engine bay. Tracer's fuel-injected 1.6-liter 4-cylinder engine and front-drive chassis are lifted from the Mazda. Mercury revised Mazda's transmission gearing and replaced some suspension pieces for its versions, but it neglected to pick up the 323's 4-speed overdrive automatic transmission, opting instead for an optional 3-speed automatic. A 5-speed manual is standard. Mercury markets Tracer as a fully-equipped subcompact, listing only a handful of individual options and option groups. Tracer lacks some of the variations that make Mazda 323 special, namely a 4-wheel-drive model, an available turbocharged engine the 4-speed automatic transmission. Of the three, Tracer needs the 4-speed automatic the most. Its 3-speed automatic has the engine running at a frantic 3300 rpm at 60 mph. The 5-speed manual runs it at a more relaxed and hushed 2600 rpm at 60. As it is, Tracer is still pretty economical with automatic, though fuel economy and performance are better with the 5-speed. Tracer is a generally enjoyable subcompact that handles competently, feels surefooted and rides fairly well for a small car.

Specifications

	3-door hatchback	5-door hatchback	5-door wagon
Wheelbase, in.	94.7	94.7	94.7
Overall length, in.	162.0	162.0	169.7
Overall width, in.	65.2	65.2	65.2
Overall height, in.	53.0	53.0	53.7
Turn diameter, ft.	30.8	30.8	30.8
Curb weight, lbs.	2158	2185	2233
Cargo vol., cu. ft.	28.9	28.9	57.6
Fuel capacity, gal.	11.9	11.9	11.9
Seating capacity	5	5	5
Front headroom, in.	38.3	38.3	38.2
Front shoulder room, in.	51.9	51.9	51.9
Front legroom, max., in.	41.5	41.5	41.5
Rear headroom, in.	37.0	37.0	38.1
Rear shoulder room, in.	51.9	51.9	51.9
Rear legroom, min., in.	34.7	34.7	34.7

Engines

	ohc I-4
Size, liters/cu. in.	1.6/97
Fuel delivery	PFI
Horsepower @ rpm	82 @ 5000
Torque (lbs./ft.) @ rpm	92 @ 2500
Availability	S

EPA city/highway mpg

5-speed OD manual	26/29
3-speed automatic	26/29

Prices

Mercury Tracer	Retail Price	Dealer Invoice	Low Price
3-door hatchback	$8556	$7714	$8135
5-door hatchback	9242	8324	8783
5-door wagon	9726	8755	9241
Destination charge	335	335	335

Standard Equipment:

1.6-liter PFI 4-cylinder engine, 5-speed manual transmission, tachometer, trip odometer, coolant temperature gauge, digital clock, tinted glass, cloth reclining front bucket seats, driver's seat height and lumbar support adjustments. split folding rear seatback with headrests and recliners, AM/FM ST ET, rear defogger, power mirrors, map lights, center console with storage, remote fuel door and liftgate releases, right visor mirror, cargo area cover, P175/70R13 tires on steel wheels (hatchbacks; alloy on wagon), full wheel covers.

Optional Equipment:

3-speed automatic transmission	415	352	384
Air conditioning	688	585	637
AM/FM ST ET cassette	137	116	127
AM/FM ST ET delete (credit)	(206)	(175)	(175)
Preferred Pkg. 551A	235	200	218
Power steering.			
Sport Pkg., exc. wagon	268	228	248
Two-tone paint, alloy wheels, tape stripe.			
Cruise control	182	154	168
Alloy wheels (std. wagon)	183	155	169

Merkur Scorpio and XR4Ti

The XR4Ti is to die off after the 1989 model year, but it's back along with its larger Scorpio companion with only mild changes. Both these rear-drive hatchbacks are imported from Ford of Germany and sold through Lincoln-Mercury dealers with Merkur franchises. Merkur (pronounced mare-COOR) is the German word for Mercury. Scorpio is a luxury 5-door with a 2.9-liter V-6 engine and standard anti-lock disc brakes. XR4Ti is a 3-door sport sedan with a turbocharged

Prices are accurate at time of printing; subject to manufacturer's change

Merkur Scorpio

2.3-liter 4-cylinder. Known in Europe as the Sierra, XR4Ti kicked off the Merkur line in 1985, but never sold well in the U.S. Most of what's new for '89 was added to XR4Ti as a running change during the 1988 model year. Cosworth-style cast aluminum wheels replaced thick-spoked alloys, and speedometer graphics changed from an 85-mph top speed to 150 mph. Cruise control also was added as an option. Scorpio additions for '89 include emergency tensioning retractors for front seatbelts and newly optional heated front seats. Gas hood struts replaced the prop rod in mid-'88, the power front seats got a power recliner, and the automatic climate control system got an "Off" setting. Scorpio has split rear seatbacks that fold for extra cargo room and have separate power recliners for each side. Ford now advertises Scorpio and XR4Ti without using the Merkur name, though it continues to appear on the cars and on dealers' signs. That's an indication of the muddled marketing that has contributed to lackluster sales for both of these credible "captive imports." XR4Ti is a roadworthy and spacious sports sedan that's quick but suffers a lack of refinement under the hood. Our major complaint with the Scorpio also is under the hood, where its V-6 provides only adequate performance for this price class. Scorpio is otherwise a fine luxury tourer, with a cavernous and well-appointed cabin and confidence-inspiring road manners. Ford now indexes Scorpio's resale value to that of the Mercedes-Benz 190E and pays any difference in cash to Scorpio owners who trade for a new Lincoln, Mercury or Merkur. Ford is said to be testing a V-8 for use in the Scorpio, among other cars, after 1990.

Specifications

	XR4Ti 3-door hatchback	Scorpio 5-door hatchback
Wheelbase, in.	102.7	108.7
Overall length, in.	178.4	186.4
Overall width, in.	68.0	69.5
Overall height, in.	53.8	54.6
Turn diameter, ft.	35.4	34.1
Curb weight, lbs.	2920	3230
Cargo vol., cu. ft.	35.5	37.2
Fuel capacity, gal.	15.0	16.9
Seating capacity	5	5
Front headroom, in.	38.5	37.0
Front shoulder room, in.	53.9	56.4
Front legroom, max., in.	41.0	41.3
Rear headroom, in.	37.7	37.3
Rear shoulder room, in.	54.1	56.4
Rear legroom, min., in.	34.4	38.6

Engines

	ohv V-6	Turbo ohc I-4
Size, liters/cu. in.	2.9/177	2.3/140
Fuel delivery	PFI	PFI
Horsepower @ rpm	144 @ 5500	175 @ 5000[1]
Torque (lbs./ft.) @ rpm	162 @ 3000	200 @ 3000[1]
Availability	S[2]	S[3]

EPA city/highway mpg

5-speed OD manual	17/23	19/25
3-speed automatic		18/21
4-speed OD automatic	17/23	

1. 145 horsepower and 180 lbs./ft. torque with automatic transmission   *2. Scorpio*
3. XR4Ti

Prices

Merkur Scorpio	Retail Price	Dealer Invoice	Low Price
5-door hatchback	$25052	$20543	$22798
Destination charge	170	170	170

Standard Equipment:

2.9-liter PFI V-6 engine, 5-speed manual transmission, power steering, 4-wheel disc brakes, anti-lock braking system, power windows and locks, automatic climate control, front bucket seats with 16-way adjustments, 60/40 split folding rear seatback with electric recliners, cruise control, tilt/

Prices are accurate at time of printing; subject to manufacturer's change

telescopic steering column, heated power mirrors, remote fuel door release, intermittent wipers, rear wiper/washer, AM/FM ST ET cassette, overhead console with digital clock, calendar, stopwatch and outside thermometer, P205/60HR15 Pirelli P6 tires on cast aluminum wheels.

Optional Equipment:

	Retail Price	Dealer Invoice	Low Price
4-speed automatic transmission	550	468	510
Power moonroof	1125	957	1041
Touring Pkg.	2635	2240	2438
Power moonroof with shade, leather seats, trip computer.			
Heated front seats	225	192	209

Merkur XR4Ti

3-door hatchback	$19759	$17580	$18670
Destination charge	170	170	170

Standard Equipment:

2.3-liter turbocharged PFI 4-cylinder engine, 5-speed manual transmission, power steering, air conditioning, cloth reclining front bucket seats, driver's seat height adjustment, asymmetrically split folding rear seatback, rear defogger and wiper/washer, bronze tinted glass, intermittent wipers, console with armrest and storage, tachometer, coolant temperature and turbo boost gauges, cargo tiedowns and net, lighted right visor mirror, AM/FM ST ET cassette, 195/60HR15 Pirelli P6 tires on alloy wheels.

Optional Equipment:

3-speed automatic transmission	479	407	443
Heated front seats	225	192	209
Leather interior	989	841	715
Tilt/slide screened moonroof	549	466	505
Cruise control	182	154	168

Mitsubishi Eclipse

This new sporty coupe is the first car built by Diamond-Star Motors, a 50-50 partnership between Chrysler and Japan's Mitsubishi Motors. Chrysler-Plymouth dealers will sell a nearly identical version as the Plymouth Laser. Both are built at the new Diamond-Star plant in Illinois, and will go

Prices are accurate at time of printing; subject to manufacturer's change

1990 Mitsubishi Eclipse

on sale in January as 1990 models. Mitsubishi designed the interior and supplies the powertrains while the 3-door hatchback body is the result of a styling collaboration between Mitsubishi and Chrysler. Eclipse and Laser differ only slightly in trim. Their front-drive platform is taken from the Mitsubishi Galant compact sedan. At 170 inches overall, Eclipse is seven inches shorter than the Ford Probe, one of its principal targets. A 90-horsepower 1.8-liter 4-cylinder powers base and upgraded GS Eclipses. The Eclipse GS DOHC 16 Valve takes its name from its double-overhead cam 135-horsepower 2.0-liter four. A turbocharged and intercooled 2.0 DOHC four rated at 190 horsepower forms the basis for the GS Turbo. All but the turbo are available with an optional 4-speed automatic transmission. Four-wheel disc brakes are standard on all models; Mitsubishi says an anti-lock system is in the works for 1991. A 4-wheel-drive turbo model is to be introduced in the fall of 1989. Prices had not been announced at publication time, but Mitsubishi says the base Eclipse will start at $10,000 or less, while a fully optioned turbo will go for around $15,000. That would undercut such competitors as the Probe, Toyota Celica and Acura Integra—cars the Eclipse equals or exceeds on most points by which sporty coupes are measured. The best-balanced Eclipse is the GS DOHC 16 Valve equipped with the slick-shifting 5-speed. It has significantly more muscle than the 1.8-liter version, but does without the feistiness under full power that can make the Turbo a demanding car to drive fast. Its firm ride is only marginally stiffer than the base car's, but wider, lower-profile tires puts its handling among the best in the class. The power steering is a touch light for some drivers.

Specifications

	3-door hatchback
Wheelbase, in.	92.7
Overall length, in.	170.5
Overall width, in.	66.5
Overall height, in.	51.4
Turn diameter, ft.	NA
Curb weight, lbs.	2524
Cargo vol., cu. ft.	10.2
Fuel capacity, gal.	15.9
Seating capacity	4
Front headroom, in.	37.9
Front shoulder room, in.	55.1
Front legroom, max., in.	43.8
Rear headroom, in.	34.1
Rear shoulder room, in.	45.7
Rear legroom, min., in.	28.5

Engines

	ohc I-4	dohc I-4	Turbo dohc I-4
Size, liters/cu. in.	1.8/107	2.0/122	2.0/122
Fuel delivery	PFI	PFI	PFI
Horsepower @ rpm	92 @ 5000	135 @ 6000	190 @ 6000
Torque (lbs./ft.) @ rpm	107 @ 3500	125 @ 5000	190 @ 5000
Availability	S	S	S
EPA city/highway mpg			
5-speed OD manual	26/37	24/36	24/36
4-speed OD automatic	26/37	24/34	

Prices not available at time of publication.

Mitsubishi Galant

On sale since May, Galant is a front-drive compact sedan that replaced the smaller Tredia to give Mitsubishi a rival for cars such as the Honda Accord, Toyota Camry and Mazda 626. All Galants are 4-door notchbacks in base, luxury LS or sporty GS form. Base and LS use a 102-horsepower 2.0-liter 4-cylinder engine. A 5-speed manual transmission is standard on the base Galant, a 4-speed automatic

Mitsubishi Galant GS

Specifications

	4-door notchback
Wheelbase, in.	102.4
Overall length, in.	183.9
Overall width, in.	66.7
Overall height, in.	53.5
Turn diameter, ft.	34.8
Curb weight, lbs.	2601
Cargo vol., cu. ft.	12.3
Fuel capacity, gal.	15.9
Seating capacity	5
Front headroom, in.	38.6
Front shoulder room, in.	54.7
Front legroom, max., in.	41.9
Rear headroom, in.	37.4
Rear shoulder room, in.	54.4
Rear legroom, min., in.	36.0

Engines

	ohc I-4	dohc I-4
Size, liters/cu. in.	2.0/122	2.0/122
Fuel delivery	PFI	PFI
Horsepower @ rpm	102 @ 5000	135 @ 6000
Torque (lbs./ft.) @ rpm	116 @ 4500	125 @ 5000
Availability	S[1]	S[2]
EPA city/highway mpg		
5-speed OD manual	23/30	21/27
4-speed OD automatic	22/28	

1. Base, LS 2. GS

is standard on the LS, optional on the base. A 135-horsepower double-overhead cam, 16-valve 2.0 powers the GS. The GS is to get an automatic-transmission option late in the model year. GS standards include 4-wheel disc brakes, high-performance tires and Mitsubishi's Active-Electronically Controlled Suspension. Anti-lock brakes are a GS option. The new Galant is roomy, comfortable, solid and competent. The base engine is adequate, though automatic transmission hinders it on hills and in fast-paced expressway traffic. The GS has outstanding acceleration. Its 5-speed manual allows the fine engine's power to be tapped, but the delayed availability of automatic will limit the car's sales appeal. Base and LS models have controlled rides and handle turns well. The GS increases their cornering limits, but we're not convinced the electronically controlled suspension on the GS is the right choice for low-cost, long-term reliability. Inside, there's ample room for four adults, plenty of cargo space, and well-designed controls that have easy operation and a precision feel. Galant isn't a revolutionary compact sedan, but it's good in many ways and competitively priced.

Prices

Mitsubishi Galant	Retail Price	Dealer Invoice	Low Price
4-door notchback, 5-speed	$10971	—	—
4-door notchback, automatic	11819	—	—
LS 4-door notchback, automatic	13579	—	—
GS 4-door notchback, 5-speed	15269	—	—
Destination charge	265	265	265

Dealer invoice and low price not available at time of publication.

Standard Equipment:

2.0-liter PFI 4-cylinder engine, 5-speed manual transmission, power steering and brakes, cloth reclining front bucket seats, outboard rear lap/shoulder belts, tachometer and coolant temperature gauge, dual trip odometers, intermittent wipers, optical horn, automatic-off headlamps, digital clock, tinted glass, remote mirrors, tilt steering column, center console with covered storage, cup and coin holders, remote fuel door and decklid releases, right visor mirror, rear defogger, 185/70SR14 all-season SBR tires. **LS** adds: 4-speed automatic transmission with power and economy modes, variable intermittent wipers, cruise control, power windows and locks, power

Prices are accurate at time of printing; subject to manufacturer's change

mirrors, front spot lamps, driver's seat height and lumbar support adjustments, velour upholstery, rear center armrest with trunk-through, front seatback pockets, storage tray under passenger seat, bilevel console, AM/FM ST ET cassette with power antenna, rear heat ducts. **GS** adds to base: DOHC 16-valve engine, 4-wheel disc brakes, variable-assist steering, electronically controlled suspension, electronic time and alarm system, leather-wrapped steering wheel and shift knob, switchable green or orange instrument lighting, cruise control, power windows and locks, power mirrors, front and rear spot lamps, driver's seat height adjustment, contoured rear seat, sport cloth upholstery, power antenna, front mud guards, rear heat ducts, 195/60HR15 SBR performance tires on alloy wheels.

Optional Equipment:	Retail Price	Dealer Invoice	Low Price
Anti-lock braking system, GS	1495	—	—
Air conditioning	790	—	—
AM/FM ST ET cassette, base	552	—	—
w/EQ, LS & GS	316	—	—
Power sunroof, LS & GS	685	—	—
Wheel covers, base	78	—	—
Floormats	67	—	—
Mud guards, base & LS	98	—	—

Mitsubishi Mirage

Mitsubishi Mirage 4-door

Mirage has been redesigned and repositioned upmarket from Mitsubishi's Korean-built Precis subcompact. Its front-drive platform no longer forms the basis for the Precis, which also is sold as the Hyundai Excel. Mirage comes as a

Prices are accurate at time of printing; subject to manufacturer's change.

3-door hatchback or a 4-door sedan. Four-door models have a 96.7-inch wheelbase, versus 93.9 for hatchbacks, and at 170.1 inches bumper-to-bumper, are nearly a foot longer than the 3-doors. Base hatchbacks have a 1.5-liter 4-cylinder engine and a 3-speed automatic transmission as standard. Sedans come in base and LS trim with the same 1.5 engine, but offer a choice of a 5-speed manual or the 3-speed automatic. The Mirage Turbo hatchback has a turbocharged 16-valve 1.6-liter four and is available only with a 5-speed manual. Mirage hatchbacks with slightly revised content are sold as Colts by Dodge and Plymouth. Jeep-Eagle dealers sell a version of the 4-door as the Summit. All Mirages are now imported from Japan, but eventually 4-door models and

Specifications

	3-door hatchback	4-door notchback
Wheelbase, in.	93.9	96.7
Overall length, in.	158.7	170.1
Overall width, in.	65.7	65.7
Overall height, in.	52.0	52.8
Turn diameter, ft.	30.2	30.8
Curb weight, lbs.	2238	2271
Cargo vol., cu. ft.	11.5	10.3
Fuel capacity, gal.	13.2	13.2
Seating capacity	5	5
Front headroom, in.	38.3	39.1
Front shoulder room, in.	53.5	53.5
Front legroom, max., in.	41.9	41.9
Rear headroom, in.	36.9	37.5
Rear shoulder room, in.	50.7	53.1
Rear legroom, min., in.	32.5	34.4

Engines

	ohc I-4	Turbo dohc I-4
Size, liters/cu. in.	1.5/90	1.6/97
Fuel delivery	PFI	PFI
Horsepower @ rpm	81 @ 5500	135 @ 6000
Torque (lbs./ft.) @ rpm	91 @ 3000	141 @ 3000
Availability	S	S

EPA city/highway mpg

5-speed OD manual	29/35	23/29
3-speed automatic	27/29	

Summits will be built at Diamond-Star Motors, the Mitsubishi/Chrysler Corporation joint-venture plant in Illinois. While plowing no new ground, base and LS Mirages are comfortable and generally competent modern Japanese subcompacts. The 1.5 runs smoothly, but has little power to spare with automatic transmission. The 4-door has decent passenger room for a small sedan, and on the LS version, the convenience of split, fold-down rear seatbacks for extra cargo space. Base and LS Mirages trail the trend-setting Honda Civic in performance, but offer comparable interior room and longer warranties. The quick and nimble Turbo hatchback, meanwhile, enjoys power over a broad range of engine speeds with minimal turbo lag. Smoothness and refinement characterize a delightful turbo package that outruns most rivals.

Prices

Mitsubishi Mirage	Retail Price	Dealer Invoice	Low Price
3-door hatchback, automatic	$9159	—	—
4-door notchback, 5-speed	8859	—	—
4-door notchback, automatic	9329	—	—
LS 4-door notchback, 5-speed	10209	—	—
LS 4-door notchback, automatic	10699	—	—
Turbo 3-door hatchback, 5-speed	11969	—	—
Destination charge	265	265	265

Dealer invoice and low price not available at time of publication.

Standard Equipment:

1.5-liter PFI 4-cylinder engine, 3-speed automatic transmission (hatchback; 5-speed manual on 4-door), power brakes, reclining front bucket seats, cloth upholstery (vinyl with cloth inserts on 4-door), coolant temperature gauge, trip odometer, outboard rear lap/shoulder belts, rear defogger, console with storage bin, split folding rear seat (hatchback), remote hatch release, tinted glass, optical horn, 155/80SR13 all-season tires. **LS** adds: 5-speed manual or 3-speed automatic transmission, power steering, velour upholstery, split folding rear seat, tachometer, digital clock, intermittent wipers, remote fuel door and trunk releases, right outside mirror, 175/70SR13 tires. **Turbo** adds to base: 1.6-liter PFI DOHC PFI turbocharged engine, 5-speed manual transmission, power steering, power 4-wheel disc brakes, sport suspension, tachometer, sport seats, digital clock, anti-lift windshield wipers, intermittent wipers, rear wiper/washer, tilt/telescopic steering column, air dam and sill extensions, rear spoiler, remote fuel door release, 195/60HR14 performance tires on alloy wheels.

Prices are accurate at time of printing; subject to manufacturer's change.

Optional Equipment:	Retail Price	Dealer Invoice	Low Price
Air conditioning	744	—	—
Power steering, base	262	—	—
4-door requires automatic transmission.			
AM/FM ST ET, base	353	—	—
AM/FM ST ET cassette	552	—	—
Digital clock, base	56	—	—
Rear wiper/washer, 3-doors	138	—	—
Floormats	63	—	—
Mud guards	67	—	—
Trim rings, base 4-door	58	—	—

Mitsubishi Sigma

Mitsubishi Sigma

Formerly known as Galant, and for most of 1988 as the
Galant Sigma, this front-drive sedan now is simply the
Sigma. It returns little changed in content after giving up its
Galant name to a new Mitsubishi compact. The two cars
share the same 102.4-inch wheelbase, but Sigma's body is
two inches longer at 185.8 inches overall. And where Galant
is aimed at the likes of the Honda Accord, Sigma is positioned to challenge larger, more upscale Japanese sedans
such as the Nissan Maxima and Toyota Cressida. Sigma has
a 3.0-liter V-6 as standard equipment. For '89 anti-lock
brakes are available as an individual option as well as part of
the Eurotech Package, which includes Mitsubishi's Elec-

Prices are accurate at time of printing; subject to manufacturer's change.

tronically Controlled Suspension (ECS). ECS lets the driver choose from soft, medium or firm suspension modes, or it can automatically adjust firmness and ride height. Also new for '89 is the capability to arm the standard theft-deterrent system by key-locking the doors. And the power sunroof can now be closed up to 30 seconds after turning off the ignition. Mitsubishi's refined V-6 works in concert with the automatic transmission to deliver smooth, potent power. We're glad anti-lock brakes are now a separate option instead of being part of the expensive Eurotech Package with its ECS. We don't notice enough benefit from ECS to make it worthwhile. Sigma's cabin remains cramped front and rear, however. The driver's seat doesn't go back far enough for tall people to have a comfortable reach to the wheel and pedals, plus the optional power sunroof leaves inadequate head

Specifications

	4-door notchback
Wheelbase, in.	102.4
Overall length, in.	185.8
Overall width, in.	66.7
Overall height, in.	51.6
Turn diameter, ft.	34.8
Curb weight, lbs.	3075
Cargo vol., cu. ft.	12.4
Fuel capacity, gal.	15.9
Seating capacity	5
Front headroom, in.	37.5
Front shoulder room, in.	53.5
Front legroom, max., in.	40.3
Rear headroom, in.	36.7
Rear shoulder room, in.	53.2
Rear legroom, min., in.	36.4

Engines

	ohc V-6
Size, liters/cu. in.	3.0/181
Fuel delivery	PFI
Horsepower @ rpm	142 @ 5000
Torque (lbs./ft.) @ rpm	168 @ 2500
Availability	S

EPA city/highway mpg
4-speed OD automatic	18/22

room for most. Rear seat passengers are squeezed unless the front seats are moved well forward. Though short on room, Sigma offers good performance and optional anti-lock braking at reasonable cost.

Prices

Mitsubishi Sigma	Retail Price	Dealer Invoice	Low Price
4-door notchback	$17069	—	—
Destination charge	265	265	265

Dealer invoice and low price not available at time of publication.

Standard Equipment:

3.0-liter PFI V-6 engine, 4-speed automatic transmission, power steering and brakes, reclining front bucket seats, 8-way adjustable driver's seat, velour trim, underseat tray, seatback pockets, folding rear seatbacks, rear armrest, door pockets, rear heat ducts, power windows and locks, heated power mirrors, tinted glass with dark upper band, tilt steering column, rear defogger, speed-sensitive variable intermittent wipers, digital clock, trip odometer, tachometer, coolant temperature gauge, voltmeter, cruise control, low fuel and washer fluid lights, AM/FM ST ET cassette, power antenna, theft deterrent system, remote fuel door and decklid releases, 195/60HR15 tires on alloy wheels.

Optional Equipment:

Anti-lock brakes	1495	—	—
Eurotech Pkg.	2042	—	—
Electronically controlled suspension, anti-lock brakes.			
Power sunroof	685	—	—
Leather seats	816	—	—
AM/FM ST ET cassette w/EQ	361	—	—
Floormats	80	—	—

Mitsubishi Wagon

This rear-drive minivan gets some minor equipment revisions and what Mitsubishi calls "racoon" blackout exterior trim around the windows. Seven-seat passenger versions are called Wagons and 2-seat cargo models are Vans. New

Prices are accurate at time of printing; subject to manufacturer's change.

Mitsubishi Wagon

standard features include a high-mounted stop lamp, heavy-duty rear defroster with timer, cargo-bay tie-down hooks, a new on-board engine diagnostics system, and one-touch front door locks. The top-line LS Wagon also gains power mirrors and an auto-down power driver's window. Mitsubishi's minivan layout is similar to the mid-engine, rear-drive form used by Nissan and Toyota. A 2.4-liter 4-cylinder engine is mounted behind the front axle and between the front seats. A 4-speed automatic is the sole transmission and all models have a sliding side door and a rear liftgate. Passenger models have reclining front bucket seats, two middle-place captain's chairs that recline, swivel and slide fore and aft, and a 3-place rear bench with reclining seatback. The rear bench can also be removed to improve cargo room, which is minimal with all seats in place. The common layout of all Japanese minivans, except the new front-engine Mazda MPV, gives them a short wheelbase and considerable body overhang. The result is a tight turning circle and good low-speed maneuverability, but a ride that's bouncy, pitchy and uncomfortable under most conditions. Mitsubishi's Wagon outhandles the Toyota Van, feels more stable and has less body lean in turns. But it shares such common shortfalls as a high-step up over the front wheels to the front seats, a cramped, bus-like driving position, and an engine cover that thwarts passage between the cabin's front and rear seats. Mitsubishi gets credit for highly flexible seating, but the front-drive Dodge Caravan/Plymouth Voyager, and now the MPV, are better choices for passenger use.

Specifications

	4-door van
Wheelbase, in.	88.0
Overall length, in.	175.2
Overall width, in.	66.5
Overall height, in.	71.3
Turn diameter, ft.	29.5
Curb weight, lbs.	3285
Cargo vol., cu. ft.	161.6
Fuel capacity, gal.	14.2
Seating capacity	7
Front headroom, in.	38.6
Front shoulder room, in.	57.3
Front legroom, max., in.	40.0
Rear headroom, in.	39.0
Rear shoulder room, in.	60.6
Rear legroom, min., in.	41.1

Engines

	ohc I-4
Size, liters/cu. in.	2.4/143
Fuel delivery	PFI
Horsepower @ rpm	107 @ 5000
Torque (lbs./ft.) @ rpm	132 @ 3500
Availability	S

EPA city/highway mpg

4-speed OD automatic	18/21

Prices

Mitsubishi Wagon	Retail Price	Dealer Invoice	Low Price
4-door van	$14929	—	—
4-door van w/LS Pkg.	16579	—	—
Destination charge	265	265	265

Dealer invoice and low price not available at time of publication.

Standard Equipment:

2.4-liter PFI 4-cylinder engine, 4-speed automatic transmission, power brakes, carpeting, console with storage compartment, rear defogger, remote fuel door release, tinted glass, rear heater, dual outside mirrors, velour upholstery, two recline/swivel/slide middle seats, third fold-down, removable bench seat, tilt steering column, rear side storage bins, variable intermittent

Prices are accurate at time of printing; subject to manufacturer's change.

wipers, P205/75R14 tires. **LS Pkg.** adds: power steering, digital clock, cruise control, power windows and door locks, bronze tinted glass, bodyside molding, AM/FM ST ET cassette.

Optional Equipment:	Retail Price	Dealer Invoice	Low Price
Dual air conditioning	1426	—	—
AM/FM ST ET cassette, base	511	—	—
Power sunroof	685	—	—
Alloy wheels, LS	335	—	—
Power steering, base	268	—	—
Power mirrors, base	65	—	—
Digital clock, base	56	—	—
Floormats	52	—	—

Nissan Maxima

Nissan Maxima GXE

Redesigned for 1989, Maxima's boxy styling is discarded in favor of all-new aero sheetmetal. Last year's 5-door wagon has been dropped, so all '89s are 4-door sedans. Maxima retains its predecessor's front-drive layout, but grows enough to climb from the compact- to the mid-size class. The wheelbase is stretched by four inches and the new body is longer by six and wider by three. Every interior dimension is up as well, though curb weight increases only 46 pounds. Carried over is the 3.0-liter V-6 that's essentially the same engine used in the 300ZX sports car. Two trim levels are

Prices are accurate at time of printing; subject to manufacturer's change.

offered: luxury GXE, which comes only with a 4-speed automatic transmission; and sporty SE, with a choice of 5-speed manual or automatic. The automatics have a shift lock that requires the driver to place a foot on the brake pedal before shifting from park. SE's standard 4-wheel disc brakes have an anti-lock option; GXEs are available only with a front disc/rear drum set up. An Electronics Package optional for the GXE includes a new heads-up display that reflects the dashboard's digital speedometer reading onto the lower-left corner of the windshield, in the driver's field of vision. The package also includes Sonar Suspension II that uses a sonar sensor under the front bumper to "read" the road surface and adjust shock-absorber damping to try and maintain a supple ride. Standard on SE and optional on GXE is a new

Specifications

	4-door notchback
Wheelbase, in.	104.3
Overall length, in.	187.6
Overall width, in.	69.3
Overall height, in.	55.1
Turn diameter, ft.	36.7
Curb weight, lbs.	3086
Cargo vol., cu. ft.	14.5
Fuel capacity, gal.	18.5
Seating capacity	5
Front headroom, in.	39.5
Front shoulder room, in.	NA
Front legroom, max., in.	43.7
Rear headroom, in.	36.9
Rear shoulder room, in.	NA
Rear legroom, min., in.	33.2

Engines

	ohc V-6
Size, liters/cu. in.	3.0/181
Fuel delivery	PFI
Horsepower @ rpm	160 @ 5200
Torque (lbs./ft.) @ rpm	181 @ 3200
Availability	S

EPA city/highway mpg

5-speed OD manual	20/26
4-speed OD automatic	19/26

Bose stereo system. Motorized front shoulder belts are standard. The SE with a 5-speed is a credible sports sedan. It's agile and sure-footed and enjoys the security of optional anti-lock brakes. A harsh ride over rough pavement is its only major flaw. The GXE is softer by nature, with a ride that's almost too pliant, though we'd expect it to be comfortable and competent in most city and highway travel. Some flaws: The automatic transmission is slow to downshift for passing. And there's no surplus of rear-seat headroom, a drawback in a mid-size sedan. GXE's heads-up display does indeed make speedometer-watching easier.

Prices

Nissan Maxima	Retail Price	Dealer Invoice	Low Price
GXE 4-door notchback, automatic	$16999	—	—
SE 4-door notchback, 5-speed	17999	—	—
SE 4-door notchback, automatic	18899	—	—
Destination charge	250	250	250

Dealer invoice and low price not available at time of publication.

Standard Equipment:

3.0-liter PFI V-6, 4-speed automatic transmission, power steering, air conditioning, power windows and locks with keyless entry, velour reclining front bucket seats, driver's seat height and lumbar adjustments, split folding rear seat, power mirrors, cruise control, tinted glass, AM/FM ST ET cassette with diversity antenna, motorized front shoulder belts with manual lap belts, theft deterrent system, tilt steering column, variable intermittent wipers, rear defogger, remote fuel door and decklid releases, illuminated entry, tachometer, dual trip odometers, coolant temperature gauge, digital clock, 195/60R16 tires on alloy wheels. **SE** adds: 5-speed manual or 4-speed automatic transmission, 4-wheel disc brakes, Nissan-Bose audio system, leather-wrapped steering wheel and shift knob, power glass sunroof, fog lights.

Optional Equipment:

Anti-lock brakes, SE	1450	—	—
Luxury Pkg., GXE	1800	—	—
Power front seats, power sunroof, Nissan-Bose audio system.			
Electronic Equipment Pkg., GXE	1500	—	—
Digital instruments with head-up display, automatic temperature control, sonar suspension; requires Luxury Pkg.			
Leather trim, GXE	900	—	—
Pearl glow paint	350	—	—

Prices are accurate at time of printing; subject to manufacturer's change

Nissan Pulsar NX

Nissan Pulsar NX SE

This front-drive sporty coupe loses its Sportbak option but gains more power for its base engine. Pulsar, a 4-seater built off the subcompact Sentra platform, comes in base XE and more powerful SE guise. Both models are 3-door hatchbacks with a removable hatch lid and T-top roof panels that allow a quasi-convertible configuration. The discontinued Sportbak was a removable fiberglass rear-roof section that turned Pulsar into a mini-station wagon. A new cylinder head for the XE's 1.6-liter 4-cylinder engine boosts horsepower from 69 to 90. The head has three valves per cylinder—two intake and one exhaust—instead of two. The 1.6 is available with a 5-speed manual or 3-speed automatic transmission. The SE returns with a 125-horsepower double-overhead cam, 16-valve 1.8-liter four. SE transmission choices are a 5-speed manual or a 4-speed automatic. A folding 2-place rear seat is standard on both models. For 1989, Pulsar is covered by Nissan's new 36-month/ 36,000-mile basic warranty on the entire car. It replaces a 12-month, 12,500-mile warranty. We haven't yet sampled the 90-horsepower 1.6, but the 1.8 coupled to a 5-speed manual gives pleasing if unspectacular performance. Handling is above average and the ride is generally compliant. A supportive front bucket places the driver within perfect reach of the smooth-working and excellently located controls, though visibility is hampered by the low seating position. The 2-place rear seat is fine for children.

There's lots of wind and road noise even before you start removing roof panels. Popping the T-tops is simple; taking off the heavy rear hatch is much more of a chore. Overall, Pulsar NX is a solidly built, fun-to-drive junior sports car.

Specifications

	3-door hatchback
Wheelbase, in.	95.7
Overall length, in.	166.5
Overall width, in.	65.7
Overall height, in.	50.8
Turn diameter, ft.	33.5
Curb weight, lbs.	2388
Cargo vol., cu. ft.	7.0
Fuel capacity, gal.	13.2
Seating capacity	4
Front headroom, in.	38.0
Front shoulder room, in.	NA
Front legroom, max., in.	44.2
Rear headroom, in.	33.9
Rear shoulder room, in.	NA
Rear legroom, min., in.	31.1

Engines

	ohc I-4	dohc I-4
Size, liters/cu. in.	1.6/97	1.8/110
Fuel delivery	TBI	PFI
Horsepower @ rpm	90 @ 6000	125 @ 6400
Torque (lbs./ft.) @ rpm	96 @ 3200	112 @ 4800
Availability	S	S[1]

EPA city/highway mpg

5-speed OD manual	26/34	23/29
3-speed automatic	24/29	
4-speed OD automatic		21/28

1. SE

Prices

Nissan Pulsar NX	Retail Price	Dealer Invoice	Low Price
XE 3-door hatchback, 5-speed	$11749	$10280	$11015
XE 3-door hatchback, automatic	12269	10735	11502
SE 3-door hatchback, 5-speed	12999	11374	12187
SE 3-door hatchback, automatic	13754	12035	12895
Destination charge	250	250	250

Prices are accurate at time of printing; subject to manufacturer's change.

Standard Equipment:

XE: 1.6-liter TBI 4-cylinder engine, 5-speed manual or 3-speed automatic transmission, power steering and brakes, T-bar roof, removable hatchback lid, variable intermittent wipers, tachometer, coolant temperature gauge, trip odometer, AM/FM ST ET with diversity antenna, power mirrors, tilt steering column, center console, remote fuel door and hatch releases, reclining front cloth bucket seats, 185/70R13 tires. **SE** adds: 1.8-liter DOHC 16-valve PFI engine, 5-speed manual or 4-speed automatic transmission, tweed-type upholstery, 195/60R14 tires on alloy wheels.

Optional Equipment:	Retail Price	Dealer Invoice	Low Price
Air conditioning	795	660	728
Security system/alloy wheel locks, SE . . .	199	165	182
Fog lights, SE	145	120	133
Sport graphics	105	87	96

Nissan Sentra

Nissan Sentra Standard 2-door

Nissan's most popular U.S. model line, the subcompact Sentra, gets a facelift and more power, while the 4-wheel-drive station wagon gains an improved 4WD system. Horsepower on Sentra's 1.6-liter 4-cylinder engine jumps from 69 to 90 thanks to a new cylinder head with three valves per cylinder instead of two. The 4WD wagon trades its on-demand, part-time 4WD set up for a new permanently engaged system. It has a viscous coupling that splits torque between the front and rear wheels as needed to maintain traction. Nissan now

Prices are accurate at time of printing; subject to manufacturer's change.

Specifications

	2-door notchback	4-door notchback	3-door Sport Coupe	5-door wagon
Wheelbase, in.	95.7	95.7	95.7	95.7
Overall length, in.	168.7	168.7	166.5	172.2
Overall width, in.	64.6	64.6	65.6	64.6
Overall height, in.	54.3	54.3	52.2	54.3
Turn diameter, ft.	30.2	30.2	30.2	30.2
Curb weight, lbs.	2200	2231	2258	2304
Cargo vol., cu. ft.	12.0	12.0	16.0	24.0
Fuel capacity, gal.	13.2	13.2	13.2	13.2
Seating capacity	5	5	4	5
Front headroom, in. . . .	38.2	38.2	37.0	38.2
Front shoulder room, in. .	52.1	52.1	52.3	52.1
Front legroom, max., in. .	41.8	41.8	41.6	41.8
Rear headroom, in.	36.8	36.8	29.2	39.3
Rear shoulder room, in. .	51.3	52.1	50.3	52.1
Rear legroom, min., in. .	31.4	31.4	NA	31.4

Engines

	ohc I-4
Size, liters/cu. in.	1.6/97
Fuel delivery	TBI
Horsepower @ rpm	90 @ 6000
Torque (lbs./ft.) @ rpm	96 @ 3200
Availability	S

EPA city/highway mpg

5-speed OD manual	28/36
3-speed automatic	26/30

calls it the All-Wheel Drive wagon and sells it only with a 5-speed manual transmission. All other Sentras are front-wheel drive and are available with manual or a 3-speed automatic. In addition to the 5-door wagon, Sentra body styles include 2- and 4-door sedans, a 3-door hatchback sedan and a 3-door hatchback Sport Coupe. All have new grilles and tail-lamps, the first appearance change since Sentra was redesigned for 1987. Sentra gets a 36-month/36,000-mile basic warranty for 1989, in place of the 12-month/12,500-mile coverage Nissan used previously. Some Sentras are built at Nissan's Tennessee assembly plant and some are imported from Japan. Sentra doesn't offer extraordinary performance or have exceptionally low prices, but it does stand as a pretty good value among subcompacts. And it rates highly among cars under $20,000 in J.D. Power & Associates customer satisfaction surveys. All Sentra's can use the extra 21 horsepower, especially with three or four aboard and the air conditioner on. Ride, room, comfort and road manners are middle-of-the-subcompact-pack: not up with the Honda Civic or Volkswagen Golf, but comparable to Ford Escort or Hyundai Excel. We rate the Standard 2-door sedan and E models as the best Sentra values.

Prices

Nissan Sentra	Retail Price	Dealer Invoice	Low Price
Standard 2-door notchback, 4-speed	$6849	$6438	$6644
E 2-door notchback, 5-speed	7999	7039	7519
E 2-door notchback, automatic	8869	7805	8337
XE 2-door notchback, 5-speed	9649	8443	9046
XE 2-door notchback, automatic	10544	9226	9885
E 4-door notchback, 5-speed	8549	7523	8036
E 4-door notchback, automatic	9419	8289	8854
XE 4-door notchback, 5-speed	10299	9012	9656
XE 4-door notchback, automatic	11194	9795	10495
E 5-door wagon, 5-speed	9224	8117	8671
E 5-door wagon, automatic	10094	8883	9489
XE 5-door wagon, 5-speed	10724	9348	10054
XE 5-door wagon, automatic	11619	10167	10893
XE 4WD 5-door wagon, 5-speed	11524	10084	10804
XE 4WD 5-door wagon, automatic	12419	10867	11643
XE 3-door coupe, 5-speed	10674	9340	10007
XE 3-door coupe, automatic	11569	10123	10846
SE 3-door coupe, 5-speed	11924	10374	11149
SE 3-door coupe, automatic	12444	10826	11635
Destination charge	250	250	250

Standard Equipment:

Standard: 1.6-liter TBI 4-cylinder engine, 4-speed manual transmission, power brakes, coolant temperature gauge, rear defogger, taillamp/brake failure warning, headlamps-on tone, reclining front bucket seats, center console, 155R13 all-season SBR tires. **E** adds: 5-speed manual or 3-speed automatic transmission, power steering and tilt steering column (with automatic transmission only), tinted glass, dual outside mirrors, black bodyside moldings, trip odometer, intermittent wipers. **XE** adds: dual remote mirrors, cloth upholstery, tilt steering column, tachometer (coupe), remote decklid/hatch releases, AM/FM ST (with automatic transmission only), power steering, rear wiper/washer (coupe), 175/70R13 all-season tires. **GXE** adds: wide

Prices are accurate at time of printing; subject to manufacturer's change.

CONSUMER GUIDE®

bodyside moldings, upgraded cloth upholstery, AM/FM ST ET with diversity antenna, variable intermittent wipers, driver's seat lumbar support, tachometer, visor mirrors, large console with lid, digital clock. **SE** adds to XE coupe: pop-up sunroof, multiple driver's seat adjustments, visor mirrors, digital clock, large console with lid, AM/FM ST ET with diversity antenna, variable intermittent wipers, 185/60R14 tires on alloy wheels. **All Wheel Drive** wagon has permanent, full-time 4-wheel drive.

Optional Equipment:	Retail Price	Dealer Invoice	Low Price
Air conditioning	795	660	728
Removable glass sunroof, XE coupe	450	374	412
Two-tone paint, SE coupe	300	249	275
Metallic paint, Standard	100	83	92

Nissan Stanza

Nissan Stanza GXE

The 5-door wagon has been dropped, but Nissan plans a replacement under a new model name in the spring of '89. Carried over is the 4-door notchback sedan in base E and more-expensive GXE trim. A new grille, taillamps and interior fabrics are the only changes. While the wagon was available with front- or 4-wheel drive, the sedan comes only with front-drive. Stanza uses a 2.0-liter 4-cylinder engine and a 5-speed manual or 4-speed automatic transmission. All Nissans are now covered by a 36-month/36,000-mile

Prices are accurate at time of printing; subject to manufacturer's change.

basic warranty. It replaces a 12-month/12,500-mile plan. Since an all-new wagon is on the way, we'll confine our remarks to the Stanza sedan. It's a pleasant, well-equipped compact priced below such Japanese rivals as the Honda Accord and Toyota Camry. Its main shortcoming is a lack of muscle: 97 horsepower for 2800 pounds. You frequently have to floor the throttle pedal to keep pace with traffic. The automatic transmission further handcuffs performance. It changes too quickly to the higher gears and is reluctant to downshift promptly for passing. The car is at least economical; we averaged 27 mpg in our last test, which included a lot of city miles. Body lean is well controlled in turns but the power steering is light and the tires let you know early that they're not up to hard cornering. The penal-

Specifications

	4-door notchback
Wheelbase, in.	100.4
Overall length, in.	177.8
Overall width, in.	66.5
Overall height, in.	54.9
Turn diameter, ft.	32.2
Curb weight, lbs.	2770
Cargo vol., cu. ft.	12.0
Fuel capacity, gal.	16.1
Seating capacity	5
Front headroom, in.	38.9
Front shoulder room, in.	NA
Front legroom, max., in.	42.0
Rear headroom, in.	37.4
Rear shoulder room, in.	NA
Rear legroom, min., in.	33.0

Engines

	ohc I-4
Size, liters/cu. in.	2.0/120
Fuel delivery	PFI
Horsepower @ rpm	97 @ 5200
Torque (lbs./ft.) @ rpm	114 @ 2800
Availability	S

EPA city/highway mpg

5-speed OD manual	22/28
4-speed OD automatic	21/27

ty for the soft ride is a little too much bouncing over freeway dips. The driving position is workable, with a comfortable seat, clear and sensibly designed controls, and good outward visibility. Interior room is fine for four adults and the trunk has more usable space than its 12-cubic foot volume would indicate, plus, the rear seatbacks fold for extra cargo room. Stanza is a comfortable, well-built compact that simply needs more power.

Prices

Nissan Stanza	Retail Price	Dealer Invoice	Low Price
E 4-door notchback, 5-speed	$11849	$10368	$11109
E 4-door notchback, automatic	12599	11024	11812
GXE 4-door notchback, 5-speed	13799	12074	12937
GXE 4-door notchback, automatic	14549	12730	13640
Destination charge	250	250	250

Standard Equipment:

2.0-liter PFI 4-cylinder engine, 5-speed manual or 4-speed automatic transmission, power steering and brakes, tinted glass, reclining front bucket seats, coolant temperature gauge, dual trip odometers, tilt steering column, intermittent wipers, rear defogger, 185/70R14 tires. **GXE** adds: power mirrors, tinted upper windshield band, upgraded upholstery and carpet, cruise control, AM/FM cassette with diversity power antenna, variable intermittent wipers, tachometer, oil pressure and voltage gauges, driver's seat height and lumbar support adjustments, split folding rear seatbacks, visor mirrors.

Optional Equipment:

Air conditioning	795	660	728
Alloy wheels, GXE	420	328	374
Value Option Pkg., GXE	999	959	979
Air conditioning, power glass sunroof, vehicle security system, pinstripe.			
Two-tone paint, GXE	300	249	275

Nissan Van

Nissan's compact Van gets only minor equipment revisions for '89. Returning are base XE and plusher GXE models; the XE comes with a 5-speed manual or 4-speed automatic transmission, while the GXE comes only with the automatic. The

Nissan Van GXE

Nissan Van's mechanical layout is similar to that of the compact vans from Mitsubishi and Toyota. The rear wheels are driven by a 4-cylinder engine mounted behind the front axle and between the front seats. Nissan has standard seating for seven, in a 2-2-3 configuration, front to rear. The XE has a 2-place removable center bench seat. The GXE substitutes removable, swiveling captain's chairs. The 3-place rear bench standard on both models also is removable. There's a sliding side door and a unique-to-Nissan split rear liftgate with a window that opens separately. Front and rear air conditioning units are standard. The Van has Nissan's new 36-month/36,000-mile basic warranty in place of the previous 12-month/12,500-mile coverage. The mid-engine design has some serious compromises. You've got to climb over the front wheel wells to get in and out the front doors. Once in, the engine blocks access to the rear compartment and engine servicing requires the removal of cumbersome interior panels. The Nissan Van's unique liftgate is a plus, as is a cabin that devotes an uncommon amount of space to passengers, albeit at the expense of luggage capacity. On the road, the 2.4-liter four gives adequate acceleration, and while the Nissan's ride isn't as bouncy as the Mitsubishi Wagon's, its suspension is less absorbent, so it bangs over bumps rather than soaking them up. The Japanese mini-vans have quality assembly and low-speed maneuverability on their side, but for daily passenger duty, we prefer the front-engine/front-drive design of the Dodge Caravan and Plymouth Voyager.

Specifications

	4-door van
Wheelbase, in.	92.5
Overall length, in.	178.0
Overall width, in.	66.5
Overall height, in.	72.4
Turn diameter, ft.	30.2
Curb weight, lbs.	3330
Cargo vol., cu. ft.	157.6
Fuel capacity, gal.	17.7
Seating capacity	7
Front headroom, in.	39.0
Front shoulder room, in.	57.1
Front legroom, max., in.	39.8
Rear headroom, in.	39.0
Rear shoulder room, in.	57.7
Rear legroom, min., in.	31.3

Engines

	ohc I-4
Size, liters/cu. in.	2.4/146
Fuel delivery	TBI
Horsepower @ rpm	106 @ 4800
Torque (lbs./ft.) @ rpm	137 @ 2000
Availability	S

EPA city/highway mpg

5-speed OD manual	18/22
4-speed OD automatic	18/21

Prices

Nissan Van (1988 prices)	Retail Price	Dealer Invoice	Low Price
XE 4-door van, 5-speed	$14799	$12807	$13803
XE 4-door van, automatic	15744	13624	14684
GXE 4-door van, automatic	17099	14797	15948
Destination charge	250	250	250

Standard Equipment:

2.4-liter TBI 4-cylinder engine, 5-speed manual or 4-speed automatic transmission, power steering, power brakes, front and rear air conditioning,

Prices are accurate at time of printing; subject to manufacturer's change

7-passenger seating including cloth reclining front bucket seats with driver's seat lumbar support, reclining rear bench seats, AM/FM ST ET with clock, cruise control (with automatic transmission only), tinted glass, front and rear heaters, dual outside mirrors with power right, tilt/swing-up steering column, tachometer, coolant temperature gauge, trip odometer, headlamps-on warning, variable intermittent wipers, full wheel covers, P195/75R14 tires. **GXE** adds: second-row captain's chairs, power windows and locks, privacy glass, dual power mirrors, AM/FM ST ET cassette, rear wiper/washer.

Optional Equipment:	Retail Price	Dealer Invoice	Low Price
Dual sunroofs & alloy wheels, GXE	1300	1066	1183
Includes flip-up front sunroof, sliding rear sunroof and 205/70R14 tires.			
Two-tone paint	300	246	273
Roof luggage rack	155	127	141

Nissan 240SX

Nissan 240SX SE

Replacing the 200SX is an all-new sports coupe, the 240SX, so named for its 2.4-liter 4-cylinder engine and to conjure the memory of Nissan's classic 1970s 240Z sports car. The new car retains rear-wheel drive and is available as a 2-door XE Coupe or a 3-door SE hatchback. Their 97.4-inch wheelbase is nearly two inches longer than the 200SX's and overall length is up by 3.6 inches. The 2.4, the only engine offered, has three valves per cylinder—two intake, one exhaust. It makes 140 horsepower, 41 more than the 2.0 four standard in '88, but 25 fewer than last year's optional 3.0-liter V-6. Transmission choices are a 5-speed manual and 4-speed

Prices are accurate at time of printing; subject to manufacturer's change.

automatic. Four-wheel disc brakes are standard; the SE has an optional anti-lock system. Last year's independent rear suspension is replaced by an all-new multi-link, independent design. An optional heads-up instrument display is available only on the XE coupe. It projects the digital speedometer reading onto the lower left corner of the windshield, in the driver's field of vision. Nissan has replaced its previous 12-month/12,500-mile warranty with a 36-month/36,000 plan for 1989. On the road, the 240SX has a rough, unforgiving ride, though handling is balanced and predictable, and high-speed stability is outstanding. The engine sacrifices high-rev power and personality for good low- and mid-range performance. We think the hot styling calls out for more spirit under the hood. The cockpit is well-suited to

Specifications

	2-door notchback	3-door hatchback
Wheelbase, in.	97.4	97.4
Overall length, in.	178.0	178.0
Overall width, in.	66.5	66.5
Overall height, in.	50.8	50.8
Turn diameter, ft.	30.8	30.8
Curb weight, lbs.	2657	2690
Cargo vol., cu. ft.	8.6	14.2
Fuel capacity, gal.	15.9	15.9
Seating capacity	4	4
Front headroom, in.	37.8	37.8
Front shoulder room, in.	52.0	52.0
Front legroom, max., in.	42.0	42.0
Rear headroom, in.	34.5	33.3
Rear shoulder room, in.	52.0	51.8
Rear legroom, min., in.	23.8	23.8

Engines

	ohc I-4
Size, liters/cu. in.	2.4/146
Fuel delivery	PFI
Horsepower @ rpm	140 @ 5600
Torque (lbs./ft.) @ rpm	152 @ 4400
Availability	S

EPA city/highway mpg

5-speed OD manual	20/26
4-speed OD automatic	20/25

spirited driving, however, with clear gauges, gimmick-free controls and supportive seats. The rear seat is child-sized, and the air conditioner feels weak in hot, muggy conditions. The 240SX doesn't hit the high notes of some rivals, but its balance and pleasing design are not to be dismissed. And in a world of front-drive sporty coupes, its rear-wheel drive is a plus for some drivers.

Prices

Nissan 240SX	Retail Price	Dealer Invoice	Low Price
XE 2-door notchback, 5-speed	$12999	$11309	—
XE 2-door notchback, automatic	13759	11970	—
SE 3-door hatchback, 5-speed	13199	11483	—
SE 3-door hatchback, automatic	13959	12144	—
Destination charge	250	250	250

Low price not available at time of publication.

Standard Equipment:

XE: 2.4-liter PFI 4-cylinder engine, 5-speed manual or 4-speed automatic transmission, power steering, power 4-wheel disc brakes, reclining front bucket seats with driver's side lumbar support adjustment, motorized front shoulder belts with manual lap belts, outboard rear lap/shoulder belts, tilt steering column, tachometer, coolant temperature gauge, trip odometer, digital clock, variable intermittent wipers, tinted glass, dual remote mirrors, AM/FM ST ET with diversity antenna, rear defogger, door pockets, remote fuel door and decklid/liftgate releases, 195/60R15 all-season M + S SBR tires.

Optional Equipment:

Anti-lock braking system, SE	1400	1162	—
Requires Sport Pkg. & air conditioning.			
Air conditioning	795	660	—
Power Convenience Group, XE	999	899	—
Active speakers, head-up display, cruise control, power windows and locks, power mirrors, radio upgrade with cassette, map and footwell courtesy lights.			
Power Convenience Group, SE	799	719	—
Cruise control, power windows and locks, power mirrors, radio upgrade with cassette, rear wiper/washer.			
Sport Pkg., SE	799	719	—
Cruise control, sport suspension, front air dam, rear spoiler, leather-wrapped steering wheel and shift knob, upgraded upholstery.			
Power Convenience Group & Sport Pkg., SE	1399	1259	—

Prices are accurate at time of printing; subject to manufacturer's change.

	Retail Price	Dealer Invoice	Low Price
Two-tone paint	300	249	—
Power glass sunroof, XE	800	664	—
Removable glass sunroof, SE	450	374	—

XE requires Power Convenience Group; SE requires Power Convenience Group or Sport Pkg.

Nissan 300ZX

Nissan 300ZX Turbo

Nissan's rear-drive sports car is carried over unchanged in anticipation of an all-new model due in the spring of '89. Nissan has released no information on the new Z-car, except to acknowledge that while the current one has grown into somewhat of a hefty grand tourer, the new car will be oriented toward outright performance. For 1989, the base engine stays a 165-horsepower 3.0-liter V-6; the optional 205-horsepower turbocharged 3.0 also is carried over. The naturally aspirated 300ZX is available in 2+2 or 2-seat versions, while the 300ZX Turbo only comes as a 2-seater. The 300ZX is covered by Nissan's new basic 36-month/36,000 warranty, which replaces the previous 12-month/12,500-mile coverage. The 300ZX is competitive in price and performance with its nearest rival, the Toyota Supra. Both offer base models with naturally aspirated 6-cylinder engines and high-performance editions with turbocharged engines. Nissan has the better seller, despite several Supra advantages.

Prices are accurate at time of printing; subject to manufacturer's change.

Supra is available with anti-lock brakes, it rides better and the interior is more modern and harmonious. A Mazda RX-7 also gives the 300ZX a run for its money, and offers a turbo model with optional anti-lock brakes. Yes, the 300ZX looks and feels somewhat dated. But its performance and handling still overshadow that of most cars; especially in turbo trim. It's just that the 300ZX goes about its business with a nod toward comfort and convenience features that others in its class might overlook. That doesn't make it bad, just different. Rumors about the bare-knuckles nature of the all-new 1990 Z-car, however, indicate that even Nissan believes it's time for a change.

Specifications

	3-door hatchback	3-door 2 + 2 hatchback
Wheelbase, in.	91.3	99.2
Overall length, in.	170.7	178.5
Overall width, in.	67.9	67.9
Overall height, in.	49.7	49.7
Turn diameter, ft.	32.2	34.8
Curb weight, lbs.	3139	3265
Cargo vol., cu. ft.	14.7	20.3
Fuel capacity, gal.	19.0	19.0
Seating capacity	2	4
Front headroom, in.	36.6	37.2
Front shoulder room, in.	54.0	54.2
Front legroom, max., in.	43.6	43.6
Rear headroom, in.	—	34.3
Rear shoulder room, in.	—	NA
Rear legroom, min., in.	—	25.3

Engines	ohc V-6	Turbo ohc V-6
Size, liters/cu. in.	3.0/181	3.0/181
Fuel delivery	PFI	PFI
Horsepower @ rpm	165 @ 5200	205 @ 5300
Torque (lbs./ft.) @ rpm	173 @ 4000	227 @ 3600
Availability	S	S[1]

EPA city/highway mpg

5-speed OD manual	17/25	17/25
4-speed OD automatic	18/26	17/24

1. Turbo

Prices

Nissan 300ZX

	Retail Price	Dealer Invoice	Low Price
GS 3-door hatchback, 5-speed	$22299	$18954	$20627
GS 3-door hatchback, automatic	23049	19592	21321
Turbo 3-door hatchback, 5-speed	24699	20994	22847
Turbo 3-door hatchback, automatic	25499	21632	23566
GS 2+2 3-door hatchback, 5-speed	23499	19932	21691
GS 2+2 3-door hatchback, automatic . . .	24199	20570	22385
Destination charge	250	250	250

Standard Equipment:

GS: 3.0-liter PFI V-6 engine, 5-speed manual or 4-speed automatic transmission, 4-wheel power disc brakes, power steering, air conditioning, AM/FM ST ET cassette, cloth reclining front bucket seats with 8-way adjustments, front seats, tilt steering column, theft-deterrent system, power windows and locks, tachometer, trip odometer, coolant temperature and oil pressure gauges, tinted glass, 215/60R15 tires on alloy wheels. **Turbo** adds: turbocharged engine, adjustable shock absorbers, uprated brakes, headlight washers, turbo boost gauge, 225/50VR16 tires.

Optional Equipment:

Electronic Equipment Pkg.	1375	1141	1258

Premium stereo with EQ, automatic temperature control, audio and cruise control switches in steering wheel hub, power driver's seat, heated mirrors, illuminated entry, left visor mirror.

Leather Trim Pkg., 2-seat	1055	876	966
2+2s	1215	1008	1112

Partial leather seating surfaces, imitation leather door panel inserts, cargo area cover, bronze-tinted glass; requires Electronic Equipment Pkg.

Digital instrumentation pkg	710	589	650

Digital instruments, trip computer, Auto Check System, oil temperature gauge; requires Electronic Equipment and Leather Pkg.

Pearlglow paint	350	291	321

Oldsmobile Cutlass Supreme

Several important changes under the skin and some new features mark Cutlass Supreme's second season as a front-drive coupe. The car debuted last year along with the Buick Regal and Pontiac Grand Prix as replacements for rear-drive

Oldsmobile Cutlass Supreme

GM intermediates. For '89, all three get anti-lock brakes as
an option; 4-wheel disc brakes are standard. At mid-year a
138-horsepower 3.1-liter V-6 will replace a 130-horsepower
2.8 V-6 as the Cutlass Supreme's standard engine with automatic transmission. The 2.8 will still come with the 5-speed
manual transmission (standard on the International Series,
a credit option on the base and SL). Air conditioning and
3-point rear shoulder belts are now standard. A power sunroof, remote-control entry system using radio signals, electronic climate control (required with the keyless entry system), compact disc player, 8-speaker sound system,
steering-wheel mounted stereo controls and Driver Information System trip computer are among the new options.
Late in the year, a heads-up instrument display will be offered as a limited-production option. The HUD projects
digital speedometer, turn signal indicators, low-fuel warning and high-beam indicator onto the windshield in the
driver's field of vision. Oldsmobile will sell a 4-door sedan
built from this design for the 1990 or 1991 model year as a
replacement for the Cutlass Ciera 4-door. Any small power
gain provided by the 3.1 V-6 is welcome. The 2.8 sounds and
feels overtaxed by the big coupe's 3000-pound curb weight.
Despite a general competence, the Cutlass Supreme and its
Pontiac and Buick siblings are off to slow sales starts. Adding a 4-door version probably will help, but initially, there
really was nothing special about these cars except their
sleek-for-GM styling. The new V-6 and anti-lock brake option help nudge them away from the mundane.

Specifications

	2-door notchback
Wheelbase, in.	107.5
Overall length, in.	192.1
Overall width, in.	71.0
Overall height, in.	52.8
Turn diameter, ft.	39.0
Curb weight, lbs.	3084
Cargo vol., cu. ft.	15.5
Fuel capacity, gal.	16.6
Seating capacity	6
Front headroom, in.	37.8
Front shoulder room, in.	57.6
Front legroom, max., in.	42.3
Rear headroom, in.	37.1
Rear shoulder room, in.	57.2
Rear legroom, min., in.	34.8

Engines

	ohv V-6	ohv V-6
Size, liters/cu. in.	2.8/173	3.1/189
Fuel delivery	PFI	PFI
Horsepower @ rpm	130 @ 4500	138 @ 4800
Torque (lbs./ft.) @ rpm	170 @ 3600	183 @ 3600
Availability	S	S[1]

EPA city/highway mpg

5-speed OD manual	18/30	
4-speed OD automatic	20/29	NA

1. Mid-year, with automatic transmission

Prices

Oldsmobile Cutlass Supreme	Retail Price	Dealer Invoice	Low Price
2-door notchback	$14295	$12337	$13316
SL 2-door notchback	15195	13113	14154
I Series 2-door notchback	16995	14667	15831
Destination charge	455	455	455

Standard Equipment:

2.8-liter PFI V-6, 4-speed automatic transmission, power steering, power 4-wheel disc brakes, air conditioning, 55/45 front seat with storage armrest, trip odometer, left remote and right manual mirrors, AM/FM ST ET, automatic front seatbelts, outboard rear lap/shoulder belts, tinted glass, 195/75R14

Prices are accurate at time of printing; subject to manufacturer's change.

all-season SBR tires. **SL** adds: Convenience Group (reading lamps, right visor mirror, misc. lights), AM/FM ST ET cassette, power decklid release, alloy wheels. **International Series** adds: 5-speed manual transmission, FE3 suspension, fast-ratio steering, Driver Information System (trip computer and service reminder), electronic instruments (tachometer, coolant temperature, oil pressure, voltmeter), power locks with remote control, rocker panel extensions, power front bucket seats, rear bucket seats, tilt steering column, intermittent wipers, 215/60R16 tires on alloy wheels.

Optional Equipment:

	Retail Price	Dealer Invoice	Low Price
4-speed auto trans, I Series	615	523	566
5-speed manual trans, base & SL (credit) .	(615)	(523)	(523)
Anti-lock braking system	925	786	851
Option Pkg. 1SB, base	327	278	301
Tilt steering column, intermittent wiper, Convenience Group, bodyside moldings, door edge guards, power antenna, cruise control.			
Option Pkg. 1SC, base	979	832	901
Pkg. 1SB plus power windows and locks, remote lock control, power decklid release, floormats, power driver's seat, power mirrors.			
Option Pkg. 1SB, SL	295	251	271
Cruise control, tilt steering column, floormats, intermittent wipers, bodyside moldings, door edge guards, power antenna.			
Option Pkg. 1SC, SL	1082	920	995
Pkg. 1SB plus power windows and locks, remote lock control, power mirrors, power driver's seat, steering wheel touch control.			
Power locks, base & SL	145	123	133
Power windows	220	187	202
Power sunroof, SL & I Series	650	553	598
Rear defogger	145	123	133
FE3 suspension pkg., base & SL	284	241	261
Alloy wheels w/locks, base	215	183	198
Rallye instruments, base & SL	265	225	244
AM/FM ST ET cassette, base	147	125	135
w/EQ, SL & I Series	255	217	235
AM/FM ST ET w/CD player, SL & Series . .	399	339	367
Driver Information System, SL	150	128	138
Custom leather trim, SL	454	386	418
I Series	364	309	335

Oldsmobile Toronado/Trofeo

A color cathode ray tube (CRT) called the Visual Information Center is optional on the Toronado/Trofeo front-drive luxury coupe this year. Buick has been criticized for the CRT on its similar Riviera, and Oldsmobile is stressing

Oldsmobile Trofeo

how its CRT is different. Both mount in the center of the
dashboard, but Olds uses color graphics to Buick's monochrome display and the Olds touch points are larger and
easier to trigger. Significantly, Olds retains 17 conventional
dashboard buttons for functions such as climate control,
stereo and trip computer. Also new this year are steering-
wheel controls for some of those stereo and climate functions. They're standard on Trofeo and optional on Toronado, and can be ordered with or without the CRT. The
flagship Trofeo also gets anti-lock brakes, automatic door
locks and an oil-level sensor as standard equipment. On
Toronado, bucket seats and a console, 15-inch aluminum
wheels, monochromatic paint, and the oil-level sensor are
new standard items. A front bench seat, formerly standard,
is now optional on Toronado. Anti-lock brakes remain optional on Toronado. The lone powertrain is a 165-horse-
power 3.8-liter V-6 and 4-speed automatic. Toronado sales
have languished since the car's 1986 downsizing and a restyling for 1990 is forecast. As it stands, there's a decent car
under this dull sheetmetal. Performance is subdued, but
balanced and competent. Trofeo's firmer suspension improves handling at the expense of ride comfort. Gadgets furnish the comfort and convenience expected of the price
class, though rear-seat room and trunk space are modest.
Olds has improved upon Buick's CRT, but we still prefer
simple, convenient, conventional controls—and the fewer
the better—to electronic toys.

Specifications

	2-door notchback
Wheelbase, in.	108.0
Overall length, in.	187.5
Overall width, in.	70.8
Overall height, in.	53.0
Turn diameter, ft.	38.7
Curb weight, lbs.	3361
Cargo vol., cu. ft.	14.1
Fuel capacity, gal.	18.8
Seating capacity	6
Front headroom, in.	37.8
Front shoulder room, in.	58.3
Front legroom, max., in.	43.0
Rear headroom, in.	37.8
Rear shoulder room, in.	57.3
Rear legroom, min., in.	35.7

Engines

	ohv V-6
Size, liters/cu. in.	3.8/231
Fuel delivery	PFI
Horsepower @ rpm	165 @ 5200
Torque (lbs./ft.) @ rpm	210 @ 2000
Availability	S

EPA city/highway mpg

4-speed OD automatic	19/28

Prices

Oldsmobile Toronado	Retail Price	Dealer Invoice	Low Price
2-door notchback	$21995	$18982	$20488
Trofeo 2-door notchback	24995	21571	23283
Destination charge	550	550	550

Standard Equipment:

3.8-liter PFI V-6 engine, 4-speed automatic transmission, power steering, power 4-wheel disc brakes, air conditioning, tinted glass, power windows and locks, reclining front bucket seats, outboard rear lap/shoulder belts, front and rear armrests, bumper rub strips, Convenience Group (lamps, visor mirror, chime tones), cruise control, electronic gauge cluster including tachometer and Reminder Package, courtesy lamps, dual remote mirrors, automatic leveling system, AM/FM ST ET cassette with power antenna,

Prices are accurate at time of printing; subject to manufacturer's change.

power driver's seat, tilt steering column, header panel storage unit, intermittent wipers, 205/75R15 tires. **Trofeo** adds: anti-lock braking system, FE3 suspension, front air dam with fog lamps, rocker panel extensions, electrochromic day/night mirror, perforated leather bucket seats, power passenger seat, emergency kit, power fuel door release, floormats, power decklid pulldown, lighted front door locks, lighted visor mirrors, 215/60R14 tires on alloy wheels.

Optional Equipment:

	Retail Price	Dealer Invoice	Low Price
Anti-lock braking system, base	925	786	851
Option Pkg. 1SB, base	587	499	540
Power passenger seat, courtesy and reading lamps, Illumination Pkg., lighted visor mirrors, power mirrors, power decklid pulldown.			
Option Pkg. 1SC, base	967	822	890
Pkg. 1SB plus Twilight Sentinel, automatic power locks, automatic day/night mirror, remote fuel door release, steering wheel touch controls.			
Divided bench seat, base (credit)	(110)	(94)	(94)
Power sunroof, Trofeo	1230	1046	1132
Accent stripe, base	45	38	41
FE3 suspension pkg., base	126	107	116
Engine block heater	18	15	17
Delco/Bose music system	703	—	—
AM/FM ST ET cassette w/EQ	120	—	—
Mobile telephone	1795	1526	1651
Visual Information Center	1295	1101	1191
HD cooling, base	40	34	37
Glamour metallic paint, base	210	179	193
Custom leather trim, base	384	326	353
California emissions pkg.	100	85	92

Peugeot 405

Peugeot's newest U.S. offering was voted 1987 European Car of the Year. It's a front-drive 4-door sedan aimed at the likes of the Audi 80/90 and Saab 900. All 405s have a 1.9-liter 4-cylinder engine. The 8-valve version in base DL and midline S models has 110 horsepower; the 16-valver in the Mi 16 makes 150. A 5-speed manual transmission is standard; a 4-speed automatic is optional for DL and S. An all-independent suspension and 4-wheel disc brakes are standard. Anti-lock brakes (ABS) are optional on the Mi 16. Optional for the S is a Luxury Touring Package that includes ABS plus other Mi 16 features. Peugeot hopes to sell about 14,000 405s dur-

Prices are accurate at time of printing; subject to manufacturer's change.

Peugeot 405 Mi 16

ing its introductory year; only about 1000 will be Mi 16s. The only 405 we've driven is an Mi 16. Its engine pulls quickly and smoothly to higher speeds, where it develops most of its power. Unlike some other multi-valve engines, this one doesn't feel lifeless below 3000 rpm, so you can keep pace with traffic with a light throttle foot. The Mi 16 lacks any truly outstanding dynamic qualities, yet it is highly competent in all. Responsive steering, surefooted handling and great brakes are highlights, an occasionally notchy shift action was a minus. The ride is not so stiff that you'll dread bumps or rail crossings, but it is much firmer than we've come to expect from Peugeot. DL and S models probably won't be as frisky or tenacious around corners because of their lower power and slightly narrower tires and wheels, but they're likely to have a more absorbent ride. The airy cabin accommodates four adults in comfort; the trunk is spacious. The arms-out driving position takes some getting used to, as do some of the traditionally French controls, including a horn button on the end of the turn-signal stalk and power window buttons relegated to the far ends of the center console. We're impressed with the car and we aren't put off by the prices. Peugeot parts and service are not common, however, and the French automaker has yet to establish a reputation for reliability in the U.S.

Specifications

	4-door notchback
Wheelbase, in.	105.1
Overall length, in.	177.7
Overall width, in.	67.6
Overall height, in.	55.4
Turn diameter, ft.	36.1
Curb weight, lbs.	2460[1]
Cargo vol., cu. ft.	13.7
Fuel capacity, gal.	17.2
Seating capacity	5
Front headroom, in.	36.5
Front shoulder room, in.	NA
Front legroom, max., in.	41.4
Rear headroom, in.	36.9
Rear shoulder room, in.	NA
Rear legroom, min., in.	34.4

1. 2580 lbs., S; 2715 lbs., Mi 16

Engines

	ohc I-4	dohc I-4
Size, liters/cu. in.	1.9/116	1.9/116
Fuel delivery	PFI	PFI
Horsepower @ rpm	110 @ 5200	150 @ 6400
Torque (lbs./ft.) @ rpm	120 @ 4250	128 @ 5000
Availability	S[1]	S[2]

EPA city/highway mpg

	ohc I-4	dohc I-4
5-speed OD manual	20/26	20/27
4-speed OD automatic	20/24	

1. DL and S   2. Mi 16

Prices

Peugeot 405	Retail Price	Dealer Invoice	Low Price
DL 4-door notchback	$14500	$12833	NA
S 4-door notchback	17700	15576	NA
Mi 16 4-door notchback	20700	18113	NA
Destination charge	400	400	400

Low price not available at time of publication.

Standard Equipment:

DL: 1.9-liter PFI 4-cylinder engine, 5-speed manual transmission, power steering, power 4-wheel disc brakes, air conditioning, power locks, velour reclining front bucket seats, tilt steering column, dual remote mirrors,

Prices are accurate at time of printing; subject to manufacturer's change.

tachometer, coolant temperature and oil level gauges, trip odometer, tinted glass, intermittent wipers, rear defogger, lighted visor mirrors, digital clock, Michelin MXV 185/65R14 tires with full-size spare. **S** adds: power windows, remote power locks, cruise control, heated front seats, automatic front shoulder belts, outboard rear lap/shoulder belts, center armrest, rear armrest with trunk-through, power sunroof, heated power mirrors, Clarion AM/FM ST ET cassette, alloy wheels. **Mi 16** adds: DOHC 16-valve engine, 3-point front lap/shoulder belts, leather upholstery, leather-wrapped steering wheel, power driver's seat, driver's lumbar and side bolster adjustments, oil temperature gauge, Alpine AM/FM ST ET cassette, 195/60R14 tires on alloy wheels.

Optional Equipment:

	Retail Price	Dealer Invoice	Low Price
4-speed auto trans, DL & S	650	573	NA
Anti-lock brakes, Mi 16	NA	NA	NA
Metallic paint	375	330	NA
Leather Pkg., S	1300	1144	NA
Leather sport seats, Alpine AM/FM ST ET cassette.			
Luxury Touring Pkg., S	NA	NA	NA
Leather Pkg. plus anti-lock brakes.			

Plymouth Laser

1990 Plymouth Laser RS Turbo

The new Laser front-drive sports coupe is touted as the "first Plymouth of the '90s." It'll debut in California in January as a 1990 model, then spread from there. Buyers age 25 to 35 are targets, and women are expected to account for up to 60 percent of sales. Plymouth has slotted the Laser

Prices are accurate at time of printing; subject to manufacturer's change.

Specifications

	3-door hatchback
Wheelbase, in.	97.2
Overall length, in.	170.5
Overall width, in.	66.5
Overall height, in.	49.8
Turn diameter, ft.	34.0
Curb weight, lbs.	2410
Cargo vol., cu. ft.	10.2
Fuel capacity, gal.	15.8
Seating capacity	4
Front headroom, in.	33.9
Front shoulder room, in.	53.9
Front legroom, max., in.	42.5
Rear headroom, in.	30.1
Rear shoulder room, in.	53.1
Rear legroom, min., in.	29.6

Engines

	ohc I-4	dohc I-4	Turbo dohc I-4
Size, liters/cu. in.	1.8/107	2.0/122	2.0/122
Fuel delivery	PFI	PFI	PFI
Horsepower @ rpm	92 @ 5000	135 @ 6000	190 @ 6000
Torque (lbs./ft.) @ rpm	107 @ 3500	125 @ 5000	203 @ 5000
Availability	S	O[1]	O[1]

EPA city/highway mpg

5-speed OD manual	26/37	24/36	24/36
4-speed OD automatic	26/37	24/34	

1. RS

against the Ford Probe, Toyota Celica, Nissan 240SX, Acura Integra, Mazda MX-6, and even corporate sibling Dodge Daytona. Built in Normal, Ill., at a Chrysler-Mitsubishi joint venture plant, Laser is nearly identical to the new Mitsubishi Eclipse. The '90 Laser is unrelated to 1984-86 Chrysler Laser, which was a Daytona clone. Plymouth's Laser is based on a Mitsubishi Galant chassis and uses Mitsubishi engines and transmissions. A 1.8-liter 92-horsepower 4-cylinder is standard on both the base model and the top-line RS. Optional on the RS is a 2.0-liter 16-valve double-overhead can four that makes 135 horsepower in naturally aspirated form, and 190 with a turbocharger and intercooler. A 5-

speed manual is standard, 4-speed automatic optional (except with the turbo motor until June). Four-wheel-disc brakes are standard on all models. RS and Turbo Lasers have wider tires and firmer suspensions to improve handling. Prices (not announced as of this writing) are expected to range from $10,000 to $15,000, undercutting most competitors. Performance meets or exceeds class standards—with the turbo, Laser zips from 0-60 mph in 6.9 seconds and tops out at 143 mph, according to Plymouth. Price, performance, and styling should make the Laser a contender in its class. For further comments see the Mitsubishi Eclipse.

Specifications and prices not available at time of publication.

Pontiac Grand Am

Pontiac Grand Am LE

Revamped front and rear styling, more powerful engines and fewer models sum up the changes for Grand Am, the sporty front-drive compact that's Pontiac's best seller. Last year's base series is dropped, leaving LE and SE versions in either 2-door coupe or 4-door sedan styling. The facelift includes a new, lower hood and new fenders made of 2-sided galvanized steel for longer corrosion resistance. Modifications to the cylinder head and fuel-injection system increase horsepower on the base 2.5-liter 4-cylinder engine from 98 to 110. The 2.5 is standard on the LE. A 165-horsepower turbocharged 2.0-liter four is standard on the performance-oriented SE. The 150-horsepower 2.3-liter Quad 4 dual-cam

4-cylinder is optional on all models. Late in the year, about 200 SEs are to get a 185-horsepower high-output version of the Quad 4, a preview of the power more widely available for 1990. Grand Am is similar to the Buick Skylark and Oldsmobile Calais, which comprise GM's N-body family of cars. Buick and Olds offer the 2.5-liter four and the 2.3-liter Quad 4, plus a new 3.3-liter V-6 engine in their versions. Grand Am is by far the most successful of the three. Pontiac has the most focused marketing, aiming Grand Am at younger buyers who want hot performance, or at least the appearance of hot performance. Grand Am is lukewarm with the base 2.5. The turbo 2.0 and the Quad 4 do sizzle, though lots of noise accompanies their abundant power. We prefer the Quad 4

Specifications

	2-door notchback	4-door notchback
Wheelbase, in.	103.4	103.4
Overall length, in.	180.1	180.1
Overall width, in.	66.5	66.5
Overall height, in.	52.5	52.5
Turn diameter, ft.	37.8	37.8
Curb weight, lbs.	2508	2592
Cargo vol., cu. ft.	13.1	13.1
Fuel capacity, gal.	13.6	13.6
Seating capacity	5	5
Front headroom, in.	37.7	37.7
Front shoulder room, in.	52.6	52.6
Front legroom, max., in.	42.9	42.9
Rear headroom, in.	37.1	37.1
Rear shoulder room, in.	55.2	55.2
Rear legroom, min., in.	34.3	34.3

Engines

	ohv I-4	Turbo ohc I-4	dohc I-4
Size, liters/cu. in.	2.5/151	2.0/122	2.3/138
Fuel delivery	TBI	PFI	PFI
Horsepower @ rpm	110 @ 5200	165 @ 5600	150 @ 5200
Torque (lbs./ft.) @ rpm	135 @ 3200	175 @ 4000	160 @ 4000
Availability	S[1]	S[2]	O

EPA city/highway mpg

5-speed OD manual	23/33	21/30	24/35
3-speed automatic	23/30	21/28	23/32

1. LE   2. SE

over the more trouble-prone turbo, though as with other multi-valvers, the power isn't uncorked until above 3000 rpm or so. Grand Am shares with the Skylark and Calais a shortage of interior and trunk space. We're not enthused about these cars, but concede that Grand Am is a logical choice for the young and young at heart.

Prices

Pontiac Grand Am	Retail Price	Dealer Invoice	Low Price
LE 2-door notchback	$10469	$9349	$9909
LE 4-door notchback	10669	9527	10098
SE 2-door notchback	13599	12144	12872
SE 4-door notchback	13799	12323	13061
Destination charge	425	425	425

Standard Equipment:

2.5-liter TBI 4-cylinder engine, 5-speed manual transmission, power steering and brakes, outboard rear lap/shoulder belts, tinted glass, headlamps-on tone, upshift indicator light, dual outside mirrors, AM/FM ST ET, cloth reclining front bucket seats, 185/80R13 all-season SBR tires. **SE** adds: 2.0-liter turbocharged PFI engine, WS6 sport suspension, monotone exterior treatment, sill moldings, fog lamps, power locks, split folding rear seat, tachometer, trip odometer, coolant temperature and oil pressure gauges, voltmeter, 215/60R14 tires on alloy wheels.

Optional Equipment:

2.3-liter DOHC Quad 4 engine, LE	660	561	607
SE (credit)	(108)	(92)	(92)
3-speed automatic transmission	490	417	451
Air conditioning	675	574	621
Option Pkg. 1SA, LE	408	347	375
Air conditioning, console, tilt steering column.			
Option Pkg. 1SB, LE	484	411	445
Pkg. 1SA plus intermittent wipers, cruise control, Lamp Group.			
Option Pkg. 1SC, LE	670	570	616
Pkg. 1SB plus remote fuel door and decklid releases, split folding rear seat.			
Option Pkg. 1SD, LE 2-door	1112	945	1023
LE 4-door	1037	881	954
Pkg. 1SC plus power windows and locks, fog lamps, power driver's seat.			
Option Pkg. 1SA, SE 2-door	431	366	397
SE 4-door	506	430	466
Air conditioning, Lamp Group, power windows.			

Prices are accurate at time of printing; subject to manufacturer's change.

	Retail Price	Dealer Invoice	Low Price
Option Pkg. 1SB, SE 2-door	560	476	515
SE 4-door	635	540	584
* Pkg. 1SA plus power driver's seat, lighted right visor mirror, power mirrors.*			
Value Option Pkg., LE	341	290	314
* AM/FM ST ET cassette, 195/70R14 tires on alloy wheels.*			
Rear defogger	145	123	133
California emissions pkg	100	85	92
Rally instruments, LE	127	108	117
Decklid luggage rack	115	98	106
Two-tone paint, LE	101	86	93
Power locks, LE 2-door	145	123	133
LE 4-door	195	166	179
Power windows, 2-doors	210	179	193
4-doors	285	242	262
AM/FM ST ET cassette	122	104	112
AM/FM ST ET cassette w/EQ	272	231	250
LE w/VOP	150	128	138
AM/FM ST ET w/CD & EQ	545	463	501
LE w/VOP	423	360	389
Performance Sound System	125	106	115
* Requires power windows.*			
Articulated sport seats, SE	450	383	414
SE w/Pkg. 1SB	245	208	225
Custom Interior Trim, LE	269	229	247
LE w/Pkg. 1SC or 1SD	119	101	109
Removable glass sunroof	350	298	322
WSW tires, LE	68	58	63
195/70R14 tires, LE	104	88	96
215/60R14 tires, LE	278	236	256
LE w/VOP	174	148	160
w/white letters & WS6 Pkg., LE	370	315	340
w/white letters & WS6 Pkg., LE w/VOP .	266	226	245
* 60-series tires require alloy wheels.*			
14" alloy wheels, LE	215	183	198

Pontiac Grand Prix

Grand Prix gets an anti-lock brake (ABS) option and the forecast of more power. ABS is optional on all Grand Prix models: base, LE and SE. Four-wheel disc brakes are standard. Around January, a 140-horsepower 3.1-liter V-6 will

Pontiac Grand Prix

replace a 130-horsepower 2.8 V-6 as the standard engine with automatic transmission. The 2.8 will continue in models with the 5-speed manual transmission. In spring 1989, about 2000 McLaren Turbo Grand Prixs will go on sale. Developed by the McLaren division of ASC, a specialty-car builder, the car's turbocharged and intercooled 3.1 V-6 will produce over 200 horsepower—more than any other front-drive GM car—and have a 4-speed automatic transmission. ABS, 245/50ZR16 tires, power sunroof, tan leather interior and aero body trim will be standard. Bright red and metallic black will be the only colors offered. Air conditioning is standard for '89 on all Grand Prixs; on LE and SE it's a new electronically-controlled climate system. Rear shoulder belts are also standard. New options include a power sunroof, steering-wheel controls for the stereo system, and a remote keyless entry system that uses radio signals to lock or unlock the doors and trunk from up to 30 feet away. GM's W-body program saw Grand Prix redesigned to front-drive last year along with the Buick Regal and Oldsmobile Cutlass Supreme. All are 2-door coupes. All four GM divisions will eventually get 4-door W-body sedans; the Chevrolet Lumina due in the spring of '89 will be first. Grand Prix handles well, especially in SE form, but its 2.8 can't motivate this big coupe in a style befitting its racy looks. The 3.1 should help; the McClaren turbo is certain to help. We also find fault with the SE's multi-adjustable but still-uncomfortable front seats and with its pseudo-high-tech dashboard. The sportiest of GM's W-bodies needs more gumption and fewer gimmicks. The new 3.1 and ABS is a worthy start.

Specifications

	2-door notchback
Wheelbase, in.	107.5
Overall length, in.	193.9
Overall width, in.	70.9
Overall height, in.	53.3
Turn diameter, ft.	39.7
Curb weight, lbs.	3167
Cargo vol., cu. ft.	15.0
Fuel capacity, gal.	16.0
Seating capacity	6
Front headroom, in.	37.8
Front shoulder room, in.	57.3
Front legroom, max., in.	42.3
Rear headroom, in.	36.7
Rear shoulder room, in.	57.3
Rear legroom, min., in.	34.8

Engines

	ohv V-6	ohv V-6
Size, liters/cu. in.	2.8/173	3.1/191
Fuel delivery	PFI	PFI
Horsepower @ rpm	130 @ 4500	140 @ 4500
Torque (lbs./ft.) @ rpm	170 @ 3600	185 @ 3600
Availability	S	S[1]

EPA city/highway mpg

5-speed OD manual	18/30	
4-speed OD automatic	20/29	NA

1. Mid-year, with automatic transmission.

Prices

Pontiac Grand Prix	Retail Price	Dealer Invoice	Low Price
2-door notchback	$13899	$11995	$12947
LE 2-door notchback	14849	12815	13832
SE 2-door notchback	15999	13807	14903
Destination charge	455	455	455

Standard Equipment:

2.8-liter PFI V-6 engine, 4-speed automatic transmission (5-speed manual may be substituted for credit), power steering, power 4-wheel disc brakes, air conditioning, cloth split bench seat with folding armrest, AM/FM ST ET, electronic instruments, remote fuel door release, tinted glass, left remote and right manual mirrors, automatic front seatbelts, outboard rear lap/shoul-

Prices are accurate at time of printing; subject to manufacturer's change.

der belts, 195/75R14 tires. **LE** adds: power windows, light group, map pockets, tachometer and trip odometer, 60/40 front seats with recliners, folding rear seatback. **SE** adds: 5-speed manual transmission, cruise control, articulating power front bucket seats, contoured rear seats with head restraints, power mirrors, front floor and rear overhead consoles, analog instruments, front and rear reading lamps, tilt steering column, leather-wrapped steering wheel, fog lamps, intermittent wipers, Rally Tuned Suspension, 215/60R16 Goodyear Eagle GT + 4 tires on alloy wheels.

Optional Equipment:

	Retail Price	Dealer Invoice	Low Price
4-speed automatic transmission, SE	615	523	566
5-speed manual transmission, base & LE (credit)	(615)	(522)	(522)
Anti-lock brakes	925	786	851
Option Pkg. 1SA, base	183	156	168
Tilt steering column, Lamp Group.			
Option Pkg. 1SB, base	188	160	173
Pkg. 1SA plus intermittent wipers, cruise control.			
Option Pkg. 1SC, base	378	321	348
Pkg. 1SB plus power windows and locks, remote decklid release.			
Option Pkg. 1SA, LE	275	234	253
Tilt steering column, intermittent wipers, cruise control, power locks.			
Option Pkg. 1SB, LE	383	326	352
Pkg. 1SA plus remote decklid release, power driver's seat, lighted right visor mirror.			
Option Pkg. 1SC, LE	594	505	546
Pkg. 1SB plus reading lamps, leather-wrapped steering wheel and shift handle, power mirrors, remote keyless entry.			
Option Pkg. 1SA, SE	260	221	239
Power locks, remote decklid release, power driver's seat.			
Option Pkg. 1SB, SE	563	479	518
Pkg. 1SA plus lighted right visor mirror, remote keyless entry, electronic compass with trip computer and service reminder.			
Value Option Pkg., base	393	334	362
40/60 seat, AM/FM ST ET cassette, gauge pkg., 195/70R15 tires on styled steel wheels.			
Value Option Pkg., LE	375	319	345
AM/FM ST ET cassette, two-tone paint, 195/70R15 tires on alloy wheels.			
Rear defogger	145	123	133
California emissions pkg.	100	85	92
Gauge cluster w/tachometer, base	85	72	78
Decklid luggage rack	115	98	106
Two-tone paint	105	89	97
Power locks	145	123	133
Power glass sunroof, base & LE	675	574	621
LE w/Pkg. 1SC, SE	650	553	598
Power windows, base	220	187	202
AM/FM ST ET cassette	122	104	112

Prices are accurate at time of printing; subject to manufacturer's change.

	Retail Price	Dealer Invoice	Low Price
AM/FM ST ET cassette w/EQ, base & LE	447	380	411
Base & LE w/VOP	325	276	299
LE w/Pkg. 1SC, SE	397	337	365
LE w/Pkg. 1SC & VOP	275	234	253
Performance Sound System, LE & SE	125	106	115
Power antenna	70	60	64
40/60 seat, base	133	113	122
Bucket seats, base	193	164	178
Base w/VOP	60	51	55
LE	110	94	101
Leather bucket seats, SE	375	319	345
WSW tires, base & LE	72	61	66
195/70R15 tires, base & LE	48	41	44
215/60R16 tires, base & LE	232	197	213
Base & LE w/VOP	184	156	169
15″ styled wheels, base & LE	130	111	120
15″ alloy wheels, base & LE	215	183	198
Base w/VOP	85	72	78
Requires 195/70R15 tires.			
16″ alloy wheels, base & LE	250	213	230
Base w/VOP	120	102	110
LE w/VOP	35	30	32
Requires 205/60R16 tires.			

Pontiac LeMans

Pontiac Le Mans SE

A removable glass sunroof due as a mid-year option is the only news for Pontiac's Korean-built front-drive subcompact. Built in Korea by Daewoo (partly owned by GM), LeMans was designed by GM's Opel division in West Ger-

Prices are accurate at time of printing; subject to manufacturer's change.

many. The lineup consists of the Aerocoupe Value Leader 3-door hatchback; plusher LE hatchback; LE and sporty SE 4-door sedans; and the GSE hatchback. All except the GSE use a 1.6-liter 4-cylinder engine. The GSE comes with a 2.0-liter four, plus larger tires, firmer suspension and racy exterior trim. All models are available with either a 5-speed manual or 3-speed automatic transmission except the Value Leader, which comes only with a 4-speed manual. Our test of an '88 SE revealed an agile, surefooted car that's stingy with fuel, but inordinately slow with automatic transmission. A 5-speed we tested was much faster and provided acceptable acceleration, plus even better fuel economy. The SE's

Specifications

	3-door hatchback	4-door notchback
Wheelbase, in.	99.2	99.2
Overall length, in.	163.7	172.4
Overall width, in.	65.5	65.7
Overall height, in.	53.5	53.7
Turn diameter, ft.	32.8	32.8
Curb weight, lbs.	2136[1]	2235[2]
Cargo vol., cu. ft.	18.8	18.4
Fuel capacity, gal.	13.2	13.2
Seating capacity	5	5
Front headroom, in.	38.8	38.8
Front shoulder room, in.	53.5	53.5
Front legroom, max., in.	42.0	42.0
Rear headroom, in.	38.0	38.0
Rear shoulder room, in.	53.4	53.4
Rear legroom, min., in.	32.8	32.8

1. 2302 lbs., GSE.   2. 2357 lbs., SE.

Engines

	ohc I-4	ohc I-4
Size, liters/cu. in.	1.6/98	2.0/121
Fuel delivery	TBI	TBI
Horsepower @ rpm	74 @ 5600	96 @ 4800
Torque (lbs./ft.) @ rpm	90 @ 2800	118 @ 3600
Availability	S	S[1]

EPA city/highway mpg

4-speed OD manual	30/39	
5-speed OD manual	31/40	24/30
3-speed automatic	27/31	22/28

1. GSE

175/70R13 all-season tires and firm suspension return responsive handling in exchange for a stiff, jiggly ride on bumpy pavement. LeMans has a 99.2-inch wheelbase, long for a subcompact, so there's more leg room than in some rivals, but the rear doors are narrow for tight access to the back seat. Cargo room is above average for a small car. The base LeMans is attractively priced, but not as well furnished as a base Hyundai Excel, also made in Korea. A top-line LeMans SE with automatic transmission, power steering and air conditioning runs well over $10,000, which isn't a bargain in this class.

Prices

Pontiac Le Mans

	Retail Price	Dealer Invoice	Low Price
Aerocoupe Value Leader 3-door hatchback .	$6399	$5919	$6159
Aerocoupe LE 3-door hatchback	7699	7083	7391
LE 4-door notchback	7999	7359	7679
SE 4-door notchback	9429	8486	8958
Aerocoupe GSE 3-door hatchback	9149	8234	8692
Destination charge	315	315	315

Standard Equipment:

Value Leader: 1.6-liter TBI 4-cylinder engine, 4-speed manual transmission, power brakes, reclining front bucket seats, rear defogger, tachometer, trip odometer, outboard rear lap/shoulder belts, cargo area cover, 175/70SR13 tires with full-size spare. **LE** adds: 5-speed manual transmission, tinted glass, dual remote mirrors, right visor mirror, AM/FM ST ET with clock, swing-out rear side windows (Aerocoupe; roll-down on 4-door). **SE** adds: 2.0-liter engine, sport suspension, sport seats with height adjusters, 60/40 folding rear seat, tilt steering column, fog lamps, 185/60HR14 tires. **GSE** adds: front air dam with fog lamps, sill extensions, rear spoiler, alloy wheels.

Optional Equipment:

3-speed automatic transmission (NA VL) .	420	357	386
Air conditioning	660	561	607
Requires power steering; not available on VL).			
Power steering, LE & SE	214	182	197
Cruise control	175	149	161
AM/FM ST ET, VL	307	261	282
AM/FM ST ET cassette, VL	429	365	395
Others	122	104	112
Luggage carrier	95	81	87
Removable sunroof	350	298	322

Prices are accurate at time of printing; subject to manufacturer's change.

Pontiac Sunbird

Pontiac Sunbird LE 2-door

A juggled lineup and a new dashboard are the major changes for Sunbird, Pontiac's J-body front-drive subcompact. All five GM divisions introduced J-bodes for 1982, but the slow-selling Cadillac Cimarron and Oldsmobile Firenza have been dropped for 1989, leaving the Buick Skyhawk, Chevrolet Cavalier and Sunbird. Pontiac kills the 5-door wagon for '89, leaving a 2-door coupe, 4-door sedan and 2-door convertible. Last year's base sedan is replaced by a reinstated LE series as the low-priced Sunbird. LE coupes and sedans sport a nose, composite headlamps and twin-outlet grille new to the Sunbird line. The SE coupe and GT coupe and convertible return unchanged from last year. All get a new instrument panel that mimics the Grand Prix's, with analog gauges flanked by controls for lights and windshield wiper/washers. The stereo and heat/vent controls are also relocated and a redesigned center console includes a new horseshoe-shaped parking brake lever. A compact disc player is to be available later in the year. A 2.0-liter 4-cylinder is standard on LEs and SEs. A turbocharged 2.0 four is standard on GTs and optional on the SE. The non-turbo engine is available as a credit option on the GTs. A 5-speed manual transmission is standard and a 3-speed automatic optional on all. Sunbird differs from its Cavalier and Skyhawk cousins by virtue of its overhead-cam engines (Chevrolet and Buick use overhead-valve engines) and a marketing approach that leans more toward sport and performance than value or luxury. The zesty turbo GT hits its mark, though its power wrenches the front tires off course in hard acceleration.

Specifications

	2-door notchback	4-door notchback	2-door conv.
Wheelbase, in.	101.2	101.2	101.2
Overall length, in.	178.2	181.7	178.2
Overall width, in.	66.0	65.0	66.0
Overall height, in.	50.4	53.8	51.9
Turn diameter, ft.	34.7	34.7	34.7
Curb weight, lbs.	2418	2433	2577
Cargo vol., cu. ft.	14.0	15.2	10.4
Fuel capacity, gal.	13.6	13.6	13.6
Seating capacity	5	5	4
Front headroom, in.	37.7	38.6	38.5
Front shoulder room, in.	53.7	53.7	53.7
Front legroom, max., in.	42.9	42.2	42.2
Rear headroom, in.	36.1	37.9	37.4
Rear shoulder room, in.	52.6	53.7	38.0
Rear legroom, min., in.	31.6	34.3	31.1

Engines

	ohc I-4	Turbo ohc I-4
Size, liters/cu. in.	2.0/121	2.0/121
Fuel delivery	TBI	PFI
Horsepower @ rpm	96 @ 4800	165 @ 5500
Torque (lbs./ft.) @ rpm	118 @ 3600	175 @ 4000
Availability	S	S[1]

EPA city/highway mpg

	ohc I-4	Turbo ohc I-4
5-speed OD manual	27/36	21/31
3-speed automatic	23/31	20/27

1. GT; optional, SE

Prices

Pontiac Sunbird	Retail Price	Dealer Invoice	Low Price
LE 2-door notchback	$8849	$7902	$8376
LE 4-door notchback	8949	7991	8470
SE 2-door notchback	9099	8125	8612
GT 2-door notchback	11399	10179	10789
GT 2-door convertible	16899	15091	15995
Destination charge	425	425	425

Prices are accurate at time of printing; subject to manufacturer's change.

Standard Equipment:

5.0-liter 4bbl. V-8 engine, 4-speed automatic transmission, power steering and brakes, air conditioning, tinted glass, courtesy lights, left remote and right manual mirrors, bodyside moldings, AM/FM ST ET, cloth split bench seat with center armrest, rear-facing third seat, outboard rear lap/shoulder belts, custom wheel covers, 225/75R15 tires.

Optional Equipment:	Retail Price	Dealer Invoice	Low Price
Turbo Pkg., SE	1384	1176	1273
SE w/VOP	1169	994	1075
2.0-liter turbo engine, power steering, Rally Gauge Cluster, engine block heater, WS6 Performance Pkg. (215/60R14 tires on alloy wheels).			
Turbo engine delete (credit), GT	(768)	(653)	(653)
Air conditioning	675	574	621
Option Pkg. 1SA, LE & SE	233	198	214
SE w/Turbo Pkg.	158	134	145
Tinted glass, power steering, left remote and right manual mirrors.			
Option Pkg. 1SB, LE & SE	330	281	304
SE w/Turbo Pkg.	205	174	189
Pkg. 1SA plus tilt steering column, intermittent wipers, front armrest, floormats.			
Option Pkg. 1SC, SE & LE 2-door	769	654	707
LE 4-door	775	659	713
SE w/Turbo Pkg.	544	462	500
Pkg. 1SB plus rally steering wheel, air conditioning, Lamp Group, cruise control.			
Option Pkg. 1SA, GT notchback	268	228	247
Tinted glass, tilt steering column, intermittent wipers, floormats, air conditioning.			
Option Pkg. 1SB, GT notchback	456	388	420
Pkg. 1SA plus Lamp Group, cruise control, remote decklid release.			
Option Pkg. 1SC, GT notchback	811	689	746
Pkg. 1SB plus power windows and locks, leather-wrapped steering wheel.			
Option Pkg. 1SA, GT conv.	163	139	150
Tilt steering column, intermittent wipers, floormats, air conditioning.			
Option Pkg. 1SB, GT conv.	401	341	369
Pkg. 1SA plus Lamp Group, cruise control, remote decklid release, leather-wrapped steering wheel.			
Value Option Pkg., LE	370	315	340
AM/FM ST ET cassette, rally gauge pkg., 195/70R14 tires on alloy wheels.			
Value Option Pkg., SE	392	333	361
Split folding rear seat, AM/FM ST ET cassette, alloy wheels.			
Rear defogger (NA conv.)	145	123	133
California emissions pkg	100	85	92
Rally gauge cluster, LE	49	42	45
Decklid luggage rack	115	98	106
Two-tone paint, LE	101	86	93

Prices are accurate at time of printing; subject to manufacturer's change.

	Retail Price	Dealer Invoice	Low Price
Power locks, 2-doors	145	123	133
LE 4-door	195	166	179
Power windows, 2-doors	210	179	193
LE 4-door	285	242	262
AM/FM ST ET cassette	152	129	140
AM/FM ST ET cassette w/CD player	396	337	364
SE & LE w/VOP	244	207	224
Custom Interior Trim, GT notchback	335	285	308

Upgraded door panels with pockets, split folding rear seat, added sound insulation.

	Retail Price	Dealer Invoice	Low Price
Custom Interior Trim, GT conv.	142	121	131

Upgraded door panels with pockets.

	Retail Price	Dealer Invoice	Low Price
Split folding rear seat (NA conv.)	150	128	138
Removable glass sunroof	350	298	322
WSW tires, LE	68	58	63
195/70R14 tires, LE	104	88	96
215/60R14 tires, SE w/o Turbo Pkg.	184	156	169
w/white letters, SE w/o Turbo Pkg.	276	235	254
w/white letters, SE w/Turbo Pkg., GT	102	87	94

Includes WS6 Performance Pkg.; requires alloy wheels.

	Retail Price	Dealer Invoice	Low Price
13″ alloy wheels, LE, SE w/o Turbo Pkg.	215	183	198

Saab 900

Saab 900 3-door

The 900 Turbo 4-door sedan returns after a 3-year absence and all 900s now have 16-valve engines. The Turbo 4-door shares its 160-horsepower, turbocharged and intercooled 2.0-liter four with the 900 Turbo 3-door hatchback and the

1988 Specifications

	3-door hatchback	4-door notchback	2-door convertible
Wheelbase, in.	99.1	99.1	99.1
Overall length, in.	184.5	184.3	184.3
Overall width, in.	66.5	66.5	66.5
Overall height, in.	56.1	56.1	56.1
Turn diameter, ft.	33.8	33.8	33.8
Curb weight, lbs.	2695	2735	2985
Cargo vol., cu. ft.	56.5	53.0	9.9
Fuel capacity, gal.	16.6	16.6	16.6
Seating capacity	5	5	4
Front headroom, in.	36.8	36.8	36.8
Front shoulder room, in.	52.2	53.0	52.2
Front legroom, max., in.	41.7	41.7	41.7
Rear headroom, in.	37.4	37.4	NA
Rear shoulder room, in.	53.5	54.5	NA
Rear legroom, min., in.	36.2	36.2	NA

Engines

	dohc I-4	Turbo dohc I-4
Size, liters/cu. in.	2.0/121	2.0/121
Fuel delivery	PFI	PFI
Horsepower @ rpm	125 @ 5500	160 @ 5500
Torque (lbs./ft.) @ rpm	125 @ 3000	188 @ 3000
Availability	S	S

EPA city/highway mpg

5-speed OD manual	22/28	21/28
3-speed automatic	19/22	19/23

2-door convertible. The only other Turbo news is that the optional high-performance SPG package for the 3-door gets a leather-wrapped steering wheel and shift knob and is now available in black as well as gray exterior paint. On naturally aspirated 900s, the 16-valve 2.0-liter four previously standard on the 900S becomes standard on base models as well. Horsepower increases from 125 to 128 and hydraulic engine mounts replace rubber ones. The 8-valve, 110-horsepower naturally aspirated 2.0-liter four is shelved. Among other changes, the base 900 gains stabilizer bars front and rear, and high-pressure gas shock absorbers. And the convertible gets the upgraded leather upholstery used in the SPG. Saab's decision to scrap the 8-valve engine is a wise one, given the tepid performance it generated in the base 900.

The 16 valver feels adequate for these cars, but it hardly pins your ears back the way the turbo does. We prefer automatic transmission with the turbo because of the 5-speed's notchy shift linkage. All models handle well, with sharp steering and a firm but absorbent ride. An anti-lock braking system is unfortunately unavailable to augment the already-capable standard 4-wheel discs. The 900 traces its lineage to the Saab 99, introduced in 1968. Kudos to Saab for keeping the surprisingly roomy cabin updated with fine controls, though some criticize it for continuing to place the power window switches and (on 5-speed models) the ignition lock on the floor between the front seats.

Prices

Saab 900	Retail Price	Dealer Invoice	Low Price
3-door hatchback	$16995	—	—
4-door notchback	17515	—	—
S 3-door hatchback	19695	—	—
S 4-door notchback	20245	—	—
Turbo 3-door hatchback	23795	—	—
Turbo 4-door notchback	24345	—	—
Turbo convertible	32095	—	—
Turbo SPG 3-door hatchback	26895	—	—
Destination charge	359	—	—

Dealer invoice and low price not available at time of publication.

Standard Equipment:

2.0-liter DOHC 16-valve PFI 4-cylinder engine, 5-speed manual or 3-speed automatic transmission, power steering, power 4-wheel disc brakes, air conditioning, tachometer, coolant temperature gauge, trip odometer, analog clock, rear defogger, intermittent wipers, power locks, tinted glass, driver's seat tilt/height adjustment, cloth heated reclining front bucket seats, folding rear seat, AM/FM ST ET, 185/65R15 SBR tires. **S** adds: cruise control, folding rear armrest, power windows and mirrors, AM/FM ST ET cassette, manual sunroof, alloy wheels. **Turbo** adds: turbocharged engine, sport seats, upgraded stereo with EQ; convertible has power top and leather interior. **Turbo SPG** has: higher-output engine, sport suspension, leather-wrapped steering wheel and shift knob, aero body addenda, wider tires.

Optional Equipment:

3-speed automatic transmission (NA SPG) .	525	—	—
Metallic or special black paint	485	—	—
Leather Pkg., Turbos exc. conv.	1295	—	—

Prices are accurate at time of printing; subject to manufacturer's change.

Saab 9000

1988 Saab 9000S

Saab adds a trunk and a full complement of standard equipment to create a 4-door notchback version of its 9000. Positioned as the line's new flagship, the 9000CD joins 5-door hatchback 9000S and 9000 Turbo models. The CD's body is about 6.5 inches longer than the hatchbacks, though curb weight is within a few pounds. Its trunk has 19.8 cubic feet of storage space, versus the 15.9 cubic feet of space available in the hatchback with the rear seatback upright. The CD's rear seatback does not fold for access to the trunk, though there is a small pass-through for skis and other long objects. Other features unique to the CD include a slightly revised grille and front bumper, plus a front spoiler and fog lamps. The bodyside moldings are wider and a rear accent panel bridges the taillamps, which are smoked in the CD. All 9000 CDs use the turbocharged and intercooled 2.0-liter 4-cylinder engine standard in the 9000 Turbo. CD has more sound insulation and softer suspension settings than other 9000s. Among other changes, the 9000 Turbo 5-door gets Saab's first power seats ever as standard. The naturally aspirated 9000S has a new option package that includes leather upholstery, which was previously a separate option, and adds for the first time fog lamps and a power driver's seat as options. We haven't seen a CD yet, but 9000 hatchbacks have extremely roomy cabins and can easily double as small station wagons with the rear seatback folded. Saab's assembly quality and grade of materials are top notch. And the cars have excellent road manners. The turbo is quite fast, though its turbo lag and torque steer can be unseemly in a $30,000-plus car. The 9000S has acceptable power, but most rivals are quicker.

1988 Specifications

	5-door hatchback
Wheelbase, in.	105.2
Overall length, in.	181.9
Overall width, in.	69.4
Overall height, in.	55.9
Turn diameter, ft.	35.8
Curb weight, lbs.	3022
Cargo vol., cu. ft.	56.5
Fuel capacity, gal.	17.9
Seating capacity	5
Front headroom, in.	38.5
Front shoulder room, in.	NA
Front legroom, max., in.	41.5
Rear headroom, in.	37.4
Rear shoulder room, in.	NA
Rear legroom, min., in.	38.7

Engines

	dohc I-4	Turbo dohc I-4
Size, liters/cu. in.	2.0/121	2.0/121
Fuel delivery	PFI	PFI
Horsepower @ rpm	125 @ 5500	160 @ 5500
Torque (lbs./ft.) @ rpm	125 @ 3000	188 @ 3000
Availability	S	S

EPA city/highway mpg

5-speed OD manual	22/28	22/28
4-speed OD automatic	18/24	19/26

Prices

Saab 9000	Retail Price	Dealer Invoice	Low Price
S 5-door hatchback	$24445	—	—
Turbo 5-door hatchback	30795	—	—
CD 4-door notchback	31995	—	—
Destination charge	359	—	—

Dealer invoice and low price not available at time of publication.

Prices are accurate at time of printing; subject to manufacturer's change.

Standard Equipment:

2.0-liter DOHC 16-valve PFI 4-cylinder engine, 5-speed manual or 4-speed automatic transmission, power steering, anti-lock braking system, 4-wheel disc brakes, automatic air conditioning, AM/FM ST ET cassette, power antenna, trip computer, trip odometer, tachometer, coolant temperature gauge, front and rear reading lights, reclining front bucket seats, driver's seat height/tilt, lumbar and lateral support adjustments, velour upholstery, emergency tensioning front seatbelt retractors, rear shoulder belts, telescopic steering column, power tilt/slide steel sunroof, 185/65R15 SBR tires on alloy wheels. **Turbo and CD** add: turbocharged engine, leather upholstery, fog lights, power glass sunroof, upgraded stereo, 205/55VR15 tires.

Optional Equipment:

4-speed automatic transmission	695	—	—
Leather Pkg., S	1595	—	—
Metallic or special black paint	485	—	—

Sterling 827

1988 Sterling 825SL

A 5-door hatchback body style joins the 4-door sedan and all versions of this front-drive luxury car from England get a larger, more powerful engine. Sterling's chassis and drive-train are shared with the Acura Legend Sedan in a joint venture between the British manufacturer Austin Rover and Honda, which builds Acura. The Sterling 825 debuted in the U.S. in early 1987 as a 4-door notchback that used the Legend Sedan's 151-horsepower 2.5-liter V-6. The Legend Sedan got a 161-horsepower 2.7-liter V-6 for '88, and Sterling gets it for '89, becoming the 827. Two notchbacks are available. Standard on the flagship 827SL are anti-lock brakes, 4-speed overdrive automatic transmission and leather upholstery, all of which are optional on the base 827S. The new hatchback is called the 827SLi. Its rear suspension lacks the self-leveling feature of the sedan's, but Sterling says the ride is tuned for a sportier feel. No other details or specifications were available at publication time. This year's larger engine should make Sterling quicker off the line and more compatible with automatic transmission. But based on our experiences with the 2.7 in the Legend, we're not certain the harsh-shifting Honda automatic is the best transmission for this high-revving engine. The engine itself is a silken jewel, with abundant power above 3000 rpm. Like Legends, Sterlings have generally outstanding road manners, though the

Specifications

	4-door notchback
Wheelbase, in.	108.6
Overall length, in.	188.8
Overall width, in.	76.8
Overall height, in.	54.8
Turn diameter, ft.	36.5
Curb weight, lbs.	3164
Cargo vol., cu. ft.	12.1
Fuel capacity, gal.	17.0
Seating capacity	5
Front headroom, in.	37.8
Front shoulder room, in.	54.9
Front legroom, max., in.	41.2
Rear headroom, in.	36.3
Rear shoulder room, in.	54.3
Rear legroom, min., in.	36.4

Engines

	ohc V-6
Size, liters/cu. in.	2.7/163
Fuel delivery	PFI
Horsepower @ rpm	161 @ 5900
Torque (lbs./ft.) @ rpm	162 @ 4500
Availability	S

EPA city/highway mpg

5-speed OD manual	19/24
4-speed OD automatic	18/23

ride quality is not up to such European competitors as Audi or Saab. Sterling's leather and wood interior does more to lend the car a highbrow British air than to improve upon the efficiency of Acura's control layout.

Prices

Sterling (1988 prices)	Retail Price	Dealer Invoice	Low Price
825S 4-door sedan	$20804	$17995	$19200
825SL 4-door sedan	25995	22356	23976
Destination charge	435	435	435

Standard Equipment:

825S: 2.5-liter PFI 24-valve V-6 engine, 5-speed manual transmission, power steering, power brakes, cruise control, intermittent wipers, remote fuel filler release, locking remote trunk release, gauges (tachometer, coolant temperature, oil pressure and voltage), Philips 6-speaker AM/FM ST ET cassette, courtesy delay interior lights, tilt steering column, reclining front bucket seats with adjustable lumbar support, burled walnut interior trim, coin tray, front and rear map/reading lights, composite halogen headlamps, heated power mirrors, central locking with infrared remote control, theft deterrent system, power moonroof with louvered blind, tinted glass, P195/65VR15 Goodyear tires. **825SL** adds: 4-speed automatic transmission (5-speed manual may be substituted at no charge), anti-lock braking system, Connolly leather upholstery, metallic paint, curbside illumination, power driver's seat with 4-position memory (includes mirrors), power passenger seat, trip computer, graphic display for fluid levels, door ajar and outside air temperature, courtesy delay headlight switch, 8-speaker stereo with upgraded amplifier, alloy wheels.

Optional Equipment:

Connolly leather upholstery, 825S	1025	861	943
Anti-lock braking system, 825S	1150	966	1058
4-speed automatic transmission, 825S	625	525	575
Metallic paint, 825S	400	336	368
Power rear seat, 825SL	375	315	345

Subaru Justy

An electronic continuously variable transmission (ECVT) will be optional on the front-drive Justy GL, and Subaru says it's nothing short of revolutionary. ECVT is essentially a "gearless" automatic transmission that uses pulleys to con-

Prices are accurate at time of printing; subject to manufacturer's change.

Subaru Justy GL

tinuously vary the ratio of engine speed to drive-wheel speed, operating without any shifting or interruption of power flow. Conventional automatics have three or four predetermined gear ratios that are engaged according to throttle position, engine load, vehicle speed and other factors. Subaru says the ECVT has a much wider spread of gear ratios and also provides livelier acceleration and lower engine speeds at cruising speed than conventional automatics. The ECVT has fewer moving parts than a conventional transmission, and is lighter and more compact. Justy also is restyled for 1989, gaining six inches in overall length to 145 and a more rounded appearance for its 3-door hatchback body. Subaru says there's now more passenger head room and more luggage space behind the folding rear seat. All models have new rear suspension geometry that's supposed to improve handling, while GL and RS models also get a new rear stabilizer bar and 13-inch wheels and tires (instead of 12-inchers). The base DL hatchback comes with front-wheel drive, and the mid-level GL model is available with either front-drive or on-demand 4WD that's engaged by a button on the shift lever. The sporty RS comes only with 4WD. A 1.2-liter 3-cylinder engine and 5-speed manual transmission are standard on all versions. We haven't driven the new ECVT, but it's another innovation for Subaru, which pioneered 4WD in small passenger cars in 1975. Justy is in fact the smallest passenger car sold with 4WD. The engine is gutsy and Justy holds its own in city traffic. Try anything really demanding, however, and you'll quickly discover its poor control in hard braking or cornering.

Specifications

	3-door hatchback
Wheelbase, in.	90.0
Overall length, in.	145.5
Overall width, in.	60.4
Overall height, in.	55.9
Turn diameter, ft.	32.2
Curb weight, lbs.	1745[1]
Cargo vol., cu. ft.	21.9
Fuel capacity, gal.	9.2
Seating capacity	4
Front headroom, in.	38.0
Front shoulder room, in.	51.9
Front legroom, max., in.	41.5
Rear headroom, in.	37.0
Rear shoulder room, in.	51.0
Rear legroom, min., in.	30.2

1. 1920 lbs., 4WD

Engines

	ohc I-3
Size, liters/cu. in.	1.2/73
Fuel delivery	2 bbl.
Horsepower @ rpm	66 @ 5200
Torque (lbs./ft.) @ rpm	70 @ 3600
Availability	S

EPA city/highway mpg

5-speed OD manual	34/37
ECVT automatic	34/35

Prices

Subaru Justy (1988 prices)	Retail Price	Dealer Invoice	Low Price
DL 3-door hatchback	$5666	$5221	$5444
GL 3-door hatchback	6666	5987	6327
RS 4WD 3-door hatchback	7666	6868	7267

Destination charge varies by region.

Standard Equipment:

DL: 1.3-liter 2bbl. 3-cylinder engine, 5-speed manual transmission, power brakes, locking fuel door, reclining front bucket seats, one-piece folding rear seat, SBR tires. **GL** adds: rear defogger, tachometer, intermittent wipers, rear wiper, digital clock, AM/FM ST ET, 50/50 folding rear seat, luggage shelf, remote hatch release. **RS** adds: monochrome exterior, AM/FM ST ET, remote mirrors, carpet, digital clock, cloth and vinyl upholstery, graphic monitor, full wheel covers, all-season tires.

Prices are accurate at time of printing; subject to manufacturer's change.

Optional Equipment:

	Retail Price	Dealer Invoice	Low Price
On-Demand 4WD, GL	600	400	500
Air conditioning	685	NA	NA
Alloy wheels	550	NA	NA

Subaru Sedan/Wagon/ 3-Door Coupe & Hatchback

Subaru RX 3-Door Coupe

Subaru's high-volume line gains a Touring Wagon for 1989 with new rear styling that adds three inches of head room, more cargo room and larger rear windows. The Touring Wagon is available in GL and GL-10 trim with front-drive or 4-wheel-drive. The regular 5-door wagon returns as well. The sporty RX 3-Door Coupe this year gains as an option Subaru's Active 4WD system, a permanently engaged, full-time system with a 4-speed overdrive automatic transmission. The sedan, wagon and coupe are available with front-wheel-drive; Active 4WD; on-demand 4WD, which is engaged by a shift-lever button; or Continuous 4WD, which comes with a 5-speed manual transmission and splits power permanently 50/50 between the front and rear wheels. Two versions of the same 1.8-liter flat (horizontally opposed) 4-cylinder engine are offered: a 90-horsepower naturally aspirated version and a 115-horsepower turbocharged one. Subaru's venerable Hatchback, the oldest model in its line, returns with only minor changes. Its size and price place it

Prices are accurate at time of printing; subject to manufacturer's change.

between the minicompact Justy and the larger Subaru Sedan/Wagon/3-Door Coupe trio. It's available in front-drive or on-demand, part-time 4-wheel drive and uses a 73-horsepower version of the 1.8. Subaru has announced it will introduce a new 4-door sedan and station wagon, called Legacy, in the spring of '89. The Legacy models will be larger than the current sedan, wagon and 3-door coupe, which will continue for 1990 as the Loyale line. None of these Subarus is very sporty or quick, but they are solid small cars with a natural allure to folks in snow states.

Specifications

	3-door hatchback	3-door Coupe	4-door notchback	5-door wagon
Wheelbase, in.	93.7	97.2	97.2	97.2
Overall length, in.	157.9	174.6	174.6	176.8
Overall width, in.	63.4	65.4	65.4	65.4
Overall height, in.	53.7	51.8	52.5	53.0
Turn diameter, ft.	30.8	34.8	34.8	34.8
Curb weight, lbs.	2120[1]	2280	2240	2370
Cargo vol., cu. ft.	33.9	39.8	14.9	70.3
Fuel capacity, gal.	13.2	15.9	15.9	15.9
Seating capacity	4	5	5	5
Front headroom, in.	38.2	37.6	37.6	37.6
Front shoulder room, in.	51.0	53.5	53.5	53.5
Front legroom, max., in.	39.3	42.2	41.7	41.7
Rear headroom, in.	36.6	35.8	36.5	37.7
Rear shoulder room, in.	52.4	52.8	53.5	53.5
Rear legroom, min., in.	30.2	32.6	35.2	35.2

1. 2240 lbs., 4WD

Engines

	ohv flat-4	ohc flat-4	Turbo ohc flat-4
Size, liters/cu. in.	1.8/109	1.8/109	1.8/109
Fuel delivery	2 bbl.	TBI	PFI
Horsepower @ rpm	73 @ 4400	90 @ 5200	115 @ 5200
Torque (lbs./ft.) @ rpm	94 @ 2400	101 @ 2800	134 @ 2800
Availability	S[1]	S	O

EPA city/highway mpg

4-speed OD manual	25/29		
5-speed OD manual	26/31	25/31	22/25
3-speed automatic	23/25	25/27	22/24
4-speed OD automatic			20/26

1. Hatchback

Prices

Subaru Hatchback

	Retail Price	Dealer Invoice	Low Price
GL 3-door hatchback	$8596	—	—

Dealer invoice and low price not available at time of publication. Destination charge varies by region.

Standard Equipment:

1.8-liter 2bbl. 4-cylinder engine, 5-speed manual transmission, power brakes, Hill Holder, cloth and vinyl reclining front bucket seats, driver's seat lumbar support adjustment, tachometer, coolant temperature and oil pressure gauges, trip odometer, tilt steering column, rear defogger, intermittent wipers, right visor mirror, 50/50 folding rear seat, AM/FM stereo, rear wiper, dual outside mirrors, 175/70SR13 tires.

Optional Equipment:

3-speed automatic transmission	560	—	—
On-Demand 4WD w/4-speed manual	700	—	—

Subaru Sedan, Wagon & 3-door Coupe

	Retail Price	Dealer Invoice	Low Price
DL 4-door notchback	$9731	—	—
GL 4-door notchback	11521	—	—
GL-10 Turbo 4-door notchback	16401	—	—
DL 3-door hatchback	10031	—	—
GL 3-door hatchback	11821	—	—
RX 3-door hatchback	16361	—	—
DL 5-door wagon	10181	—	—
GL 5-door wagon	11971	—	—
GL-10 Turbo 5-door wagon	16851	—	—

Dealer invoice and low price not available at time of publication. Destination charge varies by region.

Standard Equipment:

DL: 1.8-liter TBI 4-cylinder engine, 5-speed manual transmission, power steering and brakes, reclining front bucket seats, cloth upholstery, tinted glass, digital clock, rear defogger, remote fuel door and hatch/trunk releases, bodyside moldings, trip odometer, 50/50 folding rear seat (wagon), rear wiper (wagon), 155SR13 all-season SBR tires. **GL** adds: power mirrors, tachometer, power windows and locks, AM/FM stereo, memory tilt steering column, 50/50 folding rear seat (except 4-door), driver's seat lumbar support adjustment, 175/70SR13 tires. **GL-10 Turbo** adds: PFI turbocharged engine, 4-wheel disc brakes, variable intermittent wipers, power sunroof, air condi-

Prices are accurate at time of printing; subject to manufacturer's change.

tioning, cruise control, digital instruments with trip computer, upgraded stereo. **RX** adds: Continuous 4WD, 5-speed dual-range manual transmission, upgraded suspension, white monochrome exterior treatment, analog instruments, performance tires.

Optional Equipment:	Retail Price	Dealer Invoice	Low Price
3-speed automatic transmission, DL & GL .	560	—	—
4-speed automatic transmission, RX	760	—	—
On-Demand 4WD, GL	700	—	—
Continuous 4WD/5-speed, GL-10 Turbo . .	1600	—	—
Active 4WD/4-speed automatic, GL-10 Turbo	2360	—	—
Continuous 4WD Turbo/5-speed pkg.,			
GL wagon	2475	—	—
Touring Wagon Pkg., GL	200	—	—
GL-10 Turbo	NC	—	—

Subaru XT

Subaru XT6

The 2-seat DL model has been killed, so all XTs now have seating for four. Little else has changed. New high-performance, all-season tires are standard this year on XT6 4-wheel-drive models, and all models now have rear shoulder belts. The new tires are Goodyear Eagle GT+4s; size is the same as last year, 205/60HR14. XT6 takes its name from its 2.7-liter horizontally opposed, or flat, 6-cylinder engine. Base (GL) XT models use a 1.8-liter flat 4-cylinder. GL comes with front-wheel drive or on-demand 4WD. The XT6 comes three ways: front-drive; Continuous 4WD with a 5-speed

Prices are accurate at time of printing; subject to manufacturer's change.

Specifications

	2-door notchback
Wheelbase, in.	97.0
Overall length, in.	177.6
Overall width, in.	66.5
Overall height, in.	49.4
Turn diameter, ft.	34.1
Curb weight, lbs.	2455
Cargo vol., cu. ft.	11.6
Fuel capacity, gal.	15.9
Seating capacity	4
Front headroom, in.	37.4
Front shoulder room, in.	52.8
Front legroom, max., in.	43.3
Rear headroom, in.	34.4
Rear shoulder room, in.	52.8
Rear legroom, min., in.	26.2

Engines

	ohc flat-4	ohc flat-6
Size, liters/cu. in.	1.8/109	2.7/163
Fuel delivery	PFI	PFI
Horsepower @ rpm	97 @ 5200	145 @ 5200
Torque (lbs./ft.) @ rpm	103 @ 3200	156 @ 4000
Availability	S	O

EPA city/highway mpg

5-speed OD manual	24/28	18/25
4-speed OD automatic	23/30	20/28

manual transmission; and Active 4WD with a 4-speed overdrive automatic transmission. Continuous and Active 4WD are permanently engaged systems, but the first splits power 50/50 between the front and rear wheels, while the second varies the power split according to road conditions. The 6-cylinder engine that arrived last year gives the XT performance that comes much closer to matching its racy looks than previous engines. Compared to the four, the six makes for a much more refined and fun-to-drive package. The front-drive model handles capably, though its front tires plow in hard turns. The XT's electronic power steering system is accurate and returns good road feel. Adding 4WD increases the price by several hundred dollars, but also improves the XT's usefulness in foul weather. Inside, there's not much head or leg room even in front, and the tiny back seat is suitable for children only. An attractive analog gauge cluster is surrounded by a complicated control layout and a multitude of small buttons that are hard to find and operate while driving. While the interior still needs work, the XT offers respectable performance with the 6-cylinder and option of 4WD.

Prices

Subaru XT	Retail Price	Dealer Invoice	Low Price
GL 2-door notchback	$13071	—	—
XT6 2-door notchback	17111	—	—

Dealer invoice and low price not available at time of publication. Destination charge varies by region.

Standard Equipment:

1.8-liter PFI 4-cylinder engine, 5-speed manual transmission, power steering and brakes, cloth reclining front bucket seats, passive restraint system (automatic front shoulder and manual lap belts), console, Hill Holder, tinted glass, remote fuel door and trunk releases, dual spot lamps, memory tilt steering column, coolant temperature gauge, trip odometer, tachometer, digital clock, rear defogger, telltale graphic monitor, variable intermittent wipers, AM/FM ST ET, power windows and locks, power mirrors, driver's seat lumbar and height adjustments, one-piece folding rear seat, oil pressure gauge, voltmeter, 185/70HR13 all-season tires. **XT6** adds: 2.7-liter PFI 6-cylinder engine, 4-wheel disc brakes, air conditioning, fog lamps, cruise control, upgraded stereo with cassette and EQ, headlamp washers, trip computer, 195/60HR14 all-season tires on alloy wheels.

Optional Equipment:

4-speed automatic transmission, GL	760	—	—
On-Demand 4WD, GL	700	—	—
Active 4WD/4-speed automatic	1660	—	—
Continuous 4WD/5-speed, XT6	840	—	—

Suzuki Swift

Swift is Suzuki's version of the minicompact sold by Chevrolet dealers as the new Geo Metro, and the first passenger car sold in the U.S. by Suzuki. Both Swift and Metro share a front-drive design evolved from that of the first-generation

Prices are accurate at time of printing; subject to manufacturer's change.

Suzuki Swift GTi

Suzuki Cultus, which only GM sold here before as the Chevy Sprint (GM owns a small piece of Suzuki). Where Chevy pitches Metro in the economy-car sector, Suzuki is aiming Swift at two different niches. The Swift GLX comes only as a 5-door hatchback with a new 70-horsepower 1.3-liter 4-cylinder engine and a 3-speed automatic transmission. Standard equipment includes power door locks, rear wiper/washer, rear defogger, electric mirrors and a tachometer. The GLX is supposed to go on sale in November '88 with a base price of $7495. The Swift GTi, a 3-door hatchback priced at $8995 for its October introduction, sports racy rocker-panel extensions and a modest front spoiler holding a pair of foglamps. Under the hood, GTi uses a 1.3-liter engine with multi-point injection, twin overhead camshafts and four valves per cylinder. Suzuki claims a healthy 100 horsepower with this engine and a 0-60 mph time of 8.2 seconds with the standard 5-speed overdrive manual transaxle. An electronically controlled 3-speed automatic is optional. Matching this extra performance are standard all-disc brakes (versus the GLX's front-disc/rear-drum system), a firmer suspension, and 14-inch wheels with 175/60R14 tires, instead of the GLX's 13-inchers and skinny 155/80R rubber. The GTi is also sportier than the GLX inside, with more heavily bolstered front bucket seats. Paint choices are limited to red, white and black on the GTi. We haven't driven either version of the Swift, so we cannot comment on the performance of these cars.

Specifications

	GTi 3-door hatchback	GLX 5-door hatchback
Wheelbase, in.	89.2	93.1
Overall length, in.	146.1	150.0
Overall width, in.	62.4	62.6
Overall height, in.	53.1	54.3
Turn diameter, ft.	30.2	31.4
Curb weight, lbs.	1768	1741
Cargo vol., cu. ft.	NA	NA
Fuel capacity, gal.	10.6	10.6
Seating capacity	4	4
Front headroom, in.	NA	NA
Front shoulder room, in.	NA	NA
Front legroom, max., in.	NA	NA
Rear headroom, in.	NA	NA
Rear shoulder room, in.	NA	NA
Rear legroom, min., in.	NA	NA

Engines

	ohc I-4	dohc I-4
Size, liters/cu. in.	1.3/79	1.3/79
Fuel delivery	TBI	PFI
Horsepower @ rpm	70 @ 6000	100 @ 6500
Torque (lbs./ft.) @ rpm	74 @ 3500	83 @ 5000
Availability	S[1]	S[2]

EPA city/highway mpg

	GTi	GLX
5-speed OD manual		29/36
3-speed automatic	31/34	25/28

1. GLX   2. GTi

Prices not available at time of publication.

Toyota Camry

Automatic transmission is now available for the 4-wheel-drive All-Trac Camry sedan, and all All-Tracs are now available with anti-lock brakes. The 4-speed automatic is mandatory on the top-line LE All-Trac and optional on the less costly Deluxe All-Trac, which retains the 5-speed as standard. The previous 5-speed-manual LE All-Trac is dropped. The permanently engaged 4WD All-Trac system was added to the front-drive Camry line in '88. Later in the model year, Toyota made available a 24-valve, double-overhead cam 2.5-

Toyota Camry V6 4-door

Specifications

	4-door notchback	5-door wagon
Wheelbase, in.	102.4	102.4
Overall length, in.	182.1	183.1
Overall width, in.	67.4	67.4
Overall height, in.	54.1	54.5
Turn diameter, ft.	34.8	34.8
Curb weight, lbs.	2690[1]	2855
Cargo vol., cu. ft.	15.4	65.1
Fuel capacity, gal.	15.9	15.9
Seating capacity	5	5
Front headroom, in.	37.9	38.2
Front shoulder room, in.	54.3	54.3
Front legroom, max., in.	42.9	42.9
Rear headroom, in.	36.6	37.7
Rear shoulder room, in.	53.7	53.7
Rear legroom, min., in.	34.4	34.4

1. *3086 lbs., All-Trac*

Engines

	dohc I-4	dohc V-6
Size, liters/cu. in.	2.0/122	2.5/153
Fuel delivery	PFI	PFI
Horsepower @ rpm	115 @ 5200	153 @ 5600
Torque (lbs./ft.) @ rpm	124 @ 4400	155 @ 4400
Availability	S	O

EPA city/highway mpg

5-speed OD manual	26/32	19/24
4-speed OD automatic	24/30	19/24

liter V-6 engine. The V-6 is available only in 2WD Deluxe and LE sedans and wagons; all other sedans and wagons use the 115-horsepower, double-overhead cam 2.0-liter 4-cylinder. Toyota says high price and the resulting low demand rule out a V-6 All-Trac Camry. Anti-lock brakes (ABS), also added mid-1988, remain optional for the V-6 LE sedan and now are available on All-Trac models as well. ABS costs $1280 on the All-Trac and $1130 on the LE, down from $1250 last year. Camry is Toyota's best-selling U.S. line and a fine compact that offers several features not available on its strongest competitor, the Honda Accord: anti-lock brakes, a V-6 engine, 4WD and a station wagon body style. The V-6 engine is smooth, strong and flexible—much better suited than the weaker 4-cylinder for duty with automatic transmission. The four, however, still is adequate for Camry and returns good gas mileage. Note that ABS is available only on two of the more expensive models, which are quite pricey for the compact class. A loaded V-6 LE with ABS is around $20,000. Look to a V-6 Deluxe with fewer options or a 4-cylinder Deluxe, the latter competitive with a Honda Accord LX at around $15,000 fully equipped. Camry is competitive with Accord in most other areas as well, including assembly quality, reliability and resale value.

Prices

Toyota Camry	Retail Price	Dealer Invoice	Low Price
4-door notchback, 5-speed	$11488	9880	10884
4-door notchback, automatic	12158	10456	11507
Deluxe 4-door notchback, 5-speed	12328	10503	11616
Deluxe 4-door notchback, automatic	13078	11142	12310
LE 4-door notchback, automatic	14658	12415	13737
Deluxe All-Trac 4-door notchback, 5-speed .	14108	12020	13264
Deluxe All-Trac 4-door notchback, automatic	15058	12829	14144
LE All-Trac 4-door notchback, automatic .	16648	14101	15575
Deluxe 5-door wagon, 5-speed	13018	11091	12255
Deluxe 5-door wagon, automatic	13768	11730	12949
LE 5-door wagon, automatic	15438	13076	14457
Deluxe V6 4-door notchback, 5-speed . . .	13638	11620	12829
Deluxe V6 4-door notchback, automatic . .	14388	12259	13524
LE V6 4-door notchback, automatic	16428	13915	15372
Deluxe V6 5-door wagon, automatic	15078	12846	14162
LE V6 5-door wagon, automatic	17218	14584	16101

Dealer invoice and destination charge may vary by region.

Prices are accurate at time of printing; subject to manufacturer's change.

Standard Equipment:

2.0-liter DOHC 16-valve PFI 4-cylinder engine, 5-speed manual or 4-speed automatic transmission, power steering, narrow bodyside moldings, coolant temperature gauge, trip odometer, tilt steering column, center console with storage bin, velour reclining front bucket seats with driver's seat height adjustment, passive restraint system (motorized front shoulder belts and manual lap belts), rear lap/shoulder belts, remote fuel door and trunk/liftgate releases, rear defogger, tinted glass, P185/70SR13 all-season SBR tires. **Deluxe** adds: 2.0-liter DOHC 16-valve PFI 4-cylinder or 2.5-liter DOHC 24-valve PFI V-6 engine, wide bodyside moldings, dual remote mirrors, tilt steering column, automatic-off headlamp feature, folding rear seatbacks (wagon), rear wiper/washer (wagon), digital clock, right visor mirror, cup holder. **LE** adds: air conditioning (V6), power mirrors, tachometer, console armrest, multi-adjustable driver's seat, folding rear armrest, cargo cover (wagon), illuminated entry with fadeout, upper windshield tint band, AM/FM ST ET with power antenna. **All-Trac** models have full-time 4-wheel drive.

Optional Equipment:	Retail Price	Dealer Invoice	Low Price
Anti-lock brakes, LE All-Trac	1280	1024	1152
LE V6 4-door	1130	904	1017
Air conditioning (std. LE V6)	795	636	716
All Weather Guard Pkg., base	55	46	51
California emissions pkg	70	59	65
Power sunroof (NA base)	700	560	630
Cruise control	210	168	189
Power Pkg., Deluxe	520	416	468
LE	565	452	509
Power windows and locks; LE includes lighted visor mirrors.			
Power Seat Pkg., LE	230	184	207
Power driver's seat, lighted visor mirrors; requires Power Value Pkg.			
Leather Pkg., LE 4-door	230	184	207
Requires Power Pkg. and Power Seat Pkg. or Power Seat Pkg. and Value Pkg.			
Alloy wheels, LE 4-cyl.	360	288	324
LE V6	380	304	342
AM/FM ST ET, base & Deluxe 4-doors	330	247	289
Deluxe wagons	360	270	315
AM/FM ST ET cassette, base	480	360	420
Deluxe 4-doors	520	390	455
Deluxe wagons	550	412	481
LE	190	142	166
AM/FM cassette w/EQ & diversity antenna, LE	470	352	411
Speaker upgrade, base & Deluxe 4-doors	140	112	126
Deluxe wagons	170	136	153
Cargo deck cover, Deluxe wagons	50	41	46
Two-Tone Paint Pkg., LE 4-doors	245	196	221
Full wheel covers, Deluxe 4-cyl. 4-doors	75	60	68

Prices are accurate at time of printing; subject to manufacturer's change.

	Retail Price	Dealer Invoice	Low Price
Tachometer, Deluxe w/5-speed	60	48	54
CQ Convenience Pkg., base	195	156	176
Full-size spare tire, dual remote mirrors, digital clock.			
Tilt steering column, base	105	90	98
Mudguards	30	24	27
Fall 1989 Value Pkg., Deluxe 4-cyl. 4-doors .	1580	1346	1463
Deluxe 4-cyl. wagons	1600	1363	1482
Deluxe V6 4-doors	1530	1304	1417
LE 4-cyl. 4-doors	1190	1008	1099
LE V6 4-door exc. All-Trac	650	551	601
Air conditioning, cruise control, AM/FM ST ET, full wheel covers, Power Pkg.			

Toyota Celica

Toyota Celica All-Trac Turbo

Only detail changes attend Toyota's front-drive and All-Trac 4-wheel-drive sporty coupes. Full wheel covers are newly standard for the base ST and midrange GT models, and all but the ST have new interior fabric trim. A rear spoiler is a new option for GTs. The All-Trac Turbo, which has a permanently engaged 4WD system, comes only with a 5-speed manual transmission; optional for others is a 4-speed automatic. Anti-lock brakes remain an option for GT-S and All-Trac. Celica STs and GTs use a 115-horse-power 16-valve twin-cam 2.0-liter 4-cylinder. GT-S models get a 135-horsepower version of that engine, while the All-Trac Turbo has a 190-horsepower turbocharged and inter-

Specifications

	2-door notchback	3-door hatchback	2-door convertible
Wheelbase, in.	99.4	99.4	99.4
Overall length, in.	173.6	171.9	173.6
Overall width, in.	67.3	67.3	67.3
Overall height, in.	49.8	49.8	49.8
Turn diameter, ft.	35.4	35.4	35.4
Curb weight, lbs.	2436	2524[1]	2680
Cargo vol., cu. ft.	NA	25.2	NA
Fuel capacity, gal.	15.9	15.9	15.9
Seating capacity	5	5	4
Front headroom, in.	37.8	37.8	38.4
Front shoulder room, in.	52.1	52.1	52.1
Front legroom, max., in.	44.4	44.4	44.4
Rear headroom, in.	33.9	33.9	35.8
Rear shoulder room, in.	50.9	50.9	36.6
Rear legroom, min., in.	27.9	27.9	27.9

1. 3197 lbs., All-Trac

Engines

	dohc I-4	dohc I-4	Turbo dohc I-4
Size, liters/cu. in.	2.0/122	2.0/122	2.0/122
Fuel delivery	PFI	PFI	PFI
Horsepower @ rpm	115 @ 5200	135 @ 6000	190 @ 6000
Torque (lbs./ft.) @ rpm	124 @ 4400	125 @ 4800	190 @ 3200
Availability	S[1]	S[2]	S[3]

EPA city/highway mpg

5-speed OD manual	26/32	22/28	19/26
4-speed OD automatic	26/32	22/28	

1. ST, GT   2. GT-S   3. All-Trac

cooled version. Celica appeals mainly to younger drivers, and thus sales have dropped as its prices have increased. While the ST and GT have sporty looks, they lack sporty performance. Their 115-horsepower engine is economical but hardly exciting, especially with automatic transmission. The GT-S and All-Trac models elevate performance considerably, but GT-S prices start at more than $15,000 and the All-Trac Turbo is more than $20,000, putting it in the same league as the Mazda RX-7. Still, the All-Trac is quite a package: a high-powered, responsive engine, pavement-hugging 4WD system and optional anti-lock brakes. The GT-S is more reasonably priced and still provides brisk performance, plus you can order anti-lock brakes. Even so, you're probably looking at spending at least $17,000. At that price there are several alternatives, including a Ford Mustang GT or a low-line RX-7. For less than $17,000 you can get an Acura Integra, Chevrolet Beretta GT, Honda Prelude, Ford Probe or Mazda MX-6. Despite Celica's reputation for longevity, today's price is too high for what it delivers.

Prices

Toyota Celica	Retail Price	Dealer Invoice	Low Price
ST 2-door notchback, 5-speed	$11808	$10096	$10952
ST 2-door notchback, automatic	12478	10665	11572
GT 2-door notchback, 5-speed	13408	11397	12403
GT 2-door notchback, automatic	14078	11966	13022
GT 3-door hatchback, 5-speed	13658	11609	12634
GT 3-door hatchback, automatic	14328	12178	13253
GT 2-door convertible, 5-speed	18318	15570	16944
GT 2-door convertible, automatic	18988	16139	17564
GS-S 2-door notchback, 5-speed	15388	13003	14196
GT-S 2-door notchback, automatic	16138	13636	14887
GT-S 3-door hatchback, 5-speed	15738	13299	14519
All-Trac Turbo 3-door hatchback, 5-speed .	20878	17642	19260

Dealer invoice and destination charge may vary by region.

Standard Equipment:

2.0iter DOHC 16-valve PFI engine, 5-speed manual or 4-speed automatic transmission, power steering, tinted glass, console, rear defogger, remote fuel door and decklid/liftgate releases, fabric reclining front bucket seats, one-piece folding rear seatback, automatic headlamps off, trip odometer, tachometer, coolant temperature and oil pressure gauges, voltmeter, digital clock, AM/FM ST ET, 165SR13 tires. **GT** adds: split folding rear seatback, right visor mirror, pushbutton heating/ventilation controls, power mirrors, memory tilt steering column, cargo cover (3-door), cargo area carpet, 185/70SR13 tires; convertible has power top and power rear windows. **GT** adds: higher-output engine, rear wiper/washer (3-door), variable intermittent wipers, sport seats with power lumbar and lateral supports, tilt/telescopic steering column with memory, 205/60HR14 tires on alloy wheels. **All-Trac Turbo** adds: turbocharged, intercooled engine, permanent 4-wheel drive, 205/60VR14 tires.

Optional Equipment:

Anti-lock brakes, GT-S, All-Trac	1130	904	1017
Air conditioning, ST & GT	795	636	716
w/auto temp, GT-S & All-Trac	960	768	864

Prices are accurate at time of printing; subject to manufacturer's change.

	Retail Price	Dealer Invoice	Low Price
Power Pkg., ST & GT exc. conv.	415	332	374
Power windows and locks, heated power mirrors.			
Power Pkg., GT conv.	490	392	441
Power windows, locks and mirrors.			
Power Pkg., GT-S	390	312	351
Power windows and locks.			
Power Pkg. 2, GT exc. conv.	390	312	351
Power windows and locks.			
AM/FM ST ET cassette (std. All-Trac) . . .	190	142	166
w/EQ, GT & GT-S	430	322	376
w/EQ & diversity antenna, All-Trac	280	210	245
CD player, All-Trac	800	600	700
Alloy wheels, GT	340	272	306
GT conv.	370	296	333
Power sunroof	675	540	608
Cruise control	210	168	189
Color-Keyed Pkg., GT-S	50	40	45
Leather Sport Seat Pkg., GT-S	1550	1240	1395
All-Trac	1160	928	1044
Includes cruise control, power windows and locks.			
Two-tone paint	215	172	194
Rear wiper/washer, GT 3-door	135	111	123
Tilt/telescopic steering column, GT exc. conv.	70	60	65
Rear spoiler, GT	225	180	203
ST Value Pkg. 1 or 2	510	500	510
Pkg. 1: AM/FM ST ET cassette, air conditioner, pinstripe. Pkg. 2 deletes air conditioner and adds sunroof.			
GT Value Pkg.	620	610	620
AM/FM ST ET cassette, air conditioning, cruise control, rear spoiler, GT stripe.			
GT-S Value Pkg.	700	690	700
AM/FM ST ET cassette, automatic air conditioning, cruise control, Power Pkg.			

Toyota Corolla

A new 4-wheel-drive All-Trac Deluxe sedan joins the two All-Trac wagons this year as the major news for the subcompact Corolla. The line is otherwise unchanged following last year's redesign. Deluxe and SR5 All-Trac wagons arrived during 1988 to replace the 4WD Tercel wagons. The All-Trac 4-door sedan uses the same permanently engaged 4WD system as the wagons. It includes a center differential that

Prices are accurate at time of printing; subject to manufacturer's change.

Toyota Corolla All-Trac 4-door

Specifications

	2-door notchback	4-door notchback	5-door wagon
Wheelbase, in.	95.7	95.7	95.7
Overall length, in.	172.3	170.3	171.5
Overall width, in.	65.6	65.2	65.2
Overall height, in.	49.6	52.4	54.5
Turn diameter, ft.	NA	NA	NA
Curb weight, lbs.	2242	2207[1]	2282[2]
Cargo vol., cu. ft.	12.0	11.0	26.0
Fuel capacity, gal.	13.2	13.2	13.2
Seating capacity	5	5	5
Front headroom, in.	37.9	38.4	39.6
Front shoulder room, in.	51.0	53.2	53.2
Front legroom, max., in.	42.9	40.9	40.9
Rear headroom, in.	35.3	36.4	39.3
Rear shoulder room, in.	51.0	52.3	52.7
Rear legroom, min., in.	25.8	31.6	31.6

1. 2606 lbs., All-Trac   2. 2690 lbs., All-Trac

Engines

	dohc I-4	dohc I-4	dohc I-4
Size, liters/cu. in.	1.6/97	1.6/97	1.6/97
Fuel delivery	2 bbl.	PFI	PFI
Horsepower @ rpm	90 @ 6000	100 @ 5600	115 @ 6600
Torque (lbs./ft.) @ rpm	95 @ 3600	101 @ 4400	100 @ 4800
Availability	S[1]	S[2]	S[3]

EPA city/highway mpg

5-speed OD manual	30/35	23/28	26/31
3-speed automatic	27/30		
4-speed OD automatic	27/34	23/29	

1. Deluxe, LE, SR5   2. All-Trac   3. GT-S

can be locked for maximum traction. With manual shift this is accomplished by a dashboard switch; with automatic, by electronic control. All-Trac Corollas are powered by a fuel-injected, 100-horsepower 1.6-liter four with dual overhead cams. The top-line GT-S coupe continues with a 115-horsepower version of the 1.6. A carbureted 90-horsepower version is used in the rest of the line. A 5-speed manual transmission is standard across the board and is mandatory on the GT-S and SR5 All-Trac wagon. All the others have a 4-speed overdrive automatic as optional, except the front-drive Deluxe sedan and wagon, on which a 3-speed automatic is optional. Not having yet driven an All-Trac model or one of the coupes, we'll address the front-drive 4-door sedans, which we find competent and comfortable. The overdrive top gear on the LE's 4-speed automatic allows quieter, more economical highway cruising than the Deluxe's 3-speed. Stick with the 5-speed manual for best performance and maximum economy. The LE's wider tires don't seem to improve cornering or roadholding compared to the Deluxe. Interior room is comparable to other subcompact sedans. Corolla is priced higher than most other small sedans, though a good reliability record and good resale value compensate in the long run.

Prices

Toyota Corolla	Retail Price	Dealer Invoice	Low Price
Deluxe 4-door notchback, 5-speed	$9198	$7909	$8554
Deluxe 4-door notchback, automatic	9668	8314	8991
LE 4-door notchback, 5-speed	10418	8928	9673
LE 4-door notchback, automatic	11088	9502	10295
Deluxe 5-door wagon, 5-speed	9788	8417	9103
Deluxe 5-door wagon, automatic	10258	8822	9540
Deluxe All-Trac 5-door wagon, 5-speed . .	11498	9887	10693
Deluxe All-Trac 5-door wagon, automatic .	12268	10549	11409
SR5 All-Trac 5-door wagon, 5-speed	13088	11216	12152
Deluxe All-Trac 4-door notchback, 5-speed .	10608	9122	9865
Deluxe All-Trac 4-door notchback, automatic	11378	9784	10581

Dealer invoice and destination charge may vary by region.

Standard Equipment:

Deluxe: 1.6-liter DOHC 16-valve 2bbl. 4-cylinder engine, 5-speed manual or 3-speed automatic transmission, power brakes, cloth reclining front bucket seats (vinyl on wagons), split folding rear seatback (wagons), tinted

Prices are accurate at time of printing; subject to manufacturer's change.

glass, console with storage, door map pockets, cup holder, remote fuel door and trunk releases, trip odometer, coolant temperature gauge, 155SR13 tires. **LE** adds: 5-speed manual or 4-speed automatic transmission, tachometer, intermittent wipers, digital clock, 60/40 folding rear seatbacks, bodyside molding, remote mirrors, driver's seat height and lumbar support adjustments, upgraded trunk trim, 175/70SR13 all-season tires. **Deluxe All-Trac** models have: PFI engine, permanent 4-wheel drive, 5-speed manual or 4-speed automatic transmission. **SR5 All-Trac wagon** adds: power steering, cruise control, digital clock, AM/FM ST ET, cloth upholstery, tilt steering column, remote mirrors, intermittent wipers, rear wiper.

Optional Equipment:

	Retail Price	Dealer Invoice	Low Price
Air conditioning	745	596	671
All-Weather Guard Pkg. (std. All-Trac) . . .	55	46	51
California emissions pkg.	70	59	65
CQ Convenience Pkg., Deluxe w/5-speed .	195	156	176
Deluxe w/automatic	135	108	122
Intermittent wipers, dual remote mirrors, digital clock, tachometer (w/5-speed).			
Power steering (std. SR5)	250	214	232
Power sunroof	530	424	477
CL Convenience Pkg., Deluxe w/5-speed .	385	308	347
Deluxe w/automatic	325	260	293
LE, SR5	210	168	189
Cruise control, intermittent wipers, digital clock, dual remote mirrors, tachometer (w/5-speed).			
Alloy wheels w/tire upgrade, LE 4-doors . .	370	296	333
SR5	415	332	374
AM/FM ST (4 speakers; std. LE &			
SR5; NA wagons)	330	247	289
w/2 speakers, Deluxe	210	157	184
AM/FM cassette, Deluxe 4-door &			
All-Trac wagon	480	360	420
Deluxe wagons	380	285	333
SR5	190	142	166
LE	150	112	131
Tilt steering column (std. SR5)	85	73	79
Power Pkg., LE 4-doors & SR5	570	456	513
Power windows, locks and mirrors.			
Two-Tone Paint Pkg., SR5	320	256	288
Cargo deck cover, wagons (std. SR5) . . .	50	41	46
Fabric seats	70	60	65
RQ Convenience Pkg., Deluxe wagons			
w/5-speed	520	419	470
Deluxe wagons w/automatic	460	371	416
Rear wiper, cruise control, CQ Pkg.			
Rear wiper, wagons	155	127	141
Exterior Appearance Pkg., LE 4-doors . . .	85	68	77

Prices are accurate at time of printing; subject to manufacturer's change.

	Retail Price	Dealer Invoice	Low Price
Speaker upgrade, Deluxe All-Trac wagons .	115	92	104
Value Pkg., Deluxe	449	386	418
LE 4-doors	659	575	617
Deluxe 2WD wagons	599	515	557
Deluxe All-Trac wagons	539	464	502

Power steering, digital clock, dual remote mirrors, AM/FM ST, intermittent wipers, cargo cover (wagons), fabric seats (wagons), tilt steering column (LE), Power Pkg. (LE), trim rings (Deluxe), roof rack (2WD wagons).

Toyota Corolla Sport

	Retail Price	Dealer Invoice	Low Price
SR5 2-door notchback, 5-speed	$10628	$9108	$9868
SR5 2-door notchback, automatic	11298	9682	10490
GT-S 2-door notchback, 5-speed	12728	10882	11805

Dealer invoice and destination charge may vary by region.

Standard Equipment:

SR5: 1.6-liter DOHC 16-valve 2bbl. 4-cylinder engine, 5-speed manual or 4-speed automatic transmission, cloth reclining front bucket seats, trip odometer, coolant temperature gauge, tachometer, 175/70SR13 tires. **GT-S** adds: higher-output PFI engine, oil pressure gauge, voltmeter, tilt steering column, automatic headlights-off system, power mirrors, leather steering wheel trim, intermittent wipers, 185/60R14 tires.

Optional Equipment:

Air conditioning	596	745	671
Power steering	250	214	232
Power sunroof	530	424	477
CL Pkg., SR5 5-speed	365	292	329
SR5 automatic	305	244	275
GT-S	210	168	189

Cruise control, variable intermittent wipers, digital clock, dual remote mirrors.

CQ Convenience Pkg., SR5	240	199	220

Intermittent wipers, digital clock, split folding rear seat, dual remote mirrors, driver's seat lumbar and height adjustments.

Alloy wheels, SR5	445	356	401
GT-S	435	348	392
AM/FM ST ET, SR5	330	247	289
AM/FM ST ET cassette, SR5	520	390	455
GT-S	190	142	166
w/EQ, GT-S	430	322	376
Tilt steering column, SR5	85	73	79
Power Pkg.	390	312	351

Power windows and locks.

Prices are accurate at time of printing; subject to manufacturer's change.

	Retail Price	Dealer Invoice	Low Price
Two-Tone Paint Pkg.	215	172	194
Sport seat, GT-S	180	144	162
KQ Pkg., SR5	415	339	377
Exterior Appearance Pkg., CQ Pkg., power mirrors.			
KL Pkg., SR5	480	384	432
Exterior Appearance Pkg., CL Pkg., power mirrors.			
All Weather Guard Pkg.	55	46	51
California emissions pkg.	70	59	65

Toyota Cressida

Toyota Cressida

Toyota's luxury flagship is all new this year. It remains a rear-drive 4-door notchback sedan, but gets slightly more rounded styling and a new engine. Compared to its 1985-88 predecessor, the new Cressida has an inch-longer wheelbase and a body that's 1.8 inches longer and 1.2 inches wider. Curb weight is up about 100 pounds. Four-wheel disc brakes are standard and anti-lock control is a new option. As before, standard equipment is comprehensive. Replacing the 156-horsepower 2.8-liter 12-valve inline 6-cylinder of previous models is a slightly detuned version of the 3.0-liter six from the Supra, also an inline design but with four valves per cylinder and 190 horsepower. It teams exclusively with Toyota's 4-speed automatic transmission, now with a shift lock that freezes it in "park" unless the brakes are applied. The new Cressida is no big advance on the old one, which was a surprisingly capable sedan, staid looks notwithstanding. Cressida's new engine delivers more than adequate

Prices are accurate at time of printing; subject to manufacturer's change.

punch, and the transmission provides prompt, super-smooth shifts. Despite its slightly greater heft and bulk, the new Cressida feels more agile than the old. Braking is fine, the ride is firm but supple. The new Cressida's cabin seems about as large as the Acura Legend's, slightly smaller than the Mazda 929's. The driving position, seat comfort and general ergonomics prompt little complaint—with two exceptions. The automatic-climate-control panel slides out like a drawer to reveal its manual fan-speed and mode buttons. The panel won't extend or retract with the ignition off. Equally silly is the bank of duplicate sound system controls just under the center dash vents. In all, this new Cressida is as much an enigma as the equally conservative 929: a wolverine in sheep's clothing—a smooth, competent and luxurious upscale sedan rendered almost invisible by unimaginative styling.

Specifications

	4-door notchback
Wheelbase, in.	105.5
Overall length, in.	189.6
Overall width, in.	67.3
Overall height, in.	53.7
Turn diameter, ft.	NA
Curb weight, lbs.	3417
Cargo vol., cu. ft.	12.0
Fuel capacity, gal.	18.5
Seating capacity	5
Front headroom, in.	38.4
Front shoulder room, in.	54.6
Front legroom, max., in.	42.8
Rear headroom, in.	37.1
Rear shoulder room, in.	54.4
Rear legroom, min., in.	35.0

Engines

	dohc I-6
Size, liters/cu. in.	3.0/180
Fuel delivery	PFI
Horsepower @ rpm	190 @ 5600
Torque (lbs./ft.) @ rpm	185 @ 4400
Availability	S

EPA city/highway mpg

4-speed OD automatic	19/24

Prices

Toyota Cressida

	Retail Price	Dealer Invoice	Low Price
4-door notchback	$21498	$17628	$19563

Dealer invoice and destination charge may vary by region.

Standard Equipment:

3.0-liter DOHC 24-valve PFI 6-cylinder engine, 4-speed automatic transmission, power steering, power 4-wheel disc brakes, shift lock, automatic air conditioning, reclining front bucket seats, passive restraint system (motorized front shoulder belts, manual lap belts), rear lap/shoulder belts, cruise control, variable intermittent wipers, trip odometer, coolant temperature gauge, tachometer, AM/FM ST ET cassette with EQ, power antenna, power windows and locks, heated power mirrors, tilt/telescopic steering column, 205/60R15 tires.

Optional Equipment:

Anti-lock brakes	1130	904	1017
CD player	800	600	700
Power sunroof	810	648	729
Leather Pkg.	905	724	815
Power Seat Pkg.	540	432	486
Leather Power Seat Pkg.	1245	996	1121

Toyota MR2

Toyota's mid-engine 2-seat sports car gets only two minor changes for '89. All models get a center high-mount stop lamp that employs light-emitting diodes (LEDs) instead of conventional bulbs. The feature had been included with the optional Aerodynamic Spoiler Package only. And the Supercharged version gains a standard rear stabilizer bar. The base engine is a naturally aspirated 115-horsepower 1.6-liter, twin-cam 4-cylinder. The supercharged version of that engine has 145 horsepower. A choice of 5-speed manual or 4-speed automatic transmissions continues, as do standard all-disc brakes. Toyota blames high sports-car insurance rates for declining MR2 sales, but climbing prices certainly aren't helping. We prefer the MR2's supercharged engine to most turbocharged engines because of its smooth rush of

Toyota MR2

Specifications

	2-door notchback
Wheelbase, in.	91.3
Overall length, in.	155.5
Overall width, in.	65.6
Overall height, in.	48.6
Turn diameter, ft.	31.5
Curb weight, lbs.	2350[1]
Cargo vol., cu. ft.	7.8
Fuel capacity, gal.	10.8
Seating capacity	2
Front headroom, in.	37.4
Front shoulder room, in.	52.4
Front legroom, max., in.	43.0
Rear headroom, in.	—
Rear shoulder room, in.	—
Rear legroom, min., in.	—

1. 2493 lbs., Supercharged MR2

Engines

	dohc I-4	Supercharged dohc I-4
Size, liters/cu. in.	1.6/97	1.6/97
Fuel delivery	PFI	PFI
Horsepower @ rpm	115 @ 6600	145 @ 6400
Torque (lbs./ft.) @ rpm	100 @ 4800	140 @ 4000
Availability	S	S

EPA city/highway mpg

5-speed OD manual	26/31	24/30
4-speed OD automatic	25/30	22/27

power, even at low speeds. Luckily, the base engine delivers almost as much pleasure for substantially less money. Our staff is divided on the MR2's handling and roadholding; some rate both as excellent, others claim it feels loose in corners, lacks straight-line stability and has vague steering. The criticisms seem directed more at the supercharged model, and that car's new stabilizer bar may be Toyota's response. (A rear stabilizer was standard on early MR2s, but was removed as a running change). Most drivers find a workable position in the tight cockpit. The gauges are clearly marked, all controls are within easy reach, except for the low-mounted stereo. A low build makes getting in or out a chore, and despite trunks in the front and rear, cargo space is minimal. Of course, MR2s are bought for driving pleasure, not cargo carrying. This well-designed 2-seater will make the sporting driver smile.

Prices

Toyota MR2	Retail Price	Dealer Invoice	Low Price
2-door, 5-speed	$13798	$11659	$12729
2-door, automatic	14548	12293	13421
2-door w/T-bar roof, 5-speed	15268	12901	14085
2-door w/T-bar roof, automatic	16018	13535	14777
Supercharged w/T-bar roof, 5-speed	17628	14896	16262
Supercharged w/T-bar roof, automatic	18378	15529	16954

Dealer invoice and destination charge may vary by region.

Standard Equipment:

1.6-liter DOHC 16-valve PFI 4-cylinder engine, 5-speed manual or 4-speed automatic transmission, 4-wheel disc brakes, reclining bucket seats, tinted glass with shaded upper windshield band, remote fuel door and decklid releases, AM/FM ST ET, intermittent wipers, trip odometer, tachometer, coolant temperature and oil pressure gauges, voltmeter, 185/60HR14 tires. **T-bar roof models** add: Performance Interior Pkg. (sport seats, leather-wrapped steering wheel and shift knob, power mirrors, rear console, automatic headlamp off). **Supercharged** models have 1.6-liter supercharged and intercooled engine, Aerodynamic Spoiler Pkg., alloy wheels.

Optional Equipment:

Air conditioning	795	636	716
Moonroof w/sunshade, base	380	304	342

Prices are accurate at time of printing; subject to manufacturer's change.

	Retail Price	Dealer Invoice	Low Price
Power Pkg., base w/T-bar	390	312	351
Base w/o T-bar	920	736	828

T-bar: power windows, locks and mirrors. Standard roof adds leather-wrapped steering wheel, automatic headlamp off and rear console.

	Retail Price	Dealer Invoice	Low Price
Performance Interior Pkg., base w/o T-bar .	530	424	477

Sport seats, leather-wrapped steering wheel, automatic headlamp off, power mirrors.

Cruise control	225	180	203
Rear spoiler, T-bar models	285	228	257
Aerodynamic Spoiler Pkg., base	560	448	504

Rear spoiler, side skirts, rear mudguards, rear sunshade.

Alloy wheels, base	435	348	392
Leather/Power/Performance Pkg.,			
base w/o T-bar	1730	1384	1557
Base w/T-bar	1200	960	1080

Power windows and locks, power mirrors, leather-wrapped steering wheel, automatic headlamp off, rear console box, leather sport seat.

Two-Tone Paint Pkg.	245	196	221
AM/FM ST ET cassette	280	210	245
w/EQ, base w/o T-bar	490	367	429
w/EQ, base w/T-bar	435	326	381
Alloy wheels & all-weather tires, base . . .	435	348	392

Toyota Supra

Toyota Supra Turbo

Toyota's rear-drive grand touring car enters its fourth season with several touchups inside and out. The turbocharged engine gets a nominal two extra horsepower for a total of 232. Supra's naturally aspirated 3.0-liter, 24-valve inline six

Prices are accurate at time of printing; subject to manufacturer's change.

is unchanged at 200 horsepower. Standard for the Turbo and optional for the base Supra is new speed-sensitive power steering. A 5-speed manual transmission is standard; the optional 4-speed automatic now has a shift lock that keeps it in park unless the brakes are applied. Rear suspension components have been revised for what Toyota says is improved handling and stability. Other changes include a thicker steering wheel with spoke-mounted cruise control switches (previously divided between a column stalk and a main dash switch); new gauge graphics, power-window switches and climate controls; and a revised 6-speaker stereo with newly optional compact-disc player. Outside is an enlarged air intake under the front bumper, a revised grille, new taillamps and, on the Turbo, a restyled 3-piece spoiler with LED center

Specifications

	3-door hatchback
Wheelbase, in.	102.2
Overall length, in.	181.9
Overall width, in.	68.7
Overall height, in.	51.6
Turn diameter, ft.	35.4
Curb weight, lbs.	3459
Cargo vol., cu. ft.	12.8
Fuel capacity, gal.	18.5
Seating capacity	4
Front headroom, in.	37.5
Front shoulder room, in.	52.5
Front legroom, max., in.	43.6
Rear headroom, in.	33.9
Rear shoulder room, in.	50.5
Rear legroom, min., in.	24.7

Engines

	dohc I-6	Turbo dohc I-6
Size, liters/cu. in.	3.0/180	3.0/180
Fuel delivery	PFI	PFI
Horsepower @ rpm	200 @ 6000	232 @ 5600
Torque (lbs./ft.) @ rpm	188 @ 3600	254 @ 3200
Availability	S	S

EPA city/highway mpg

5-speed OD manual	18/23	17/22
4-speed OD automatic	18/23	18/23

high-mount stop lamp as on the MR2. Supra succeeds despite its hefty curb weight. Performance is brisk with the base engine and quite satisfying with the turbo, but the heavy Supra feels ponderous and clumsy at lower speeds. The wide tires, while generating lots of road noise, allow impressive cornering ability, and the suspension handles demanding roads with aplomb. The optional anti-lock system will improve the already fine braking. Inside, Supra has well-shaped, supportive front seats, a comfortable driving position and simple, convenient controls.

Prices

Toyota Supra	Retail Price	Dealer Invoice	Low Price
3-door hatchback, 5-speed	$22360	$18335	$20348
3-door hatchback, automatic	23110	18950	21030
w/Sport Roof, 5-speed	23430	19213	21322
w/Sport Roof, automatic	24180	19828	22004
Turbo, 5-speed	24700	20254	22477
Turbo, automatic	25450	20869	23160
Turbo w/Sport Roof, 5-speed	25720	21090	23405
Turbo w/Sport Roof, automatic	26470	21705	24088

Dealer invoice and destination charge may vary by region.

Standard Equipment:

3.0-liter DOHC 24-valve PFI 6-cylinder engine, 5-speed manual or 4-speed automatic transmission, speed-sensitive power steering, power 4-wheel disc brakes, automatic air conditioning, power windows and locks, heated power mirrors, two-can cupholder, tilt/telescopic steering column, fog lights, theft deterrent system, bodyside moldings, tachometer, coolant temperature and oil pressure gauges, voltmeter, trip odometer, variable intermittent wipers, cruise control, console with storage area and padded armrest, cloth sport seats, driver's seat power lumbar and lateral support adjustments, folding rear seatbacks, lighted visor mirrors, remote fuel door and hatch releases, automatic-off headlight system, illuminated entry system, tinted glass with shaded upper windshield band, rear defogger, cargo cover, AM/FM ST ET cassette with EQ, diversity power antenna, 225/50VR16 Goodyear Eagle GT Gatorback tires on alloy wheels. **Turbo** adds: turbocharged, intercooled engine, oil cooler, turbo boost gauge, Sports Pkg. (Electronically Modulated Suspension, limited-slip differential, headlamp washers).

Optional Equipment:

Anti-lock brakes	1130	904	1017
Leather Seat Pkg.	1010	808	909

Prices are accurate at time of printing; subject to manufacturer's change.

	Retail Price	Dealer Invoice	Low Price
Power driver's seat	230	184	207
Sports Pkg., base	595	476	536
Turbo	360	288	324
Electronically Modulated Suspension, limited-slip differential.			
White Exterior Appearance Pkg.	40	32	36
CD player	800	600	700
Leather/Power Seat Pkg.	1240	992	1116
California emissions pkg.	70	59	65

Toyota Tercel

Toyota Tercel 2-door

Now bereft of wagons, Toyota's price-leader subcompact series gets only minor changes this year. Included are upgraded seat fabrics for Standard and Deluxe models, standard dual, manual remote-control mirrors, and newly optional full wheel covers for Deluxes. Model choices are down to a 2-door notchback coupe and 3- and 5-door hatchback sedans in standard and Deluxe trim, plus the bare-bones EZ 3-door, all with front-wheel drive. The EZ comes with a 4-speed manual transaxle instead of the others' 5-speed overdrive unit and isn't available with optional 3-speed automatic. Continuing as Tercel power is a carbureted 1.5-liter 4-cylinder engine with three valves per cylinder and 78 horsepower. Tercel is smaller, a little more basic and less expensive than the Corolla, so this is the logical choice for those on a tight budget. Fuel economy is good with either transmission, but naturally better with the overdrive manual transmissions. Acceleration is surprisingly brisk with manual shift and barely adequate with automatic. However, we've encountered power lulls during acceleration, a problem apart from the power drained by the air conditioner. The coupe has minimal rear seat room, while the hatchbacks allow enough space for two adults to sit in somewhat cramped fashion. Trunk space is modest on the coupe as well, while the hatchbacks have rear seatbacks that fold to improve cargo room. While Tercel is a competent small car, neither its performance nor its price are exceptional for today. However, an admirable record for reliability and durability make it worth looking at.

Specifications

	2-door notchback	3-door hatchback	5-door hatchback
Wheelbase, in.	93.7	93.7	93.7
Overall length, in.	166.7	157.3	157.3
Overall width, in.	64.0	64.0	64.0
Overall height, in.	51.8	52.6	52.8
Turn diameter, ft.	31.2	31.2	31.2
Curb weight, lbs.	2000	1970	2025
Cargo vol., cu. ft.	NA	36.2	37.8
Fuel capacity, gal.	11.9	11.9	11.9
Seating capacity	5	5	5
Front headroom, in.	37.8	38.4	38.5
Front shoulder room, in.	51.5	51.5	52.9
Front legroom, max., in.	40.2	40.2	40.2
Rear headroom, in.	35.9	36.6	36.3
Rear shoulder room, in.	50.7	51.5	52.4
Rear legroom, min., in.	30.8	32.1	32.1

Engines

	ohc I-4
Size, liters/cu. in.	1.5/89
Fuel delivery	1 bbl.
Horsepower @ rpm	78 @ 6000
Torque (lbs./ft.) @ rpm	87 @ 4000
Availability	S

EPA city/highway mpg

4-speed OD manual	35/41
5-speed OD manual	31/37
3-speed automatic	28/32

Prices

Toyota Tercel

	Retail Price	Dealer Invoice	Low Price
Standard 2-door notchback, 5-speed	$7338	$6604	$6971
Standard 2-door notchback, automatic ...	7798	7018	7408
Deluxe 2-door notchback, 5-speed	8398	7221	7810
Deluxe 2-door notchback, automatic	8868	7626	8247
EZ 3-door hatchback, 4-speed	6328	5789	6059
Standard 3-door hatchback, 5-speed	7178	6532	6855
Standard 3-door hatchback, automatic ...	7648	6959	7304
Deluxe 3-door hatchback, 5-speed	8298	7136	7717
Deluxe 3-door hatchback, automatic	8768	7540	8154
Deluxe 5-door hatchback, 5-speed	8538	7342	7940
Deluxe 5-door hatchback, automatic	9008	7747	8378

Dealer invoice and destination charge may vary by region.

Standard Equipment:

EZ: 1.5-liter 12-valve 4-cylinder engine, 4-speed manual transmission, power brakes, locking fuel door, trip odometer, vinyl reclining front bucket seats, door pockets, fold-down rear seatback, 145/80SR13 tires on styled steel wheels. **Standard** adds: 5-speed manual or 3-speed automatic transmission, cloth seat inserts, cup holder, door-ajar light, bodyside moldings, rear ashtray. **Deluxe** adds: cloth seat trim, folding rear seatbacks, right visor mirror, rear defogger, tinted glass, 155SR13 all-season tires.

Optional Equipment:

Air conditioning (NA EZ)	735	588	662
Power steering (NA EZ)	250	214	232
Manual sunroof, Deluxe 3-door	370	296	333
Rear wiper/washer, Std & Deluxe hatchbacks	135	111	123
Full wheel covers, Deluxe	125	100	113
AM/FM ST ET	210	157	184
AM/FM ST ET cassette, Deluxe	480	360	420
Cargo cover, Std 3-door	50	41	46
CL Pkg., Deluxe hatchbacks	355	287	321
Deluxe 2-doors	385	311	348

Cruise control, variable intermittent wipers, tilt steering column, clock, lighted cigaret lighter.

CQ Convenience Pkg., Standard	140	116	128
Deluxe hatchbacks	155	127	141
Deluxe 2-doors	185	151	168

Standard: remote left mirror, tilt steering column, remote decklid/liftgate release, full fabric seats, day/night mirror, trunk light. Deluxe adds: low-fuel warning lamp, rear console box, security latch (hatchbacks), clock, lighted cigaret lighter and trunk light.

Prices are accurate at time of printing; subject to manufacturer's change.

	Retail Price	Dealer Invoice	Low Price
All Weather Guard Pkg., Std & EZ	90	77	84
Deluxe	55	46	51
California emissions pkg.	70	59	65

Volkswagen Fox

1988 Volkswagen Fox GL wagon

A 5-speed manual transmission arrived during the summer for Fox, Volkswagen's Brazilian-built, front-drive subcompact. Coming for 1989 are a new GL trim level for the 2-door sedan, formerly available only in base trim, and a removable glass sunroof as a new option. The 5-speed manual transmission is standard on the Fox GL Sport model, which also has alloy wheels and a sport steering wheel. The 5-speed will not be offered on the GL 3-door wagon. Fox debuted in 1987 and until now has been available only with a 4-speed manual transmission, which remains standard on the base 2-door, GL 4-door and GL wagon. We welcome the 5-speed manual since the widely spaced gear ratios in the 4-speed manual leave huge gaps between the gears, so it's hard to find the right one for many occasions. Even so, Fox still easily outruns most other subcompacts. All models use an 81-horsepower 1.8-liter 4-cylinder engine similar to the ones in the Golf and Jetta. This version of VW's 1.8 lacks neck-snapping

Prices are accurate at time of printing; subject to manufacturer's change.

power, but compensates with a free-revving, hard-working nature. Fuel economy is impressive for the lively performance; we averaged nearly 28 mpg in urban driving with a 1988 wagon. On models we've tested, shift action was fine in the forward gears, but getting into reverse at times was a real wrestling match. No word yet on when automatic transmission or power steering will be offered. In size, Fox falls between the Golf hatchbacks and the Jetta sedans in overall length, but has a shorter wheelbase and is narrower overall. Head room is limited in front, so most drivers have to recline the seatback more than usual. Cargo space is skimpy on the sedans and just adequate on the wagon. Far from perfect, Fox is more fun to drive than most other cars in its size and price range.

Specifications

	2-door notchback	4-door notchback	3-door wagon
Wheelbase, in.	92.8	92.8	92.8
Overall length, in.	163.4	163.4	163.4
Overall width, in.	63.0	63.0	63.9
Overall height, in.	53.7	53.7	54.5
Turn diameter, ft.	31.5	31.5	31.5
Curb weight, lbs.	2126	2203	2203
Cargo vol., cu. ft.	9.9	9.9	61.8
Fuel capacity, gal.	12.4	12.4	12.4
Seating capacity	4	4	4
Front headroom, in.	36.6	36.6	36.6
Front shoulder room, in.	51.7	51.7	51.7
Front legroom, max., in.	41.1	41.1	41.1
Rear headroom, in.	35.4	35.4	35.8
Rear shoulder room, in.	52.1	51.1	51.5
Rear legroom, min., in.	30.2	30.2	30.2

Engines

	ohc I-4
Size, liters/cu. in.	1.8/109
Fuel delivery	PFI
Horsepower @ rpm	81 @ 5500
Torque (lbs./ft.) @ rpm	93 @ 3250
Availability	S

EPA city/highway mpg

4-speed OD manual	25/30
5-speed OD manual	24/29

Prices

Volkswagen Fox

	Retail Price	Dealer Invoice	Low Price
2-door notchback	$6590	$5966	$6278
GL 4-door sedan	7640	6796	7218
GL 3-door wagon	7770	6911	7340
GL Sport 4-door notchback	8115	7217	7666
Destination charge	320	320	320

Dealer invoice and low price not available at time of pubication.

Standard Equipment:

1.8-liter PFI 4-cylinder engine, 4-speed manual transmission, power brakes, reclining front bucket seats, tweed upholstery, tinted glass, rear defogger, intermittent wipers, carpeting, padded steering wheel, trip odometer, coolant temperature gauge, clock, swing-out rear side windows, remote left mirror, front door storage pockets, bodyside moldings, 155/80SR13 tires on steel wheels with hubcaps and full-size spare. **GL** adds: tachometer (except wagon), LCD digital clock (wagon has analog clock), velour upholstery, three-point rear seatbelts, swivel map light, trunk carpeting, wider bodyside moldings, full wheel covers, 175/70SR13 tires. **GL Sport** adds: 5-speed manual transmission, alloy wheels.

Optional Equipment:

	Retail Price	Dealer Invoice	Low Price
Heavy-Duty Cooling Pkg.	85	71	78
Air conditioning	685	575	630
AM/FM stereo cassette	415	349	382
4-speaker radio prep	110	92	101
Rear wiper/washer, wagon	145	122	134

Volkswagen Golf/Jetta

Anti-lock brakes are a new option on the Jetta Carat and GLI 16V. Volkswagen expects to eventually offer the $995 Teves-designed anti-lock system on the Golf-based GTI 16V, which, like the Carat and GLI, has 4-wheel disc brakes standard. With the Scirocco sport coupe discontinued for 1989, the GTI is VW's main performance model, using a 123-horsepower, 16-valve 1.8-liter engine. The top-line Jetta Carat becomes the stand-in for the Quantum, also dropped for '89, as a sport/luxury sedan. Golf and Jetta are built from the same

Prices are accurate at time of printing; subject to manufacturer's change.

1988 Volkswagen Golf

Specifications

	Jetta 2-door notchback	Jetta 4-door notchback	Golf 3-door hatchback	Golf 5-door hatchback
Wheelbase, in.	97.3	97.3	97.3	97.3
Overall length, in.	171.7	171.7	158.0	158.0
Overall width, in.	65.5	65.5	65.5	65.5
Overall height, in.	55.7	55.7	55.7	55.7
Turn diameter, ft.	34.4	34.4	34.4	34.4
Curb weight, lbs.	2305	2305	2194	2246
Cargo vol., cu. ft.	16.6	16.6	39.6	39.6
Fuel capacity, gal.	14.5	14.5	14.5	14.5
Seating capacity	5	5	5	5
Front headroom, in.	38.1	38.1	38.1	38.1
Front shoulder room, in. .	53.3	53.3	53.3	53.3
Front legroom, max., in. .	39.5	39.5	39.5	39.5
Rear headroom, in.	37.1	37.1	37.5	37.5
Rear shoulder room, in. .	53.3	53.3	54.3	54.3
Rear legroom, min., in. .	35.1	35.1	34.4	34.4

Engines

	ohc I-4	ohc I-4	dohc I-4
Size, liters/cu. in.	1.8/109	1.8/109	1.8/109
Fuel delivery	PFI	PFI	PFI
Horsepower @ rpm	100 @ 5400	105 @ 5400	123 @ 5800
Torque (lbs./ft.) @ rpm	107 @ 3400	110 @ 3400	120 @ 4250
Availability	S[1]	S[2]	S[3]

EPA city/highway mpg

5-speed OD manual	25/34	25/34	22/29
3-speed automatic	23/28	23/28	

1. Base Golf and Jetta, Golf GL   2. Jetta GL and Carat   3. GTI and GLI

front-drive design, but Golf comes as 3- and 5-door hatchbacks and Jetta as 2- and 4-door sedans. This year's Golf line includes base and GL hatchbacks with a 100-horsepower 1.8-liter engine, and the GTI 16V with the 123-horsepower. Last year's Golf GT hatchbacks have been dropped. Jetta's roster includes base 2- and 4-door sedans with the 100-horsepower engine, GL and Carat 4-doors with a 105-horsepower engine, and sporty GLI 16V with the 123-horsepower engine. Brisk performance, good fuel economy, capable front-drive handling, ample passenger room and generous cargo space are standard on all Golfs and Jettas. The optional anti-lock brakes make Jettas even more tempting. There isn't much difference between the 100- and 105-horsepower engines, so don't ignore the base models. Performance and fuel economy suffer noticeably with the optional automatic transmission, so we recommend the 5-speed manual. These cars are among the most frequently broken into because their stereos can be popped out of the dashboard in seconds. Volkswagen has been selling anti-theft stereos the past couple of years, but the word hasn't gotten around to everyone in the "smash-and-grab" crowd.

Prices

Volkswagen Golf	Retail Price	Dealer Invoice	Low Price
3-door hatchback, 5-speed	$8465	$7823	$8144
3-door hatchback, automatic	8970	8293	8632
GL 3-door hatchback, 5-speed	9170	8242	8706
GL 3-door hatchback, automatic	9675	8712	9194
GL 5-door hatchback, 5-speed	9380	8431	8906
GL 5-door hatchback, automatic	9885	8901	9393
GTI 16V 3-door hatchback, 5-speed	13650	11979	12815
Destination charge	320	320	320

Standard Equipment:

1.8-liter PFI 4-cylinder engine, 5-speed manual or 3-speed automatic transmission, power brakes, reclining front bucket seats, cloth upholstery, folding rear seat, tinted glass, intermittent wipers, rear defogger, rear wiper, analog clock, trip odometer, coolant temperature gauge, console, left remote mirror, wide bodyside moldings, 175/70SR13 tires. **GL** adds: digital clock, upgraded door trim with pockets, tachometer, dual remote mirrors, automatic seatbelts. **GTI 16V** adds: DOHC 16-valve engine, close-ratio 5-speed manual

Prices are accurate at time of printing; subject to manufacturer's change.

transmission, power steering, 4-wheel disc brakes, tachometer, trip computer, courtesy light with delay, lighted right visor mirror, sport seats with driver's height adjustment, 60/40 rear seat, leather-wrapped steering wheel, sport suspension, 205/55VR14 tires on alloy wheels.

Optional Equipment:

	Retail Price	Dealer Invoice	Low Price
Air conditioning	805	692	749
Power steering, base & GL	275	231	253
Cruise control, GL	225	194	210
Floormats, GL, GTI 16V	50	43	47
Metallic clearcoat paint, GL	165	142	154
Mica paint, GTI 16V	210	180	195
AM/FM ST ET cassette, base	520	447	484
GL, GTI 16V	585	503	544
4-speaker radio prep	165	142	154
Manual sliding sunroof	395	340	368
Split rear seat, GL	150	129	140
Power Pkg., GTI 16V	605	552	579
Power windows, locks and mirrors.			

Volkswagen Jetta

2-door notchback, 5-speed	$9690	$8950	$9320
2-door notchback, automatic	10195	9415	9805
4-door notchback, 5-speed	9910	9152	9531
4-door notchback, automatic	10415	9617	10016
GL 4-door notchback, 5-speed	11120	9820	10470
GL 4-door notchback, automatic	11625	10285	10955
Carat 4-door notchback, 5-speed	15140	13358	14249

1988 Volkswagen Jetta GLI 16V

Prices are accurate at time of printing; subject to manufacturer's change.

	Retail Price	Dealer Invoice	Low Price
Carat 4-door notchback, automatic	15545	13823	14684
GLI 16V 4-door notchback, 5-speed	14770	13032	13901
Destination charge	320	320	320

Standard Equipment:

1.8-liter PFI 4-cylinder engine, 5-speed manual or 3-speed automatic transmission, power brakes, reclining front bucket seats, cloth upholstery, rear defogger, tachometer, coolant temperature gauge, trip odometer, front door pockets, dual remote mirrors, wide bodyside moldings, intermittent wipers, 175/70SR13 SBR tires. **GL** adds: automatic front seatbelts, rear armrest, time-delay courtesy light, visor mirrors with lighted right, velour upholstery. **Carat** adds: 105-bhp engne, 4-wheel disc brakes, power steering, air conditioning, cruise control, AM/FM cassette, power windows and locks, power mirrors, metallic paint, manual seatbelts, sport seats with height adjustment, ski sack, leather-wrapped steering wheel, sport suspension, 185/60HR14 tires on alloy wheels. **GLI 16V** deletes air conditioning, cruise control, radio, power windows, locks and mirrors and adds: DOHC 16-valve engine, Recaro seats with height adjustment, trip computer.

Optional Equipment:

Anti-lock brakes, GLI & Carat	995	856	926
Air conditioning	805	692	749
Power Pkg.	705	644	675
Power windows, locks and mirrors.			
Power steering, base	280	241	261
Cruise control, GL & GLI 16V	225	194	210
Metallic clearcoat paint (std. Carat)	165	142	154
AM/FM ST ET cassette, base	520	447	484
GL & GTI 16V	585	503	544
4-speaker radio prep	215	185	200
Manual sliding sunroof	395	340	368
Cast alloy wheels, GL	460	377	419
Forged alloy wheels, Carat	210	180	195

Volcanic

Volvo 240

The base price on the cheapest Volvo is now more than $17,000, which isn't cheap at all. While there's nothing special about the 240's credentials, we applaud its overall competence. The 114-horsepower engine feels surprisingly

Prices are accurate at time of printing; subject to manufacturer's change.

Volvo 240 DL 4-door

adequate in the 3000-pound 240 sedan, so you can easily
keep pace with traffic and get brisk acceleration by using a
heavy throttle foot. It's also an economical engine; we averaged 23 mpg with a 1988 DL 4-door/5-speed from mostly city
and suburban driving. The base Volvo is competent and
reassuring on the road: The responsive steering has good
centering action while the firm suspension absorbs bumps
pretty well without being floppy, for a stable ride over most
surfaces. The 4-wheel disc brakes have good stopping power
and control. Changes for 1989 are minor: Rear headrests are
now standard on all 240 models, which comprise DL and GL
price levels in 4-door sedan and 5-door wagon body styles.
DL models also have new wheel covers and the DL wagon
offers cloth upholstery as a no-cost option to the standard
vinyl. DL models can now be ordered with optional factory-
installed power windows. Previously, power windows were
a dealer-installed option for DLs. With the factory-installed
option, the power window controls will be mounted on the
armrests rather than the dashboard. All models have rear-
wheel drive and the 114-horsepower 2.3-liter 4-cylinder engine. The DLs are available with a 5-speed manual or 4-
speed automatic transmission; the GLs come only with the
automatic. When we consider the 240's fine reputation for
durability and Volvo's generous warranties, and then add
other virtues such as the roomy, comfortable interior, we
find enough to justify the high price.

Specifications

	4-door notchback	5-door wagon
Wheelbase, in.	104.3	104.3
Overall length, in.	189.9	190.7
Overall width, in.	67.3	67.7
Overall height, in.	56.3	57.1
Turn diameter, ft.	32.2	32.2
Curb weight, lbs.	2919	3051
Cargo vol., cu. ft.	14.0	76.0
Fuel capacity, gal.	15.8	15.8
Seating capacity	5	5
Front headroom, in.	37.9	37.9
Front shoulder room, in.	NA	NA
Front legroom, max., in.	40.1	40.1
Rear headroom, in.	36.1	36.8
Rear shoulder room, in.	NA	NA
Rear legroom, min., in.	36.4	36.1

Engines

	ohc I-4
Size, liters/cu. in.	2.3/140
Fuel delivery	PFI
Horsepower @ rpm	114 @ 5400
Torque (lbs./ft.) @ rpm	136 @ 2750
Availability	S

EPA city/highway mpg

5-speed OD manual	21/27
4-speed OD automatic	19/24

Prices

Volvo 240	Retail Price	Dealer Invoice	Low Price
DL 4-door notchback, 5-speed	$17250	—	—
DL 4-door notchback, automatic	17820	—	—
DL 5-door wagon, 5-speed	17740	—	—
DL 5-door wagon, automatic	18310	—	—
GL 4-door notchback, automatic	20035	—	—
GL 5-door wagon, automatic	20775	—	—
Destination charge	350	350	350

Dealer invoice and low price not available at time of publication.

Standard Equipment:

DL: 2.3-liter PFI 4-cylinder engine, 5-speed manual or 4-speed automatic transmission, power steering, power 4-wheel disc brakes, air conditioning,

Prices are accurate at time of printing; subject to manufacturer's change.

power door locks, analog clock, trip odometer, rear defogger, tinted glass, dual remote mirrors, driver's seat height adjustment, cloth reclining heated front bucket seats, rear head restraints, AM/FM ST ET cassette, 185/70R14 tires (4-door), 185R14 tires (wagon). **GL** adds: 4-speed automatic transmission, manual sunroof (4-door), leather upholstery (wagon), power windows, tachometer, alloy wheels.

Optional Equipment:	Retail Price	Dealer Invoice	Low Price
Power windows, DL	275	—	—
Metallic paint	380	—	—
Leather upholstery, GL 4-door	785	—	—

Volvo 740/760/780

Volvo 740 GL wagon

A new 16-valve engine becomes standard on the 740 GLE sedan and wagon after January 1, while new 740 GL models have been slotted below the GLEs in equipment and price. The new engine for the 740 GLE uses the same block as last year's 2.3-liter 4-cylinder, but is topped by a dual-cam, 16-valve cylinder head that boosts horsepower from 114 to 153. The 16-valve engine is available with a 5-speed manual or a 4-speed automatic transmission, which gains a lockup torque converter this year. Other changes for the 740 GLE are that a driver's-side air bag is standard instead of op-

Specifications

	780 2-door notchback	740/760 4-door notchback	740/760 5-door wagon
Wheelbase, in.	109.1	109.1	109.1
Overall length, in.	188.8	188.4	188.4
Overall width, in.	69.3	69.3	69.3
Overall height, in.	55.1	55.5	56.5
Turn diameter, ft.	32.2	32.2	32.2
Curb weight, lbs.	3415	2954	3082
Cargo vol., cu. ft.	14.9	16.8	74.9
Fuel capacity, gal.	15.8	15.8[1]	15.8
Seating capacity	4	5	5
Front headroom, in.	37.2	38.6	38.6
Front shoulder room, in.	NA	NA	NA
Front legroom, max., in.	41.0	41.0	41.0
Rear headroom, in.	35.8	37.1	37.6
Rear shoulder room, in.	NA	NA	NA
Rear legroom, min., in.	34.7	34.7	34.7

1. 21.0 gals with turbo engine or V-6.

Engines

	ohc I-4	dohc I-4	Turbo ohc I-4	ohc V-6
Size, liters/cu. in.	2.3/140	2.3/140	2.3/140	2.8/176
Fuel delivery	PFI	PFI	PFI	PFI
Horsepower @ rpm	114 @ 5400	153 @ 5700	160 @ 5300[1]	144 @ 5100
Torque (lbs./ft.) @ rpm	136 @ 2750	150 @ 4450	187 @ 2900	173 @ 3750
Availability	S[2]	S[3]	S[4]	S[5]

EPA city/highway mpg

	ohc I-4	dohc I-4	Turbo ohc I-4	ohc V-6
4-speed manual + OD			20/25	
5-speed OD manual	21/27	NA/NA		
4-speed OD automatic	20/26	NA/NA	19/23	17/21

1. 175 horsepower in 780   2. 740 GL   3. 740 GLE   4. Turbo models
5. 760 GLE, 780

tional and tire size has been increased from 185/70R14 to 185/65R15. The new base model in this range is the 740 GL, with a 114-horsepower, single-cam, 8-valve engine. Carry-over models include the 740 Turbo sedan and wagon, 760 GLE sedan, and 760 Turbo sedan and wagon. Turbo models use a 160-horsepower turbocharged 2.3, while the 760 GLE uses a 144-horsepower 2.8-liter V-6. Volvo's highest-priced model, the Bertone-built 780 2-door, is available this year with a turbocharged 2.3 that benefits from different elec-

Volvo 740 Turbo 4-door

tronic engine controls to boost horsepower to 175 and provide a flatter torque curve. A 780 with the 144-horsepower V-6 engine returns from last year; only automatic transmission is available with either 780 engine. The 114-horsepower 740 GLs are underpowered for this price; nice cars, but we want more for our $20,000. All models are highly capable otherwise. Anti-lock brakes and a driver's-side air bag are standard on all but the GL, where they're optional. Overall, these high-priced Swedish cars are refined, roomy and well-built, and they're backed by generous warranties.

Prices

Volvo 740/760/780	Retail Price	Dealer Invoice	Low Price
740 GL 4-door notchback, 5-speed	$19985	—	—
GL 4-door notchback, automatic	20555	—	—
740 GL 5-door wagon, 5-speed	20665	—	—
740 GL 5-door wagon, automatic	21235	—	—
740 GLE 4-door notchback, 5-speed	NA	—	—
740 GLE 4-door notchback, automatic . . .	NA	—	—
740 GLE 5-door wagon, 5-speed	NA	—	—
740 GLE 5-door wagon, automatic	NA	—	—
740 Turbo 4-door notchback, 5-speed . . .	24925	—	—
740 Turbo 4-door notchback, automatic . .	25405	—	—
740 Turbo 5-door wagon, 5-speed	25605	—	—

Prices are accurate at time of printing; subject to manufacturer's change.

Volvo 780 Turbo

	Retail Price	Dealer Invoice	Low Price
740 Turbo 5-door wagon, automatic	26085	—	—
760 GLE 4-door notchback	32155	—	—
760 GLE Turbo 4-door notchback	32940	—	—
760 GLE Turbo 5-door wagon	32940	—	—
780 2-door notchback	37790	—	—
780 Turbo 2-door notchback	38975	—	—
Destination charge	350	350	350
Gas Guzzler Tax, 760 & 780 V-6	500	500	500

Dealer invoice and low price not available at time of publication.

Standard Equipment:

740 GL: 2.3-liter PFI 4-cylinder engine, power steering, power 4-wheel disc brakes, air conditioning, cloth reclining front bucket seats, power windows and locks, tachometer, coolant temperature gauge, trip odometer, analog clock, AM/FM ST ET cassette, power antenna, 185/70R14 tires. **740 GLE** adds: DOHC 16-valve engine, anti-lock braking system, Supplemental Restraint System, cruise control, 185/65R15 tires on alloy wheels. **740 Turbo** adds: turbocharged, intercooled engine, 4-speed manual plus overdrive or 4-speed automatic transmission, power sunroof, power mirrors, velour and leather upholstery, 195/60R15 tires. **760** adds: 2.8-liter PFI V-6 or 2.3-liter turbocharged 4-cylinder engine, 4-speed automatic transmission, independent rear suspension, automatic air conditioning, leather upholstery, power seats, tilt steering column, upgraded stereo with EQ, front map lights, rear reading lights (Turbo). **780** adds: power moonroof, elm burl accents.

Optional Equipment:

Anti-lock brakes, 740 GL	1175	—	—
Supplemental Restraint System, 740 GL . .	850	—	—
Pearlescent paint, 780	320	—	—

Prices are accurate at time of printing; subject to manufacturer's change.

Yugo

Yugo GVX

Yugo plans to offer an automatic transmission and a new convertible during the 1989 model year. Yugo's lineup at the end of 1988 included the base GV and more expensive GVL and GVS versions of the same car. All three use the same front-drive chassis, 3-door hatchback body, 52-horsepower 1.1-liter 4-cylinder engine and 4-speed manual transmission. New for a spring 1988 release was the GVX, powered by a 64-horsepower 1.3-liter four with a 5-speed overdrive manual transmission. The GVX also has a front air dam, fog lamps, aero body trim and 13-inch tires instead of 12-inch. A 3-speed automatic transmission is supposed to eventually be available on all models, though different transmissions may be offered for the 1.1- and 1.3-liter engines. Also promised for the 1989 model year is the GVC, a convertible based on the GV design. Yugo is estimating the GVC's base price at $8300, which would make it the lowest-priced convertible car in the U.S. The GVC will use the 1.3-liter engine and 5-speed manual transmission, plus it will have a power folding top and a heated glass rear window. We're impressed by the 1.3-liter engine's adequate performance, commendable smoothness and good gas mileage (31.4 mpg overall in our test). However, the shift linkage on a 1988 GVX was vague and rubbery; the ride was stiff and the little

Yugo could easily be jarred off course by sharp bumps; the steering wheel was angled too far forward; wind and engine noise were quite high; the cramped interior had thinly padded seats, cheap materials, and no glovebox. If this was a $4000 car, we could overlook some of those flaws. However, this was a $7200 Yugo (including optional air conditioning and stereo, plus the destination charge); too much for us to be interested.

Specifications

	3-door hatchback
Wheelbase, in.	84.6
Overall length, in.	139.0
Overall width, in.	60.7
Overall height, in.	54.7
Turn diameter, ft.	31.2
Curb weight, lbs.	1832
Cargo vol., cu. ft.	27.5
Fuel capacity, gal.	8.4
Seating capacity	4
Front headroom, in.	37.0
Front shoulder room, in.	NA
Front legroom, max., in.	39.0
Rear headroom, in.	36.0
Rear shoulder room, in.	NA
Rear legroom, min., in.	NA

Engines

	ohc I-4	ohc I-4
Size, liters/cu. in.	1.1/68	1.3/79
Fuel delivery	2 bbl.	2 bbl.
Horsepower @ rpm	52 @ 5000	64 @ 5800
Torque (lbs./ft.) @ rpm	52 @ 4600	68 @ 4000
Availability	S[1]	S[2]

EPA city/highway mpg

4-speed manual	28/31	
5-speed OD manual		26/29

1. GV, GVL, GVS   2. GVX

Prices

Yugo (1988 prices)	Retail Price	Dealer Invoice	Low Price
GV 3-door hatchback	$4349	$3979	$4164
GVL 3-door hatchback	4599	4158	4379

Prices are accurate at time of printing; subject to manufacturer's change.

	Retail Price	Dealer Invoice	Low Price
GVS 3-door hatchback	4699	4230	4465
GVX 3-door hatchback	5699	5149	5424
Destination charge	400	400	400

Standard Equipment:

GV: 1.1-liter 2bbl. 4-cylinder engine, 4-speed manual transmission, power brakes, rear defogger, bodyside molding, reclining front seats, fabric upholstery, folding rear seats, console, right visor mirror, locking fuel cap, tool kit, 145SR13 all-season SBR tires with full-size spare. **GVL** adds: upgraded seats and upholstery. **GVS** adds: AM/FM ST cassette, velour upholstery, wheel covers. **GVX** adds: 1.3-liter engine, uprated suspension, front air dam, fog lamps, sill extensions, rear spoiler, 155/70SR13 tires.

Optional Equipment:

Comfort & Sound Pkg., GV	999	749	874
GVL, GVX	1099	825	962
Air conditioning, AM/FM stereo.			
Rear wiper/washer, GV, GVS	139	112	126
Air conditioning, GVS	799	639	719
AM/FM ST cassette, GV	239	160	200
GVL, GVX	379	254	317
Sport Pkg., GV	229	160	195
GVL	189	132	161
Right outside mirror, wheel covers, luggage rack, rear louvers.			
Appearance Pkg., GV	99	74	87
Wheel covers, right mirror.			
Tourister Pkg., GV	229	160	195
Right outside mirror, wheel covers, luggage rack.			
Alloy wheels, GVL	349	244	297
GVS	299	224	262
Metallic paint (NA GV)	149	125	137
Passive restraint, GVS & GVX	99	89	94
Right outside mirror, GVS	39	29	34
Luggage rack, GVS	119	89	104
Travel Pkg., GVL	189	132	161
Luggage rack and right outside mirror.			
Premium Travel Pkg., GVL	249	174	212
Travel Pkg. plus rear louvers.			
Catapult seats, GVL	149	112	131
Easy-entry feature with memory.			
Rear louver, GVX	149	89	119

Prices are accurate at time of printing; subject to manufacturer's change

RATINGS CHART

SCALE 5 = Exceptional; 4 = Above average; 3 = Average; 2 = Below average; 1 = Poor

MAKE AND MODEL	Performance							Accommodations						Workmanship			TOTAL
	Acceleration	Economy	Driveability	Ride	Steering/handling	Braking	Noise	Driver seating	Instruments/controls	Visibility	Room/comfort	Entry/exit	Cargo room	Exterior	Interior	Value	
Acura Integra	4	4	4	3	4	4	2	3	4	4	3	3	3	3	4	4	56
Acura Legend (Sedan)	4	2	4	4	4	5	4	4	4	4	4	4	4	4	4	4	63
Audi 80/90 (90)	4	3	4	4	5	5	3	3	4	4	3	3	2	5	5	3	60
Audi 100/200 (200 Quattro)	4	2	4	5	4	5	4	2	4	3	4	4	5	5	4	3	62
BMW 3-Series (325i)	4	3	4	4	4	5	3	3	5	4	3	3	3	5	4	3	60
BMW 5-Series (535i)	4	2	4	5	4	5	5	4	5	4	4	4	4	5	4	3	65
BMW 7-Series (750iL)	5	1	5	5	4	5	5	5	4	4	5	5	4	5	5	2	69
Buick Century/Oldsmobile Cutlass Ciera (2.8 V-6)	4	2	4	3	3	3	4	4	3	4	4	4	4	3	4	3	56
Buick Electra/Oldsmobile Ninety-Eight (ABS)	4	2	4	4	4	5	4	3	3	4	4	4	4	3	4	3	59

RATINGS CHART

SCALE 5 = Exceptional; 4 = Above average; 3 = Average; 2 = Below average; 1 = Poor

MAKE AND MODEL	Performance							Accommodations						Workmanship			TOTAL
	Acceleration	Economy	Driveability	Ride	Steering/handling	Braking	Noise	Driver seating	Instruments/controls	Visibility	Room/comfort	Entry/exit	Cargo room	Exterior	Interior	Value	
Buick Estate/Oldsmobile Custom Cruiser/Pontiac Safari	3	2	4	4	2	3	4	3	3	3	5	5	5	3	4	4	57
Buick LeSabre/Oldsmobile 88 Royale/Pontiac Bonneville (Bonneville SSE)	4	2	3	3	4	4	3	4	3	4	4	4	4	4	3	3	56
Buick Reatta	4	2	4	3	4	5	4	4	2	4	4	3	3	4	4	3	57
Buick Regal	3	2	4	3	4	4	3	3	2	4	4	3	4	4	3	3	53
Buick Riviera	4	2	4	4	4	3	4	4	2	4	3	3	3	4	4	3	55
Buick Skyhawk	2	4	3	3	3	3	3	3	4	5	3	3	3	3	4	3	52
Buick Skylark/Oldsmobile Cutlass Calais	4	3	3	3	4	3	2	3	3	4	3	3	3	3	4	3	51

Make / Model																	Total
Cadillac Allante	4	2	4	4	4	5	3	4	3	3	4	3	3	5	4	2	57
Cadillac Brougham	3	1	3	2	2	2	5	3	2	3	4	5	4	3	4	3	49
Cadillac De Ville/ Fleetwood (ABS)	4	2	4	4	4	5	4	3	3	3	4	4	4	4	4	3	59
Cadillac Eldorado/ Seville (Eldorado, ABS)	4	2	4	3	4	4	4	3	4	3	3	3	3	4	4	3	55
Chevrolet Astro/ GMC Safari	3	4	4	3	4	4	3	4	3	2	2	3	3	4	3	3	55
Chevrolet Camaro/ Pontiac Firebird (IROC-Z)	5	2	4	1	4	4	2	3	3	3	2	2	2	4	3	3	48
Chevrolet Caprice (V-8)	4	2	3	3	3	3	5	2	2	4	4	5	4	3	3	4	54
Chevrolet Cavalier	2	3	3	3	3	3	3	3	4	4	3	3	3	3	3	3	48
Chevrolet Celebrity/Pontiac 6000 (V-6 Celebrity)	3	2	4	4	3	3	4	3	2	4	4	4	4	4	4	4	56
Chevrolet Corsica/Beretta (V-6 Corsica)	4	2	3	3	4	3	3	3	3	4	3	4	3	4	3	4	53
Chevrolet Corvette	5	2	4	2	4	5	2	4	3	3	3	3	2	4	4	3	53
Chrysler Conquest TSi/ Mitsubishi Starion	5	2	3	2	4	4	2	4	3	2	3	3	3	4	4	3	52
Chrysler Fifth Avenue/ Dodge Diplomat/Plymouth Gran Fury	3	2	4	3	2	3	5	3	3	4	4	4	3	4	3	3	52

RATINGS CHART

SCALE 5 = Exceptional; 4 = Above average; 3 = Average; 2 = Below average; 1 = Poor

MAKE AND MODEL	Performance							Accommodations						Workmanship		Value	TOTAL
	Acceleration	Economy	Driveability	Ride	Steering/handling	Braking	Noise	Driver seating	Instruments/controls	Visibility	Room/comfort	Entry/exit	Cargo room	Exterior	Interior		
Chrysler LeBaron (Coupe Turbo)	4	3	3	3	4	3	2	2	3	3	3	3	4	4	4	3	51
Chrysler New Yorker (ABS)	3	2	4	4	3	4	4	3	3	2	4	4	4	4	3	3	54
Daihatsu Charade	2	5	3	2	2	3	1	3	3	3	2	3	2	3	3	2	42
Dodge Aries America/ Plymouth Reliant America (4-dr, 2.5)	3	3	4	3	3	3	3	4	4	5	4	3	3	4	3	5	57
Dodge Caravan/ Plymouth Voyager (Grand Caravan V-6)	4	2	4	4	3	3	3	3	3	3	5	3	5	4	3	4	56
Dodge/Plymouth Colt (3-dr)	3	5	4	3	3	4	2	3	3	4	3	3	3	4	3	4	54
Dodge/Plymouth Colt Vista (4WD)	2	3	4	3	4	3	2	3	4	4	4	4	4	4	4	3	55

CONSUMER GUIDE®

Dodge Daytona (turbo)	5	2	3	2	4	4	2	3	4	3	2	2	3	49
Dodge Dynasty (4 cyl.)	2	3	3	4	3	4	3	4	4	4	4	4	3	55
Dodge Lancer (ES Turbo)	4	2	4	3	4	3	2	3	3	4	3	4	4	55
Dodge Omni America/ Plymouth Horizon America	4	3	3	3	3	4	3	3	5	3	3	3	5	55
Dodge Shadow/ Plymouth Sundance (Shadow ES Turbo)	4	2	3	4	4	3	2	3	3	3	3	4	4	53
Dodge Spirit/ Plymouth Acclaim (V-6)	4	2	3	3	3	3	4	4	4	3	3	3	4	54
Eagle Medallion	2	2	4	4	3	3	3	2	3	4	4	3	3	48
Eagle Premier	4	3	4	4	3	3	4	2	4	4	4	4	4	58
Eagle Summit (1.6 DOHC)	3	3	3	4	4	3	3	4	4	3	3	3	3	51
Ford Aerostar	3	2	4	3	3	3	3	3	3	5	5	2	4	53
Ford Escort (GT)	3	3	3	2	3	3	2	2	3	2	2	2	3	41
Ford Festiva	3	5	3	3	3	3	2	3	4	3	3	3	4	54
Ford LTD Crown Victoria/ Mercury Grand Marquis	4	2	5	3	2	3	4	2	4	5	5	5	4	60
Ford Mustang (GT)	5	2	4	2	4	3	2	3	2	2	3	3	4	50
Ford Probe (GL)	2	2	3	4	3	3	2	3	4	3	4	3	3	46
Ford Taurus/ Mercury Sable (3.0 V-6)	4	2	4	4	3	3	4	4	4	4	4	3	4	57

RATINGS CHART

SCALE 5 = Exceptional; 4 = Above average; 3 = Average; 2 = Below average; 1 = Poor

MAKE AND MODEL	Performance							Accommodations						Workmanship			TOTAL
	Acceleration	Economy	Driveability	Ride	Steering/handling	Braking	Noise	Driver seating	Instruments/controls	Visibility	Room/comfort	Entry/exit	Cargo room	Exterior	Interior	Value	
Ford Tempo/Mercury Topaz	2	4	3	3	2	3	3	4	4	3	3	3	3	2	3	3	48
Ford Thunderbird/Mercury Cougar	3	2	3	3	3	2	3	3	3	3	4	3	3	3	3	3	47
Geo Metro	3	5	3	2	3	4	1	3	3	5	2	3	3	3	3	4	50
Geo Spectrum	2	5	3	2	3	4	1	3	3	4	3	3	3	4	3	3	49
Honda Accord (LX)	3	3	4	4	4	3	3	4	4	4	4	4	4	4	4	5	61
Honda Civic (DX 3-dr)	4	4	4	3	4	4	3	3	3	5	3	3	3	4	4	4	58
Honda CRX (Si)	4	4	4	2	4	4	1	3	4	2	4	2	3	4	3	4	52
Honda Prelude (4WS)	4	3	3	3	4	4	3	3	4	4	2	3	3	4	3	2	52
Hyundai Excel/Mitsubishi Precis	2	5	3	3	3	3	3	4	3	5	3	4	3	4	3	4	55
Isuzu I-Mark	2	5	3	2	3	4	1	3	3	4	3	3	3	4	3	3	49

Model																			Page
Isuzu Impulse (turbo)	4	3	4	2	3	4	2	3	4	3	3	3	3	4	3	3	4	3	52
Lincoln Continental	4	2	4	4	4	4	2	4	4	4	4	4	4	4	4	4	5	3	59
Lincoln Mark VII (LSC)	5	2	4	4	4	5	4	3	5	4	3	3	3	4	3	5	5	4	62
Lincoln Town Car	4	2	5	4	2	3	4	2	5	3	5	5	4	5	5	4	5	4	60
Mazda MPV (V-6)	3	2	4	3	3	3	3	4	3	4	4	5	4	4	4	4	4	4	56
Mazda RX-7 (Turbo)	5	2	4	2	5	4	5	3	4	3	4	3	2	3	4	4	4	4	54
Mazda 323 (LX 4-dr)	3	5	4	3	3	4	3	3	4	5	3	3	4	4	4	4	4	4	57
Mazda 626 (LX 4-dr)	3	3	3	3	4	4	4	3	4	3	4	4	4	4	4	4	4	4	59
Mazda 929	4	2	4	4	4	4	4	3	4	4	4	4	4	4	4	4	4	4	61
Mercedes-Benz S-Class (560 SEL)	5	1	5	3	4	5	5	5	5	5	5	4	4	5	5	5	5	2	67
Mercedes-Benz 190 (2.6)	4	2	3	4	4	5	4	3	3	4	3	3	4	3	5	5	4	3	58
Mercedes-Benz 260/300 (300E)	4	2	4	4	4	5	4	4	4	4	4	4	4	4	5	4	4	3	63
Mercury Tracer (Auto)	2	4	4	3	3	3	2	3	3	4	2	3	3	3	3	3	3	4	48
Merkur Scorpio and XR4Ti (Scorpio)	3	2	3	4	4	4	5	4	3	3	4	4	4	4	4	4	4	3	57
Mitsubishi Eclipse (DOHC 16-V)	4	3	4	2	4	4	2	4	3	4	2	3	2	4	3	4	3	4	50
Mitsubishi Galant (GS)	4	3	3	3	3	5	4	3	4	3	4	4	4	3	4	3	3	3	57
Mitsubishi Mirage (4-dr)	3	4	3	3	3	2	3	2	3	4	3	3	3	4	3	4	3	3	49

RATINGS CHART

SCALE 5 = Exceptional; 4 = Above average; 3 = Average; 2 = Below average; 1 = Poor

MAKE AND MODEL	Performance							Accommodations						Workmanship		Value	TOTAL
	Acceleration	Economy	Driveability	Ride	Steering/handling	Braking	Noise	Driver seating	Instruments/controls	Visibility	Room/comfort	Entry/exit	Cargo room	Exterior	Interior		
Mitsubishi Wagon/Van (LS Wagon)	3	2	4	2	2	2	3	2	3	4	5	1	5	4	4	3	49
Nissan Maxima (SE, ABS)	4	2	4	3	4	5	3	3	4	3	3	4	4	4	4	4	58
Nissan Pulsar (SE)	4	4	3	3	4	4	2	3	3	2	3	2	3	4	4	3	51
Nissan Sentra	3	5	3	3	3	3	2	3	3	5	2	2	2	2	2	3	52
Nissan Stanza	3	3	3	4	3	3	4	3	4	5	4	4	4	4	3	4	58
Nissan Van	2	2	4	2	2	3	3	3	3	3	5	1	5	4	3	3	48
Nissan 240SX	4	3	4	3	4	4	3	4	4	4	2	2	3	4	4	3	55
Nissan 300ZX (Turbo)	5	2	5	2	4	4	3	4	3	3	3	2	2	5	4	3	54
Oldsmobile Cutlass Supreme	3	3	3	4	3	4	4	2	3	4	4	3	4	4	4	3	55
Oldsmobile Toronado/Trofeo	4	2	4	3	4	4	4	4	3	4	3	3	3	4	4	3	55
Plymouth Laser (Turbo)	5	3	3	2	4	4	2	3	4	2	2	2	2	4	3	3	48

Plymouth Laser (Turbo)	5	3	3	2	4	4	2	3	4	2	2	2	4	3	3	48
Peugeot 405 (Mi 16)	4	3	4	3	4	4	3	4	3	4	4	3	4	3	3	57
Pontiac Grand Am (SE/Quad 4)	4	3	3	2	4	3	3	3	4	3	3	3	4	4	4	53
Pontiac Grand Prix (SE)	3	2	3	4	4	4	2	3	4	3	3	3	4	4	3	53
Pontiac LeMans (SE/auto)	2	4	2	3	4	3	4	2	4	3	3	3	4	3	3	51
Pontiac Sunbird (GT)	4	2	3	2	4	3	4	3	4	3	2	3	5	4	4	51
Saab 900 (900S)	3	3	4	3	4	4	3	4	3	3	4	4	4	3	3	56
Saab 9000 (Turbo)	5	3	3	4	4	5	3	3	4	4	3	4	4	4	3	61
Sterling 827	4	2	4	3	4	5	3	3	4	4	4	3	4	3	4	58
Subaru Justy	3	5	3	2	3	4	1	3	3	2	3	2	3	3	4	49
Subaru Sedan/Wagon/3-Door Coupe & Hatchback (4WD Turbo wagon)	3	2	4	4	3	3	3	3	5	3	3	4	4	4	3	56
Subaru XT (XT6)	4	2	4	4	4	3	3	3	4	2	2	3	4	4	3	52
Suzuki Swift (GTi)	4	4	3	3	4	2	3	4	4	2	3	3	3	3	3	51
Toyota Camry (V-6)	4	3	4	4	4	4	4	4	4	4	4	4	4	4	4	63
Toyota Celica (GT 2-dr)	3	3	3	4	4	3	3	3	4	2	2	3	4	4	3	52
Toyota Corolla	3	4	4	4	4	3	4	3	5	3	3	3	4	3	4	57
Toyota Cressida	4	2	4	3	4	4	4	4	4	4	4	3	4	4	3	59
Toyota MR2 (Supercharged)	4	4	3	3	4	2	4	3	4	3	2	1	4	4	3	53

RATINGS CHART

SCALE 5 = Exceptional; 4 = Above average; 3 = Average; 2 = Below average; 1 = Poor

MAKE AND MODEL	Performance							Accommodations						Workmanship		Value	TOTAL
	Acceleration	Economy	Driveability	Ride	Steering/handling	Braking	Noise	Driver seating	Instruments/controls	Visibility	Room/comfort	Entry/exit	Cargo room	Exterior	Interior		
Toyota Supra (Turbo)	5	2	4	2	4	5	2	4	5	3	2	2	2	4	4	3	53
Toyota Tercel (2-dr)	2	5	3	3	3	4	2	3	3	5	2	3	3	4	4	4	53
Volkswagen Fox (wagon)	4	4	3	3	3	3	3	3	3	4	3	3	3	3	3	4	52
Volkswagen Golf/Jetta (Jetta Carat)	4	4	4	3	4	4	3	4	4	3	3	3	4	4	4	4	59
Volvo 240	3	3	4	4	3	4	3	4	3	5	4	3	3	5	4	3	58
Volvo 740/760/780 (760 Turbo)	4	2	4	4	4	5	3	4	4	4	4	4	4	5	4	3	62
Yugo (GVX)	3	5	4	2	2	3	2	2	2	5	2	3	2	3	2	2	44